Coyote's GUIDE

TO CONNECTING WITH NATURE

OWLINK MEDIA CORPORATION
849 Almar Avenue
Suite C #468
Santa Cruz, California 95060

OWLink Media formed to help Our World Learn (OWL) through all forms of media, broadcasting and publishing utilizing successful techniques gained from the Art of Mentoring. If you are interested in finding out more about OWLink Media, visit www.OWlinkMedia.com.

Wilderness Awareness School fosters understanding and appreciation of nature, community, and self. The School is a division of The Awareness Society, a Nonprofit Corporation recognized as a Federal Tax Exempt organization under I.R.S. code section 501(c)(3). If you are interested in finding out more about Wilderness Awareness School, visit www.WildernessAwareness.org.

ISBN Number: 978-1-57994-025-6

Printed in South Korea.

Coyote's GUIDE

TO CONNECTING WITH NATURE

SECOND EDITION

Jon Young, Ellen Haas, Evan McGown
FORWARD BY **Richard Louv**

OWLink Media

PERMISSION TO PRINT THE FOLLOWING IS GRATEFULLY ACKNOWLEDGED.

PUBLISHED MATERIAL:

Abram, David. Excerpt from *The Spell of the Sensuous: Perception and Language in a More-than-Human World*. Pantheon Books, Random House, Inc. (1996)

Cohen, Michael. Excerpt from *Reconnecting with Nature*. EcoPress. (2007)

Cornell, Joseph. *Excerpt from Sharing Nature with Children Volume 2 and Sharing Nature with Children, 20th Anniversary Edition*. Dawn Publications. (1989, 1998)

Eaton, Randall. Excerpt from *From Boys to Men*. OWLink Media. (2009)

Leslie, Clare Walker. Excerpt from *Keeping a Nature Journal: Discover a Whole New Way of Seeing the World Around You*. Storey Publishing. (2003)

Lopez, Barry. Excerpt from *Arctic Dreams*. Reprinted by permission of SLL/Sterling Lord Literistic, Inc. (1986)

Lopez, Barry. Excerpt from *Patriotism and The American Land*. Copyright 1986 Barry Lopez. Reprinted by permission of The Orion Society. (2002)

Louv, Richard. Excerpt from *Last Child in the Woods: Saving Our Children from Nature - Deficit Disorder*. Houghton Mifflin, (1990)

Nachmanovitch, Stephen. Excerpt from *Free Play: Improvisation in Life and Art*. Penguin Putnam Inc. (1990)

Nelson, Richard K. Excerpt from *The Island Within*. Copyright © 1989 by Richard Nelson. Published by Vintage Books, a division of Random House, Inc. NY, and originally by North Point Press. Reprinted by permission of Susan Bergholz Literary Services, New York, NY and Lamy, NM. All Rights reserved. (1989)

Olson, Sigurd. Excerpts from *Open Horizons*. Permission granted by Robert K. Olson on behalf of the Olson family. University of Minnesota Press. (1998)

Philips, Mick. Caterpillar Photograph from *Field and Swamp: Animals and Their Habitats*. (www.dpughphoto.com)

Powell, "Ingwe" Norman. "I Revere" from *Echoes of Kenya*. OWLink Media. (2002) Learn to Hear Voices in the Wind (anecdote) (1996)

Pyle, Robert Michael. Excerpt from *The Thunder Tree*. Houghton Mifflin Co. (1993)

Stafford, William. "Listening" copyright 1954, 1998 by the Estate of William Stafford. Reprinted from *The Way It Is: New & Selected Poems* with the permission of Graywolf Press, Saint Paul, MN.

Swamp, Jake. Excerpt from *The Art of Mentoring & Coyote Teaching*. OWLink Media. (1997)

Weed, Tim. *Coyote*. (www.timweed.com) (2008)

Wilson, E.O. Excerpt from *Writing Natural History*, Dialogues With Authors, by Edward Lueders. Permission granted by Copyright Clearance Center. University of Utah Press. (1989)

Young, Jon. Alarm Call Graphics from *Animal Tracking Basics*. Stackpole Books. (2006)

NON-PUBLISHED MATERIAL:

Bird, Wendolyn. What does Coyote Mentoring look like when working with the 3 to 5 year old? (anecdote) (1997)

Burkett, Gail. An Imperative (anecdote) (2008)

Chilkotowsky, John. Who You Are Being? (anecdote) (2006)

Cleveland, Richard. What am I Missing? (anecdote) (2006)

Collins, Arianna Alexsandra. *A-Buzzing We Will Go, Promise of the Acorn* and Song Writing (anecdote) (2003)

Doran, Sol. *Welcoming Song* (2006)

Dranginis, Kristi. www.kristidranginis.com Photo Contribution: Page No's: xx, xxxiv, 20, 65, 77, 78, 122-123, 169, 223, 224, 227, 285, 290, 345, 359, 417, 475

Eaton, Randall. Team Sailing (anecdote) (2007)

Forthoffer, David. Brain Patterning and Fifty-Fifty Principle (anecdote) (2007)

Grindrod, Frank. Amphibian Etiquette and A Frog Stalking Challenge (anecdote) (2007)

Kiselyk, Dale. Plant ID Lesson from Kamana journals. (2004)

Moskowitz, David. www.davidmoskowitz.net Photo Contribution Page No. 288-289

Stonefelt, Julie. Photo Contribution: Page No. 109

Thompson, Patricia. Washington Department of Fish and Wildlife. Professional Field Report (anecdote) (2002)

CHILDREN'S CONTRIBUTIONS:

Davidoff, Addy. The Song of Nature (poem) (2002)

Helmann, Sierra. This Tree (poem) (2007)

Ross, Kim. Dabo's Story — written by Evan McGown (anecdote) (2007)

DEDICATED TO

Tom Brown Jr., Jon Young's Mentor
and
Ingwe, Our Beloved Grandfather

HOW TO USE THIS BOOK

To mentors, teachers, parents, counselors and other kinds of guides who work with kids of all ages, from one to a hundred:

This book is split into two main parts, each complementing the other.

Part *One*, the **Mentor's Manual**, reveals through stories and discussion the principles of Coyote Mentoring. These are "layers" of learning and human development that underlie all practice, often invisible to participants, but alive in the awareness of a mentor.

Part *Two* of this book, the **Activity Guide,** is an offering of games and other exercises that show how these "layers" of learning actually get implemented into practice—without participants even realizing it.

The trick is to interweave underlying principles (Part One) with practice (Part Two). The whole book is color-coded for this purpose, linking the principles embedded within each activity to their explanations in the Mentor's Manual. The color-coding goes like this:

Core Routines ◎ = Blue

Child Passions ↑ = Yellow

Book of Nature 🌿 = Green

Natural Cycle ↺ = Purple

Indicators of Awareness ⚡ = Red

Activity Guide ● = Brown/Beige

The Foreword by Richard Louv and our Introductions provide background information on the emergent movement of regenerative, nature-based education. Read these if this bigger picture interests you.

After that, we suggest reading through the Mentor's Manual. If any one part seems too technical, just skip it for now.

Once you are familiar with the basic concepts from the Mentor's Manual, the Activity Guide (and perhaps any other book of activities) becomes an open tool-box—or a collection of basic recipes—fully accessible for your own practice, experimentation and adaptation.

We don't intend to simply provide more "recipes" for nature connection—instead, we want to help you learn *how to cook*. Treat this book like a Field Guide, using the Index and the color-coded pages to flip back and forth between principles and practice, theory and action, study and play—as they inform and strengthen each other over time.

At the end of the book you'll find resources that will enrich your principles and practice even further.

The **Epilogue** written by Jon Young, looks at the role of Coyote Mentoring within the big picture of societal change and regenerative human living. **Suggested Reading** provides a long list of selected resources, many of them regionally based. **Affiliated Programs** shows organizations across the US, Canada, and the world, where these principles are being applied. An **Index** helps you locate key concepts and cross references.

Our most important advice for using this book—have fun!

Keep a look out for Coyote…and let your curiosity lead the way.

CONTENTS

PART ONE: MENTOR'S MANUAL

CORE ROUTINES

CHILD PASSIONS

BOOK OF NATURE

THE NATURAL CYCLE

INDICATORS OF AWARENESS

PART TWO: ACTIVITY GUIDE

GIVING THANKS

Many hands and hearts have touched this book. To name them all, we must cast a wide net. We want to start with grateful acknowledgment to everyone who has, over time and place, contributed to the creation of *Coyote's Guide*; that would include every star or dewy blade of grass who ever winked or wagged at us.

We send thanksgiving to the Elders who have given their sacred guidance to our schools and The Art of Mentoring community:

Tom Brown, Jr., (who was mentored by Stalking Wolf in the way of the Coyote, and is Jon's mentor), for his commitment to sharing the vision that underlies these teachings.

Norman "Ingwe" Powell & Elizabeth, Ingwe is the Grandfather and co-founder of Wilderness Awareness School, and gave us hope and stories.

Jake & Judy Swamp, Jake is former sub-chief of the Wolf Clan of the Mohawk Nation. He gave us our Central Fire, Peacemaking Principles, and the Thanksgiving Address.

Gilbert Walking Bull & Diane Marie, Gilbert was a tradition-ally raised Lakota Sacred Man from North Dakota. He gave us the Seven Sacred Symptoms and many good traditions.

Paul Raphael, a Peacemaker of the Grand Traverse Band of the Odawa Nation. He warmed our sacred fires and helped us understand how to heal grief, and how to take on the roles of Elders.

We send thanksgiving to those who sparked and fed the fire to pro-duce Coyote's Guide:

Richard Louv, author of *Last Child in the Woods*, who so gra-ciously wrote our Foreword, for valiantly leading the "No Child Left Inside" movement and the Children and Nature Network.

Karen Dvornich, of the University of Washington's NatureMapping Program, and **Margaret Tudor**, of the Pacific Education Institute, who passionately wanted this book for schools and their kids.

Warren Moon, Executive Director of Wilderness Awareness School, thank you for your depth of soul and clarity of mind, and for your continual support.

Mark Smythe, Past Board Chairman; **John Chilkotowsky**, Program Director; and **Dan Rain**, Outreach Director, of Wilderness Awareness School, thank you for mentoring us through all the stages. **Chris Laliberte, Tony & Margaret Laliberte**, thank you for providing the framework.

We send thanks to our long-term moral supporters, the people who have kept badgering and believing in this book for years, most especially:

John Gallagher, most beloved, who has scouted us into production for two decades.

Frank Grindrod, of Massachusetts, whose EarthWork Programs exemplify this teaching.

Dale Kiselyk, of Alberta, who lives this teaching.

Daniel Kirchhof of Montana, whose pure spirit over lights this work.

Amy Marchegiani, who helped us see it in the beginning.

Rees Maxwell, who dreamed it with his heart and soul.

We thank those who have moved the book from draft to production through OWLink Media:

Deb Winters, Project Manager, thanks for diving in with a powerfully peaceful mind and steady common sense, to get the job done.

Mariko Schmidtauer, thanks for brightly coaxing a network of Affiliates into naming themselves.

DixieLynn Gleason and **Arianna Husband**, thanks for your persistence in obtaining permissions for copyrighted quotations.

Josh Lane and **Caitlin Williams**, thanks for jumping in when needed.

Kiliii Yu, of Question Oxygen Design, thank you for your continued support.

Randall Eaton, for navigating our team through this 2nd Edition and providing critical feedback.

Mark J. Harlow, whose extraordinary photographic artwork is a testimony to his ethics, his skill and his presence.

theBookDesigners team and **Kit Cooley** of **Dream Lizard Creations,** for bringing a new level of sophistication to Coyote's Guide.

To the many people who helped at various points to add their talents and bright minds, and their important critical feedback, including but certainly not limited to: **Nicole Young, Mark Morey, James Stark, Penny Livingston-Stark, Nathan Meffert, Tony Deis, Kirsten Segler, Miki Dedijer,** and **Alan Brisley**. And to all the people that we mentor and work with who looked this over and gave feedback.

We greatly appreciate our many editors, knowing the time and mental focus you gave to reviewing and revising words:

Gail Burkett, for encouragement and elegant editing of the complete manuscript.

Nate Summers, for writing the first and last activities and managing completion of the Activities section.

Daniel Evans, for waiting impatiently and writing many activities and stories.

Dan Gardoqui, for completing the Book of Nature chapter and beginning the bibliography.

John Chilkotowsky, **Amara Oden**, and **Dan Rain** for editing everything several times.

To the individual chapter editors who volunteered their insight during winter holidays and beyond:

Wes Geitz, Margaret Alvarez, Louis Berner, Jane Bernstein, Peter Bettman-Kerson, Dan Corcoran, Sol Doran, David Forthoffer, Emily Gibson, Frank Grindrod, Laura Gunion, Pam Hawes, Corrie Hayes Stuck, Susie Hillman, Arianna Husband, Lindsay Huettman, Mark Jordahl, Angie Jordan, Dale Kiselyk, Jason Knight, Chris Laliberte, Kimberly Leeper, Francine Leiphard, Pam Leiter, Kylie Loynd, Rees Maxwell, Tony Moon, Dave Moskowitz, Karen Dvornich, Melissa Mueller, Todd Peterson, Mike Prince, Barbara Russell, Liz Sinclair, Connor Stedman, Alexia Stevens, Glendora Trescher, Lorene Wapotich, Kim Wilkinson, and **Dave Wilson.**

We thank our photo contributors:

Mark Harlow, David Moskowitz, Kristi Dranginis, Emily Gibson, Linda Bittle, Laurie Nelson, Alexander, Kiliii Yu, Frank Grindrod, DeAnna Dailey, Filip Tkaczyk, John Chilkotowsky, Dan Rain, Julie Stonefelt and the Wilderness Awareness School staff.

Finally, we three authors send our personal thanksgiving:

Jon Young –

To my mentor, **Tom Brown, Jr.**, whose commitment to Coyote's path, and ultimately to me, caused this book to exist and this movement to happen. Can we ever thank Tom enough?

To **Ingwe and Gilbert Walking Bull**, beloved elders who have traveled to the other side—and who gave so much to this movement. To **Paul Raphael** for helping us tighten our Cultural Mentoring strings, to **Jake & Judy Swamp** and the **Tree of Peace Society** for helping us learn how to build a foundation. To my **Hawaiian Ohana** who share so much with us about love and healing.

To **my parents** for supporting a naturalist in the modern days. To my **family elders**, **Grandmother Nanny Cecil** and **Great Aunt Carrie**, who held my hand when I was a toddler and just let me listen to the birds, and hear the sounds of the gentle waves of the bay on the shore, encouraged me to catch things and bring them home and care for them with love. To my wife **Nicole** and **all my children**, thanks for loving, supporting and believing in me too! To all the committed folks who dared to set down an anchor in their communities.

Evan McGown –

To my family: **Joe & Henrietta Foster** for their financial support and belief in me, **Hewitt & Jane McGown** for their musical selves, **Great Grandma B.B.** for opening nature's doors to me, and my mother & father, **Jane & Jim McGown** for their unwavering love and support. My brother **Todd** for inspiring me to search out my own path.

To my many mentors, who collectively embody Coyote: **Terry Nestor, Dorothy Granham, Sally Krisel, Harry Sims, Marianne Causey, Peggy Lowry, Chris Mason, Kirk Duncan, Steve Brooks, Tony Rucker, Carl Lindberg, Whit Browne, Tim Smalley, Chris Laliberte, Jason Knight, Angie Jordan, John Chilkotowsky, Warren Moon, Walt Hoesel, Sol Doran**, all my friends and teachers at **Wilderness Awareness School** and **Power of Hope, Soasis Sukuweh, Michael Meade, Allison Holmes, William Stafford, Victor Wooten**, and most especially **Ellen Haas** and **Jon Young** for hooking me with that old *Art of Mentoring* tape cassette and for believing in my abilities as a writer.

To the children I've been blessed to work with in Seattle, Duvall, Vashon Island, and elsewhere, whose stories run throughout this book. You have truly been my teachers. To the owls. To all that have touched and supported me, thank you.

Ellen Haas –

To all the passionate people I've encountered over the many years of writing this book, you have called it into being. By telling your stories of what you are trying to do, who you teach, and what you need, you've kept up the breath of inspiration and given shape to the book. Thank you for your daily brave gestures on behalf of the earth and our children. Together, it is you who turn the tide.

To my beloved co-authors, thank you **Jon Young** for your uplifting spirit, and love you **Evan McGown** for the sweet earthy voice of this book.

To my mother, **Glendora Trescher**, who let me loose to trust nature: how blessed I am to be under your wing. Thank you for your continuous moral, spiritual, and financial support of this project. To my son **Will**, my joy in life, to my caretaking sister, **Tory Agnich**, and to **Susie & Matt Hillman** and my grandchildren, **Jonah** and **Audrey**, deep thanks for your life support throughout these writing years.

To everyone in the **Wilderness Awareness School community**, you are my mentors, my role-models, and my family. Thanks for surrounding me with love, patience, and encouragement.

Left to Right: Jon Young, Ellen Haas, Evan McGown, Deb Winters & Gail Burkett

Not long ago, the director of a school camp told me about a sixth-grader who attended his camp who had seldom if ever walked on uneven ground. "He spent all of his time in front of his computer, or doing homework, or playing video games. He was literally unstable on his feet when he left the sidewalk, and frightened," the camp director said. "It took him a while to get used to the trails, but after a while he was running and playing—he came fully alive."

That was an extreme example of what I documented in *Last Child in the Woods: Saving Our Children from Nature-Deficit Disorder*, published in 2005.

The broad—even international—interest in *Last Child* came as a surprise to me, but in retrospect it probably shouldn't have. Many dedicated people, including the hard-working folks at Wilderness Awareness School and its many affiliates, have been reconnecting children to the natural world for a long while. My book amplified these voices, documented the scientific research and offered possible solutions—and hope—at a moment when a lot of people knew something was seriously wrong with the nature connection but couldn't define what that something was. They did know they wanted to help make things better for their children. Thanks to the creators of *Coyote's Guide to Connecting with Nature*, kids of all ages and their mentors now have a powerful set of tools to help them with their task.

No question about it: We need to restore the broken bond between children and nature. The status quo isn't working, despite the best intentions of parents, teachers and others who devote time and energy to help children succeed in life. We see the evidence of this break in many ways: decreasing use of National Parks, falling enrollment in undergraduate college conservation programs, and plummeting sales of entry-level outdoor equipment. Even bike riding and Little League teams, one-time benchmarks of an active childhood, are losing their appeal to youngsters. Not coincidentally, obesity in children is at an all-time high, along with associated

FOREWORD
by Richard Louv

Author of *Last Child in the Woods: Saving Our Children from Nature-Deficit Disorder* and chairman of the Children & Nature Network (www.cnaturenet.org)

increases in diabetes and other health problems, including attention-deficit disorders.

Organized activities aside, unstructured time to just mess around outdoors—free play—seems to be in free-fall, despite a clinical report released not long ago by The American Academy of Pediatrics stating that play, especially free play, is "essential to development, as it contributes to the cognitive, physical, social, and emotional well-being of children and youth." Other recent research links children's and adults' physical and mental health, as well as cognitive functioning and creativity, directly to experiences in nature. It's not much of a leap to say that a creative and intelligent individual holds the keys to a high-quality life. And, too, there are planetary emergencies to be dealt with. We certainly need young people with all of their available brain neurons firing to help solve these problems. Wildlife reserves, parks and greenbelts—and the creatures and plants that live within—also depend on an alert and caring political constituency—informed people—for their continued survival.

Jon Young's Art of Mentoring and Coyote Teaching approach puts into print what this network of teachers has transmitted orally for the last 25 years.

In nature, life seems to explode at the cusp of forest and meadow, or ocean and beach. At the verge, Coyote Teaching is similarly energetic with the possibility of discovery.

As Coyote's authors write: "The real-life coyotes lurk on the edge of the human village, always just beyond sight or reach. They keep a close and wary eye on danger and opportunity in all directions. That's how they hunt; that's how they live. Coyote's edge-walk is a perfect metaphor for nature educators to use as a guide…"

Coyote's Guide entices us off the familiar path—off the sidewalk and onto uneven ground—and encourages us to experiment with creative approaches to reintroduce children to nature. The spirit of Coyote goads teachers to have "a true sense of play and abandon...and leads us to connect in an intimate and meaningful way" with nature, and with our natural selves.

This teaching "is a radical approach that uses no textbooks or tests, but simply starts at the roots of nature education by engaging people in direct experience with the plants and animals just beyond the edge of their back yards."

By learning to think like Coyote the Trickster, mentors are inspired to drop the know-it-all mentality and see nature with fresh eyes. Here is where story and play merge with fact and science. This is not the interactive learning of yesterday, but a guide to the Invisible School, which teaches knowing in a deep way.

Because the methods suggested in this book have been field-tested for decades—in truth, for thousands of years—this guide should become an essential resource for mentors, teachers, parents, and outdoor educators—anyone who wants to revive their sense of kinship with nature but needs some help.

This is good medicine for nature-deficit disorder.

Nature-deficit disorder describes the human costs of alienation from nature ... but deficit is only one side of the coin. We can also become more aware of how blessed our children can be—biologically, cognitively and spiritually—through positive physical connection to nature.

RICHARD LOUV, *Last Child in the Woods: Saving Our Children from Nature-Deficit Disorder*

A long, long time ago, maybe two hundred thousand years ago, and in a few places still today, the native people who lived off their land schooled their children, but they did it invisibly. Our ancestors' children didn't go to school. School surrounded them. Nature was a living teacher. There were many relatives for every child and every relative was a mentor. Stories filled the air and ceremonies of gratitude filled mundane lives.

Wouldn't it brighten our horizons to see more of this kind of teaching in our suburbs and cities today?

ELLEN HAAS, *The Art of Mentoring and Coyote Teaching* audiotape with Jon Young, 1995

No Child Left Inside

Coyote's Guide finally puts into print our extended community's long story of connecting people with nature. Thanks to a climate change in environmental education that is now calling for "No Child Left Inside," the time is ripe for writing down our oral tradition. This Mentor's Manual and Activities Guide offers vital and effective ways to restore the bond between people and the rest of nature. It sets fresh standards for environmental literacy that engages body, mind, and spirit with the natural world.

I first met the pioneers of Wilderness Awareness School when they came west from New Jersey to Washington in 1994, a bunch of barefoot trackers with a haywire organization and a worldwide vision. They were led by a skinny fellow with bright eyes and body language that brought to life whatever plant or animal he was imagining as he told its story. As a veteran high school English teacher, a recent author of a book about building a school from the ground up, and an active environmental organizer, I saw in a blink that these folks were hatching something vibrant and important. They had the answer to our culture's educational and environmental woes.

It was called "nature awareness" and was really as simple as that: Go outside and stop-look-and-listen. But Coyote Mentoring was an edgy approach to developing "the naturalist intelligence." It was so different in attitude, in pacing, in depth, in quality, and in sparkle-in-the-eye, from traditional approaches that it required no small degree of craziness to take it seriously as "educational method."

Who are You?

Fifteen years later, this book takes it seriously. Until now, Wilderness Awareness School and its affiliates have passed on teachings about *The Art of Mentoring and Coyote Teaching* only through experiential workshops. Yet, from my desk at the center of the school's office, I keep hearing the insistent pleas of countless amazing mentors out there who aren't able to get here for a program, have students just waiting to get started, and want our blueprint for design and construction of a profound learning experience.

Your cries for help have called out *Coyote's Guide*.
Your stories are wonderful:

You've started a weekend year-round program for families in Massachusetts.
You lead an after-school outdoor club of teens in Indiana.
You run a summer canoeing camp in Alberta.
You're networking trackers from the Netherlands to Romania.
You coordinate rites-of-passage journeys for adults in New Mexico.
You're a wildlife biologist educating your public.
You're a team of teachers Nature-Mapping your region.
You're facilitating a permaculture community.
You're honing your nature skills on your own.
You mentor your grandchildren who want to play outside.
You homeschool your kids who love nature.
You're an environmental education graduate looking for a job that uses your gifts and fulfils your calling.

Bottom line, you feel deeply the value of direct experience with nature in your own life and want to transmit it to others. Some of you were fortunate to grow up free to roam and hunt and fish and build tree houses in the wild places near your home with parents and mentors who encouraged you—and you want to pass on the tradition. More of you are members of the first generation that didn't have that privilege and you want to resurrect the tradition.

Parents, teachers, counselors, guides, and mentors, all who find this book in your hand, Jon, Evan, and I have written it for you. We want you to be confident that *Coyote's Guide* can be adapted to work wherever you are, in situations as diverse as we can imagine.

Translating an Oral Tradition

Translating our oral tradition has challenged the writing team (which includes many co-conspirators and contributors) to scale it down, widen it out, and then distil it down again, until we've come to the bright life and voice and shape of this book.

Last summer we went to a workshop with Joseph Cornell, author of the classic, *Sharing the Joy of Nature with Children*, and we asked his advice for our book. He said "Remember your reader and keep it very simple. Go to the universal principles."

This large book tries to capture our universal principles in printed words with a magical voice and a bundle of stories. Through living in the landscape, questioning, storytelling, adventuring, and inquiring, mythical Coyote inspires the learners. Through wise and specific limit-setting, guidance, and counsel, Mentor steers the raft.

As Mowgli says in the *Jungle Book*, "Good hunting to you" as you absorb these principles and put these activities into practice. At our core, we all want to restore a culture of people who live what Aldo Leopold named "the land ethic," "a tendency to preserve the integrity, stability and beauty of the biotic community." Without politics or dogma, we want people to learn from Mother Nature that childlike wisdom about where they fit, how resilient life is, and how they can help.

We hope these materials will help our modern culture bring back the children's trails that used to line the fences and fields and cut across the neighborhood woods. We can't go in there as adults and clear the old trails but we can invite kids of all ages to wander back and bushwhack their own.

Now Chil the Kite brings home the night
That Mang the Bat sets free –
The herds are shut in byre and hut
For loosed till dawn are we.
This is the hour of pride and power,
Talon and tush and claw.
Oh, hear the call! – Good hunting all
That keep the Jungle Law!

RUDYARD KIPLING,
"Night-Song in the Jungle"
The Jungle Books

Coyote Mentoring—An Ancient Lineage

WHO ARE WE?
by Jon Young

This book reveals the ancient way of passing on, from one generation to the next, knowledge of and connection to nature. As our great legacy, these hunter-gatherer ways come to us from all over the world and reflect the oldest ways of being, learning, and connecting with nature. I am glad to say this cultural treasure of Coyote Mentoring thrives today at the heart of a vibrant educational movement spreading through learning communities and wilderness schools across continents.

At its very best, Coyote Mentoring helps individuals realize their full potential to the benefit of their community. It consists of a powerful set of tools for coaxing out of individuals what nature has provided and stored away. The mentoring draws people gently to the edge of their knowledge and experience, and guides them into new territory. This repeats through a cyclical pattern of visits, explorations, and relationship-building that allows for real connection to occur in its own organic way. In previous centuries, this connection happened naturally as families in a community depended on natural resources and the ingenuity to know when, where, and how to hunt, trap, fish, and gather what they needed, while they cared for the natural world at the same time.

In our modern life, Coyote Mentoring emulates the goals of our ancestors: With very specific patterns or repetitions, we help people re-connect their sensory systems, rational processes, and imagination to the world around them. Each individual's family history and experience require an equally unique strategy by the Coyote Mentor. Perhaps it is still about survival—this time for a different reason. Maybe it is about human beings reclaiming their love of the creation to better tend nature's precious resources for our future generations. To get us there, we all need the most fundamental building blocks of nature connection.

The Challenges of Coyote Mentoring

Mentoring helps people grow more fully into their gifts. Whether it's sports, music, business, or nature connection, as a mentor, our first strategy focuses on what's happening with the other person. It is not about dwelling on our own expectations and agendas. We need to be fully present for those we mentor in the moment. We look for signs of comprehension and opportunities to guide their next steps. We help by asking them questions that will nurture self-sufficiency. In time, mentoring uncovers the gifts of creativity and power that lie within each individual.

Initially, each Coyote Mentor will be challenged by old habits and expectations built up over years on their own learning experiences. However, Coyote Mentoring, a highly personalized journey that emphasizes sensory awareness and curiosity depends on spontaneity and improvisation. Consider the power of nature connection on our development as humans. In ancient lore, Coyote helps people transform through ingenuity, cleverness, and sometimes trickery. Coyote represents someone who lives on the edge of a wild landscape. To fully connect to nature in the most powerful way, all sensory systems must be engaged and developed, and pattern recognition must be infused with both imagination and rational processes. Coyote's power of nature connection and transformation is critical to motivate this Coyote Mentoring journey.

With the broad, rich palette of nature connection, the Coyote Mentor needs no agenda to guide a person through patterns of seasonal realities, natural inhabitants, and tracking with all the senses. To gauge development, the Coyote Mentor looks for qualities of awareness, enthusiasm, health, and vitality, rather than measuring a skill, or testing for information storage ability. We know people learn what they need to learn, in their own time. How can we set a time limit on building relationships through all our senses with trees, birds, grasses, herbs, insects, lizards, creeks, wind, and mammals? We need to give these relationships the unstructured time they need to develop—it's an organic, unfolding process; the result is authentic nature connection.

How It Works

When a person I am working with comes in from the field—most often they have been there without me—I begin to ask questions. I want to know where they were and what they saw. How they answer and what they say is both a diagnostic for me as the mentor, and a way for them to learn more deeply. Their story is as important to their learning as their field experiences. I watch and I listen carefully for cues that tell me what got them really excited and curious, what made them most uncomfortable, and what really has them stumped. By simply listening to their story in a gentle way, asking questions, and finding the blank spots in their memory, they realize what their awareness missed. If they noticed no birds on a warm, spring morning in a diverse forest environment, I want to know why they didn't hear them. If they noticed one kind of bird, such as a jay or crow (loud and obvious), and no others, I will ask them about the sparrows and thrushes that I know were there. Tomorrow, when that individual returns to the field, he or she will want to pay much closer attention.

Experience has taught me that Coyote Mentoring, working on so many levels, is by far the most effective learning and healing journey I have yet to encounter. I have seen people fully connect to the birds of their landscape, discovering hawks, foxes, and owls with the help of birds and other animals. They also connect to themselves differently. Individuals who develop authentic depth in their nature awareness, especially through the bird language journey, will also notice they cause waves in the world around them. They see that a song sparrow mirrors back to them how they are being in the world. This is significant. A natural desire to reduce those waves emerges with such sensitivity that people begin to really look at themselves differently. They begin to rethink their priorities, how they show up, and for more than just the sparrows. This leads to deeper levels of awareness and tracking, both on the inner and outer landscapes—it becomes a process of healing.

Tom Brown, Jr. and a Vision for a Coyote Mentoring Culture

My induction into this lineage began in 1971 when I set out on an eight-year learning journey with my own mentor and carrier of this mentoring way—Tom Brown, Jr. In his small New Jersey neighborhood, Tom grew up next to a very large wilderness area called the Pine Barrens. He was mentored there in the Coyote tradition by an Apache elder he calls "Grandfather." At age 21, after he moved an hour north to my neighborhood, where Tom met me on a street corner. His first words to me on that day came through a question, "What have you got there?" My answer, "A common eastern snapping turtle." That's how much information I gave him in that moment. He immediately knew I had field guides at home, I like turtles, and I was good at catching stuff. He arrived at this understanding through the words I spoke, the inflection of my voice, my body language, and the clothes I wore which all told a story of a boy who played a lot in the forest and around mud. He saw my rudimentary, improvised tackle and read a lot from that. He continued with more questions from that day on for the next eight years.

Tom really never gave answers. Instead he shared interesting stories. He met me at my edges and asked amazing, inspiring questions: One by one, day by day, I learned the names of all the hazards, all the mammals of my region, and their track and sign, and how to find and catch them if I wanted. He helped me improve my fishing and hunting skills and guided me to acquire knowledge about gathering plants for food, for medicine, and for crafts such as cordage and baskets. He helped deepen my appreciation for landscape, ecology, and survival in challenging times; he strengthened my courage, creativity, and storytelling; and ultimately he ignited a passion for learning and living.

Ingwe and Wilderness Awareness School

As a boy growing up fishing, hunting, gathering and trapping live animals for pets, I directly experienced many of the elements of the village culture, but so many threads were already missing from the whole cord. It became my life's work to identify these threads and weave them back into the whole, thus expanding the lineage for the future generations to enjoy once more. My own personal vision was and is to hold the lineage true and re-build strong connections to nature—even stronger than my own—with as many people in as many places as possible. I felt highly committed to understanding how this connection to nature happens, how Coyote Mentoring works, and how to pass all this forward to the next generation in a regenerative way to ensure this lineage continues to grow into the future. I became convinced that connection to nature could once more become commonplace, and so I began to create the foundations for a school.

In 1984, Ingwe joined me and we formally started Wilderness Awareness School to share the lessons learned with his Akamba people and through building the Scouting movement in Africa. Born M. Norman Powell in 1914 of British ancestry, Ingwe spent his childhood running barefoot through the plains of Kenya with the young warriors of the neighboring Akamba tribe. Adopted into their tribe, Ingwe learned how to live close to the Earth. He spoke their language fluently and his heart and soul grew truly wise through his immersion experience in indigenous Cultural Mentoring—he was authentic and powerful to the core. Ingwe fully experienced the context of village and tribe—the grandmothers, grandfathers, uncles and aunts—and he even had the peers. He hunted, he gathered, he wandered the wilderness.

Together, Ingwe and I pulled together the many threads of cultural wisdom—diverse features born of good values and peaceful relationships. We found most exciting that the elements of mentoring were virtually identical from continent to continent—elements of culture and wisdom overlap and resonate in perfect harmony. Soon we were featured in our local newspaper and word spread—children of all ages gathered around for mentoring. The home-schooling community found us too, so we had all ages working together. Through our programs, we had, in some ways, recreated a virtual village.

The Art of Mentoring and a Worldwide Movement

In 1995, I taught the first Art of Mentoring for adults in Washington. Soon a team of us were teaching Art of Mentoring all over the United States, with a few courses in Canada as well. Working with long-time naturalists and tracking trainees, and with Tom and Debbie Brown's help, we piloted a leadership training series and worked with about 100 folks from across North America. These people took multiple Art of Mentoring classes with Wilderness Awareness School, enrolled in the *Kamana Naturalist Training Program*, and attended classes at Tom Brown's Tracker School.

Out of this initiative, many little projects emerged around the world based on the Art of Mentoring model of cultural and Coyote Mentoring. Soon, thousands and thousands of adults and children were enjoying the power of this experience. Many of these people now run wilderness schools and sister organizations throughout the world.

Thanks to Richard Louv's work, we are finally seeing how our children suffer as a consequence of widespread disregard for our biological needs and capacities. When people lose connection to nature they no longer experience or love this amazing life system that supports us. There is a great difference between a person who grows up without a mentor, and one who is coaxed to tap his or her deepest resources by experiencing nature through all the senses. If we don't use all of what we've got, we end up with a very different worldview and set of ethics than if we are connected to nature through all our sensory capacities. We become what our experiences provide—that's our nature.

Now that Coyote Mentoring is resurging in a wide variety of learning environments, many of us see how this lineage may be just what we need to restore health and happiness in our communities. This book gathers the many building blocks that make up the foundation of Coyote Mentoring. It will help you rediscover the power of this ancient mentoring, learning and teaching medicine. You will find yourself in good company: Since the early1980's, when only a few of us knew of Coyote Mentoring, the lineage has expanded to tens of thousands of children and adults globally. I feel so honored and encouraged to see these old and powerful ways applied in truly modern circumstances with tremendous results. For thousands of years, the Coyote Mentoring lineage showed us how to nurture the gifts of the individual in service to future generations.

We hope that Coyote's Guide will be your gateway to this lineage, whether you are new to this tradition, or you are already on this journey. With this book in hand and some direct experience in Coyote Mentoring, you will become an important link in the chain of restoring nature connection in yourself, your family, your learning community, and your neighborhood.

ABOUT THE AUTHORS

Through this book, we truly celebrate our collaboration in the important, powerful, and eternal work of Coyote Mentoring. Early in the 1990's when we first met, Ellen Haas began asking me to write all this down. She worked hard with me, and with so many others, re-iterating this amorphous mass of wisdom until we found a form that could hold the oral tradition. This work is largely her vision and passion; I am just a behind-the-scenes consultant and engineer of Coyote Mentoring.

Evan McGown, a talented young instructor at Wilderness Awareness School, stepped forward as a good storyteller ready to interlock the complex pieces of education, culture, and relationship with nature. Evan was a veteran of many Art of Mentoring programs, and a Wilderness Awareness School Residential Program graduate. Evan told this story from his own experience as a naturalist, a mentor, and a musician—the perfect metaphorical journey for mirroring Coyote Mentoring in nature.

I read every sentence that Evan wrote, and then worked with a shared document on the internet to fill in areas where there needed filling, and to adjust some voicing here and there. Ellen edited it all through many versions, gathering feedback from a wide circle of reviewers, wove in the logic, and filled in the gaps from chapter to chapter.

A team of skilled Coyote Mentors from Wilderness Awareness School wrote down all the exercises they could muster for this work. Many of the exercises in this book were introduced in 1995 to the first summer camp staff in Washington. These exercises come from so many places it is almost impossible to track them all back to their source—some go back to my childhood with Tom Brown, others to Ingwe's experiences with the Akamba, many to camps all over the US.

The Epilogue, Coyote in Context was written by collaboration as well—this time with many experienced veterans of both Coyote and Cultural Mentoring who came to consensus on key points to make. Then, while teaching a peace-making course in Steyerberg, Germany, a team gathered around to help with the closing words. This included a professional writer, Kirsten Segler, and an experienced journalist, Miki Dedijer, founder of a Wilderness & Permaculture program in Sweden, who helped me trim and empower the words of this chapter.

Throughout the entire writing of this book, many have read over our shoulders, reviewed versions of the chapters, and given generous feedback and criticism. So many, many people, it is difficult to name them all, though in Giving Thanks, we try! I am behind every one of the words in this book, and so are Ellen and Evan. We are authors, writers and Coyote engineers together. I am proud of this team, I feel joyous and tearfully grateful for the incredible impact this vision is having on the world. The children and nature both rejoice in the return of this wonderful way of being.

Jon Young

MENTOR'S MANUAL

Written in the voice of Evan McGown

Chapter 1

COYOTE AS OUR GUIDE

Why Coyote?

In the beginning stages of writing this *Coyote's Guide*, I met with my boss at the time, Warren Moon, Executive Director of Wilderness Awareness School, to discuss the title of this book.

For years our founder and co-author, Jon Young, had been guiding workshops known as "Coyote Mentoring" through Wilderness Awareness School and our sister schools.

But Warren and I weren't sure about "Coyote." After all, in many Native American stories and modern cartoons, he's depicted as a mangy scavenger or a wily, manipulating, often selfish—even lascivious—fool. By the end of our meeting, we left each other in agreement: "Yes, there's no need to have 'Coyote' in the title of the book; it will just confuse people and distract from what we really want to say."

Coyote, are you the trickster they say,
Stealing the night from the day?
Coyote, are you the wandering sage,
Willing to show us the way?

You're the sound of the wild
You're the voice of the free
You're the song in the night that calls out to me -
forget our travails as we follow your trails
Shout out Coyote wails

Coyote, Coyote, Coyote, Coyote . . .

Coyote, the moon shines in your eyes
The land is your soul and your heart is the sky
Coyote, they're giving you a bad name,
But I love you just the same

Tim Weed,
Coyote (a song for banjo, fiddle, and bass)

A Story that Instigates

Right after that meeting, I got in my car to run some errands. I drove a winding road from my foothill-nestled, rural home in Duvall, into the Seattle suburb of Redmond, the home of our technology giant, Microsoft, and its expanding suburbs of employees' homes.

Although rapidly being converted into logged plats for a new subdivision, forests of towering evergreens still lined each side of the road like a great hall. As my little Honda hurtled around a curve, something darted across the road a few cars ahead of me. I barely caught the flash of movement in the edge of my peripheral vision. Probably no other driver saw it. Yet in only that flash, I instantly knew—*but could it be?*

As I slowed down, I saw it clearly, just standing there on the side-walk: Coyote.

In all my time spent outdoors, I've seen quite a few animals, but I never see coyotes. My friends and students often do, but for some reason I never run across them. Just minutes before, we had decided to cut Coyote out of our story. Right then I had to wonder: was Coyote trying to tell me something?

My heart beating, I pulled off and parked on a patch of gravel made for construction trucks. When I got out, Coyote was still standing there. Once or twice he glanced over his shoulder in my direction, as if to size me up. Then he looked both ways and casually ambled back across the road, back where he had come from.

Half a football field up the road from him, I crossed too. Now he had disappeared past a layer of bushes. I followed into the bushes and came out into a bulldozed clearing. Coyote was gone. There was some mud near where he had entered, and I logically thought, "I should go look for tracks." But then some instinctive part of me disagreed, "No, walk across the clearing toward those far trees."

Turning into that stand of trees, I saw a grass clearing

When we get out of the glass bottles of our ego,
When we escape like squirrels
Turning in the cages of our personality
And get into the forests again,
We shall shiver with cold and fright
But things will happen to us
So that we don't know ourselves.

Cool, unlying life will rush in,
And, passion will make our bodies taut with power,
We shall stamp our feet with new power
And old things will fall down,
We shall laugh, and institutions will curl up like burnt paper.

D.H. LAWRENCE, *"Get Into the Forests Again"*

beyond and standing in it was Coyote. I walked closer; he just stood still and studied me back.

Then he trotted on—or maybe he walked, I can't quite remember the gait, but it was relaxed and unhurried—over the bulldozed hill, out of sight again. Following his trail, I climbed over the hill, now so far from the road I couldn't see any cars. Here, I found a newly paved, barren road, surrounded by forest. I could still smell the fresh, black asphalt. But again, once I got there, Coyote was nowhere to be seen.

Right next to the road was a stretch of bulldozed orange-colored mud. This time I couldn't help but look down for tracks. For fifteen minutes I followed different trails of coyote tracks through the mud, but lost the trail each time. In the forests around me I listened for bird language that might tell me where Coyote had gone. I heard calls that might have been alarms, but I wasn't sure of anything.

"It's getting late," I started to think, and "Evan, you have things you need to do in Redmond. Let's go." As I started to turn away, some other part of me wanted to walk up that new, shiny-black, resin-smelling road for one more look. So I did, moving even further away from where I started.

A few paces up, my head lifted to the peak of the hill. There, silhouetted against the western sunset sky, was Coyote, standing in the middle of the asphalt, just looking back at me. He casually wagged the tip of his low-hanging tail.

As soon as I saw him, he sauntered off into the thicker woods across the street. This time, there was no internal argument: I followed to where he had stood. Yep, he'd been right here: an apple-filled scat was plopped right on the sidewalk. How sweet of him.

Then I turned and walked into the forest where he had gone, asking myself, "If I were Coyote, where would I go?" With my eyes and ears alert, following my curiosity, I walked deeper and farther into the forest. My car was far behind me now.

Soon I came upon a well-worn deer trail and began to trace it. A few feet down the trail, just off to the side, I found a pile of bones. As I stooped puzzling over them and their story, suddenly a flock of kinglets—small, chickadee-sized birds with

What being a naturalist has come to mean to me, sitting my mornings and evening by the river, hearing the clack of herons through the creak of swallows over the screams of osprey under the purl of fox sparrow, … is this: Pay attention to the mystery. Apprentice to the best apprentices. Rediscover in nature your own biology. Write and speak with appreciation for all you have been gifted.

Barry Lopez, *Patriotism and the American Land*

flares of gold on their heads—swooped in and began hopping all around me, twinkling their music like little angels.

In that moment, I suddenly woke up to where I was: to the sculpted trunks of cedar trees, the fern-covered floor, and the sweet sounds of those precious little birds. I could have been in the farthest wilderness. For untold minutes I was lost in the wondrous spell of that place, its moment-to-moment dance of birds, ferns, breeze, bones and textured trees.

I soon realized I could hear cars in the deep distance; and I also realized that the tasks of my day were forgotten completely. My mind was clear and content. My body was relaxed, at ease. I had even forgotten about finding the trail of Coyote.

As I took in this mossy heaven, I had to laugh and wonder: why was I here in this place, in this moment? Of all the places I could have been, and with all the duties of life tugging at my sleeves, why was I sitting here in an old cedar grove in the Redmond suburbs, reveling in tracks and mysterious bones, alive to my senses, alive to my curiosity, alive to the world? On that day, there was one reason: Coyote.

Why Tell You this Story?

I tell you this story because stories make our world and this is the story that wanted to make the little world inside this book.

This story is why, in the end, we decided to title the book "Coyote's Guide." It's the story that taught me who Coyote is, and perhaps more importantly, who Coyote can be for us as educators, mentors, or parents who care about the future of this earth and our children.

Here I was, on the edge of the ever-developing epicenter of the computer industry, with busy, important things to do—and what happened? I was led, from street edge, to clearing edge, to forest edge, into another world. Coyote had brought me home.

Nature Deficit Disorder

The developed world we live in largely ignores the need for connection with nature. Sadly, the terrain of childhood is dominated more and more by technology and indoor focus. TV, internet, pink polka-dotted cell-phones, video games—all these electronics distract children from attending to the natural world around them. Electronics lure children's attention away from playing with mud and catching frogs, from sitting under trees, musing about the clouds or the mysteries of the animals surrounding them. And now, generations of adults are sadly disconnected from nature as well.

There are other factors that contribute to the trend that Richard Louv so compellingly describes in his book, *Last Child in the Woods: Saving Our Children from Nature-Deficit Disorder*. There are fears—child kidnappers, parks being trampled to death if kids go off-trail, or stray outside of safely controlled places. There are simple facts—growing population that replaces forests with houses and concrete roads, growing emphasis on test scores translating into more time in classrooms and less time playing outside, or schedules busy with soccer practices, music recitals, and extra-curricular projects. These things each have value. But collectively they result in no time left for children to bond with nature. Playful, meaningful connection with the wild world outdoors needs to be a fundamental ingredient of every childhood. We cannot let it invisibly slip away. We must consciously choose it for our children, our communities and ourselves.

Why? Direct experience with nature is primary learning. Human beings share many traits with animals, such as bone-structures, sensory perceptions, and footprints that mirror every hairy mammal on this earth. We have become who we are by living outdoors for hundreds of thousands, perhaps even millions of years. Just as a baby begins to breathe simply by being in a world of oxygen and letting its body respond, so do our bodies and brains have millions of built in neurological connections with the environment, waiting to be activated. Growing into and remaining as healthy and fully functional human animals requires ample time interacting with wild nature, time to play, be curious, be open-eyed and alive, and discover how we fit in, how we are connected with our biological world.

We've gradually allowed exploratory experience outdoors to be traded for indoor, largely sedentary experiences that depend on learning tools imagined and manufactured by humans.

What are the results? Not only do kids get the short-end of the developmental stick, but the natural world has fewer people who know and love it, fewer adults who have nature built into their habits of awareness, and therefore fewer humans who care to be good tenders of their habitat. The current trend of humans moving away from the rest of nature is so pervasive, it can seem overwhelming, like a tide we can't turn.

Turning the Tide

But we can turn the tide. We can, we must—and we are. By taking the first step off the beaten path and into the woods again, we've already begun.

More and more people are realizing this need and calling for direct experience outdoors to be a basic part of childhood. Parents, educators, psychologists and authors are all buzzing with the same message as Richard Louv: we need to restore the bond between children and nature. The emphatic statement broadcast across the Western world is more than "No Child Left Behind," we need, "No Child Left Inside." Knowing adults needs this too, and that younger people model what older people do, makes it imperative that the grown-ups make nature connection a priority in their lives as well.

But how do you do that? How do you get kids and their adults outside and into the nearby woods, or even out to the backyard? Who can lead them into the forests and fields and deserts, giving them the chance—like me that day in Redmond—to touch unfiltered wilderness, and be touched in return?

If anyone holds the antidote to Nature Deficit Disorder, if anyone can lead us and our children out from our concrete roads into the beating heart of our natural habitat, and wake us up to life—Coyote can.

Who is Coyote?

Coyote, also known as *Canis latrans*, is a common mammal of North America. It's a Canid—a member of the dog family. Generally, a coyote is about the size of a small golden retriever, about four feet from head to tail. It often trots with its tail down, over its bottom and between its legs, as if it's just done something sneaky and needs to slink away from the scene. Coyote's dominant sense, smell, is signaled by its long nose, and it uses that natural gift to hunt rabbits, rodents, and the occasional small deer, as well as to scavenge and eat seasonal fruits and berries. Undeniably, Coyotes also nab their share of pets, sheep, chickens, and other domestic livestock. Using that keen nose and also sharp hearing, Coyote travels alone or in pairs and lives a secretive life-style. As well as it can, it remains on the edge of awareness—of both potential predator and potential prey.

This wild dog with four-toed tracks has adapted well to human development across the continent, and can even be found thriving in the heart of some of America's largest cities. Just a few years ago, one ran into an elevator inside a Seattle skyscraper and took a ride. Not long after that, another one was found taking another ride—this time in the luggage compartment of an airport shuttle tram. Coyote is known for cunning adaptability, craftiness, and ability to survive anywhere. These qualities likely led to Coyote's mythic connotations among the indigenous people of North America.

The Trickster

In many Native American stories, Coyote uses his unorthodox foolery to save the humans in a pinch. He brings fire to the teeth-chattering, shivering humans in one story. In another story, when no human man can interest the most beautiful and artistic woman, Coyote uses tricks to attract her attention, marry her, bear her children, and so preserve the source of cultural creativity. And in yet another story, after the Creator made a little mistake in the initial creation of animals, Coyote is the one who makes sure every animal receives an anus. In some stories, the Trickster is the Creator. Nearly every tribe tells innumerable stories of Trickster, the foolish bringer of lessons.

Coyote is just one version, one manifestation, of this ubiquitous Trickster. On every continent of this planet, trickster shows up as different animals: Jackal, Raven, Rabbit, Raccoon, Spider, Fox, and many others. The trends in the Trickster stories are the same, however. When things go wrong and humans or animals don't know what to do, when none of the traditional approaches work, the Trickster shows up. With some wacky, out-of-the-box approach that at first seems ridiculous, Trickster cleverly makes things right.

The worldwide presence of such stories tells us the Trickster is a vital figure in human societies. In fact, Trickster in human form, almost always causes the huge leaps in cultural change. Gandhi played his Trickster card when he said he'd topple the British oppression by marching to the sea and making salt. Jesus, as the Trickster, threw the money-changers out of the temple, and allowed himself be led to death when no one else understood why. Buddha became the Trickster when he denounced the luxuries of the most sought-after position of Prince in order to free humans from suffering. Even Bill Gates of Microsoft was the Trickster when he dreamed of a computer in every home and began selling strange clunky boxes with screens and keyboards. Can't you hear the laughter aimed at these fools?

Yes, at first they seem a little crazy, a little off their rocker, a few cards short of a deck. But Trickster is the driving force

Trickster has a bad reputation. He is conniving, lying, cheating, falsifying, lazy, and good-for-nothing. He is also a god with quite a lot of power. He can die and be born again. He can shift his shape. He has a plan, but you don't know what it is. Through shifty means, he guides folks through the low roads of transformation. Quick-witted and convincing, he brings them out the other side, bright as butterflies.

ELLEN HAAS, Trickster has a Bad Reputation

of evolution. Trickster energy creates change by doing the outlandish so well that the outlandish becomes the new accepted norm. Then another Trickster comes along to shift that norm, and on and on.

Why this is Coyote's Guide

To make a long story short, we call this *Coyote's Guide* because it entices each of us off our beaten path, to experiment with creative approaches, to do something different from what's generally being tried. Coyote goads us to be willing to have a true sense of play and abandon, knowing that this new, uncharted way will truly be the only way out.

The mentoring approach in *Coyote's Guide to Connecting with Nature* challenges convention. It requires that we who wish to mentor others get in touch with and trust in our own Coyote selves—teasing us out of our indoor worlds and leading us all to connect in an intimate and meaningful way with the natural world and our natural selves.

We use a radical approach without textbooks or tests; we simply begin with the roots of nature education by engaging people in direct experience with the plants and animals just beyond the edge of their back yards. This book hopes to inspire you and coach you into stretching your own creativity. We offer you a bunch of tools and strip them down to underlying principles that you can apply to your situation. Like a book on gardening, we don't know what exactly will grow in your place, but we can give you the principles and encourage you to innovate with them. Then these tools will become yours.

That day in Redmond as Coyote led me from edge to edge deeper into the forest I learned this: he is the edge-walker, he-who-walks-around-the-edges. The Lakota song honoring the wolf, fox, and coyote species suggests how coyote does his magic. Real-life coyotes lurk on the edge of our human villages, always just beyond sight or reach. They keep a close and suspicious eye on danger and opportunity in all directions. They hunt and live wary around the edges. Coyote's edge-walk works as a perfect metaphor for nature educators to use as a guide.

Around the Edge I am Traveling,
Around the Edge I am Traveling,
In a Sacred Manner
I am Traveling.

"Traditional Lakota Song"
honoring the Wolf, Fox and
Coyote Nations

Translated by
Gilbert Walking Bull

How to Mentor as a Guide: Stretching Peoples' Edges

The first facet to the edge-walking metaphor suggests *how to mentor as a guide*. By circling around the periphery of those you mentor, you can guide them out from their indoor comfort zones, to the edge and farther edge of their experience and knowledge, just as Coyote did with me that day. He first met me where I was, then, staying a few steps ahead, he gently pulled me along. *Coyote's Guide* will encourage you to do the same thing: meet people where they are, and then intrigue them and entice them into ever-widening connection with the wilderness beyond the edge of town.

"Mentoring," is the appropriate word for this process, corresponding to a vigilant guide-to-explorer, or master-to-apprentice relationship. The most profound education will occur when you get to know the person you mentor the way medieval guild masters got to know their apprentices. Masters trained journeymen by living with them night and day, through work and play, and discovering their special gifts and challenges.

First and foremost, guiding like Coyote requires that you get to *know* the people you mentor. You have to watch carefully for what will capture their curiosity, engage their natural gifts, and challenge them in ways they can handle in their personal learning journey. Look for their edges: the edge of their comfort zone, the edge of their awareness, the edge of their knowledge, the edge of their experience. Then, you can stretch and pull them to a new edge, and then another, deeper and deeper into a sense of comfort and kinship with the wildness of the natural world.

To explain why anyone is a conservationist and what motivates him … means going back to the very beginning of his involvement with the natural scene. I believe one of the basic tenets … is to have a love for the land, which comes through a long intimacy with natural beauty and living things.

Only if there is understanding can there by reverence and only where there is deep emotional feeling is anyone willing to do battle.

SIGURD OLSON, *Open Horizons*

Melanie's story

Here's an example: at a summer camp in a park in the heart of big-city Seattle, one girl in my group named Melanie wouldn't even sit on the ground to eat lunch, so I asked her about it. She said she was scared of spiders and thought they might crawl on her if she sat on the ground. That was her edge.

So after lunch (she stood the whole time), I asked my group of kids if they wanted to play a hiding game. They all yelped in delight, "Yeah!"

The inspiration was so high that I could see the excitement creep into her face. When it dawned on her, her face suddenly changed—hiding would mean her lying in the bushes and on the ground. She told me she wasn't going to play. But I could see her wavering now, on her edge, ready to push through.

So once the "seeker" had closed her eyes and started counting, and all the kids dashed into the bushes to hide, I leaned over to her and whispered, "If you point to where you want to hide, I'll go search it real good for spiders to make sure none are there, and then you can hide."

She hesitated, and I could physically see the conflict within her. Finally, she nodded, "Okay," and looking around, pointed to a huge sword fern behind a fallen log.

I went over, got down on my knees, and then on my belly, looking all around. Not finding any spiders, I got up, brushed the dirt off my shirt, and smiled, "It's all clear." She walked over and carefully squatted down on her knees, her head and body covered now by fern leaves.

Out of the corner of my eye, I watched her squirm and worry her way through that first round of hiding. But by the fourth or fifth round, she was diving in the thickest bushes without hesitation.

I wish you could have seen the smile on her face when the game was over, the sparkle in her eye. She had pushed through her edge. In what had seemed like a scary wilderness, she could now be comfortable. So, the Coyote Mentoring mind then asks, "What's her next edge?"

The trick to Coyote Mentoring is to watch and listen and get to know well the people you guide. Then to continually stay a couple steps ahead and guide them, edge by edge, into ever-expanding orbits.

The Art of Mentoring and Coyote Teaching is about the process by which we stretch and stretch a person, in their awareness, in their use of senses, in their search imagery, in their appreciation of where they fit, in their knowledge of self, and in the understanding and telling of their own story within the story of life.

Jon Young

What to Learn: Straddling the Edge of Two Worlds

A second facet of the edge-walking metaphor suggests *what is being learned*. Coyote teaches us to straddle the edge between "two worlds"— the ancient, primitive world of wilderness and instinct, and the modern, civilized world of science and technology.

When I followed Coyote that day in Redmond, I remember wondering about his scat full of apples. Were there any fruiting apple trees around? Nope. It wasn't the season. I don't know where he could have found those apples. But *he did*, because Coyote knows intimately both where to hide in the dark forests and where to raid the compost piles in the suburban back yards. Many indigenous cultures see Coyote as the epitome of knowledge of place; their legends hold many stories of his amazing ability to adapt to almost any landscape.

Coyote's Guide does not call you to go backwards to nature, to run off to the woods to survive. The ideal learning journey for connection to nature embraces the solid scientific curriculum that qualifies a well-trained naturalist—such as cross-referencing information, using technical names, and replicating results. However, a felt sense of connection and kinship will always remain at the root of Coyote Mentoring.

Along with teaching methodologies drawn from the scientific paradigm, we also borrow from world-wide indigenous cultures who demonstrate, like Coyote, strong kinship with their landscapes. All native cultures have much to teach about connecting with nature. The word *native* shares its root word with the word *nativity*; meaning *born into*. People born and raised with the land who feel kinship with its elements are truly natives. But to us, a quality of awareness, a quality of connection to the place, defines being native to a place. By using this Guide, you will be mentoring yourself and others in the art of "Seeing Through Native Eyes" (the audio series written and narrated by Jon Young, used as the core of our *Kamana Naturalist Training Program*).

This Guide encourages you to straddle the edge and walk in both worlds: the human-made world with its vast scientific vocabulary and technology, and the instinctive, imagination-based world of our ancestors. Both worlds offer rich, educational potential. As a Coyote Mentor, you will tap into zoology and botany textbooks, field guides, the scientific method, child development theories, and wildlife videos. Yet you will also explore the ancient cultural wisdom from around the world, its mythic animal stories, nature-based ceremonies, and tools for survival. By using

Coyote as our guide, we learn both the scientific map and our landscape terrain. When we embrace *fact* with *imagination*, and combine *logical evidence* with *intuition*, we develop intellectual *understanding* through first-hand *experience*.

How to Act: Pushing Our Own Edges

Watch these facets build on one another: first *how to mentor as a guide*, then comes the content of *what to learn*. The third facet to the edge-walking metaphor refers to the Trickster aspect of Coyote. It involves role-modeling, *how to* act as mentoring guides. Coyote teaches us to go out on a limb, to do things that can seem a little scary, like telling a personal a story in front of a bunch of people, getting completely covered in mud, spending all day playing hiding games in the bushes, or getting your explorers all riled up with excitement. As a Trickster, you will embody the same humble curiosity and willingness to stretch beyond your comfort zone that you want to pass on to those you mentor.

Like the Trickster, being a Coyote Mentor implies play. Find that child inside of yourself who loves adventure and mysteries and playing outside. Improvise in the moment with courage and humility. Being a Coyote Guide calls for serious fun.

The whole purpose of this book helps you find your own creative Coyote side, so you can adapt activities to your personal style, your place, your specific purpose. Play and experimentation are the only way to get there. If you follow the guidance of this book, you will stretch your own edges continually, growing fiercely into your unique self. So, Coyote Mentoring involves a commitment to your own journey of self-knowledge as well as that of those you mentor. This Guide encourages you to let loose your own Trickster talents, edge-by-fragile-edge, until you can express them unabashedly.

Here's a poem I jotted down in the midst of writing this book:

Burn This Book
This book is not for anyone to make a banner out of,
To quote at length as some new bible.
It is a gentle companion in your own process,
A process of dancing alive in the moment
With children, squirrel tracks and clouds, a falling leaf.
If anything, let this book bump you along
Into your own way of doing things,
Into your own way of being the mentor you already are.

This book will teach you a few dances,
But we really want you to remember the place
Where dances are made, before the first step.
When you start to move to your own steps,
Burn this book. Please.

This book is an introduction, not a complete guide. Where these ideas take you will be completely up to you. This book is just the beginning of a conversation, a conversation we've been having for years, and one that will never stop.

Oh, and perhaps it's more sustainable—even *regenerative*—to pass this book on to another…

The Invisible School

In many of the old Coyote stories a dynamic repeats with Coyote acting a bit too playful for his own good. With all that play, how can anything get done? But a deeper purpose below the surface can only be realized at the end of the story—when, thanks to Coyote's great and bewildering efforts, things are made right. With Coyote Mentoring, your deeper purpose unfolds, not all that differently from the Trickster stories.

To the people you serve, it may seem like nothing but running through woods, playing games, and listening to stories. An underlying intention they never realize lies beneath this surface evidence. By subtly and invisibly using Child Passions to get people to practice Core Routines and so read the Book of Nature, you engage them in learning without them ever knowing it. You are running an "Invisible School."

Jon Young coined this term, "Invisible School," after completing his college degree studying indigenous cultures' methods of cultivating a continuous, in-depth understanding of natural history within their villages. In his research, he found no formal "schools," and rarely any formal "teachers." Yet everyone he met from such cultures, and those documented by anthropologists, demonstrated a knowledge of their natural world surpassing any modern Ph.D. in Ecology. Today Jon realizes this depth of pure understanding goes beyond simple knowledge and far into the realm of *connection*. Indigenous mentors know how the land breaths and flows through seasons and days; they can track and hunt and make complicated medicines from plants; they can read the weather and navigate by the stars. Their knowledge of and deep connection to place is intricately ingrained in every member of the culture, without schools. So how do these cultures *teach* their youth? How do they connect them so potently to the environment with no schools or teachers?

Cultural Mentoring

Jon realized the "school" of nature lived in the culture itself. "Teaching" came through the ceremonies that required certain plants to be used and honored the four directions of the sun or the cycles of the moon. The "school" lived in stories that taught volumes while enchanting listeners. Their descriptive, nature-based language spoke through the customs of naming people based on plants and animals. Great teachings flowed from the games kids played, and the errands of gathering that grandparents sent them on. Obviously teachings happened because of the intense need of the whole culture to track or hunt, and to know a wide variety of plant communities and their uses.

All of this together surrounded everyone with an Invisible School, instilling an understanding and appreciation of the environment unparalleled by any formal education. The people just lived day-to-day life and nature wove itself into a part of everything, inseparable in their very being.

This Guide intends to pass on this method of Invisible Schooling, so people will connect with nature without knowing it. They'll soak up the language of plants and animals as naturally as you or any of us learned our native language. Do you remember learning to talk? Probably not. Spoken language happened around you all the time, and allowed you to experiment with words, make mistakes, and every single day grow vocabulary. Mentoring with the language of nature happens just the same. With stories, games, songs, place-names, animal names, and more, you invisibly and subtly stretch their language edges. Just like Trickster Coyote, a lot more happens below the surface because you are the cultural conductor.

Growth and learning occur so gradually and invisibly, that people express shock when they finally realize the depth of the education and the connections they have formed. Parents often worry in the beginning, "They're just messing around all day—how can they be learning?" Then the day comes when they are out in the woods or the backyard trails with their child, who brings plant after plant with detailed knowledge about its uses, or shows them track after track, following and interpreting the trail, or effortlessly identifies trees by name. Parents then become our

Soon your people will flood the land like a river after a downpour. But my people and I we are the ebbing tide. This destiny is a mystery to the Red Man. We might be able to understand it if we knew the White Man's dreams -- the hopes and expectations about which he talks to his children in the long winter evenings -- what visions he engraves in their hearts so that they look forward eagerly to the coming day.

Chief Sealth

most ardent supporters. The same story repeats when we work this way with adults—at first they think "This is just wandering around outside." But then they say, "This is the most I have learned about nature in my life, and it is the most fun I have had in years." Nature connection through this kind of mentoring proves to be more than just effective, it is also fun, healing, and empowering. Like the Coyote whose methods at first seem unorthodox or even foolish, in the end, it works better than anyone could dream.

Using this Book

We wrote this book to "unveil" the Invisible School. Our intention reveals the unseen, as Dorothy saw the man-behind-the-green-curtain at the end of the *Wizard of Oz*, so you too, can invisibly orchestrate a grand drama of opportunities for the people you guide outdoors.

The Mentor's Manual and Activities Guide work hand-in-hand to show you the multiple intentions that go into designing and guiding a story, a lesson, or a game. As we stated at the very beginning in "How to Use This Book," the idea is not to provide yet another book of "recipes." Instead, we want to help you learn *how to cook*. We want you to see what each activity teaches below the surface, and how you can alter or create your own activities to accomplish your specific goals for those you guide.

Each activity, therefore, has a key-like heading of five elements of education that are happening "invisibly." We designed the remaining chapters of this Mentor's Manual to carefully explain those elements:

+ **Shifting Routines and Core Routines of Nature Connection** explain the practices that learners do. Repeating these invisibly and visibly all the time, in every way and in every situation, develops good habits for connecting with nature.

+ **Child Passions as Mentoring Tools, Questioning and Answering, Storytelling**, and **Music Making** highlight the universal instincts that children and playful adults possess, and show how to use these as doorways through

Our commitment in this project is restoring the children's trails. Let's dare to try. We'll reintroduce them. We'll catch and rear children, and then we'll release them.

Jon Young

Ua Mau ke Ea o ka Āina i ka Pono "The life of the land is perpetuated by the health of the people"

The State motto of Hawaii

which Core Routines and knowledge of natural history may enter the lives of children from 1 to 100, that is, *everyone.*

- **The Book of Nature** points to the most fertile places to start when connecting people with natural history. It narrows down the infinite possibilities by emphasizing meaningful relationships.

- **Orienting to the Natural Cycle** holds more than one key to understanding this Coyote's Guide. A close study of the Cycle's implications for mentoring organization will be worthwhile.

- **The Natural Cycle of Learning** conveys a vision of how energies move through a day, a week, or a lifetime, giving you a feel for the rhythm that allows you both to plan and improvise for success.

- **Indicators of Awareness** paints a handful of universal character traits fostered through connecting with nature. They describe the goals of Coyote Mentoring in terms of personal growth that emerges naturally through practicing these routines and activities.

Each activity in the Activities Guide cross-references to the key sections of the Mentor's Manual. As you choose activities for your lesson plan, consider which Core Routines to practice through the activity, which Child Passions to tap into, which parts of the Book of Nature could be emphasized, where the activity fits in the Natural Cycle, and which Indicators of Awareness you want to cultivate. This interweaving allows you to adapt your own activities in your own local ecosystem.

All together then, *Coyote's Guide* happens in the way of Coyote by guiding from behind-the-scenes. Just as the Coyote disappeared that day with me in Redmond, once you wake up the edge-stretching curiosity inside each person you mentor, you can step away. Once people break out of their indoor comfort zones, develop habits of awareness, and realize their own fascination to learn more, nature will do the rest.

Coyote's Challenge

By naming Coyote as our guide, we are invoking something that challenges each of us to grow. Coyote challenges us to break from old habits of awareness and to see with fresh eyes:

- Brightly calling us to re-imagine how we learn natural history, helping to weave us more strongly into the web of connection between ourselves, our fellow humans, and all the creatures and elements around us.

- Motivating us to frolic timelessly in the wilderness—that the fire of curiosity may light every eye and that myth and play may merge with fact and science.

- Nudging us to take up the scent, the meandering but purposeful trail, to the source of our own self-guidance, to the fount of unique gifts that each person carries.

- Sharpening our eyes to see beyond the rim of the wild hill, beyond the skyline where the modern world fades against the setting sun sky, to the possibility of a long and healthy human existence on this earth, a conscious regeneration of land and culture for generations to come.

Warren and I tried to take this book in another direction that day, just before I drove into Redmond, but thank goodness Coyote showed up to change our minds. Coyote doesn't distract from what we want to say—<u>it is</u> what we want to say. The archetype of Coyote empowers radical medicine—root-based, environmental education that restores the original bond between humans and the rest of nature.

We have never needed it more than now.

Chapter 2

SHIFTING ROUTINES

Coyote calls us off the beaten path. An Ojibway legend prophesies that the green paths the People walk will become charred and blackened, and their hearts will grow heavy. Then the time will come to turn back on the charred and blackened trail and turn off into the small green byways again. It foresees that in the small green byways the People will recover their strength, and with lifted hearts return to restore the blackened highways. The premise of this chapter is that we do need to turn back and reconnect with our natural roots, in order to recover and restore. And that means shifting our routines. This chapter includes some heady theory about how learning happens, what we're really teaching, and why to shift routines. The next chapter will launch into useful descriptions of the thirteen Core Routines of Nature Connection that underlie every moment of Coyote's mentoring approach. If you don't need to know the *why* and just want the *how*, it's okay to skip these pages; just remember to practice these Core Routines with those you mentor every day, in every way.

Rachel Carson's book, Silent Spring was written because as a citizen and a scientist, she noticed there were no frogs singing in her neighborhood spring.

Why was it that no one else had noticed this? This crisis was not in a remote Brazilian rainforest. DDT's effect was in everyone's back yard—in the vacant lot next door, in the ditches and creeks that kids played in.

People didn't notice because they didn't grow up developing the sensory perception and mental search imagery that would make the silence of the frogs apparent.

Jon Young, The Silence of Frogs

Core Routines in Any Field

Some synonyms:
Core – Heart – Center – Foundation – Middle
Routine – Round – Cycle – Habit – Practice – Discipline
Connection – Bond – Relationship – Communication – Union

As a jazz musician in college, I was taught to practice certain "core routines:" listening to music, doing finger exercises, ear-training, practicing scales, and jamming with other musicians. Poets, painters, hunters, gardeners, and even football players I have met report the same emphasis from their mentors on regular habits for learning. I am convinced curious educators can find "core routines" in just about any field of learning.

How We Learn: Brain Patterning

We humans practice routines to gain mastery in a discipline. Our tendency to form habits through repeated behavior endows us with skills and it also shapes and defines our perceptions, which is why we notice things that are important to us. For years we have referred to the process of learning-through-habit as "Brain Patterning." Some would prefer to call it "Mind Patterning" in order to align with emerging evidence that consciousness may have roots beyond the physical brain. (There is now evidence of neurons within the heart, suggesting consciousness may reside there, while other scientists think that the mind must exist outside of the body in both individual and collective fields—for more information on alternative theories of mind, see the works of Joseph Chilton Pierce and Rupert Sheldrake.) No matter how we may define brain or mind—and we leave this up to each reader to do for themselves—there is a consensus that we are habit-forming creatures. And these habits reinforce themselves, and influence our perceptions and our behaviors.

As an image, *brain patterning* brings home the message that through our habits we physically shape and change ourselves—continually.

Brain Patterning for Skill Development

Our brains take in everything we experience, far beyond our conscious awareness. If we repeat an activity, a mental image, or idea over a period of time, then our brain's neurological pathways form a shortcut so we don't need to *think* about it. This repetition acts like a computer shortcut that saves searching through a maze to find our application, or like the kids' shortcut through the neighbor's yards that bypasses streets to get to school. Such shortcuts streamline behavior: that's what we're calling "brain patterning."

Consider how *you* learn and your own neurological shortcuts will come into view. Remember learning how to ride a tricycle? When your shiny red tricycle arrived in the driveway, you danced with glee. With excitement, focused attention, and Mom and Dad showing you how to set your feet on the pedals, you threw your brain and body into the awkward task of pushing those pedals round. The tricycle bolted forward: you did it! All that afternoon, they couldn't get you off that trike as you practiced and practiced. By the end of day, you could scoot all the way up and down the driveway.

On the morning of day two, you focused excitement and attention to navigate the bumps and pits of the driveway, *while* pedaling. By the afternoon, your learning goal shifted to making the turn at both ends of the driveway, *while* pedaling *and* avoiding bumps and pits. Desire and concentration, added emotion from falling and getting back up, and a little more help from Mom and Dad, and you taught yourself to turn the handlebars just so and lean your body slightly to the inner side of the turn. Pedaling itself became second nature, which left your thinking mind to focus on the new subtleties.

This is how core routines work to condition the brain towards the development of a skill. First inherited biological potential, stimulated by mental focus and emotional excitement, plus a little help from a mentor, forges a neuronal pathway. Then repetition reinforces it into a brain pattern or unconscious mental habit, wrapped in a myelin sheath, like electrical tape. Now, with no thought about the original, basic pattern, you can add subtlety and complexity. This is how we learned to walk, how we learned to talk, how we learned to read words, and then read a whole book. Similarly, we learned to add and subtract and progressed to calculus. In exactly this way, once my fingers learned the basic routines, my mind and soul were free to play jazz.

Nobel laureate Paul MacLean a scientific authority on the human brain, along with others are well aware that brain patterning may be a manifestation of mind. In any case, it seems important to note that the heart is also a brain with neurons comprising fifty percent or more of its cells—with a new medical specialty called cardioneurology. If the body is entrained to the brain, the brain is entrained to the heart, which is to say the heart, not the brain, is the cardinal organ of the human body. If Joseph Chilton Pearce is right, bonding during infancy may influence the heart's connection between the mid-brain and the cerebral cortex thus building a foundation for heart-intelligence or thinking with the heart.

RANDALL L. EATON, Brain, Mind, or Heart?

The Brain Patterning Cycle

I remember returning from my first weeklong "nature awareness" class in New Jersey with Tom Brown, Jr. where I learned about the everyday dandelion plant: I tasted its bitter, yummy taste; I learned that dandelion leaves offer one of the most abundant plant sources of vitamin A known to humans. All through the week I would pick a few leaves a day to eat as a general health tonic. I returned home to my house in Georgia where I had lived for eighteen years, and as I walked through my yard, I suddenly froze in astonishment: dandelion suddenly grew all over my yard! I had never noticed it, but now that I had a brain pattern, in this case, a search image for dandelion, and I found it everywhere.

We see this over and over, as people come to learn with us and return home convinced that red-tail hawks or American robins have suddenly moved into their area. In truth, the robins, red-tails, and dandelions lived there all along, but because our brains were not yet patterned on them, our perceptions did not include these natural elements.

These observations caused us to formulate the following Brain Patterning Cycle:

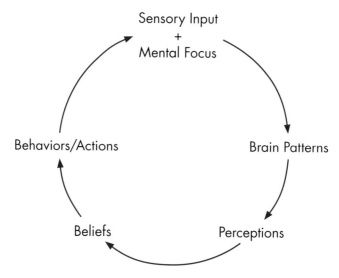

Everything we take in with our senses, combined with what we focus our mental attention on, results in brain patterns. Brain patterns, in turn, determine our perceptions, how we see the world. Our beliefs about the world are formed this way. See this transformation of my beliefs: before that Tom Brown class, I believed food and medicine came from grocery stores and pharmacies and I believed my yard was only good for soccer games. New brain patterns opened my eyes to new perceptions, which changed my beliefs: I began to believe that food could come for free out of my own backyard.

Our beliefs, in turn, determine our actions and behaviors. Previously, if I wanted to make a salad, I'd drive to the store; now, I can take a walk in the back yard. The next consequence is fairly obvious: our actions and behaviors determine our sensory input (grocery store florescent lights vs. dappled sunshine and birdsong in the backyard) and our mental focus (iceberg lettuce vs. dandelions). Now we are back at the beginning of the cycle, now we understand how our behaviors fortify our habits over time, and make them stronger through repetition.

What we Miss: The Flip Side of Brain Patterning

When we apply this Brain Patterning theory to connecting with nature, we discover its flip side. Brain patterns causing us to notice specific things implying that we will not notice almost everything else. It's like a magic trick. As observers, our brains recognize movements we expect to see. These mental habits cause us to miss the subtle sleights of hand that engage the "magic"— really just clever maneuvering around our conditioning. However, once we recognize how the trick works, we know what to look for and the veil is lifted. So as members of the modern world, what are we missing?

As the old saying goes, "We are what we eat." In terms of sensory input and mental focus, it seems to be true: our beliefs and behaviors are a reflection of our brain patterning. If we spend most of our time in our houses and buildings, in our living rooms and bedrooms, we almost literally *are* our living rooms and bedrooms. If our culture's gaze has turned inside, we won't notice the natural world.

For many people in urbanized areas nowadays, wild nature doesn't really exist in their perceptions of the world. We find this to be an enlightening and yet also scary realization. No surprise then that very few people notice when the landscape starts to change in response to our human actions, when rabbits lose their habitats and disappear, when frogs stop singing. Yes, a few—the scientists trained to see such things—will notice. To almost everyone else, those subtle happenings in nature are lost. As a culture, unless we can shift our focus of attention, we'll continue basing our choices on a sense of reality that doesn't include the rest of nature.

We miss much more than just the crises in nature. Children grow up not noticing the beauty of a robin song in the morning, or the fragile first

Without brain patterning, your brain is incapable of thinking about more than one task at a time, though you can fake it, poorly. But why can you talk, walk, chew gum, and breathe all at the same time? Walking, chewing gum, and breathing are all practiced activities. If you practice an activity until it becomes a brain pattern, you can do it without actually thinking.

If you sit in the woods, hear a bird singing, and try to recognize it, then your brain becomes preoccupied thinking about the notes, cadence, etc., which means you will miss any new sound. But if you have patterned your brain to recognize common bird songs then it will automatically hear "Wrentit," so you can calmly remember that while remaining aware enough to catch the song sparrow's call.

Brain patterning is the key to higher awareness.

DAVID FORTHOFFER, Kamana Student, Brain Patterning

'Nature' should be avoided in such vague expressions as 'a lover of nature,' 'poems about nature.' Unless more specific statements follow, the reader cannot tell whether the poems have to do with natural scenery, rural life, the sunset, the untouched wilderness, or the habits of squirrels.

STRUNK & WHITE, *The Elements of Style*, 3rd edition, 1979

flowers of spring. Grownups walk through streets blind to the hawks soaring majestically overhead, or the fox tracks lacing the back alleys with stories. The hills and clouds stop speaking to our imagination and the paths to the streams and forests get overgrown.

Toward a Culture of Nature Awareness

Until recently, humans' primary brain patterns were based on keen daily awareness of the expansive world of nature. Do these drastic and sudden shifts in mental habits benefit our health and functioning? Can we claim to be better and more evolved because modern patterns focus on indoor activities and electronic literacy? Richard Louv's book clearly documents the answer—decidedly not. Nature is an essential nutrient to the health of each human.

Good news, though. We can intervene in the brain patterning cycle. The solution requires only a shift in our routine behaviors. This is where the Core Routines of Nature Awareness enter the picture. We simply take the same cycle, and for our behaviors and actions, we insert the Core Routines:

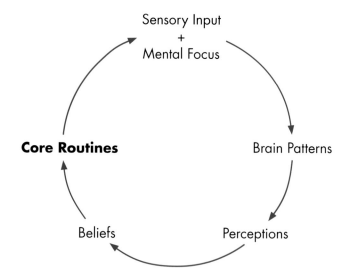

Sensory Input + Mental Focus

Brain Patterns

Core Routines

Perceptions

Beliefs

Even a conscious and quiet sit on a balcony in a skyscraper will provide connections with crows, the moods of wind and weather, and the movements of sun, moon, and stars. If—that is—we look for it.

Our goal in practicing and reinforcing the Core Routines of Nature Connection is to restore finely tuned habits of awareness based on nature. Again we return to the image of Coyote, the one who breaks "out-of-the-box" of our cultural conditioning to see things anew. Coyote sees through the magic trick. Coyote shows us how to use our brains and bodies as they were made to be used.

Defining our Field of Learning

Cultures guide every individual to develop brain patterns—through the spoken language, the customs and ceremonies of the community, and more—all of it informing where to pay attention. Culture, we could say, is the water that every individual swims in as they grow and develop. At this point, then, we should make clear and candid the type of culture, and resulting intelligences, that we offer here for consideration. What exactly are we promoting with this guide book, *Connecting with Nature*?

We engage in a field of learning quite possibly the oldest of all the cognitive disciplines. What Coyote awakens we call "Seeing through Native Eyes," like those people, or wild animals whose whole lives and cultures respond to natural rhythms and forces. We've also called it "Wilderness Awareness," a bright, awakened native intelligence that can see a jungle in a sidewalk crack. In the eighteenth and nineteenth centuries, people passionately studied our field of learning known then as the contagious story of "Natural History." The closest name modern academia offers, "Field Ecology," aspires to develop the ability to use all one's senses out in the field to understand the interdependent web of life. Or maybe this learning could be called "Nature Literacy," a fluent ability to read the Book of Nature.

For this book we call it "Nature Connection" to show our field of discovery goes far beyond an intellectual knowledge of place, or lonely names of flowers and birds detached from their real, felt meaning. Coyote's education awakens habits of perception we call Sensory Awareness, cultivates a rich vocabulary of search images we call Knowledge of Place, and through these, connects people to the Natural World in a meaningful way.

Plants change with seasons and weather, and animals move with stealth and speed and tend to avoid human presence. Professional naturalists and wildlife biologists must use all their senses to spot wildlife on the move and notice signs that wildlife has passed by. Out in the field, they must wait quietly and see quickly. In field reports they must draw inferences from signs and tracks.

PATRICIA THOMPSON,
Washington Department of Fish and Wildlife

One of the best tools I can give anybody is this: simply stop yourself several times during each day and ask yourself this question: 'What am I missing right now?' And automatically, your awareness will shift from a regular, narrow vision to an expansive awareness, involving all your senses and taking in a larger sphere of life.

RICHARD CLEVELAND, Founder and Lead Instructor, Earth School, www.lovetheearth.com

Awakening Sensory Awareness

We began writing this book with wildlife biologists and ecology teachers who told us that The Art of Mentoring and Coyote Mentoring provides the missing puzzle pieces in many of their educational curricula—this actual attention to "awareness" out in the field.

Parents work hard to teach sensory awareness as a skill set to toddlers by surrounding them with color-coded toys in shapes of circles and triangles or sitting them in front of panels full of bells and whistles. *Hot, cold, red,* and *wet* make up children's earliest words. However, by the time children reach kindergarten, deliberate education in sensory awareness fades out. They learn their ABC's and stop there. Shouldn't this foundational intelligence be honed into literacy? Shouldn't sensory imagination be an "essential learning requirement" like reading, writing, and arithmetic?

We all inherit the potential brainpower that our hunter-gatherer ancestors used with extraordinary intelligence in order to survive. Our brain power includes a huge capacity to perceive subtle and minute details, to notice all sorts of shapes, colors, smells, sounds, designs, movements, sequences, changes, patterns, and anomalies in our environment. These sensory perceptions can be honed—with time and curiosity—into the mental habits of a well developed "naturalist intelligence." Howard Gardner's *Frames of Mind* proposed seven "intelligences"—bodily-kinesthetic, linguistic, logical-mathematical, musical, interpersonal, intrapersonal, and spatial. In 1999, in *Intelligence Reframed,* Gardner endorsed an eighth, the "naturalist intelligence" that underlies all the rest. Nature, the perfectly-matched teacher for this training, offers as diverse, spontaneous, and ever-changing a palette of sights, smells, noises, tastes, and textures as we could ever write into a textbook.

Cultivating Knowledge of Place

Although all of our ancestors were indigenous people, and their unschooled ways of knowing may be considered 'illiterate' in the

Western sense, we have found native peoples of the world to be highly competent in a far older kind of 'literacy'." Not surprisingly, the brains of illiterate trackers and gatherers show little activity involved with words and names for things, but enormous activity involved with images. Our ancestors' literacy interpreted the pictures, scents, and tastes of their world. Just as the world's oldest languages use picture-images to denote the basic units of thought (not *yellow*, but *forsythia blossom*, not *north* but *land of tall trees*), so the core subject matter for Knowledge of Place supplies an infinite vocabulary of images. This multi-sensory, dynamic literacy is far more powerful than words alone.

The Core Routines of Story of the Day, Expanding our Senses, Tracking and Questioning, Animal Forms, Mapping, Journaling—indeed, all thirteen of them—pattern the brain to learn and remember what field biologists call *search images*. Like words in Language Arts, figures in Math, and symbols in Chemistry, we first learn the foundational search imagery, then we use it with increasing sophistication. Knowledge of Place, exactly like Language Arts, accumulates with discipline. Even though we learn to write a unified and coherent paragraph in first grade, we still practice to perfect the art in graduate school.

Once you get a search image for the flight pattern of an eagle *soaring* or a chickadee *lurching*, you can identify the bird off the corner of your eye. Once you get a brain pattern for the leafing system of elderberry *opposite* or Solomon's seal *alternate*, you can identify it while running. Once you hear the difference between baseline birdsong *happy* and alarm calls *frantic*, you can begin to understand the language of birds. Once you know the different feel of a south and north slope, you can guess your location when you seem lost in the terrain. Seasoned hunters will know a bear from a mile away because darkness appears where light should be. Such wonderful tales of perception from well-trained naturalists' eyes or ears can be found everywhere.

Similar knowledge of place will be cultivated into first-sighting search images by excited, focused, mentored attention. Then repeated conscious awareness can include telling about it, questioning and comparing it with things similar though different

CORE ROUTINES

Before the myelin sheaths have hardened, while the kids are young and open-minded, we need to stretch their awareness beyond tightly wound thought patterns that are inattentive to and even fearful of natural processes. We need to teach them to reach out with their eyes.

Jon Young, Myelin

Objects are concealed from our view not so much because they are out of the curve of our visual ray as because there is no intention of the mind and eye toward them … . We cannot see anything until we are possessed with the idea of it, and then we can hardly see anything else.

Henry David Thoreau, *Walden*

in detail, identifying it in field guides, acting it out, or drawing it. Learning theory suggests new information settles down into long-term memory after we notice, forget, then remember again, preferably five times, using different modalities of perception. Once a search image settles into a brain pattern, it becomes just part of your unconscious vocabulary.

Then, you can begin to read. Barry Lopez, in *Patriotism and the American Land*, describes the literature that lies ahead: "In all the years I have spent standing or sitting on the banks of this river, I have learned this: the more knowledge I have, the greater becomes the mystery of what holds that knowledge together, this reticulated miracle called an ecosystem."

Restoring the Bond between People and the Rest of Nature

The knowledge of place we look for in people we mentor shows up through their felt, bodily relationship with nature; in their muddy knees and hair with bits of leaves in it; in plants we can eat or slap on a cut to stop the bleeding; in tracks that tell us of real animals and their lives or lead us straight to them; in tree-branches that make a sturdy survival shelter or wood that burns well; in salamanders, frogs, and lizards that beg to be caught with our hands; in birds that alarm when we sneak through the woods, or lead us to hiding owls.

Once there is a personal bond with some bit of the natural world, then (or simultaneously) we can introduce scientific names and tidbits of knowledge or skill because there will be a scaffold for that information to hang on. With even a shred of meaningful relationship present, the excited explorer becomes an inquisitive "vacuum," sucking in all the information he or she can find.

Simply put, we aim to create meaningful bonds between people and the rest of nature. When we say *connection*, we mean a familiarity, a sense of kinship, just as we all experience with our human family. The goal includes knowledge and skills, but ultimately relationships restore our bond to nature.

Building this foundational connection with nature is like any relationship—it takes time to form really true bonds. Therefore, mentoring people in nature connection requires a long-term practice. Every outdoor event adds to the accumulated knowledge that we strive for—summer camps, weekend workshops, hour-long school assembly programs—make a difference in a person's life. They do. But, a longer-term and slower-growing mentoring relationship is far more effective for the powerful development of the individual's awareness and connection to nature.

Never underestimate the effect that your mentoring actions can have—however insignificant they may seem. One story can stay in their lives forever. One leaf eaten from one edible plant; one encouragement of a particular interest, one challenge at a ripe time; any one of these or a thousand other actions can make a difference. I once told a story to a group of forty kids and one parent wrote our school a letter saying, "My child sits alone in the yard for hours, because Evan told her that if she sat still long enough, the animals would get to know her."

Beyond Nature Connection: Nature, Community, and Self

When we leave the human village behind us and give ourselves unstructured time outdoors, we are able to notice and follow our inner voice. We find our own path and we end up exactly where we need to go. Our schools trust in what we call the "Gift Principle." Simply, this idea observes that everyone comes into the world bearing unique gifts. Our job as parents, friends, teachers, or mentors helps each child discover those gifts and bring them to blossom.

We realize that nature helps this happen like nothing else. As Warren Moon likes to say, "The natural world powerfully fosters self-expression, because nature itself is so completely self-expressed." The robin doesn't wake up in the morning and think, "That sparrow over on that salmonberry bush sings so much better than me." No, no such self-doubt exists in robin. It just opens up and SINGS! The same is true with trees and storms. A tree just leafs, a storm just blows. When we spend an abundance of time around this uninhibited self-expression, we resonate like tuning forks to express who we are: we sing our own gifted songs.

CORE ROUTINES

A student that I've worked with was said to have Attention Deficit Disorder. When I brought him into the field, I noticed he had the ears of a scout. He was able to monitor all four directions at the same time, and notice bird calls from every direction.

So, I watched him over time. When we worked indoors, in the classroom, in the group, he was a bit unable to sit still. But when we got out in the field, he was always the first one to see the hawk, always the first one to spot the hiding instructor, always the first one to hear the bird warnings.

And I started to ask myself, "Is that a disorder, or a gift?

Jon Young, *Seeing Through Native Eyes*, audio

Jake Swamp refers to the idea that every person has a Natural Gift, but they don't know how to see it themselves. From this perspective (and it seems to have existed all around the world in earlier times), every person has a unique gift that they are bringing to the world, and it is exactly what the world needs right now. The Coyote Mentor is trying to lead this gift out.

Jon Young, Natural Gifts

Just as in nature, where everything fills its niche and contributes to the whole, so does each human. Connection to nature naturally invites people to appreciate the dynamics of community. They realize that every person has a place and a contribution to make, whether in the exploring group of the day, or back home among their families and friends. Our ultimate mentoring goal draws out the natural gifts of each individual and helps them discover their relationship to their various communities, both human and natural.

Really, then, the nature of our connection emerges much broader than trees and tracks, berries and birds. It is also connection to our *human* nature—the discovery of our true selves and a greater appreciation of family. Gary Riekes, founder of the Riekes Center for Human Enhancement in San Francisco, once told us that if you mentor a child other than your own, your benchmark of success comes when the parents of that child invite you to dinner. Mohawk Elder Jake Swamp told Jon Young, once he realized the depth of our mentoring commitment, "Your school needs to be dedicated to healing families." Mentoring quality relationships with nature leads naturally to developing relationships with the families of the people you serve. In long-term programs, this is essential.

Norman "Ingwe" Powell, leader in the early Boy Scout movement in both Africa and America and co-founder and Grandfather of Wilderness Awareness School, summed up mentoring by saying, "We must all learn again to reach out, to touch, and to love."

Indicators of Success

Shifting into practice of the Core Routines of Nature Connection includes developing Howard Gardner's "naturalist intelligence," and much more. Ultimately, Core Routines cultivate whole human beings who appreciate and contribute to family and community by fully expressing and sharing their innate gifts and talents.

Over the years, we have observed a set of character qualities that consistently emerge as a natural side-effect of meaningful connection with nature. We call these "Indicators of

Awareness" and they are our criteria for success developed in the last chapter of this manual. When those you mentor manifest these qualities, this indicates your program is shifting brain patterns and turning the tide. You're going in the right direction to create a culture with the will to restore the charred and blackened places.

Chapter 3
CORE ROUTINES OF NATURE CONNECTION

Remembering Original Instructions

Some etymology:
Instruct *In + Struare = to pile in*
Educate *Ex + Ducere = to lead out*
Cultivate = *From Colere, to dwell in, cherish*

The Core Routines of Nature Connections are *things people do* to learn nature's ways. They aren't lessons. They aren't knowledge. They are learning habits.

Luckily for us as nature guides, shifting our mental habits into these Core Routines of Nature Connection comes as second nature to all human beings. This way of knowing was not born a few hundred years ago, or even with the rise of civilization thousands of years ago. Our job is not about *informing*, but about *educating* ourselves and those we mentor to discover what the Haudenosaunee people call our "original instructions." Humans evolved with original instructions designed for dynamic awareness of nature.

It seems those days all you had was the seat of your pants. That's how they like to tell it anyway... You didn't just open a book and teach. You by God were the book, out front in all ways, blunt and dogeared and coverless.

Paul Hunter, foreword to Headmaster on a Bulldozer, *Building a School from the Ground Up*

ELLEN HAAS

If we can inspire practice of these Core Routines, remembering our original instructions will happen on its own.

Decades of experimentation and wide-ranging research with people in forests and fields, deserts and coasts, as well as dialogue with elders from many traditions, have culminated in the list of Core Routines found here. They belong to no culture in particular, but are universal, belonging to all who live on the Earth.

These routines are the underlying practices we facilitate and hopefully inspire people to do whenever they go outdoors. They rest beneath all structured and seemingly unstructured lessons or activities, whether we engage one-on-one or if those we mentor cruise the trails by themselves. Routines will work magically with freedom to come and go as they please like the tides and the seasons. Some routines will jump to the forefront, begging to be practiced, while others fade in emphasis. Each human being comes into this world with an ancient blueprint for connecting with the natural world that has its own timetable for learning. Let it flow.

SOME Core Routines of Nature Connection

On the remaining pages we describe thirteen Core Routines. Our list is not THE definitive Core Routines of Nature Connection. Up until now, many affiliated organizations and teachers have shared Core Routines as part of a liquid, ever-changing body of oral tradition. We picked thirteen we all agree will be the most helpful for readers of this book.

This chapter transmits the spirit of these routines, what they are and why they are important. Further on in the book, you'll see these routines referred to, especially in the Book of Nature. In the Activities section called Introducing Core Routines, you'll find specific ways to start up these practices. But for now, sit back, relax, and let the unique moods and flavors of these Core Routines of Nature Connection wash over you and into you.

As you read, see if you can find versions of these routines within your own childhood or adult life, or in the stories of your friends, family, or heroes. You might be surprised. After all, these are the heritage of all us human-folk.

Sit Spot ◎

Sit Spot in a Nutshell:
Find one place in your natural world that you visit all the time and get to know it as your best friend. Let this be a place where you learn to sit still—alone, often, and quietly—before you playfully explore beyond. This will become your place of intimate connection with nature.

The Magic Pill

Sit Spot is the core of the Core Routines and the heart of this mentoring model. It's the magic pill if ever there was one. Because we've seen it, time and time again, to be so vital and enchanting to the life of both young and old children, we'll use a few more words here than with the other routines, to make sure we pass on the soul of the Sit Spot routine.

The idea is simple: guide people to find a special place in nature where they become comfortable with just being there, still and quiet. In this place, the lessons of nature will seep in. Sit Spot will become personal because it feels private and intimate; the place where they meet their curiosity; the place where they feel wonder; the place where they get eye-to-eye with a diversity of life-forms and weather-patterns; the place where they face their fears—of bugs, of being alone, of the dark—and grow past them; and the place where they meet nature as their home.

The Sit Spot routine was the heart of Jon Young's early mentoring by tracker Tom Brown, Jr., with Tom coaching from a distance, questioning and inspiring. Jon visited one spot by himself nearly every day for seven years. Jon says today that his Sit Spot in the forest near his New Jersey home had more to do with his development as a human being, not to mention as a naturalist, than anything else. The place will forever be a part of him. His relationship with that place was the pebble thrown in the pond that started Wilderness Awareness School and all its concentric rings.

Most people do not
hear the song of nature,
but, if you sit in a special place,
and notice everything around you,
sometimes you hear it. It's not
like hearing a bird sing, or bees
buzz,

It's rather a song of
understanding,
warmth, and feeling, and not of
notes and words.
So, have you heard the song of
nature?

ADDY DAVIDOFF, "The Song of
Nature" (written at age 8)
Secret Spot Prose written by
Earth Arts youth, Ithaca, NY

The Essential Attitude of Sit Spot

The essential attitude of this routine is getting to know one place really well—one biome, one community of soils and plants and animals and trees and birds and weather systems—at all times of day and night, and in every season and weather. In other words, the place becomes your nesting niche, your study site, your tracking playground, and your retreat and renewal center. The Spot itself becomes the home base from which you explore outward—where you leave your upright human self

It seems likely that the Sit Spot, vision quest and various forms of meditation have their origin in still hunting. The extreme alertness associated with these practices quiets the mind and promotes inner peace, the goal of numerous spiritual and religious traditions around the world.

RANDALL L. EATON

behind and get down and crawl on hands and knees, raccoon style, to sniff and feel around.

While it is very important to have one's own oft-visited Sit Spot, we can apply the attitude of Sit Spot to any place with similar ecological features, not just our own special place. The place feels of familiarity, relationship, and in-depth knowledge, and when you go to it your attitude overflows with childlike curiosity, discovery, and uninhibited playfulness.

Sitting Still

The other part to this routine is about sitting, about stillness. On the simplest level, to sit silent and still for a long period of time will slip open the door of a world that most humans never know: the private world of wild animals and the language of the birds. Sunrise and Sunset are especially magical times, when wildlife actively pulses with life. Once you sit quietly long enough, the birds sort of shrug you off and accept the fact that you're there, and there for good. As they return to their daily tasks, a previously hidden dimension of your landscape opens up.

Wild animals—weasels, raccoons, bobcats, owls, for example—know the patterns of human activity and move out to its edge to go unseen. Sitting still initiates you into their undomesticated realm, a wild place that plays by different rules than the human world. By being a quiet, unobtrusive guest, you will come to know Baloo's "Jungle Law," and learn to make yourself welcome again, as an accepted member of the natural community.

Sneaking into Sit Spot Time

We never want to force people into going to their Sit Spot as if it were an assignment. Instead, we subtly guide them there by wisely playing games that build up their comfort level, telling inspiring Sit Spot stories, and asking questions about the activities of squirrels and birds and dandelions. If you, the mentor, also spend time in your own Sit Spot and tell fresh stories about what happened earlier this very morning, then of course your stories provide an invaluable role modeling tool.

Many of the activities here are games that will help us lead people into the Sit Spot routine in a roundabout, unconscious way. Hiding or sneaking games require stillness for long periods while crouching in a bush, or lying silently on the ground. With the adrenaline of a game rushing through, participants hardly noticed the bugs crawling over their skin and soon they feel a new comfort level in nature.

Finding the Right Spot

We recommend you find a good spot near water, shelter, and food for wildlife, that you can get to easily and often without doing damage to a fragile landscape, with little danger of predators or other hazards.

But this can be found almost anywhere. Our co-author, Ellen Haas, has an elderly mother who takes endless delight in observing the birds feed, the ducks breed, the butterflies emerge, and the bees pollinate from her spot on her patio of a Dallas retirement community. City dwellers can find vacant lots, ditches off the local baseball fields, or sidewalk gardens that, if invested with quiet attention, brim with wild life. Folks who live in wild landscapes full of ticks or bears or snakes can find safe paths and shelters from which to bathe in their wilderness. For young children, help them find little places in the back yard where they can be safe and still and alert and enchanted. It's not about the quality of the spot; it's about the quality of attention within it.

Our four-year Kamana Naturalist Training Program is predicated on visiting a Sit Spot daily, so thousands of our friends have established regular Sit Spot routines. We could go on for pages with their powerfully appreciative testimony. It is amazing, however, what terrible wailing and lamentation go on in the beginning as each individual tries to find the perfect spot. In the end, if all our kinder guidance fails, we advise, "If you can't be with the one you love, love the one you're with."

Hitting Cruise Control

If we can get people going to a Sit Spot near their home on a regular basis, then the learning journey takes on a life of its

Danger

Don't Kill The Sit Spot!

We have seen parents become militant about their children's Sit Spot time: "You can't eat your dessert unless you've been to your Sit Spot!" PLEASE DO NOT DO THIS!

The Sit Spot works because of magic. As soon as it becomes a chore or a punishment, the magic dies. Use cleverness to get them there, not the crack of a whip.

own. We've hit cruise control at that point, then we simply and eagerly listen to their stories, ask questions about subtleties, and send them on errands that deepen the complexity of their Sit.

I remember one of my seven-year-old learners, Mira: her parents told me that she hardly ever spent time outdoors, and then only when accompanied by her parents. For a few months, we played a lot of those comfort-enhancing games, and then Mira's parents came to me with a new story from home.

"Whenever Mira gets home now, she doesn't say a word, she just puts her stuff down and runs outside to the back yard and into the trees. She stays out there for hours all by herself. We see her sometimes: she sits for a while, she climbs trees, she goes around looking at things. Before she wouldn't go out alone—now it's hard to get her to come inside!"

Even my own mother, whom you would definitely not consider the "outdoorsy" type, confided in me a couple of years ago: "I had a Sit Spot, too, when I was a child. There was an oak tree in our back yard, and everyday I would get home from school and run out to sit under that tree. Sometimes I would read a book, other times I would just sit, thinking, taking in the world around me."

Where's Your Sit Spot?

Think back through your life and, ultimately to your childhood, and see if you have ever had a Sit Spot routine. You might be surprised. Children seem, without ever being told, to instinctively find a place of their own that they gravitate to and make their "outside home." As a kid, a gnarled old tree in my neighbor's yard that was easy to climb, secluded and sheltered, served to give me a view of the land around me. Many adults keep up a similar practice all through their lives. It may be the window by their bird feeder, the bench behind the tool shed, or the place where they take their break from work. Where's yours?

The Pipes of Pan sound early before the sense of wonder is dulled, while the world is wet with dew and still fresh as the morning … The look of wide-eyed delight in the eyes of a child is proof enough of its presence.

I heard [the Pipes of Pan] in many places as a child, but one of the best was an alder thicket where I used to hide, a veritable jungle that had never been cleared. The swamp began just beyond the garden fence and I went there often, burrowing my way through the maze into its very center.

There I had fashioned a nest on a dry little shelf. It was cozy and warm, and like any hidden creature I lay there listening and watching. Rabbit runways ran through it and birds sang in the branches around me …. The alder swamp was my refuge and no one came there but me. Only Mother knew, and she understood it was mine and mine alone.
What I heard there were the Pipes, and what I sensed, I know now, was the result of a million years of listening and being aware, the accumulated experience of the race itself and of ages when man was more a part of his ancient environment than now….

Sigurd Olson, "The Pipes of Pan" *Open Horizons*

Story of the Day ◎

Story of the Day in a Nutshell
After spending time in nature, tell the story of your day. Tell your story verbally with others, or by writing or drawing in a journal.

We'll say it one more time, so you can't say we didn't hammer it home: the Sit Spot routine is essential. But equally important to the development of sensory awareness and knowledge of place is its complementary twin, its primary dance partner, the Story of the Day. This is a core routine with which every human is familiar.

The Custom of Storytelling

Growing up, I remember routinely telling stories with my family. We would sit around the dinner table at the end of the day and share what happened at work or school. My parents would question me for more details about what I had learned, and I'd question them, too. Our stories varied: they could be somber, exciting, or sometimes get us laughing so hard we'd choke on our peas. The difference with the Core Routine here is that we want to emphasize experiences with nature.

A staple practice of hunters and gatherers around the world, storytelling knit the society together. The men go out for a day of tracking and hunting, while grandmothers and children might harvest berries, root vegetables, or bark to make thread and cloth. Around the fire at night they gather and report the stories of their days. This exchange of stories seems to be very important to humans. For millennia, survival depended on information gained about food sources and other patterns in the landscape.

Story of the Day — In Groups

A classic form of Story of the Day breaks everyone into small groups. You go out for adventures for a while and then reconvene to exchange the stories of each group's discoveries. These stories move our emotions, entertain us, and can easily turn a wet, cold, hungry experience into a memorable drama.

Natural history writers are storytellers. Scientists are storytellers. Scientists live and die by their ability to depart from the tribe and go out into an unknown terrain and bring back, like a carcass newly speared, some discovery or new fact or theoretical insight and lay it in front of the tribe; and then they all gather and dance around it. Symposia are held in the National Academy of Sciences and prizes are given. There is fundamentally no difference from a Paleolithic campsite celebration.

E.O. Wilson, in *Writing Natural History*, Dialogues With Authors, by Edward Lueders

To invite children to tell their stories to one another, we share many old tricks. You will learn them as you go. Circling up, quieting down, listening to each other, passing a talking stick, loosening stuck tongues, tightening loose tongues, drawing stories on a collective map: all these will come with practice and familiarity.

You can invite adults to tell their stories in a great variety of ways, some using art, some using computers, on-line forums, list-serve groups, graphic arts, songs, skits and just plain storytelling. Grownup storytelling produces great energy. People laugh hard, they cry, they sing, and then they sleep well at night with smiles on their faces. We always get insightful feedback from their story-of-the-day sessions. Then, the very next day they go out on the trail vigorously gathering more stories to tell.

Sharing stories with others builds a collective knowledge much greater than the isolated experience of one person. We can gain a storehouse of information from others' stories: one saw frogs by the pond with bright red legs; one made rope out of old dead cedar bark; one snuck up on coyotes and aplodontias living in the woods near the pond. Storytelling layers knowledge slowly built up over time, as a living oral library.

Sharing our personal stories inspires us on further. Group sharing affirms everyone's amazing experiences in nature can be accessible to all. "If Danny can catch a frog or Samantha can touch a deer, well then, why can't I?" Curiosity, our greatest resource for learning, becomes contagious. If you listen to someone tell about catching the frog by "the most beautiful pond just down the street," you just might want to go there soon. Or maybe you wonder, now that we've mentioned it, who ever heard of an "aplodontia?"

This constant pouring of individual experience and knowledge into a collective pot for the community unveils one of the great advantages to group learning. Many people recognize the value of and crave such a learning community. As participants begin to trust that there will be a constant rhythm to this routine, that they will get many chances to

Language clothes Nature, as the air clothes the earth, taking the exact form and pressure of every object.

Ralph Waldo Emerson

My grandmother laid the foundation for frog-catching and fishing. Grandma knew her role. Her role was to catch my stories. With a grandmother to come home to, there were a lot of things to see and learn and gather.

Jon Young, Grandmother Caught My Stories

tell their stories, the momentum builds into a palpable group zeal at story-telling time. Age matters not. All people respond to this cycle of learning and sharing in a magical way.

Story of the Day—For One

If not in a group setting, stories can be told to a journal. With young children this might be done through drawing or art, or dictating to you, the writer. Again, we share many tricks for this which may depend on your skills and the skills objectives of your program.

Older youth can journal tracks they find in the field, or write about Sit Spot experiences, keeping weekly "Field Inventories," as people do in the Kamana Naturalist Training Program. If you like to inspire sketching and drawing, let it be in the spirit of expressing a story rather than coloring inside the lines. If you love how words clothe experience, you can guide people into finding strong and vivid words and ways to unfold all the sensory input of their moment in time.

Writing and drawing can end up back in the story circle as Show-and-Tell. Something about knowing their writing will be performed or published, or their drawing displayed or mounted, fires up attention to their work—as if a predator might be watching! For some, this enhances their experience, for others it can block them with fear. Again, use this response as an opportunity to guide their paths with the intent of empowering them to find their own storytelling gifts.

How Stories Reveal Edges

Story of the Day encourages self-expression and self-confidence in the validity of each person's personal experiences. With many people, you might see a progression from trembling shyness to charismatic power. At first, some may demonstrate a collapsed, drawn inward body language. With no eye contact, their timid offer is only a low and mumbled speech. After many opportunities to listen to others and share their stories, even the shyest gradually transforms into a bright voice, a lifted chest, and sparkling eyes that pour out excitement and unerring self-assurance.

Whenever you listen to a person's story, you have a golden opportunity to discern their edges and inspire them with fitting questions. As a routine, careful listening to Story of the Day gives you, the Coyote Mentor, leisure time to hear what captures the attention, what people notice and don't notice, what they feel proud or awkward to talk about, and what words they choose to express themselves. The chapter ahead called Questioning and Answering will be a very helpful guide to place questions right at the edge of their stories. Good questions, aptly chosen and well timed, will get your people curious and push them to bring back even better stories.

We encourage you to think about this process: rather than passively listening to stories, you are pulling stories—pulling *out* stories and pulling *on* stories—to reveal all the rich gems of learning, as well as all the gaps and pockets of unawareness. As with panning for gold or kneading the bubbles out of bread dough, you, the mentor, play an active role in the evolution of the story—*and the storyteller.*

The Big Two Routines

These two routines, Sit Spot and Story of the Day, feed each other constantly, like a call and response. The other eleven Core Routines that follow can be found contained within these two, as specific techniques to enhance time spent outside and daily reflection on it.

The antidote to Nature Deficit Disorder may be this simple: get people to spend time in nature, and when they return, be there to ask good questions and catch their stories.

Expanding Our Senses ◎

Expanding Our Senses in a nutshell:
Use and expand all your senses as fully as you can. Pay attention! Look Alert! Stretch Out! Use all the senses, one at a time, and together.

Pay attention!

For nature connection, we have only one golden rule: notice everything. Get down in the dirt and feel it. Widen to Owl Eyes (a name we like to give to peripheral vision) and detect movement. Hear the far-off cry of the hawk and the wind in the trees. Smell the scent carried in the warm breeze. Feel the direction of the sun. Taste the safe wild edibles. At every opportunity, alert people to expand their senses until doing so becomes routine, a practice, a habit, a discipline, and finally, a brain pattern.

Remember the context of Expanding Our Senses. People who lived off the land instilled this skill above all: pay attention at all times to everything. E. O. Wilson describes the intensity of the state by calling it "the naturalist's trance, the hunter's trance—by which biologists locate more elusive organisms." They had the alertness of predator and prey. This continual state of being directly caused much of the awareness and naturalist knowledge learned without schooling.

If you hunt or watch birds, then you already know the drill. Perhaps you've been a photographer, or had a job watching for fires from a tower, or detecting potential avalanches at a ski slope, or maybe you've raised a toddler in a cityscape full of hazards: all of these require close attention.

As a Coyote Mentor take every opportunity to stretch everyone's sensory awareness, including your own. Your actions, however subtle, lead to alerting, discovering, invoking, evoking, reviving, appreciating, encouraging, inspiring, questioning, expanding, widening, stretching, exercising, and focusing sensory awareness. The introductory exercise on Expanding our Senses in the Activities section will give you some helpful approaches.

Forging a Different Set of Brain Patterns

The routine of Expanding Our Senses wakes us up to more fully using our amazing innate capacity for seeing, hearing, smelling, tasting, and touching. In terms of brain patterning theory, this routine excites and focuses conscious attention on our sensory neurology until reaching out with our eyes, ears, nostrils, taste buds, and skin surfaces becomes a mental habit. Throughout our lives then, we'll absorb sensory information with increasing subtlety.

After all, our senses never turn off. Our brain patterns only filter what we pay attention to. Simply, this routine breaks us out of habitual brain patterns and wakes us up to capacities we would normally ignore. Through conscious use of our senses, we can actually strengthen them, and give them full range of motion, just as you might strengthen muscles by exercising at a gym. For whole-brain learning, we want to exercise all the senses in the ever-changing, many-textured playground of nature.

Human's Dominant Sense

Each animal has a dominant sense that determines its lifestyle, how it interacts with the world. The long nose of dogs makes

What is spiritual? The more of our brain that we engage, the more of our antennae that we tune, the stronger our sensitivity to the vibrations of the life force around us.

JON YOUNG, "What is Spiritual?" *Seeing Through Native Eyes* audio

Slots between the trunks up ahead shiver with blue where a muskeg opens. I angle toward it, feeling no need to hurry, picking every footstep carefully, stopping often to stare into the dizzying crannies, listening for any splinter of sound, keeping my senses tight and concentrated.

I listen as closely as possible but hear nothing. I work my eyes into every dark crevice and slot among the snowy branches, but see nothing. I stand perfectly still and wait.

Then I see it.

RICHARD K. NELSON, *The Island Within*

There is an intimate reciprocity to the senses; as we touch the bark of a tree, we feel the tree touching us; as we lend our ears to the local sounds and ally our nose to the seasonal scents, the terrain gradually tunes us in turn.

DAVID ABRAM, *The Spell of the Sensuous: Preception and Language in a More-than Human World*

"Let's go pick berries. Do you like berries?"
"I love berries, I like sweet things."
"Let's go pick berries."

And while you're picking berries, you're asking questions. "How come this berry is different from that one and these are red and those are white?" Each time we add another meaningful awareness component, we stretch them further and further. If you could attach little strings of awareness to them, they'd look like a daisy with many petals, a three dimensional flower, a clover bloom, with many, many rays of awareness going out in all directions.

JON YOUNG, *Rays of Awareness*

for a world organized by smells, while the huge satellite-dish ears of deer mean a world full of important sounds. Humans, a lot like cats with large eyes mounted on the front of a flat face, possess the ideal set-up for a life based on vision.

Human eyes operate as acute instruments that guide our lifestyle as bipedal animals with dexterous forelimbs. However, this can become a double-edged sword, both a gift and a limiting factor. Whenever we allow one sense to be over-emphasized, it is possible for the other senses, and thus other parts of our brains, to be under-developed. Try this great practice for stealing away our dominant sense so as to awaken the others—use blindfolds. If you would like a taste of this suggestion, prepare yourself a meal at home, then sit down and eat it blindfolded. The world appears very different without eyes. (We also recommend reading Helen Keller's biography or the rather terrible picture of sudden epidemic blindness in *Blindness* by Jose Saramago.)

However, we also want to use our gift of sight fully. Our cultural influences now narrow our vision into a small range to use books, TVs, computers, and handheld electronics. If you watch a new-born baby, you'll see its huge eyes take in everything. Catching the movement of a fly or bird outside the window, they will suddenly turn with wonder to look. This peripheral vision, the ability to see "out of the corner of the eye," allows us to detect subtle movements, such as animals slinking into the bushes as we arrive near their territory. It also provides excellent vision at night. A few folks that I mentor who wear glasses have changed their prescriptions: after a few months of routinely expanding their vision, their eyes actually improved as a result of this natural way of seeing. We do need "tunnel vision," that especially narrow focus, to execute certain tasks—but there is much on the edge of our focus to take in from peripheral vision.

The Fifth, Sixth, and More Senses

Expanding Our Senses on a routine basis extends the functional use of our brain well beyond the norm in our modern society. We highly recommend reading Diane Ackerman's lively research on each of the five human senses in her book

A Natural History of the Senses. Our sidebar lists additional senses abridged from a list of fifty-three that Michael J. Cohen identifies in his writings. These give just a hint of what our biology is capable of.

Consider the possibility that our "sixth sense," the one with no name, combines the full use and coordination of our five senses. What may seem mystical to some, might be plain biology when the brain is used optimally. If anything could be called strange, it would have to be that so many humans settle for using only a tiny portion of the brain's capacity for perception.

Questioning and Tracking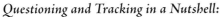

Questioning and Tracking in a Nutshell:
Become a detective and track everything as a clue to a mystery to solve. Ask questions about everything, and push your questions until they yield answers. Who? What? When? Where? Why? How?

Questioning Tracks

Tracking animals is fascinating. It's a window into wildlife. It captures imagination and empathy, and demands whole-brain intelligence and concentration. Getting down on all fours and staring at the footprints of animals offers a particular abundance of opportunity for imprinting search images. Like reading, studying the sign and following the trails of animals, develops powers of pattern recognition that stay with you for the rest of your life.

To guide your inquiry, ask the journalist's six questions: Who? What? When? Where? Why? and How? If you find a four-toed track with claw-marks, you might use a field guide to identify *who*, and you might use a ruler to measure and determine the type of gait the animal used. The gait pattern then may tell you more about *what* the animal was doing, even about its mood. Trying to figure out *when* the animal made the track also draws you in to notice the weather. Following a series of tracks may show you *where* it was headed. And this will get you wondering *why* it

Cohen lists 53 natural survival senses that connect and balance Nature within to Nature without. They include:

Sense of time
Appetite and hunger
Sense of temperature and temperature change
Sense of season, including the ability to insulate, hibernate and winter sleep
Humidity sense, including the acumen to find water or evade a flood
Hearing, including resonance, vibrations, sonar frequencies
Sense of awareness of one's own visibility and consequent camouflaging
Sense of proximity
Sense of fear
Sense of play
Sense of excessive stress
Sense of emotional place, of community belonging
Psychic capacity, such as foreknowledge, and animal instinct
Spiritual sense, including conscience, capacity for sublime love, sense of sorrow, and sacrifice.

MICHAEL J. COHEN,
Reconnecting with Nature

"Let us follow," said Mowgli, "The jungle is wet enough to hold the lightest mark."

Bagheera the Panther, trotting with his head low said, "It is single-foot" (he meant there was only one man), "and the weight of the thing he carries has pressed his heel far into the ground."

"Ha! This is as clear as summer lightning," Mowgli answered; and they fell into the quick, choppy trail-trot in and out through the checkers of the moonlight, following the marks of those two bare feet.

"Now he runs swiftly," said Mowgli. "The toes are spread apart." They went on over some wet ground. "Now why does he turn aside here?"

"Wait!" said Bagheera, and flung himself forward with one superb bound as far as ever he could. The first thing to do when a trail ceases to explain itself is to cast forward without leaving your own confusing foot-marks on the ground. Bagheera turned as he landed, and faced Mowgli, crying, "Here comes another trail to meet him. It is a smaller foot, this second trail and the toes turn inward."

Then Mowgli ran up and looked. "It is the foot of a Gond hunter," he said. "Look! Here he dragged his bow on the grass. That is why the first trail turned aside so quickly. Big Foot hid from Little Foot."

Rudyard Kipling,
The Jungle Book

was headed that way. And to answer that you'll start to notice *how* that four-toed track relates to the nearby rodent tunnels, and *how* those tunnels relate to the surrounding grasses, and *how* those grasses link to the topography. Like snowflakes or words, no two tracks, no two trails, are ever exactly the same. Tracking is the art that develops, and then infinitely complexifies, your image-vocabulary for reading the book of nature.

Tracking as Scientific Inquiry

Tracking wildlife by looking at footprints and other sign definitely offers a fertile opportunity for developing knowledge of place, but we want to expand the metaphor. We mean "tracking" in the broadest sense. The discipline of tracking nurtures quality observation, observation guided by intense curiosity, question after question. So "tracking," like scientific inquiry, always begins with a question. Then it includes gathering evidence and reasoning deductively; defining, refining, and proving hypotheses. Tracking, like playing the detective or the scientist whose discoveries are goaded on by a burning desire, leads you to find answers.

Tom Brown, Jr. likes to ask, "When are we NOT tracking?" and of course, the answer is "When we are asleep or dead!" Humans track. It is the most natural thing for us to do. We track with our eyes, ears, nose, touch, taste, emotions, minds, and bodies. Anyone can track anything. Herbalists and gardeners constantly track: through years of inquisitive observation they deepen their knowledge of plants. "What plant is this?" "Why does this plant grow so well here and not there?" "How do the different seasons affect the medicinal potency of this plant's leaves, flowers, and roots?" The technicians in the back room fixing our computers track electronic pathways. Parents track the development of their children. Youth track adults to mimic their lifestyle strategies. If your attitude is inquiring and your method is scientific, you're a tracker.

Tom has another aphorism: "We want to put the quest back in question and the search back in research." The core routine of Questioning and Tracking instills a mental habit of intense inquiry. When people relax, their naturally curiosity asks amazingly good questions. As mentors we empower that curiosity to keep their questioning alive. Role-model this enthusiastic inquisitiveness in your own life to lure them from edge to edge.

In our *Seeing Through Native Eyes* audio series, Jon Young introduces the art of tracking with as good a picture as we can give of how a person might use the classic interrogatives, "Who, What, When, Where and Why" with animal tracks. This excerpt from Part Two shows how these questions can guide your inquiry:

Jon Young on Awakening Inquiry

"Let's Look at Tracks.

On your way to your sit spot, there's that little road that you walk along, and there's that little mud puddle there. Can you picture it? You can see the raindrops like little dots all around the tracks. And in it as you look closer, you see a set of footprints. You can recognize that there are some toes there, and some claws, and you can recognize some heel pads. And you can kind of get a sense of the direction that the animal went in. And you can almost see its size; can see how big it may be. You can tell how heavy it is by pushing on the ground and saying, 'Wow, this ground is pretty firm; but notice, these tracks went in pretty deep. This animal is pretty heavy.'

Your first question you might ask is WHO? Who left this track? The identification of signs, hairs that you find stuck on a thorn, droppings that you find along the edge of a field, chews on the edge of a piece of bark: these are all signs. Holes in the ground. Who lives there? Whose trail is that? What animal is most likely to use that trail? These are all questions that are related to the first art of tracking, *identification*.

The second question you might come up with is WHAT? 'I know what kind of animal it is, but I'm really curious to know what it's doing. Is it running? Is it walking? Is it looking left or right, up or down? Is it scared? Could you tell from this track? Is that really possible?' If you had a long stretch of sand in order to understand the full length of the stories, you could do it, and that's the art of *interpretation*.

Back to your mud puddle. You've got an idea of who it is, and what it's doing. What you want to know now is, WHEN was it here? That's the third art of tracking, the art of *aging*. When did this animal go by? Ask yourself this, 'Are those raindrops I see in the mud all around that track, also in the track itself? What does that mean?' That animal came by before the rain. So if I could only figure out when it last rained, I have an idea of how old these tracks must be. Maybe the ranger who works at this park can tell me.

The next thing is, 'Hey, I don't care who made those tracks, I don't really care what that animal was doing, and I don't even care what time it was here. What I want to know is WHERE it is right now? Can I follow it? Can I take up this track right here as if it was the end of a string and follow it to its source?' A good tracker can do that. That's something the Apaches were known for. That's something the Aborigines in Australia are known for, and the Bushmen of the Kalahari. They can follow a string of footprints and lead you right to the animal. The art of *trailing* is very difficult. But you can learn that too.

So you have the Who, What, When and Where of tracking. The next one is WHY? 'Why does this animal come by here every day between 8:30 and 10:00? Why does it go down this mud road? Why is it moving at this speed and not another speed? Why does it always seem to be in the same kind of energy flow? It doesn't seem to be going anywhere except in a straight line, why is that? And why are there always human tracks next to it that seem to be from the same time?' We call this art *ecological tracking*.

The question Why always comes from the bigger picture; you'll never get the answer right from the footprint itself. Knowing what berries are ripe will tell you where the bear is going. Knowing what fish are running in the rivers will teach you about otters and about mink. Knowing about the acorns that are falling will teach you about the deer and the grouse, the turkeys, the bear. All of these things are related. And the more you know about nature, the better you will be at tracking, because you'll be able to put the whole picture together."

Animal Forms ◎

Animal Forms in a Nutshell:
Physically, mentally, and emotionally imitate any and all animals in their movements, behaviors, and personalities.

A Long Tradition of Imitation

What we call Animal Forms is simply the imitation of the physical and mental actions of animals, birds, and to some extent even grass, wind and water. This potent routine might seem a bit different from the others, more akin to dance than mental gymnastics. As a practice, animal imitations can be found in cultures across the globe. For instance, think of the many martial arts from Asia based on imitation of animals such as crane, tiger, or turtle. Also, many indigenous cultures conduct imitative dances and dramas, often with accompanying masks and costumes. The Hawaiian Hula, an ancient and modern dance form, brilliantly demonstrates such animal and nature dances. Cave paintings in Europe and old European stories indicate that the ancestors of Europeans did the same.

In the Activities section ahead, we'll emphasize some basic perceptual strategies, movements, or footprints of common North American animals: owl, deer, fox, cat, dog, raccoon, and rabbit. Also, we'll suggest games that call for imitation, pretending or play-acting how animals sneak, hide, climb, stalk, pounce, and eat. Over time, your own experiences will teach you many more.

Bodily Learning

We can "learn by feel" the anatomy behind animal movements. How do two-leggeds walk, how do four-leggeds? How do blind moles navigate? The practice of imitating animal movement, which includes its mood and strategy, creates a meaningful relationship with the animal. Combined with field guides and journaling, practicing animal forms will imprint search images—multi-dimensional, dynamic models of character and form—in both mind and body, into our very being. This is what "learning by heart" could mean: developing a stronger sense of instinct and intuition, and growing in empathy with what we imitate.

Of course, people, especially children, without ever being told naturally mimic Animal Forms. Think back to your childhood: Did you ever pretend to be an animal? Did you ever have a favorite stuffed animal that you brought to life with play-acting? Which animals did you love to be? What does your body remember today about the animal's movement? If you ever get among native folks such as the San Bushmen, you will notice that adults routinely imitate things too. In fact, their success as hunters depends on this; adult Bushman hunters have been found to accurately imitate three hundred different

Kingfishers: they make a hellacious noise, blast and rattle before them, so the whole world knows they're coming. Rest on a branch over water with their big bills, suddenly dive. Hit the water and shoot their wings back to propel themselves that extra jolt forward. Tom would say, "Let's go be kingfishers." We'd climb on the rock and dive straight down and try to catch a fish with our faces.

Jon Young

species from their environment, and many imitations serve to attract the species they are hunting. They get a great deal of humor out of it as well.

Physical Education

Why encourage the practice of animal forms? Animal Forms present a positive channel for physical development. Many of the forms we teach have some concrete, physical application, such as Raccoon Form for crawling through thickets of brush, Deer Bounding Form for jumping over logs, or Cougar Form for sneaking through low cover. Therefore, Animal Forms often make up the "Physical Education" sections of our days. The diversity of animals in the world provides a spectrum of movements that can develop all areas of a person's body, from stretching to climbing to running to lying flat and still.

Animals as Teachers

Animal Forms also establishes animals as teachers, as beings whose lifestyles offer valuable lessons for our lives. Not only physical movements, but mental attitudes can be learned from animals. For instance, watching a squirrel relentlessly harvest nuts in the fall reveals the mentality of hard work and "getting it done" when you really need to. The long-range vision of a hawk or eagle can teach us about seeing the big picture. The ferocity of the wolverine can get us in touch with that inner strength that could save our lives in extreme situations. The wiliness of coyote, the stealth of weasel, the playfulness of otter—all have lessons to teach.

Playing with the forms of different animals teaches without words that each animal presents a unique and valid way of existing in the world. It broadens our minds to realize all the multiple ways of being, multiple life-strategies—not any better than others—just different. By playing with animal forms, we can have access to all these different perspectives on how to be alive.

Staying Loose and Playful

Animal Forms keep all of us loose and playful in our self-expression. Through constant "shape-shifting" into different animals, we enliven and nourish our own and others' imaginations. Often through Animal Forms we discover those among us who have theatrical flairs and tell brilliant stories. Playing as different animals puts us just one step away from complex character-acting.

But again, just as with Sit Spot, let the magic of Animal Forms arise naturally. We will share some forms in this book, but remember the most effective Animal Forms come to life when individuals take them on as their own, creating and playing as they wish. The best thing you can do is role-model the daily play of Animal Forms in your own life. Watch animal videos and imitate movements. Or visit the zoo and watch one animal for hours until its unique style burns into your memory.

Jon Young tells of how he learned Animal Forms as a child by going in his basement, locking the door, cranking up some loud music, and losing himself in his imagination as he shape-shifted into animals, frolicking over the couch as a monkey, tromping and growling around it as a huge bear, or sneaking behind it as a bobcat on all fours. In the depths of his Mind's Eye Imagining, he developed a full sensory memory of what it was like to be different animals, birds, trees, rivers and even rocks. How can this be? Well, the imagination is powerful, just think of the writers of works like *Starwars*, *Lord of the Rings*, or *Harry Potter*: did they ever actually experience all those things they wrote about?

Wandering ◎

Wandering in a Nutshell:
Wander through the landscape without time, destination, agenda, or future purpose; be present in the moment; and go off-trail wherever curiosity leads.

Hmmm … an educational activity without purpose? A walk in nature without a destination or intent? Are we serious?

Unstructured Time

Yes, we feel so serious about this routine, that most of our programs have a built-in "wander" or "walkabout" for about half of our time out in the field. We call this "The 50-50 Principle." We plan our whole day to follow a structure, but count on fifty-percent of the time in the excitement of the moment, involving timeless, unstructured Wandering. There is nothing to accomplish, nowhere to go. By just being present in the moment, curiosity gently leads us wherever we go.

Why would we spend so much of our time wandering aimlessly?

In the modern world, we call a lot of things priorities: our agenda, our calendar, our jobs, our bills, our children, our parents, the gear we need for recreation. They push us this way and that in a direction that flows away from nature. Having an agenda or expected plan of action closes our minds to

The "wandering mentality" emerges naturally among subsistence and recreational hunters whose unparalleled alertness and total attentiveness to the environment constitute a transcendent state of consciousness.

RANDALL L. EATON, Why Hunters Save the World

Use the 50/50 principle but plan 100% of the time, with perhaps 50% of the activities being core activities such as sitting, mapping, students mentoring students, etc. For the other 50% of the time, prepare for the unexpected.

Pick from a repertoire of activities for different situations, so if an unexpected event happens, you have an appropriate lesson at your fingertips. Maybe aim for one with an inspirational hit, one with an adrenaline rush, one introducing a wholly new area, some library research, and a variety of other activities that you could change at a moment's notice.

DAVID FORTHOFFER, Kamana Student, "The Fifty-Fifty Principle"

what else may be happening at any given moment. Wandering without aim opens us to what nature wants to teach. In terms of brain patterning, Wandering is the quintessential Coyote routine, a habit to break habits, and an essential skill for allowing each person to connect with nature according to their own special gifts.

The literature of naturalists and hunters throughout time overflows with tributes to the downright spiritual—and political—value of slowing down, of living in unstructured time. A few choice tidbits describe that value:

Wendell Berry, a Kentucky farmer, conservation poet, and essayist, writes in *An Entrance to the Woods*,

"The faster one goes, the more strain there is on the senses, the more they fail to take in, the more confusion they must tolerate or gloss over—and the longer it takes to bring the mind to a stop in the presence of anything."

Sigurd Olson, canoe guide and activist who worked to save the Quetico-Boundary Waters Wilderness, writes in his biography, *Open Horizons*.

"Something grew on me during those years of roaming.… This was the sense of timelessness, a way of looking at life that truly had the power of slowing speed. In town there were always deadlines, a host of things to do, but as soon as the canoes were in the water and heading out, the tempo changed …. The coming of day and night, the eternal watching of the skies, sunrises and sunsets, the telltale story of winds in the maneuvering of clouds, the interwoven pattern of rain and mist, cycles of cold and warmth, even the changing vegetation, —all these filtered into … the comprehension of time being endless and relative with all life flowing into its stream …"

Barry Lopez, in a powerful essay in *Patriotism and the American Land*, commissioned after September 11, 2001, calls on more of us to become true naturalists, writing,

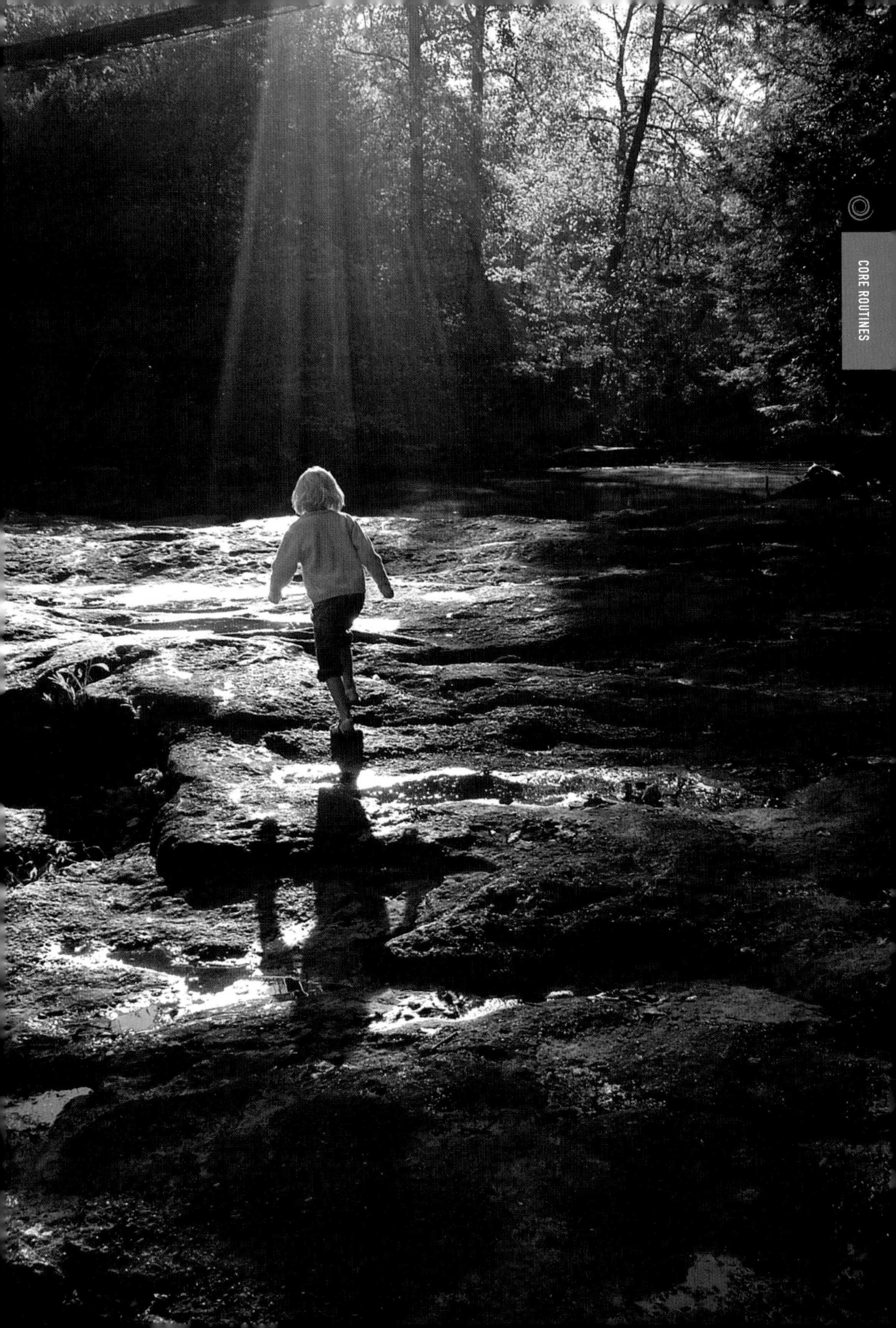

"Firsthand knowledge is enormously time consuming to acquire; with its dallying and lack of end points, it is also out of phase with the short-term demands of modern life. It teaches humility and fallibility, and so represents an antithesis to progress. It makes a stance of awe in the witness of natural process seem appropriate, and attempts at summary knowledge naïve ... Firsthand knowledge of a country's ecosystems, a rapidly diminishing pool of expertise and awareness, lies at the radical edge of any country's political thought."

Letting Curiosity Lead the Way

Wandering through a landscape being led solely by curiosity and open eyes is the fertile ground for true discovery. Wandering allows us to get in touch with what excites us. When we're not pushing a learning-agenda, curiosity comes to the forefront and guides the learning process. As mentors, we fall into the role of fellow discoverer, fellow questioner. We wait for true desire to learn about something naturally surface as we wander, and then we plant whatever seeds of meaningful knowledge we have to share. And then we ask another question.

In his book *Free Play*, Steven Nachmanovich agrees;

"Such a walk is totally different from random drifting. Leaving your eyes and ears wide open, you allow your likes and dislikes, your conscious and unconscious desires and irritations, your irrational hunches, to guide you wherever there is a choice of turning right or left. You cut a path ... that is yours alone, which brings you face to face with surprises destined for you alone. When you travel in this way ... the trip, like an improvised piece of music, reveals its own inner structures and rhythm. Thus you set the stage for fateful encounters."

The numerous "philosophical" lessons of Wandering come as rewards when people learn to trust themselves, their curiosity, their intuitions, and their personal rhythms. They discover that learning can be joyful and exciting. As Joseph Campbell said, they learn to "follow their bliss." When wandering with others, they learn to be part of a community, to be open to the interests and loves of others.

Wandering in this way invariably leads people to find the things they would never have found if they were driven by an agenda, if they had never left the trail: coyote skulls, tree frogs, the coolest hollowed-out tree to sit inside.

The wandering mentality is almost the antithesis of the dominant mentality in our hurried, businesslike, clock-timed world. It can be hard for us adults to forget our agendas and simply wander; and even if we want to, it can be very hard for teachers in formal educational environments to structure wandering into our lesson plans. We leave it to you with a will to find a way. But we do offer the following suggestions:

Going Off-Schedule

+ Stay on schedule for the start and end times of your events, especially if others are planning their time to correspond with yours.

+ Plan for un-planned time, 50% if possible. Keep your daily "measurable learning objectives" simple.

+ Plan to go off-schedule as often as possible. For instance, plan field trips, early morning bird-sits, or night-time walks.

+ Take breaks and change course when peoples' body language tells you it's time to change the tune and tempo of your lesson.

Going Off-Trail

+ Do not go off-trail in fragile areas.

+ Do not go off-trail in public parks that prohibit it or private land posted "No Trespassing." Find welcoming private land, vacant lots, or ditches off the baseball fields instead. Ask around and make friends with park managers and farm owners.

+ Preview your off-trail sites to screen for hazards such as ground-bee nests or glass splinters.

+ Arrange activities so the number of participants who go off-trail in the same place will be few and make less impact.

+ Bring a map and a compass and know how to use them.

What, to curious kids, is less vacant than a vacant lot? ... A creek bed, a weedy field or a vacant lot ... are places of initiation, where the borders between ourselves and other creatures break down, where the earth gets under our nails and a sense of place gets under our skin.

Robert Michael Pyle," Vacant Lot" *The Thunder Tree*

Mapping ◎

Mapping in a Nutshell:
Orient to the compass directions, and perceive the landscape from a bird's eye view. Draw maps to locate features of the landscape or tell stories that map your explorations.

A natural routine familiar to anyone who's ever driven in a big city, mapping orients us and shows us the gaps in what we notice. It creates a need for people to know what bird that was by the swamp, or where that creek goes. It also brings the landscape to life as the diversity of natural signposts emerges through the connections between birds and berry bushes, between coyote scat and vole-filled meadows, between bodies of water and the daily movements of animals.

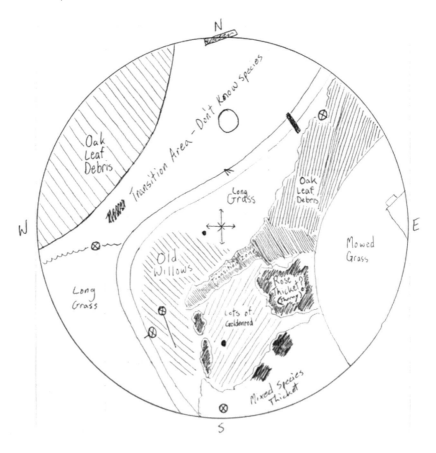

Drawing Maps

For older youth and adults, this routine comes easy. Draw maps all the time. Sketch your Sit Spot and the trails and significant features radiating out from it. Sketch your own house and yard and where it fits in your larger sphere of living. Draw the route you took on a Wander.

After a day of exploring, gather under the whiteboard and draw a collective map of where you went and what you saw. First, using the sun, stars, or a compass as a reference, identify the directions of North, South, East, and West. Then fill in your big landmarks, your trails, and the sites of the events that caught your attention.

Also, we encourage more focused groups to keep personal map-journals. They might begin with a blank slate or a store-bought contour map and fill it in with the locations of prevailing winds, ecological zones, wetlands, sunny spots, places never touched by sun, birds glimpsed, animal tracks and trails, food sources, or shelter trees. We encourage putting down everything on hand-drawn maps.

About Process, Not Product

The point is not to produce perfect maps. Rather, mapping engages us in a process infinitely beneficial to human development. Let the process evolve, and guide it with your questions. Don't get hung up on maps that "aren't right."

That said, as you practice the routine over time you will notice a marked difference in the accuracy of mapping. Every year when a new group of folks shows up at a teaching location we regularly use, they divide into groups and explore then draw a map of the small pond with a wiggly shape. After doing so, they show it to the rest of the group. Every map turns out different—one like a jelly bean, another like a long-necked goose.

Over the year, this process grows more precious to watch: every participant, including the facilitators, gradually begins to check the image in their mind with the actual reality of the pond they walk around, discussing and arguing with others, and constantly adjusting what they imagine. Through such care, all the different maps grow more uniform in shape; and the group, in a very similar manner, also congeals as a unified community.

Orienting to the Four Directions

We always draw attention to the circle of the four compass directions: East where the sun rises, South where it sits in the heat of the day, West where the sun sets, and North where it hides in the night. We'll often ask people to close their eyes and point to the compass direction for North. When eyes open to see arms flailing in every direction, they quickly realize how disoriented they are as a whole.

Every day, in every way, call attention to the four directions until this orientation settles into the brain patterns. We want people to make a habit, as their ancestors did, of orienting themselves to the sun and the stars. We constantly call attention to the way the sun moves throughout the day, or which direction we just walked from, or what direction their house lies from where they stand now. We even design our gathering spaces according to the qualities that we chose to associate with the directions: Our entry door is situated in the East; the bookshelves of field guides and journaling supplies belong in the South; the whiteboard for harvesting our stories marks the West; and the woodstove for warmth at night sits in the North. (More on using directions and directional qualities in your "Invisible School" can be found in the Natural Learning Cycle chapters.)

Navigating and Songlining

We want to take a slightly different approach to the routine of Mapping when we work with younger children or inexperienced adults. The world for younger children consists of what lies right in front of them, and often the drawing of maps will be too intellectual for their development. This can be true for beginners from any age group.

Our approach with younger children, then, is based much more on the way we communicate with them about the landscape. As we navigate through our day, we mention landmarks we passed on our wander, we ask them to lead the way back, we ask them to notice the clearing in the trees that might indicate a pond or wetland, and we tell stories about exciting things that once happened at spots on the landscape.

Traditional cultures create "Songlines" about their places with legends and songs: that mountain over there identifies where a leader goes to pray and cry for his people, and those drainage veins of snow coming down show streams of his tears; or that tree by the river with the two huge branches represents an old woman whose great arms watch over and take care of the river and its fish. In

The Practice of the Wild, Gary Snyder tells of traveling by truck in Australia with a Pintubi elder who recites the traditional Songline at truck speed. He reports, "I realized after about half an hour of this that these were tales to be told while walking, and that I was experiencing a speeded-up version of what might be leisurely told over several days of foot travel."

Take it slowly in the places you visit. "Story" your place as a means of navigating through it. Your adventures will lead to Songlines all across the landscape. Of course, name the places you go. Try naming them things you will remember, names that play off emotions of kids and adults: Death Crossing, Booger Hill, Funky Chicken Lake, Sneaking Cougar Trail.

In essence, we take the mapping mentality to "story" the landscape into one huge interconnected place that holds meaning for all of us. Whether through drawing simple maps, communicating from a bird's eye view, or paying attention to the four directions, the routine of Mapping practices, as the old saying goes, "getting to know a place like the back of your hand."

Exploring Field Guides ◎

Exploring Field Guides in a Nutshell:
Browse through field guides as treasure-chests of knowledge that fill up the vacuum of your curiosity about nature.

When people want scientific information, how can we help them find it for themselves? Leading them to Explore Field Guides makes them life-long, self-sufficient citizen-scientists of the natural world.

Field Guides as Elders

Field Guides express the amalgamation of many people's life work. They are treasure chests of hard-earned knowledge that has been passed on and built upon. Therefore they are the modern equivalent of the knowledge of an elder from a traditional culture: they hold the collective experience of many generations.

Elders from indigenous cultures have shared with us how their grandparents or aunts and uncles passed on their

The "wandering mentality" emerges naturally among subsistence and recreational hunters whose unparalleled alertness and total attentiveness to the environment constitute a transcendent state of consciousness.

RANDALL L. EATON, Why Hunters Save the World

My frog-catching was driven by my dad's mother, Nanny Cecil. My childhood years until I was ten were Nanny Cecil years. She took care of my sister and me when both my parents were working and sometimes we'd go stay with her in her little apartment on the sixth floor in the city of Asbury Park. She had grandmother magic and knew how to work it with us kids. She understood that children have these passions that she could tease them along with.

What did Nanny Cecil do that was so impressive? This shows you how her mind works. She would tell me and my sister, "You can go anywhere you want in my apartment, but whatever you do, don't go in the bottom middle drawer of my dresser." And then she'd turn, "I'm going to wash dishes." She'd sit there and wash the same two dishes over and over again for the longest time—and sing, and that would give Kim and me enough time to kind of slide up along the wall. One of us would watch for the other while we crawled on our bellies up to that middle bottom drawer and looked in.

Nanny had Golden Guides in there! The Golden Guide to Reptiles and Amphibians had drawings and maps and a picture of how frogs use their eyes. It was unbelievable treasure. And it was forbidden! Think about that. What that did for me and my sister. I'd be looking at the pictures in the book, "Oh my Gosh, look at that!"

continued...

intricate understanding of the environment through stories or by showing them things. Their descriptions of how this happened suggest that the elders only taught things when the younger people showed up ready for the lesson. The same is true with field guides. These wonderful books can be exciting to sit with, gleaning gems of information and soaking up the detail of drawings, photographs, and diagrams. But they really only teach us when we are ready to absorb.

Begin with Curiosity

Because field guides offer so much information (in small print and adult language), we need to make them fun, approachable, and accessible. We don't use them as textbooks, but rather as cherished magical books that hold innumerable secrets. We want them to be explored with wide eyes and a playful attitude.

The routine of Exploring Field Guides complements our curiosity sparked by other routines, such as Sit Spot, Questioning and Tracking, or Wandering. These other routines create an empty "vacuum" of interest primed to "suck in" information. When there is a living question, then the field guides are exciting to explore.

We encourage you to leave the field guides behind when you head out for a Wander or some Sit Spot time. Allow the field to provoke your curiosity, and when you get back you will have something to look for in the field guides. Recalling from your imagination the sight of that strange black and yellow bird engages memory—this burns the experience into the brain patterns and allows for field guide information to integrate with experience in a lasting way. Leafing through Field Guides can lead you to new questions to take back outside, and new things to watch for.

Field guides can also be great in the field, to be pulled out at lunch, or along the trail when you find a plant that might be edible. You can mix them into a game or activity. You can make a scavenger hunt with them. "Who can find these three dandelion look-a-likes?" After they huddle around your field guide, burning the images into their imagination, off they go hunting for the real things.

Soaking-In Learning

A delightful phenomenon happens when you just get people, and especially children, flipping through field guides: learning seeps in by osmosis. They might pick up a field guide to look for just one specific bird they saw or to solve a riddle you gave them. But in the process, they have to flip through and look at the pictures of dozens or hundreds of other birds. They'll often pause along the way, momentarily forgetting their goal as their curiosity overtakes them by seeing a bird with a strange feather-thing on its head. They look up its name and might read a little more, and call you over with a grin, "Look at *this* thing!" Then they keep on flipping.

Learning seeps in that wasn't planned, that couldn't be planned if you tried. This leads to an experience we witness often, and it tickles us every time. A person walks through the forest and suddenly they see a bird (or a plant, tree, track, or skull) that they've never ever seen before, and they excitedly point and blurt out without thinking, "Hey, that's a _____!" (fill in the blank with whatever they saw) Then they'll stop and a strange look will come onto their face. "I have no idea how I knew that. I've never looked up that bird or been taught it. But I'm sure I know it." They've learned it accidentally, by immersing themselves in field guides, by flipping through and letting search images develop subconsciously. Over years, this unconscious file-cabinet of images becomes huge. We have seen this with people of all ages, from very young to quite elderly. However you do it, take a hint from Jon's grandmother, Nanny Cecil, in the sidebar. Make the exploration into these treasure chests a journey of magical discovery.

Journaling ◎

Journaling in a Nutshell:
Keep a regular record, in drawings and in words, of your experience outdoors. Keep dated sketches, captions, and comments that describe your landscape. Keep it up through all the seasons until it becomes a habit you can't live without.

My sister would be on guard and she'd say, "Hurry up, hurry up, Nanny's coming!" So I'd close the book and the drawer, and she'd say, "Just kidding. My turn to look and yours to watch."

Every once in a while, Nanny would catch me. "Oh, you saw it," she'd say. "Well, we'll just have to read from it." And I sat on her lap and learned to read from these Golden Guides. Every one of the pictures in the Golden Guides is burned in my memory. They're not dead bird pictures; they're living images.

My grandmother's role from her kitchen in the city was to send me on errands and channel my stories into field guides when I came home at the end of the day. "Have you ever caught this one? Well, you should try to catch me one of those. I'd like to see one." And when I came home, she wanted to know the whole story: what did I catch, name it, use these books to find out what they eat, and go catch stuff they eat.

Little by little, the guides migrated over to my house. There was probably a rite of passage where we were allowed to look in the bottom drawer. Field Guides were my elders growing up and Nanny Cecil was the mentor who drove me to them with her questions.

Jon Young, Golden Guides

By "journaling," we do mean carrying around paper and pencil or laying open a sketchbook at the nature desk inside, next to the bookshelf stacked with field guides. Here we have the first core routine that involves *tools*. Assemble a sturdy pad of paper, a pencil or an ink pen, something to add color, and an eraser for a good beginner's toolbox.

Stretching the Imagination

Journaling is the routine that stretches and etches all the details a little further into the brain. It's the Sit Spot, Expanding Our Senses, Story of the Day, Questioning and Tracking, and Mapping all recorded in line and color and words on a page.

Look at something and then *draw it*, then look back to check on the things you weren't sure of—how that ear comes off the head, or how that leaf attaches to the stem. Can you feel your visual imagination wake up? Coloring a tree green, then looking twice, and shading the green and adding brown, activates a flurry of synaptic connections. The sketcher enters a lively image-questioning sequence with the thing observed. Because it fires up the brain's visual imagination, *drawing* imprints images in the mind's eye library.

Of course putting what you see or how you feel *into words* wakes up the linguistic brain. A five year old can learn six words for "green" and use them with delight all the rest of her life. Journaling means finding *words* that name plants and animals and birds, learning adjectives for color, inventing metaphors for smell, and growing a versatile vocabulary for movement. So much in nature is new for people that the words they find to record their experience often involve creative metaphor and little stories. So journaling, whether written or dictated, connects the language parts of the brain to sensory experiences from nature, and both bring each other alive.

Journaling as Paying Attention

The real purpose of the core routine of journaling is to train the mind to pay attention. It's important to *keep* a journal *regularly*. You want to end up with a thick book. To do that, you need to exercise some discipline. All good writers and artists and wildlife personnel practice with relentless discipline. You'll find their journals throughout the bookstores telling how journal-keeping taught them to *pay* attention.

The consistency of a nature journal lies in its dating system. At the top of every page write the date, the season, the time of day, a marker pointing north, and a note on the weather. So the very act of writing the heading calls

Go find a piece of paper; it doesn't matter what type or size. Find any pencil, marker, or drawing tool. Now gather up your eyes, take a deep breath, and ask yourself: "What is happening outdoors, this particular season, this time of day, and in this particular place where I live?"

CLARE WALKER LESLIE,
Keeping a Nature Journal

for orienting, for settling down and looking around. Then enter whatever captures your attention in the moment of journaling, in words or drawing, or both. Kept up consistently, a five-day journal tells a story, and a year-long journal records an era full of seasonal change.

Best of all, the patient and disciplined journaler imprints a mental habit of paying attention to all the fine details our five senses can perceive. Consistent journaling is a straight path to a career as a naturalist.

Writing a poem
Of seventeen syllables
Is very diffi

From a Student Assignment:
"Haiku"

Journaling as a Means of Finding One's Gift

Many people feel frustrated with the paraphernalia and change of attention needed for journaling. So let some of them off the hook. If you can, try to catch the people you are mentoring in a buttery-fly net filled with tips and allowances about how to make the journal part of their personal journey. If they produce a finished book, honor it with ceremony. Once they find a style that makes them happy, they'll demand journaling time.

So guide them to find their own special gift, their personal journaling style. There are just as many different forms of journal-keeping as there are people and snowflakes. Our Kamana Naturalist Training Program calls for journals to be submitted on a regular basis, until they turn into portfolios kept in our back office. When the "assignments" come in they are amazingly different. Some people do little flirty movement sketches in pencil with mussy handwriting and arrows pointing here and there. Some send in beautiful colored art. One drew a range map on every page, then developed it into a thematic cartoon. Some use the grid paper enclosed with the program; others combine words and sketches stretching to the outer margins of their sketchbook; while still others tap out their words on a computer with headings and bullets and even scan in their sketches.

For every different style of keeping a journal comes a choice of equipment. Consider the options: the pencil and portable memo pad in a zip lock bag; the sketchpad in an oiled leather cover; the desktop journal in a library of references; the piles of single sheets stuffed into pockets; the laptop files; the CyberTracker GPS system.

For younger children, do not burden them with equipment, but do encourage them to carry a pad and pencil, and stop once in a while to give them time to write a little heading at the top of their page. Maybe a water break will develop a habit to jot down whatever they want after the heading. If the younger ones need help, you can take dictation. Remember, as a mentor, be like Coyote: gently lure them into journaling, notice the edges of their resistance and enthusiasm. Help them discover their gifts. Let their journals go every which-way until each child discovers his or her own journaling style.

Bottom line: find a way to introduce journaling and make it a habit that those you mentor can't live without.

Survival Living

Survival Living in a nutshell:
Interact with the natural world around you on a survival basis, including all the basic human needs: shelter, water, fire, food, tools, clothing, and art.

The Original Landscape of Nature Connection

You and I wouldn't be alive if our ancestors had not practiced this Core Routine of Survival Living for all those hundreds of thousands of years before agriculture and civilization. All subsistence cultures have in common the necessity to survive in a wilderness environment, where the slopes of land and forces of climate shape brain patterns, where, according to Stalking Wolf, "the animal is an instrument played by the landscape." Indigenous cultures all share the raw experience of surging adrenaline, the "fight or flee" response. They have in common a deeply felt sense of kinship with all the elements of their natural world, a recognition that humans play only one tune among many.

The practice of survival accumulates in our bones and blood. It could be said that today's people are still hunters and gatherers, but the landscape gives us different feedback. During childhood, we learn what to click and turn, when to stop and go, how to pay attention to domestic and man made things that matter to us. But our modern systems eliminate the need to survive in direct, unmediated relationship with nature's raw elements. The mental habits that result from Survival Living have dimmed: ingenuity, self-reliance, and improvisation, and, as John Burroughs advised, "taking nature by the right handle."

Practicing Survival

Nothing gives us more meaningful relationships with nature than really putting ourselves out in the elements and living off the land. It creates the ultimate need to learn.

One of the people we mentor, Emily, went on a guided survival trip with a few other people from the same program. During their trip, they spent the night in a shelter they made out of branches

I certainly have found "good" in everything: -- in all natural processes and products, not the "good" of Sunday school books, but the good of law and order, the good of that system of things out of which we came and which is the source of our health and strength. … It is good that fire should burn, even if it consumes your house; it is good that force should crush, even if it crushes you; it is good that rain should fall, even if it destroys your crops or floods your land. Plagues and pestilences attest the constancy of natural law. They set us to cleaning our streets and houses and to readjusting our relations to outward nature.

Yes, good in everything, because law in everything, truth in everything, the sequence of cause and effect in everything, and it may all be good to me if, on the right principles, I relate my life to it. I can make the heat and the cold serve me, the winds and the floods, gravity and all the chemical and dynamical forces, serve me, if I take hold of them by the right handle.

The bad in things arises from our abuse or misuse of them or from our wrong relations to them … . Our well being consists in learning the law and adjusting our lives to it.

JOHN BURROUGHS,
The Gospel of Nature

When our son was in fourth grade he had a teacher who was game to try an idea I had for classroom environmental education. We organized a Power Outage Overnight.

After school, in the fall, we traveled from the school yard down a half-mile service road into the creek valley. We set off noisily as the sun lowered; and then as it darkened and things became odd and unfamiliar, we listened for owls and heard the creek.

Then we crept back to the blacked-out school gym, ate our Earthquake Kit food, told stories huddled around flashlights, and slept in our bags on the floor. Lots of parents came for the overnight and there were little flashlight fires all around the gym.

The Power Outage Overnight was a raving success and the third graders who are now six feet tall and halfway through college still remember it and tell me their memory of it in astonishing detail.

ELLEN HAAS, Power Outage Overnight

Without weariness there can be no real appreciation of rest, without hunger no enjoyment of food; without the ancient responses to the harsh simplicities of the kind of environment that shaped mankind, a man cannot know the urges within him.

SIGURD OLSON, *Open Horizons*

from the hemlock tree. They made a sleeping-mat floor inside their shelter from the springy green hemlock boughs, and they also made tea from the vitamin C-rich hemlock needles.

A day or two after her trip ended, I watched from a distance as Emily walked up the hill to the outdoor gathering space. Midway up the trail, she looked up and suddenly stood still, staring at the two hemlock trees. When she saw them, she told me later, she was immediately transported in her mind to the survival shelter: she could feel the soft comfort of the green hemlock boughs on her body; she could taste the citrus-tinged hemlock tea. She remembered how easily the dead twigs of the hemlock had lit up when everyone was shivering cold, struggling to make a fire. Standing there, seeing these trees she had passed so many times before without noticing, she cried. On the survival trip, Emily had created a meaningful relationship with the hemlock tree. From now on, whenever she sees a hemlock, she feels gratitude.

If you can, find a way to interact with nature in the raw. Stretch people's comfort zones by staying outside in difficult weather. Our gear lists for expeditions begins with this heading, "There is no such thing as bad weather, only inappropriate clothing!" Use wood to make fires. Use plants for food and medicine. Make leather from animal skins for clothes and drums. You might even learn how to grow your own food and learn to hunt and fish. With just a little training and practice, you can help others cultivate vegetable and herb gardens, build survival forts with sticks and leaves, and start fires in the old way, with friction methods of bow-drill or hand-drill.

Simulate a Genuine Need to Learn

These skills are valuable, ultimately, not because we need them for daily living—although they may indeed save someone's life—but for the way they help us develop connection to place and teach us to relate to nature in the oldest, most fundamental way. We learn the most when we have an intense need to learn, and nothing creates need like survival.

But if your situation won't allow actual survival learning, then try to make Knowledge of Place genuinely important to learn. Take people there through imagination: tell stories and play games based on tracking and stalking, hiding and ambushing, collecting and dissecting, finding food and making shelter. Stories of heroic deeds for survival are absolute favorites, just as they seem to be for today's audiences of the TV survival reality shows. Stories abound in the Activities section to fire up the imagination of what it would be like to survive in the wild. Many of the games simulate routines of Survival Living from deep in our DNA.

Mind's Eye Imagining ◎

Mind's Eye Imagining in a Nutshell:
Use and strengthen your imagination as much as possible, imprinting images in your mind gathered from the experience of all five senses.

Developing the Imagination

This routine develops our imagination and our ability to re-experience events with our eyes closed. If our goal is nature literacy, then we must go one step beyond plain reading into reading with the intent to "learn by heart." Not only visual images, but also smells, flavors, sounds, and textures imprint in magnificent detail in people's brain patterns when they rely on their nature literacy for survival. Routinely imagining with our Mind's Eye allows our sensory experiences to really sink in. This skill provides us with the dynamic memory required for field biology and bird watching and is the evidence of a well-developed naturalist intelligence.

This tree has been living for one hundred years, through snowstorms, standing so broad and old. If you listen you will hear her words of long ago and hear about the children that played under her when she was only a sapling and she will also tell you about the little family of doves that lived in her for so many years and how one of her branches fell off when she was playing tag with her friend the wind. If you sit there long enough, she'll also tell you about her story.

Sierra Helmann, This Tree (written at age 7)

The Mind's Eye Imagining Technique

When you come across a track while on a walk, look at it closely for a minute, then close your eyes and picture it in your mind's eye. This simple sequence intensely focuses your mind on the shapes of that track. Your mind strains to see it in full detail, preparing to re-tell the wondrous story about its every detail. When you open your eyes again, you see some things you didn't notice the first time, and when you close your eyes again, the picture in your Mind's Eye grows clearer and more vivid. Birdwatchers use this technique as they develop their eye to spot birds' flight patterns, their movement in the trees, and the slight differences in coloration among all those "Little Brown Jobbies."

The participants in our Kamana Naturalist Training Program learn to use the Mind's Eye technique to make sketches in their field journals. First, they look closely at the pictures— perhaps a Northern River Otter—in the field guides. Then, without looking at the pictures, they sketch the animal. In the act of sketching, they will notice they hadn't registered the length of tail, or the spacing of eyes, or how the otter stands up on its hind legs. Looking back at the pictures, they take note and fill the gaps in their original memory. Thus the sketch-image of the otter greatly improves, not only on paper but, more importantly, in the Mind's Eye Imagination of the artist.

Storytelling with the Mind's Eye

The Mind's Eye Imagining routine develops a filing cabinet of single images for identifying what you see in nature and it offers a potent technique for telling the Story of the Day.

Before I incorporated the use of my imagination into my nature studies as an adult, I remember how scientific reports and descriptive passages in literature bored me. I saw just a bunch of words with little behind them. After a few months of using my Mind's Eye technique to draw plants and animals, suddenly those words opened doorways into a vast landscape of images in my imagination. I was floored.

The more I used my mind's eye to remember leaf shapes and bark patterns, the more I enjoyed it when other people talked to me about these things or I read about them. It was as if suddenly I could see the movie behind the lines in a book.

Turning this around—adding all other senses and memories to the mix—I began to write and tell stories with my mind focused on the rich sensory wholeness of the experience. Since then, I've become a student of the great storytellers and speech-givers and I have discovered they all use the

Long live the weeds that overwhelm
My narrow vegetable realm!
The bitter rock, the barren soil
That force the son of man to toil;
All things unholy, marred by curse,
The ugly of the universe.
The rough, the wicked, and the wild
That keep the spirit undefiled.
With these I match my little wit
And earn the right to stand or sit
Hope, love, create, or drink and die;
These shape the creature that is I.

THEODORE ROETHKE,
Long Live the Weeds

power of their imagination, their Mind's Eye Imagining, to entrance their audience. We are image-based, sensory creatures at heart.

As people tell the stories of their day, help them ground themselves in the moment of their experience. Help them use all their senses to remember the precise angle of the harrier's tipped wings, the smell of damp earth or spring flowers, the squishy warm feeling of wet socks, the first touch of sun on their cheeks on a cold morning. Children, always so present to their experiences, are all born storytellers. But they will only truly know this about themselves when they practice using their Mind's Eye Imagining and tell their tales from a place of bright, detailed imagination.

Listening for Bird Language ◎

> *Listening for Bird Language in a Nutshell:*
> Be still and listen. Quiet down and crane your ears and eyes to notice the vocal signals and body language of birds and other animals, including humans. What message do you hear in their voice?

The Language of Birds

You know how you can talk to your best friends on the phone and just tell, by how their voices sound, they feel upset? Or surely you've seen the fast street-walk of people in business suits that says, "Don't bother me. I'm in a hurry!" This watchful interpretation of subtle signals into clear, meaning-filled communication is what the Core Routine of Listening for Bird Language is all about. We call it "Listening for Bird Language" but we extend the metaphor to include keeping our own presence quiet, and then listening, watching, and feeling all the nonverbal signals that sing and flutter about us all the time.

Much of the evolution of birds has been invested in the development of their complex vocal language. By learning how to tune into that language humans and other animals can be part of a constant many-species conversation that offers rich information about life within any landscape. Lots of other animals—squirrels, dogs, crickets, and frogs for instance—use complex vocalizations to communicate, too. All of it together creates a language in which a panoramic range of hidden meaning can be understood—if we pay attention.

Luckily, interpreting Bird Language does not require intimate knowledge of each individual bird's song or each frog's call. The two basic patterns are easy to recognize. (We develop these patterns in more detail in The Book of Nature chapter under Birds: The Messengers of the Forest.) For starters, all you need to know are *baseline* and *alarm*. Happy and comfortable birds use *baseline* songs and calls as they go about their daily business. Their songs deliver the overall feeling of peace and relaxed well-being. The *alarm* calls are the sudden piercing cries that tell you "something's up." A predator has come into the neighborhood. Cat below! Hawk above! Owl roosting too near our nest! Children abroad! These easily recognizable alarms are terrific for inspiring folks to pay attention.

Learning to Listen

As I first heard Tom Brown, Jr. say, every time an animal moves in the forest, it is like dropping a pebble into the clear surface of the pond: concentric rings go out, announcing the disturbance to everything the ring touches.

Once people see the communication possible by reading bird language, they will observe for themselves the more sophisticated nuances, the "concentric rings" of alarm that vary with the type of predator, the time of day, the time of year, and the length of time they can sit quietly without being the source of the disturbance.

Therefore, the routine practice of Listening for Bird Language begins with not creating your own disturbance. Listening for Bird Language can inspire people to walk quietly through the landscape so they don't create a "bird plow," a swath of wake before and behind them that silences or alarms all natural talk. Even the very young can be inspired to hold still a long time until they blend into the landscape and hear birds come alive again with their daily baseline twittering.

Over time, we learn to move through a forest without disturbing so many birds; we learn to blend into the landscape and relax our body language to put birds at ease. After learning how to move through the "alarm systems" of birds without setting them off, we eventually come upon stunned wildlife, whose eyes give us a quick amazed look of surprise that a human could see them first.

Learning the Language of Birds is not about you being a master birder for the Audubon Society and participating on bird counts and knowing every bird on your life list. It's about simple common sense.

And the beauty of it is that the same teachings that I learned from Tom Brown from the Apache way, I heard from Ingwe from the Akamba in Kenya. When I looked into the Bushmen of the Kalahari, they had similar teachings. When I read Jim Corbett's books about the Himalayas in India, the foothills where the tigers roamed, he described the exact same principles in action.

All of these were affirmations for me that bird language was truly universal. So learning it was not about knowing all of the birds of your area. It was about understanding patterns of voice and movement and recognizing disturbance in those patterns.

Jon Young, Universal Language of Birds

Self-Knowledge

Observing and understanding meaning in subtle patterns of sound and behavior can be applied more broadly to the rest of human life. As each person learns to be still and listen to the tones that reflect the moods of sensitive wild things, an awareness grows for the disturbances that they and others cause. People will eventually realize that their moods—fears or angers, impulsiveness or hesitancies—send off concentric rings of disturbance, both in the natural and human worlds.

Think of when you walk outside each morning to the mailbox, to your car, or to get the paper. The birds in your front yard watch you and come to expect the body language and moods you demonstrate. They react accordingly. Your bird neighbors watch you so carefully that they probably know you—in some ways—better than you know yourself.

If we don't move gently through the forest, the birds and the rest of nature give us immediate feedback. Here is the deeper lesson to the routine of Listening for Bird Language: the attitudes and body language we carry affect the world around us. Listening for Bird Language as a routine shows us that we can choose the impact we create as we move through the world.

Thanksgiving ◎

Thanksgiving in a Nutshell:
Find in yourself a grateful heart and express gratitude for any and all aspects of nature and life. Begin every episode with thanksgiving and give nods of thanks as you go about your day.

Thanksgiving as a Routine

How is "Thanksgiving" a routine for nature awareness? Taking a moment to see the grace in elements of the natural world—frogs, rain, berries, or the sun—deepens our relationships with each one. Thanksgiving reinforces the interdependence of all living things and their ground of being and reminds us of our kinship with nature.

How do you think the alarm for a cat is going to move? First, cats always seem to be up to no good, and their body language broadcasts a sneaky intent. Second, cats move in little bursts and stand still and move in little bursts and stand still. So, the alarms are going to move in little bursts and stand still and move in little bursts and stand still.

JON YOUNG, Cat Calls

If the animals can do it, you can too. You can learn to listen to the first hints of alarm, and you can also prevent the alarm. It's very similar to learning to walk by one of those motion-detector lights without flipping it on. There are motion detectors in the forest that read your intent, that read your body language, that know your mind and pass the message on as you approach.

JON YOUNG, Motion Detectors

Find a Grateful Heart

When we say "Thanksgiving," we mean routinely remembering and expressing gratitude for the things that make it possible for us to be alive. We mean generally appreciating things common to all humans, as well as those specific to each of our lives.

As the media constantly reminds us of everything going wrong in the world, the Core Routine of Thanksgiving reminds us of all the things going right: clean water comes out of faucets; birds sing beautiful songs; humans we may never meet grow plants and raise stock so that we can have food on our tables; trees bring beauty and oxygen as well as wood for houses and tools; and this very moment earthworms are decomposing matter into fertile soil. We could go on and on, and sometimes we do.

Be genuine.
Grow soft and lift your heart to feel grateful.
Stop everything and listen when someone has a story to tell.
Take time to say "thank you" and to write thank you notes.
Discover the extraordinary in the ordinary and admire it.

ELLEN HAAS

Notice the Positive

Right now, as you read this, do a little experiment. Look up and glance around your place and notice all the square or rectangular shapes around you. Can you see them? Do they pop out at you? Now turn your attention to all the round shapes in the room. Do these pop out at you? I've watched many people do this exercise with different colors or shapes and they all say they notice the same thing. Just as brain patterning theory contends, our perception of reality is determined by what we focus our attention on.

The routine of Thanksgiving simply calls our attention to the multitude of things going right with the world. We don't deny either the pain or tragedies of life; we just choose to concentrate our mental focus on all the good things that we can easily overlook. We want to help people notice the relentless springing of life all around them, with authentic hope in the rejuvenating powers of the earth.

By attending to the positive aspects of life through the routine of Thanksgiving, we apply good medicine to help heal the overwhelming sadness and anger that often shows up when we connect with nature in a deep way and realize the impact on the natural world when it is abused (even unconsciously or carelessly). Thanksgiving as a routine can shake off the eye-clouds of depression and lift our spirits toward everything good and hopeful.

Begin Everything with Thanks

Whether as an opening mini-ceremony to your program, a moment taken during the day to stop and listen, or a blessing before bed, make it a Core Routine of Nature Connection to nod a simple thanks for life.

We often begin and end each program, and even our staff meetings, by identifying specific things we feel thankful for in that moment and expressing it. The form varies; perhaps we recount mini-stories of poignant recent experiences, or go round in a circle expressing thanks with one word, or sing a song of praise. In many native and traditional cultures, they often practice thanksgiving through the songs they sing. Examples spread through all cultures: the praise-filled Psalms of the Ancient Hebrews, the nature haiku of the Japanese, the gospel praises of the African Americans, or the many songs of Indigenous people that honor the sun, the moon, the earth, water, plants, or animals.

We don't really care how it looks, as long it stays welcoming, fresh, and alive. We constantly invent new ways to acknowledge our thankfulness, and do our best to prevent our Thanksgiving from becoming a lifeless ritual.

When people share what they feel genuinely thankful for, the variation from person to person is incredible. Comments from others lead us to think of things in new ways or they expose us to new stories. It can be another form of Story of the Day. You could say that when we gather to say our thanks, the natural world speaks through all our unique selves, and reminds our collective community of the integrated beauty of our lives.

Traditional Mohawk Thanksgiving

The traditional Thanksgiving Address of the Iroquois Nation begins with the people gathering "as if they were of one mind." Then, one by one it directs greetings and thanksgiving to:

The Spirit that moves through all things

The Ancestors

The Spirits of the four directions

Moon, Sun, and Stars

Wind and Cloud

Birds

Trees

Animals

Plants

Waters

Earth

People

So as you give thanks all the way up, you browse each level of your landscape for what captures your appreciation. This provides a fan upwards through every edge of ecology. Saying your own version of it at every opportunity, as you wake, as you drive, as you begin a class, can become a wonderful mental habit.

(Jake Swamp, a former Sub-Chief of the Wolf Clan of the Mohawk Nation has written a children's version of this called *Giving Thanks, a Native American Good Morning Message*. You can buy little books by the Tree of Peace Society, in English or German, of the original Thanksgiving Address. Go to wildernessawareness.org.)

Chapter 4
CHILD PASSIONS AS MENTORING TOOLS

Child Passions as Mentoring Tools

Passion – *fervor* – *enthusiasm* – *ardor* – *zeal*
Tap into – *exploit a plentiful resource; draw sap from
a sugar maple to boil into syrup*

If Core Routines are what we do to learn nature's ways, finding ways to tap into Child Passions is what mentors do. Mentors know full well that people don't always arrive ready to focus their attention. It's our job to capture the natural passion they **do** bring and channel it into learning.

We know we want people to practice Core Routines that lead to Sensory Awareness, Knowledge of Place, and Nature Connection. But how? How do we inspire them to sit still in a Sit Spot or eagerly Explore the Field Guide's fine print? How do we stretch their passions and shift their habits toward Nature Connection—in their everyday lives, even when we're not with them?

We hope this question—how?—is always on your mind

My neighborhood was an old apple orchard that had been converted into a subdivision. They left alone the creek corridors, and people's back yards all backed up into creeks. The kids figured out after a while that there was a certain distance the parents would go beyond the house and no further; it was marked by where they went to dump the lawn clippings in their wheelbarrows. So Parent Trails poked into the back yards a little bit. But then the Children's Trails began.

If you turned left or right after going past the lawn clippings, there were these other trails. And these other trails were formed by the passage of children's feet. You never saw adults and you never saw their footprints. You saw kids' bike tracks and lots of bare feet tracks and little sneaker tracks. We children moved around in little bands and our trails connected up in these greenways. There was a small subset who were the frog catchers. They left a very particular group of footprints you recognized because they dared go out into the muck. Back there in those trails, it was kids' world.

Honestly, I don't think I ever saw an adult back there. That was symbolic of something: we as children just knew what to do. We didn't have parents instructing us. We come with instructions and they guide us to read those places. Berry bushes hung over the edges of the creek. I don't ever remember being told by anyone which berries to eat. It was just something we knew. We just ate berries. We buzzed all up and down these creek corridors eating berries.

JON YOUNG, Children's Trails

as a mentor, because the answer springs from Coyote's challenge to *meet your learners at their edge*. Start with what children of all ages naturally love to do. Using Child Passions as Mentoring Tools is Coyote's best trick for making education invisible, making it seem like just a lot of fun.

Using children's universal love of Play is the starting point. But other edges of Child Passions can also be channeled into core routines. The next few chapters give tips and tricks for using Child Passions as Mentoring Tools. Gathered together, they suggest using a bundle of styles, each in its apt moment. Each style taps into a different source of the universal pool of what children naturally love to do. *Playing* directly contributes to learning. *Questioning and Answering* calls forth their curiosity. *Storytelling* captures imagination. And *Music-Making* centers community. All of these depend upon that most natural of all human impulses—doing as we see others do, imitating our role models.

In the back section, we have keyed the Activities to show which Child Passions they engage. Just look for the Child Passions Icon at the top of each activity.

Tapping into Child Passions

This chapter shows you how to use the playful instinct to design learning experiences. Here we highlight how games factor into the practice of Core Routines of Nature Connection.

Kids in a Music Class

Let me take you back to my public elementary school in a small town, and sit there on the front row of music class, right by the teacher's upright piano, the kind with wheels on it so you can roll it around the room.

My music teacher, Mrs. Granham, undoubtedly hoped we'd love music and practice singing scales or reading music. But she knew, as many good teachers do, that she couldn't just say, "Sing the F major scales in quarter notes. Ready?" Countless adults I've talked to say their natural love of music was stamped out in their youth by being forced to practice musical "core routines." Fortunately, my teacher was a natural Coyote Mentor.

Instead, Mrs. Granham taught us catchy songs all kids love, little children's songs that had the scales and rhythms and other "routines" *built into them*. We loved singing these funny songs, we would laugh and laugh and laugh; yet all the while we unwittingly sang the F major scale in quarter note patterns. To our pride and amazement, she told us afterwards what we had done. I am eternally grateful to Mrs. Granham because she made music fun for us. She used her adult intelligence to know her students and meet us where we were.

Mrs. Granham tapped into Child Passions. Our delight in singing catchy, funny songs was the doorway through which she channeled all the learning routines she hoped we would practice. She made learning meaningful in our childlike world.

I went on a very high-minded kayak trip in Southeastern Alaska with twenty adults where we practiced early morning meditation and silent, mindful paddling for a week. We thought we were so enlightened! But when we'd break our solemnity in the free-for-all afternoons, what would we do? The women shopped for rocks on the shoreline, "Do you like this one? Oh that green is so pretty!" And the men competed, hurling rocks to hit the bullseye on outlying kelp buds!

Ellen Haas, Shopping for Rocks

What's a Child Passion?

Child Passions defines the things children world-wide love to do, no matter what their cultural background. Child Passions are those universal aspects of the childhood experience that bring children so much happiness and aliveness. Importantly, children do these things without help or prompting from adults.

As with all of nature, nothing is hard and fast, and there will always be exceptions to every rule. Some infants love being thrown in the air, while others dread it; some children thrive in competitive games, while others wilt. Each child enjoys unique passions, and different populations may have distinctive tendencies, such as with boys and girls. As many developmental psychologists have shown, kids of different ages display different Child Passions. Generally, children feel passionate about playing games, asking questions, hearing stories, singing songs, and imitating us!

What about You?

Do you remember this from your childhood? I invite you to pause here for a moment to reflect on Child Passions from your experience. Ready? Open your Mind's Eye and remember your childhood. Take out a pencil and jot down your first images.

What do your remember loving to do as a child?
What were your favorite games to play?
What did you do for fun with your friends?
What were your favorite toys?
What captured your curiosity?
What stories and songs made up your world?
Who were your favorite grownup playmates?

Now think of yourself today.
What Child Passions do you still enjoy?
Which Child Passions do the children in your life enjoy?

An Unlimited Bundle of Child Passions

Now compare your list with this list we brainstormed. Ready?

Adventuring, discovering, exploring, hiding, seeking, spying, wandering, getting lost, getting found, asking questions, being asked questions, finding answers, listening to stories, creating stories, telling stories, acting out stories, reading picture books, keeping a diary, listening to music, making music, singing, laughing, whistling, clapping, stomping, shouting, throwing things, moving/pushing things, hitting things, blowing bubbles, touching/petting things, catching little critters, seeing animals close up, climbing, swinging, riding, splashing, squirting, swimming, getting wet, getting dirty, getting muddy, spitting, flying, jumping, racing, chasing, playing tag, testing quickness, pretending, imagining, imitating, acting, performing, show-and-telling, dressing up, costuming, painting faces, making-up characters, being animals, telling secrets, keeping secrets, using secret languages, eating, tasting, cooking, gathering, smelling, painting, drawing, sculpting, building, decorating, burning, playing with fire, breaking, dissecting, making messes, cleaning up messes, trapping things, collecting, helping, carrying things, running errands, helping older folks with projects, helping each other, surprising, giving and receiving, shocking, sneaking, hiding, hunting, shooting, carving, making tools, constructing shelters, making dams, building tree houses, playing house, playing forts, whispering, joking, tricking, hugging, cuddling, holding hands, seeking treasure, detecting clues, pursuing mysteries, making dares, taking challenges, seeking adventure.

CHILD PASSIONS

Which of these do you love to do? Do you feel a response of excitement in your body? There might be some things you want to go out and do right now. Why not? Go ahead. Play!

Playing Games: The Adrenaline Secret

Kids in a Leaf Pile

As nature educators, we want to do the same thing my music teacher did: channel the practice of Core Routines through the doorway of Child Passions. Even adults, who started out as children, possess a strong root memory and can be captivated just like kids. Here's an example of how it can be done with kids outdoors.

During a summer camp in Western Washington, instructors Warren Moon and Casey MacFarland's kids discovered a huge pile of raked leaves in one corner of a wide meadow. Seeing the zeal with which the kids were jumping in the leaves, the light-bulb lit up in their heads: here is a Child Passion! The instructors asked themselves, "How can we channel this into a Core Routine?" In a few moments of brainstorming, they had it. Casey introduced the brand new game to the group.

The game was this: while the instructors walked a little ways away, the kids would all hide inside the pile of leaves,

Games give us an inside view of the way nature works—the principles of ecological systems, for example – but not in a boring, textbook way. While we play games, we act out dynamically and feel directly, the natural cycles and processes.

Joseph Cornell,
Sharing Nature with Children,
20th Anniversary Edition

And what does Coyote Mentoring look like when playing/working with the 3 to 5 year old?

ROLE MODEL – Be what you wish to see in the children. Be in the awe, wonder, curiosity, and imagination of the child. Let your senses be alive. Utilize your whole being, heart, head, mind, body when responding to the child.

PLAY – Explore, experiment, and adventure with the little ones. Release the word, "try." Adopt an attitude of expansion and possibility. Develop a willingness to observe and discover, receiving guidance from children's passions and nature itself.

SIMPLIFY - Take the essence of a core routine and bring it to its simplest, easiest form. They are still in the "duckling" phase, or "group mind," so huddle up together in your Sit Spot. Journal by drawing pictures, or pressing found leaves in a book. Draw maps on the ground. Sing Songs to the Four Directions.

MAKE IT ALL RELATIONAL - Grandfather Sun, Grandmother Moon, Brother/Sister Wind. This builds deep imaginative and relational connections.

Wendolyn Bird, Creator and Director of Tender Tracks Tales and Trails Outdoor Preschool and Summer Adventure Camps Coyote Mentoring with Little People

and then the instructors would return as "monsters" and sniff all around the pile, looking for any moving creature to eat. Therefore, the goal of the kids was to stay as hidden, and as still, as possible.

The kids yelped in excitement over the new game: they would get to hide in this enormous pile of leaves! Warren and Casey walked away so that they wouldn't witness the kids hiding, and they stood talking for at least ten minutes before even beginning to walk back to the pile.

Why would they wait so long? Because they know what kids experience in those long moments an incredibly potent form of Sit Spot. They hold absolutely still in a pile of dirty, moist leaves, with insects and spiders crawling all over them and the rich scent of decay saturating their sense of smell. They are having Sit Spot time without realizing it.

As they lie hiding in the stillness of that musty leaf pile, they begin to forge a good habit of awareness. Enveloped in sensory input, focused on staying absolutely still, and pumped with adrenaline as their hearts beat in hopes of not being found, they learn a new level of comfort in the messy natural world. Their brain patterns for comfort and stillness in nature grow stronger. And in moments as they wait, they may completely forget the game as they become rapt in the beautiful designs of an ant that crawls right in front of their nose. Because of all this, Casey and Warren wanted to prolong their waiting as long as possible.

They had gotten to know the average patience of this group of children and after ten minutes they guessed fidgeting would start. That's when the instructors began to circle in, cracking branches, grunting, and lurking around as silly monsters, which made it hard for the children not to laugh. Any kids thinking of coming out from hiding stayed still longer. So Warren and Casey pushed their edge of stillness farther and farther until, finally, kids burst out laughing or jumped out as their own brand of monster.

What Warren and Casey did that day—and what all Coyote Mentors do at every opportunity—was tap into Child Passions. The kids' spontaneous delight in the leaf pile produced energy they could funnel into an experience of the Sit

Spot routine. We want to weave the practice of Core Routines of Nature Connection into activities loaded with Child Passions so each group member leaves with such positive body memories they naturally practice Core Routines for the rest of their lives.

Adrenaline for Games

Could it be that games evolved as perfect behaviors and attitudes for learning? As humans evolved long ago, why might we have developed the instinct to run races, to hide behind bushes, or to explore under every rock? What evolutionary benefit might there be in the instinct to play games full of fight, fright, flight, and delight?

Children learned the skills they'd need as adults in serious survival situations through these games. In a world of eat or be eaten, adrenaline surges fueled the muscles to fight or flee. But clever nature prepares its young to associate those feelings of heightened excitement with fun and pleasure.

Brain research suggests that sensory input and mental focus lead to deeply imprinted pattern learning when experienced in an "adrenalated state." Who is more full of adrenaline surges than excited kids playing games? Passionate playfulness is embedded in our human blueprint for learning.

Creators of indoor toys and computer games know how to reach out to children by engaging these passions. Outdoor educators—with our different goals—can do the same, but we can do it in the original arena of forests, plains, and deserts, where the expression of passion has a full range of motion, where the energy and curiosity of childhood has a boundless playground to stretch in. Rooted in biology, Child's Play has been one of the best friends of educators, parents, grandparents, and mentors everywhere. You only have to notice and channel the energy of the game into the lesson plan.

Disclaimer: We're not encouraging you to do whatever it takes to rev up people's adrenaline. We've seen too many *macho* instructors run into disaster by playing scout games that quickly push participants over the edge, or send children crying home to their parents. However, adrenaline provides a powerful and

But, imagine! Were today's toddler's toys mounded in a landfill, you would be looking at a mountain of blue and yellow, red and green plastic. Were native toddlers' toys mounded in a landfill, there would be hardly a trace, worn and weathered corncob dolls with walnut heads, rocking horses, balls of string and broomsticks.

Jon Young, Landfill Toys

In the olden days, hunts were more real for children. Today, treasure hunts have been co-opted as Easter egg hunts, but the grass is all the same length and the eggs are bright purple. My feral children have trouble with the domestic version, they want an excuse to go out into the woods and meadows where they can collect real living frogs and lightning bugs.

Jon Young,
Treasure Hunts

Child Passions as Mentoring Tools | 85

important tool for learning, so do invoke it. Just be careful. Meet people where they are and with what they are ready to handle, and start with time-tested games and activities.

Hiding, Seeking, and Sneaking

As you look through the Activities in this Guide, you'll notice many games involve hiding, seeking, and sneaking. Why are these such wonderful forms of children's play?

As kids, we called our favorite neighborhood game "Kick the Can." We set up a tin can on the driveway, and the "It" person guarded the can. Everyone else hid around the area, in bushes or behind air conditioning units, and then we waited for our opportune moment when "It" went far enough away that we could pop out of hiding and run and kick the can before "It" ran and tagged us. If we got tagged, we went to jail—where we waited hopefully for someone to kick the can and free us!

My favorite thing to do was to hide and try to kick the can and free everyone else. I remember crouching behind this one magnolia bush that afforded good cover, so much so that I could hardly see through it to watch the guard. I would sit there absolutely silent, bugs crawling over me, bits of leaf and dirt and spider-web in my hair and clothes, and my heart beating and adrenaline pumping. In such a state, I was utterly alert: my ears strained to listen for the footsteps of the guard. I noticed how occasional gusts of wind provided a sound cover for me to adjust my position a bit; I felt the sweat on my skin and the undulations of my breathing chest. To this day, I still remember the earthy scent of that magnolia patch. With my "Spidey sense," I could judge the right time to go for it. Then bursting with excitement, I suddenly broke loose of my secretive spot and shot towards the can at full speed. Occasionally, all my intense work was rewarded—as jail-breakers hoorayed and slapped my hand "high-five" with big smiles. Nobody grinned bigger than me.

What do such games do for people? In terms of the Core Routines, they do a lot. The excitement of hiding, seeking, and sneaking pushes senses into a mode of alertness like that of predators and prey, but it's all done with a sense of fun. It's good to remember that for thousands of years, our ancestors

Being free to go fishing taught me patience. It was a slow go, teaching myself the techniques; squishing my tiny piece of white bread onto the hook; untangling lines, working with my fingers. Then, I would stand so patiently, staring in stock stillness at my fishing line and my bobber.

Patience brought awareness of things moving below the surface. I could see the surface of the water move and I could tell by the shape of it how big the fish was underneath. I could tell whether it was a turtle or a frog moving toward the bank. If you took the time, you could always identify what was going on below the surface by the surface story.

Jon Young, Fishing

were both predators and prey—so it's no accident that kids play these kinds of games. Hiding gets us to sit still for long periods of time, stretching out our short attention spans—Sit Spot time. Seeking gets our antennae sharp—Expanding the Senses. Sneaking gets us to move slowly and intentionally, with awareness to our bodies. When hiding, seeking, and sneaking link up with Animal Forms, we find ready applications for Fox-Walking, Cougar-Stalking, Worm-Crawling, or Squirrel-Climbing. Understanding Bird Language naturally mixes in also because we listen for the birds to signal that a human approaches. Tracking also gets practiced, because we learn to look for trampled plants that lead to hiding spots, or follow the trails of other sneaks and then surprise them.

Caution: Watch out for hostile competition around hiding and sneaking. Beware that some people get really upset when others jump out and scare them, beginning propaganda wars of "You are so unaware and stupid!" or "I saw you. You're terrible at hiding!" To avoid this pitfall encourage (with stories) kids to seek the self-satisfaction of staying silent and remaining invisible, just like wild animals. After all, a deer wouldn't jump out and say, "Ha-Ha! I got you!"

Also beware of kids wanting to hide from the instructor without permission. If they break the "stay where I can see you" rule by sneaking off when you turn your back, appreciate their resourcefulness, but let them know it's unsafe and unacceptable.

Hunts, Errands, and Adventures

We all love hunts. It's instinctive. Think of Easter egg hunts or following treasure maps. Look at the popularity of Geo-caching. We think people just love to explore new frontiers and experience the thrill of discovery. We want to grow, learn and push beyond the edges of the known. Hunts present us with opportunities to do exactly that.

Errands can be used as domesticated form of hunts. Most people think of errands as going shopping for a bottle of milk or swinging by the post office. The spirit behind such errands is doing something for someone, even if it's for yourself. People love to go on errands for "the village." Errand-running has the same goals and benefits as volunteering, serving others and doing good deeds, and therefore, feeling good.

Our friend, Gilbert Walking Bull, a native Lakota elder, told me how as kids he, his siblings, and cousins were all sent on lots of errands. Their grandmother, a medicine woman, sometimes sent them to pick roots, sometimes they gathered chokecherries for food dishes, and other times they delivered firewood to Elders. Their Uncles gave the kids instructions on how to move during such errands: they were to walk a certain distance apart from each other so they wouldn't talk, and they were to communicate with hand signals and eye contact, always keeping track of each other. In this way, they covered more ground as a group and shared their discoveries. The kids couldn't always be faithful to this, but when they were, it added greatly to their awareness of the places they traveled through.

Also, Gilbert said, sometimes it would take them hours to complete a single errand, and the adults didn't seem to care at all. They almost seemed to expect that.

Imagine: on the way to pick berries, a frog jumping out in front of you might side-track you into chasing it into a pond, where you silently watch as ducks swim close to you and then suddenly squawk and scatter as a hawk swoops down towards them. After reveling in the awe of such events, you suddenly remember about the berries again. So you pick up your basket and head to the berry bushes again, when suddenly you come across a fresh set of coyote tracks …

Educationally, it's not the errands themselves that are so rich. Rather, it's the adventure, the things that happen *along the way*. Kids and adults both love errands, not only because they want to contribute but because errands provide a safe format for unpredictable adventures. No wonder, then, adults from native cultures don't mind children taking a long time to return. They know invisible education was really happening.

Errands, hunts, and adventures can be exciting ways to get connected with nature, inviting the pioneer spirit of exploration within safe boundaries. In terms of Core Routines, scavenger hunts can start with Field Guides: "find me this, and one of these." They can involve Journaling: "leave the plant in the ground, but make a sketch to prove you found it." And of course they invite the practice of Mapping: "go from here, to here, to here," following clues found at each station. Errands may certainly involve Wandering along the way, whether going home or to town, or along the ditches by the sidewalk. There can be, and should be, a continual exchange between sending people on errands and asking for their Story of the Day. Once you hear the story, listen for their edges. Keep them moving by checking in and following up with a new errand, a further adventure. Remember to include your own stories and edges in your conversations too. Modeling is essential; it builds energy, faith and trust in the system of mentoring.

Make-Believe

Coming up on a long mud-puddle, a six-year old named Charlie turned to me and said, "To fairies, this is a lake. It's almost an ocean, but it's a lake." When I asked him if he sees fairies a lot, he said, "Oh yeah. I used to see them a lot when I was younger, but as I get older I don't see them as much."

This set me and all the kids talking about fairies, exchanging our bits of knowledge about them, asking questions to those who saw them more, and so on. Later that day, near the end of our lunch break, I noticed Charlie and the other kids squatting together in a huddle just on the edge of the woods. They chatted excitedly and gathered twigs they assembled together on the ground. Suddenly, one got up and started running off, in my general direction. I asked her, "What are you up to?" She was a little annoyed by having been stopped to explain, and she matter-of-factly said, "I'm going to get some moss to make a bed for the fairies." "Oh" I replied. "Can I come see it?" She nodded her head and then ran off, back to her errand.

When I walked over to see what the group was making, what I saw amazed me. Not only were they making a bed complete with twig lining and posture-pedic moss; they were also constructing a house with a kitchen, along with mini-bouquets of flowers. Their care and whole-focused absorption on the project was awesome. Realizing this as the throes of a major passion, I jumped right in. "Wow, this is so cool. You know, what if we found some really strong maple twigs to make sure the bed is strong enough?" Whoops of agreement went up, and just as a child turned to run off, he looked back and asked, "Oh yeah. I don't know what maple twigs look like. Can you show me?"

The world of children is alive with things that most adults have long lost touch with. But if we ourselves can remember the magic and mystery that the child's world holds, we will discover enormous possibility for infusing that world with nature connections. In this remembering, the kids are our best teachers.

Fairies are just one facet of this world. In a child's life, there may be gnomes, trolls, dragons, wizards, leprechauns, or pirates, arghhhhh! Kids can become so engaged in this imaginary realm that they forget about all else. Instead of dismissing these as useless child fantasies, go with them and take them into the woods with you, channeling passions into positive connections with nature.

Kid Culture

All the things mentioned above make up what we call "kid culture." In a realm of imaginary characters, fantasy is terribly important and utterly captivating to kids. Fantasy lives in the culture found in toy-stores, Disney-movies, and children's books. When your kids start talking about their video games or Harry Potter, you may initially want to steer their minds away from the technology. However, you can simply redirect these mesmerizing influences into experiences in nature.

My very first summer working with youth, I felt frustrated that my kids would rather talk about Harry Potter books than play hide-and-seek games. Not even that Child Passion power-tool would break through the spell of Hogwarts and Throw-up Flavored Jelly Beans. Suddenly, remembering something from the book, an idea struck me. "Do you remember how Harry Potter had an 'invisibility cloak' that he could wear so no one could see him?" They all knew of it intimately, expressing wishes they could have one too. "Well," I said, "you can. Except it's not a cloak—it's an invisibility fern." Their eyes lit up in surprise as they began to see the huge ferns around them in a new way. We spent the next few hours playing hiding games, ever-searching for the ideal 'invisibility fern.'

If you want to educate kids, get into their world. Immerse yourself in "kid culture." Read the books in their current rave, watch the movies they mention, buy a pack of baseball cards—so you can better understand their fantasies, heroes, and dreams. Then, you can meet them there and integrate all of their passion for pirates and fairies and heroes into meaningful connection with nature. The same holds true when you work with adults; the culture just changes forms. What are they interested in? Find out. Know those whom you mentor.

With kids, why not help them build fairy villages and earn heroic laurels? Use the chance to pass on information about survival shelters and twig identification, and get them smelling and rubbing different mosses on their cheeks. Present blind-fold games, animal forms, and physical challenges as "Jedi training," and help them learn to use "the Force." Use elements of nature to make costumes for favorite characters. Learn magic tricks. Find out about their favorite stuffed animals or play hiding games with a rubber chicken. Rediscover that eternal child in yourself, connect with the kids through their world, and make sure learning and positive memories in nature are always a foundational part of that wonder-filled world.

Imitating and Role Modeling

Which child passion embeds so deep inside we don't even realize we do it? Imitation. Young kids will imitate anything that appeals to them—the language and actions of other kids, animal movements and sounds, fashion trends, and yes, the behavior of the adults in their lives. Adults do this a bit more slyly, but still they imitate.

Start with Yourself

It is vital for every adult to grasp that kids, and also adults we mentor, view us as role models. You may want your children to grow up with a sparkle in their eye. Do you have a sparkle in yours? You may want people to have deep connection with place. How confident do you feel in your own connection with nature? You want to move those you mentor from edge to edge. How willing are you to push your own edges? You may want the people you work with to follow their passions and gifts and not give in to limiting societal norms. How alive are your gifts and how doggedly do you follow them?

You have to start with yourself. No matter how much information you offer through games, questioning, stories, or songs, your biggest influence will be *who you are* and how you live your life. As soon as you get opportunities to mentor children, they will watch you like a hawk and often imitate your ways of being. When you work with youth, their watching and imitating can be even more profound; they will imitate the faces you make, voices you use, how you walk, whether or not *you* actually visit a Sit Spot, whether or not *you* will get muddy and play games with full abandon. When you really take the act of mentoring to heart, it pushes you to constantly self-reflect. The people you mentor will hold up the mirror for you. Are you being "the change you wish to see in the world?"

Hopefully all this information will not make you balk at the prospect of mentoring, thinking you have to be perfect before you begin. If you have it in your heart, start the work. Even though you are not perfect, striving to better our world by serving as a mentor is a heroic thing to role-model. Already

If you ever run out of games or get frozen and don't know what to do with your kids, don't sweat it at all. Ultimately, it's not about what you do with students, but who you are being. That's what kids will take home.

John Chilkotowsky,
Wilderness Awareness School Program Director

CHILD PASSIONS

Be the change you want to see in the world.

Gandhi

Whatever you can do, or dream you can do, begin it. Boldness has genius, power and magic in it.

Goethe

My mother was not the kind of naturalist mentor who knows something—how to fish or hunt or harvest – and takes the child for learning forays. Instead, she gave me freedom to learn on my own. "Go explore," she told me, "Show me what you find." "Tell me your stories."

When we rented on a gentleman's estate near Philadelphia, I bounced off at five years old with the farmer on his tractor into the corn rows, waving from the shotgun seat, as my mother in red lipstick, black hair in a red bandana, waved back. I remember being allowed to toddle down the winding farm road a half mile to the pond to "watch turtles." One afternoon she found me napping among lambs and their ewe.

When we moved to the rolling rock suburbs of Mill Creek when I was seven, I fretted at the edges of the yard, so she sent me off alone through the neighborhood lanes "to find a farmer." I wandered through corridors of woods and glades and stream courses, with my lunch packed in a basket. Three hours later, beginning to hunt for me, she found me sharing my picnic on a sloping streamside lawn with the old estate gardener.

I realized when thinking about who my mentors had been, that my mother mentored me to be fearless. Fearlessness was confidence to wander. It allowed so many connections that might have been blocked. My mother was raised an Iowa farm girl with positive spirit and she gave no credence to those fears. The world was safe and welcoming. People were good. Nature and animals were friendly.

ELLEN HAAS,
Tribute to My Mother

you *are* role-modeling and mentoring everyone around you, all the time, whether it's a participant in a program or someone you chat with while in line at the grocery store.

Please consider the Kamana Naturalist Training Program, a home-study program developed by Jon Young, John Gallagher, Ellen Haas, and others. We can't recommend it enough. It will guide you to internalize the Core Routines, awaken your senses, and ground you in meaningful knowledge of your local ecosystem. It will nurture the sparkle in your eye.

You and Child Passions

As mentor, teacher, parent, counselor, or outdoor educator, Child Passions will be your best friend and an easy way to begin the journey of knowing others. Why is it easy? Because you were once a child yourself. That child still lives somewhere inside you ready to storm out and play. So accept Coyote's challenge to shapeshift yourself back to your childhood. Catch frogs, dive in muddy ponds, build forts and play pirates, go on scavenger hunts and tracking adventures, act out characters, tell stories, sing songs off key, and laugh laugh laugh!

If you want to help others come alive, *stay* alive, and be connected to nature for the rest of their lives, make sure to role-model it yourself.

Child Passions as Mentoring Tools | 93

Chapter 5
QUESTIONING
AND ANSWERING

The Art of Questioning
Childlike Curiosity

I remember when my son was about three, in the constant questioning stage. Trying to be a good mother, I dutifully answered every question with some informative explanation. Then one day in the middle of another train of questions and answers, he suddenly wailed up at me, "Mom, DON'T ANSWER!" and he burst into tears of outrage. I was stunned, but crouching down to hug his tears away, I realized that he didn't want my answers. All those questions were a plea to come into his world with him, at his level, to join with him in his curiosity.

Ellen Haas, Don't Answer!

Children are passionate about asking questions. They ask questions all the time. "Who did it?" "What is it?" "When was it?" "Where are we?" "How come?" Their favorite query comes through the wonderfully infinite question, "Why, why, why, why, why?" But notice, most of the time they don't even wait for the answer before going on to their next question. What's going on here?

When asking questions, people, and especially children, may not be asking for information so much as they are asking for you to pay attention to the world through their eyes, to get down on all fours and be curious with them. The Art of Questioning fans this flame of inquisitiveness that burns in the heart and mind of everyone.

The Art of Questioning as a Child Passions Mentoring Tool does not begin in your adult mind, but in the curiosity of those who explore with you.

Questions Before Answers

Start with their curiosity, then extend the opportunity for learning as far as it will stretch. Try to lead the answers out of people, guide them along from one logical question to the next, and throw them tidbits of partial answers on the way, until they arrive at the answer they seek for themselves.

This doesn't mean to never give answers to questions. Just remember that answers can bring about a swift end to curiosity. Sometimes, you do want to give answers and pass on information and clear instructions. However, try to wait to give answers until you see real, sincere readiness to receive them. This art is like planting seeds. No one throws seeds on unfertile, rock-hard ground. You prepare the ground for the seed before you plant it.

One of my first jobs was as an assistant at an organic farm. My boss returned one day from a national conference of organic farmers, and he told me he was amazed that hardly anyone talked about the fruits and vegetables they grew. Instead, all of the focus was on soil, how to produce good soil.

The Art of Questioning builds fertile ground for more questions. Of course, like the farmers, we want the fruit, we want people to get the information, but we focus on the soil of their curiosity. That is, we want folks to become self-sufficiently inquisitive, trusting in themselves to seek out and find answers. As the Chinese proverb says, "Give a man a fish and you feed him for a day. Teach a man to fish and you feed him for a lifetime."

Genuine Curiosity

One trick to successful questioning is to ponder every question with our own real interest, as if for the first time. Authentic curiosity is the fertile soil for the Art of Questioning. We, as mentors, must get back to "beginner's mind."

If you walk on a sandy stretch and someone in your group sees a footprint and asks, "What kind of track is that?"—and you know coyote made that track— there are a few ways you can respond.

I want to beg you, as much as I can, dear sir, to be patient toward all that is unsolved in your heart and try to love the questions themselves like locked rooms and like books that are written in a very foreign tongue...live the questions now.

RANIER MARIA RILKE,
Letters to a Young Poet

The Socratic Method of Questioning, described during the Golden Age of Greece by Plato, is our model for the Art of Questioning. In a nutshell it's a dialogue in which the mentor models curiosity about the subject, asking many questions to lead out and clarify all that the other doesn't know that he already knows about the subject. In this way, those we learn with and mentor are forced to draw answers out of themselves, as well as to re-examine the logic underlying their answers.

In nature education, our questions especially prompt people to query the knowledge of the senses. What do they smell, hear, taste, feel, or see in ever-new ways? We also like to add to this by allowing the questioning to go into the unknown, by truly embracing the mysteries of life and joining in the search ourselves.

Jon Young & Evan McGown, Socratic Questioning

You could tell them coyote came this way last night. Your response will likely induce a simple nod, a muted "oh," and a move onward. This is a blown opportunity to cultivate curiosity.

Or, you could get into the beginner's mind, the mind of humility and fresh discovery, "How can I know for sure this **was** made by a coyote? Look what a beautiful pattern it makes in the sand. I wonder what it was doing to make the track deeper on the left than the right side?" From this place of authentic curiosity, you can become partners in a joint venture of discovering the complex subtleties of the track. You might drop to a knee and bend down to look closer. "Wow, look at that. I wonder too. Who do *you* think could have made it?"

Throughout his childhood, Jon Young was mentored this way by Tom Brown, Jr. Tom could approach a coyote track for the thousandth time and sincerely study it as if for the first time. The beginner's mind engaged them both for longer and longer stretches, as over the years such genuine open-minded fascination became the norm. The more they learned, the greater their humility in realizing what they didn't know. Through Tom's modeling, Jon learned how to track, but, more importantly, *how to learn.*

Three Levels of Questioning

To walk the edge of curiosity with those you mentor, we suggest you become intentional in the use of your questions—what kind of questions you ask, when, and in what order you ask them.

These three levels of questions will help you develop your art.

Level One: Confidence Builder. Level One is where you start. Especially with beginners, meet them in their comfort zone, build confidence, and awaken the questioning reflex. Sometimes one question will work, but often a whole series of questions will help you fish around for hot topics, and answers that the person you are mentoring already knows. Answering easy questions, they feel success. Their head lifts, their shoulders square: they feel proud and literally puff up. *Do not* pop that bubble. If you start with a hard question they can't answer, they get smaller; their eyes drop down.

You'll spend the great bulk of your time, perhaps up to seventy percent, with Level One. You want to get them feeling so good about what they already know they will be self-motivated to stretch and grow and take risks. So start with self-evident facts, give them a bone, and build rapport.

Level Two: Edge Question. As soon as they're strong, look for their edge. The next question you want to ask is an "edge question." This one they can find the answer to if they do some searching. For instance, they respond at the first level saying, "Hey, it's a worm!" You hear confidence in their voice. So you ask, "Yes, where is it going?" They watch the worm and guess, "That way." "You sure?" They hesitate and start thinking about it. What did you find? Their edge. Now show more curiosity than they do. Uncross your arms, drop down on one knee, go closer. "Hey, what's this little line in the mud that's leading up to the worm?" They come down with you and their light-bulb goes on: "It's a worm track! It's going that way!" You have met them at their edge, and pushed them through. (And now their knees are a little dirty, too!)

You probably will spend around twenty-five percent of your time and energy at this level, hovering on the edge of what they know. As Coyote did with me that day in Redmond, pull them just a little bit further out into new terrain. Mentoring advanced folks who show confidence and comfort, you may spend the majority of your time right here, on their edge. Also, this isn't just about knowledge, but also sensory awareness and experience. So if you notice a person tends not to hear birdcalls or smell the air, use questions to stretch *that* edge. Look for the weaknesses in their overall sensory awareness, and pull them along, not only with questions but also with any story or information that gets them curious, that arouses the Child Passion to discover and learn.

Level Three: Beyond the Edge. Back to the worm situation—they are now on their knees with an expanding curiosity. Next you say, "I wonder how this thing **sees** where its going?" This third level of question lands just *beyond* their edge. Their jaws drop a little. Their bodies sag, and you can literally watch them hang from their spines for a moment. The essence of this level of question is to steer them to ask things they didn't know you <u>could</u> know. It keeps learners humble and reminds them to look for the not-so-obvious, the below-the-surface reality of things. This one sends them home to field guides, or maybe on to Ph.D's.

Do you want to eat some of those berries?

Can you eat those?

If they have thorny stems and the leaves are opposite each other, then we can. Let's check them out. Do you see thorns?

Yes. Ouch.

How are the leaves arranged opposite each other like arms on a person or are they alternate like stairs going up the stem?

Oh cool, they are opposite. So we can eat them, right?

Just one more thing, when you crush them they have to smell like bananas. Here, let's try it. Put a berry in your palm and squish it with your fingers. Now smell it.

Wow, it does smell like bananas. Now can we eat them?

Sure, but make sure that you save some of the berries before you leave this area.

Why should we save the berries?

Oh, they make great food for ruffed grouse and other birds. Just remember though, if there are grouse feeding on these berries, there may be bears around too.

Oh my god, I'm scared of bears!

Don't worry, the Blue Jays will tell us if there are any bears around.

In just a few moments you've inspired interest, and then have managed to take a student on a plant ID lesson; you have connected the plant ID with the sense of smell; you've introduced the idea that animals that could be in the area and what they eat. And you introduced them to bird language. All that great stuff and they don't even realize that you purposely led them through it in order to stretch their awareness.

DALE KISELYK, Kamana Student, Plant ID Lesson

Level Three questions will take up only about five percent of your time. These questions can be intimidating and should be asked only when the time is ripe. Level Three questions eventually propel people into a curiosity all their own, sending them on life-long searches for answers. Sometimes, the answers to these questions never come, and that's completely fine. The feeling of being passionately on the hunt, of being utterly alive and curious and dogged in a search, that's what we're after.

Shifting Perspectives

"What kind of track is this?" I might ask someone. "Obviously, Evan, that's a coyote. We know what coyote tracks look like." "Yeah, it's probably coyote, but what time do you think it passed here? Look at the rain drops all *around* the track, but inside it they're crushed."

This shift of perspective keeps the Art of Questioning fresh. You stand a good chance no one knows exactly what time it stopped raining. So that leads off to a search for clues that might prove when it rained. I could also ask why it's a coyote instead of a dog. How do they know for sure? "Show me each factor that gives you a clue." And on and on, with more and more refinement. When you execute the Art of Questioning well, the shifting flow of questions and answers seems perfectly natural.

Shifting Our Own Habits

That's because it *is* natural. However, it may feel contrived when you first break out of your answering habit. Check if your experience and expertise have put you deep into the brain pattern of answering questions with answers—then yourself need mentoring first. Do this two-minute exercise to help restore the innocence of your curiosity. It can be done alone, but it's intensified if you do this with a partner.

Walk outside and find an object in nature: a plant, a rock, or an acorn shell—whatever you want. For two minutes, do nothing but ask questions—out loud—about your object. Ask a question, but don't give an answer. Ask another question. Then another. Watch how your mind begins to overflow with unspoken answers that lead to new questions. Let your mind go wherever it will in its musing, but don't answer. Ask questions that use all of your senses. Your partner just remains silent and listens to the questions, but explores the object along with you as prompted by your questions. Ask question after question until the end of your two minutes. The resulting rise in heartbeat may astound you. In two minutes your brain wakes up to a whole new world of possibilities.

Long-Term Mentoring

The long-term goal of the Art of Questioning will be to turn over the reins to the learners, to light the fuse and then get out of the way. Your first goal is achieved when people feel comfortable generating their *own* Level One questions, as they show confidence in demonstrating their basic proficiency and knowledge. Your next goal is to encourage them to go to Level Two for themselves, super-charged about learning, willing to take risks, eager to make mistakes, quick to research, fired up to keep on the trail of their curiosity. The final goal is to empower them to generate their own Level Three questions, to ponder the mysteries that will captivate, motivate, and define them for the long years of their lives.

The Art of Questioning is an amazing skill-set to awaken in those you mentor. Questioning works like a muscle of the mind. Without regular exercise, it can atrophy, but with just a few continuous months of training and stick-to-it-ive-ness on your part, you'll see the questioning muscles in those your mentor operate without your help and with astonishing power.

The Place for Answers

"Didactic" is an old-fashioned word that means *instructing and informing*, although it has unfortunate overtones of *boring catechism*. In the midst of all this questioning, is there a place for informing and instructing? Is there a way for people to "actually learn" without being "talked at" or "told how it is?" Absolutely! Mentoring includes spending a great deal of time answering, informing, and instructing. This is the way of the mentor. Questions need answers, each tidbit serves as a platform to jump to the next question. Science needs good information, correct data. And learning journeys require constant monitored instruction and orientation.

When you sense people need answers, by all means seize the opportunity to respond. Of course the most memorable answers will be searched out as returning scouts pool their data in Mapping, Story of the Day, and Exploring Field Guides. But, if an eager learner or the whole community wants an educated answer from you, they deserve it. Do your research and make it an informative response. From your own treasure chest of knowledge, choose gems of answers as nutrition along the way.

However, for answering to be effective, each person must reach the level of interest to receive information. So remember to vigilantly monitor their body language, their facial expressions, and their focus of attention. Keep track of what kind of bait will "hook" their interest, and cast that out. Throw them one of those "fun factoids" about amazing animal feats. If their eyes light up, and they begin interrupting to tell you what they know, now they are engaged. They took the bait!

If your answer is a long one, allow everyone to ask questions as they come up—don't worry about "breaking your flow." If they are holding onto a question, they won't really be able to attend to the information you're offering anyway.

The Place for Information

Coyote straddles the world of experience and science. We want people we mentor to develop sensory awareness and intuition and to imprint images in their Mind's Eye, but they will need a science vocabulary to communicate. We gather information all day long, and much of the information involves naming things; we look closely to identify taxonomy, compare growth habits, or label the parts of interdependent systems. Naming will naturally channel their curiosity into an active and accurate vocabulary.

Allow even this to arise first from the imagination, so a four-year-old's words may be "puffball" or "bunny" or "birdie." Invite kids who love fantasy and creative adults to create Songlines about things they give friendly names to. Leave Field Guides out on the tables, use Journaling and Story of the Day for mystery-solving and reflection, and transmit "didactic" information through Storytelling. The names for things will come so naturally that easygoing conversation will emerge in the field using literate scientific vocabulary.

Our caution about timing your answers—restrain yourself from doing their work for them. Be conscious of *your* priority. Is it more important for information to be conveyed quickly and accurately, or do you want people you mentor to struggle with figuring it out for themselves? Go slowly and leave time for the information to sink in. Watch carefully for signs of confusion—ask them to explain in their own words what you just covered, check to see if they absorbed it. If they begin to fade, you'll just be wasting your time continuing. It will feel to them like being "talked at."

The Place for Instruction

You will also find abundant times to clearly explain the rules of the game, the boundaries of the errand, or the principles of peaceful behavior. Giving appropriate instructions and monitoring that these instructions are followed is an art just as much as questioning. Be prepared, watch their body language, and use your finest words.

In a workshop on communicating with diverse audiences, we realized the huge diversity of learning styles represented by any group of people. Asked how we'd like to get our instructions as volunteers at a food bank, some of us wanted, "Here's a kitchen, make sandwiches." Others wanted "Here's 12 jars and 6 stations; your group will make 1000 sandwiches by noon." Yet others wanted to know, "This is how you hold the knife when you spread the peanut butter." Keep an eye out to meet the needs of everyone, and deliver your instructions with clarity and improvisational wit, because you never know what to expect.

Instruction will take many shapes in your outdoor program. You need to be as diverse as your audience and your lesson plan. Instructions may look like a scavenger hunt handout or a PowerPoint presentation. They may look like Baloo in Rudyard Kipling's *Jungle Book*, teaching Mowgli "the Law of the Jungle" with a few affectionate and well-timed swats with his paw. Whether people play games by the rules, take scientific inventory of natural history, or make fire without matches in a rainstorm, they will require and welcome lots of clear instructions to show them the way.

One tip for instruction. Consider the Rule of Repetition: tell them what you are going to tell them, then tell them, then show them, then tell them what you told them. Then ask them what they heard and let them demonstrate. Repetition is the mother of mental habits!

The most beautiful emotion we can experience is the mysterious. It is the power of all true art and science. He to whom this emotion is a stranger, who can no longer wonder and stand rapt in awe, is as good as dead.

Albert Einstein

Three Mentoring Styles

In general then, we can summarize by saying over the years we have noted three main styles, or approaches, used by effective mentors. They are all valuable and their efficacy depends on the aptness and the timing of their use.

The *Didactic Approach,* we just discussed as the passing on of information. With adults, this can be done in lecture form—including some amazing factoids from natural science. With youth, telling stories laced with information may be your best opportunity for this approach.

Didactic does have its place, but we need to realize that most of us default to this approach because of its dominance in our own Western upbringing and patterning. Therefore, many mentors, when just starting out, will lean heavily on this approach, and then be frustrated when youth or adults don't listen or remember or care about an overload of information being shared.

So, watch for opportunities to transmit information and administer the correct dosage of it. Use it when people are ready to absorb it, when they have a slot in their brain patterns ready for some information. Cast your bait into the current just above your target spot at just the right time of day.

Think of me trying to show someone how to play a guitar: if someone already knows the basic chords, I can just tell them the chords straight off and they'll start playing. However, if they're just starting off, I have to change the information I give them, as well as mixing in the other two styles below so they'll not only get it, they'll also be inspired to keep going further.

The *Questioning Approach* is most effective for someone sitting on the fence between being interested and not interested, when something is needed to green-light their just-waiting curiosity. Use all the tricks of the Art of Questioning. Get them primed and ready for didactic answers. For those who are neither hot nor cold, questioning can be the perfect thing to kick them into that nice buzz and hum of experiential learning.

The final *Trickster/Transformer Approach* is emphasized throughout this book in subtle and not so subtle ways. This is the Coyote approach that busts people out of ruts and gets them to look with fresh eyes at any situation. It's the foolishness, NOT the verbal reprimands, that entices them over the edge of their comfort zone, outward on the winged edges of their curiosity.

Use this approach when your people act not at all ready or interested in whatever you are leading or presenting. Maybe they fold their arms, their eyes roll whenever you introduce an activity, or they keep looking at their watch or asking when they get to go home. The ground appears absolutely hard and not welcoming to any seeds you offer, whether questions or cool information. You need Wily Coyote now to shake things up, to play the trickster and magically transform that rock-hard clay of unwillingness into lush, loamy soils of excitement and humility.

This can be as simple as putting on blindfolds: even the simplest action of eating lunch becomes humbling when your eyes are taken away. Blindfolds offer a classic way to get people out of their ruts. But there are more sophisticated approaches too. For the person who tells you with a scarce glance and sallow tone "Those are coyote tracks," find a set of mouse tracks—whose pattern of four feet look an awful lot like the four toes of a coyote track—and with your own finger, when they aren't looking, add a little smudge of a heel-pad to lend more to the possibility of misinterpretation. Then ask them what track they see. When they say coyote, look closer and say, "But it looks like each toe of the coyote has little toes itself …" And when they eventually realize these are actually mouse tracks, their hard attitude may just crack open a bit.

So each approach, whether *Didactic, Questioning*, or *Trickster/Transformer*, has a place in the palette of an artful Coyote Mentor. Didactic is awesome when people feel genuinely ready to absorb, Questioning will bring out their latent curiosity and lead to amazing journeys of mystery and learning, and Trickster/Transformer can regularly be interspersed to loosen up the hard ground of arrogance, bust people out of ruts, and keep people excitedly looking with ever-fresh eyes.

Chapter 6
STORYTELLING

Storytelling to Capture Imagination

We've talked about Story of the Day as a Core Routine, some-thing we all do together to wrap up explorations throughout the day. Now let's turn the tables. Storytelling, **by you**, to a group circled up at the beginning of the day, or rounded up briefly between activities, or even sitting lecture-style in a hall, is a foolproof Child Passion Mentoring Tool to practice and master. The more wholeheartedly you tell stories, the more effectively they will inform and instruct, raise questions, and evoke the world of imaginative play.

I remember showing up at my first summer nature camp as a mentor. The director said we were going to get all forty kids

For unknown thousands of years the brain was expanding by genetic evolution, in part because of the palaver and increasingly extended and complex storytelling around the fire.

The storyteller has always had this central role in societies of translating that information in forms that played upon the great mythic themes and used the rhythms and the openings, the prologues, the body, the conclusion, the closures that make up literature.

So, the factual information that we get and the new metaphors created out of science somehow have to be translated into the language of the storyteller—by film, by speech, by literature, by any means that will make it meaningful and powerful for the human mind.

E.O. Wilson, *Writing Natural History, Dialogues with Authors,* by Edward Lueders

Dabo was a boy of six years when I met him. He was a bit timid at first, but had the smile of a lifetime when he got to trust me. The first day of Youth School, he pulled a "nature name" out of a hat, Raccoon. He knew a little about the animal, but he often asked me about it. I remember looking through field guides with him to find Raccoon pictures and facts, and staring in fascination at trails of Raccoon tracks we'd find along the beaches we roamed. And, he loved to hear, over and over, a story we told that featured Raccoon's ingenuity.

One day, the tide was rising very quickly, forcing our group to crawl through and over the beach debris. Dabo was near the back, moving a bit slower than the others (this was his way), but as I waited up for him, I saw a complete concentration in his eyes and in his body. The waves were crashing and coming in closer by the minute. He was clearly muttering something to himself, some sort of mantra, as you might see a determined marathon runner saying to keep himself moving. As he came closer, I could finally make out the chanted words: "Raccoon always finds a way. Raccoon always finds a way."

Evan McGown, Dabo's Story

to sit quietly outside and tell them a story for a half-hour or so. I couldn't believe it would actually work. Wouldn't they just want to run and play? But sure enough, we told them it was "time for a story," and they all eagerly plunked down to listen. From then on throughout the week, they would beg for more stories. I was floored. Jon talks about the same phenomenon with the adults he works with all over the world. They have the same eagerness to hear stories. Let a group know that there is a story ahead and they won't let you forget!

Why do we love stories so much? Ever since that day, I've watched it over and over and have become convinced; people, especially kids, are designed to love stories and to listen to them over and over. As all parents know who "have to" read their children stories before they'll consent to lie down and sleep; kids simply can't get enough of it, they can be swept away by just a few words and a wink.

Stories are everywhere, in one form or another: daily newspapers, television shows, movies, books, core myths of major religions, the funny thing that happened at work today. For the vast majority of our history, stories have been spoken or acted out, repeated, refined, and enriched with the changing colors of the seasons and the changing voices of generations of storytellers. This is "the oral tradition." It's built into our genes to respond unblinkingly to the power of live storytelling.

Here, we suggest you direct the purpose of your everyday stories towards Nature Connection. It's just like playing an instrument. If I'm in a jazz band, the way I play my bass can shift so that the bass plays jazz. Or if the band I'm in plays rock n'roll, or salsa or heavy metal, the bass can still serve its role powerfully. All I have to do is shift the way I play it. Storytelling works the same: no matter what tale you're about to tell, just shift the content and emphasis of your stories to fit your situation and your goals. In our case, we want to create connections with nature through story.

Three Levels in Storytelling

Storytelling can be approached on the same three levels that we discussed in terms of questioning.

Level One: Tell stories about doing things that anyone can do—the confidence-builders that get them exclaiming, "I've done that too. It's so fun!" This first level establishes rapport and trust. This might be, "In that rain yesterday I got so muddy and wet my housemates wouldn't let me indoors until I stripped down to my shorts. You ever done that? Ever been stopped by your Mom at the door? How'd you get her to let you in?"

Level Two: Tell stories about things right on their edge, ones that raise the ceiling of possibility in their imaginations. "When I looked down and saw I had mud all over my arms, I realized it was really good camouflage. So you know what I did? (Here comes the edge ...) I decided to get fully mudded-up, even my face and my hair, and then sprinkle grass-clippings and leaf debris all over me. After that, I could hide in the bush right by the sidewalk of my house where people would walk by, but nobody would see me."

Level Three: Tell an occasional story beyond their edge, a story about a legendary hero. During a wind storm, John Muir climbed to the top of an evergreen and was blown around twenty feet each way as he listened to the wind symphony. Hiding in his pond, Henry Thoreau breathed through a reed. Open the door to burning possibilities. "I figured if I could be invisible to humans, maybe I could be invisible to animals. So one summer, I covered myself in mud and camouflaged even my smell and waited by a deer trail before dawn until finally I actually touched a deer without it ever sensing I was there."

Mindfulness to these three levels ensures that everyone has a story to tell, but also keeps your audience continually expanding its edges.

Priming with Inspiring Stories

The most common and effective way to set up your day is with stories, which "prime" folks for the upcoming activities. If you want to focus on learning edible plants that day, tell a story about a time you (or someone else) were lost and hungry and made a meal entirely from edible plants. If you want to go animal tracking that day, tell a story about the thrill of discovering otter tracks and following them down a slippery slide.

Telling inspiring stories before an activity can make the difference between a "boring, stupid activity" and a legendary adventure they'll never forget. In the *Activities* section of this book, we offer a "Primer" (an inspirational story) for most of the games and activities. The root of the word inspire is *in* + *spiritus*, meaning spirit, or wind, or breath. In-spiration, then, means that fresh wind of spirit that suddenly sweeps into you when something excites you. This happens when people hear a story from the life of a hero or a role-model. They are struck with admiration, their eyes get brighter, and they sit up straighter. Inspirational stories wake them up; get them thinking, "I want to do that. That's amazing. How'd they do it? Could that story be true? Wow."

   Caution: You don't want to have every story be grand and glorious in its heroic feats, or else the listeners will start to think, "John Muir had amazing experiences, but I never can." Their bodies will deflate, they'll turn away. We don't want to get them comparing and belittling themselves. Always use stories to empower with role-models who show what's possible.

   So be wary of creating "celebrities" or "hero worship." 1) Tell stories of heroes who are deceased or who live in a separate community. Most traditional cultures rarely have living heroes and have avoided the celebrity-inflation phenomenon of modern society. 2) Constantly mix-up the heroes of your stories, creating an archetypal feeling of the "hero/heroine" represented by many people, rather than inflating the same individuals over and over. 3) Keep the heroes anonymous: change the names or never mention a name at all.

Didactic Lessons with Fact-filled Stories

Storytelling is the trickster Coyote's way of passing on didactic information. The listeners sit toying with blades of grass, unaware of "learning" anything, while you seed and cultivate their Mind's Eye Imaginations. Because stories bring forth vivid pictures of sight, sound, smell, touch, and taste, they have a way of slipping search images into the brain patterns that emerge sometime later, when they are able to name that bird call, or recognize that poisonous plant, or identify that track.

   Use storytelling as a subtle form of informing and instructing. Because stories engage the imagination and emotions, listeners soak up and remember little details like sponges. Throw in amazing tidbits of natural history or admirable traits of characters. To make a story a vehicle for more learning, add facts about shapes, colors, sounds, gaits, animal personalities, weather, or even your choice of gear to prolong a story that would otherwise be a quick exciting ride. It might be a tiny snippet about how Dandelions have jagged teeth like a lion, or a mention that the beaver tracks include a tail drag. Slip in all the bits of natural history you want.

You won't have any idea how much information actually sinks in to the listeners' brain patterns until months later, when you come upon a set of tracks, and someone says, "Look—it has four toes and claws, I think it's a wolf, you know, like in that story!" This has happened to me many times, sometimes years later—and I'm amazed every time. Sometimes they can remember learning it in a story, other times they don't know how they knew it. With stories, it all sinks in, and it will rise to consciousness whenever a purpose for that bit of knowledge comes along.

Of course, many stories, like fables, already have lessons built into them. You can pull out morals from stories that haven't mentioned them. Instead of spelling out the lessons of even a traditional fable, let the images speak for themselves and marinate in the listeners' subconscious. You might be surprised when they come to you with reflective lessons from the story that you never thought of before. Also, feel free to adapt stories to the needs of the people you work with, for stories can grow and evolve over time. That's the beauty and magic of the oral tradition.

Over three decades at Wilderness Awareness School, we've concocted a story that we tell in camps and college alike, of Apache Scouts and the New Jersey Pine Barrens, Tom Brown and Jon Young, Akamba trackers and wilderness survival. The stories thicken and thin into a seasonal round of hero tales and students' own stories.

We teach, in the winter wind-chill, of hazards; as days warm, of tracks; when summer's in full growth, of plants; and when it's time to sit around and enjoy the harvest and feel night and winter coming in, we move into high storytelling. In early spring, the birds bring in the big story all over again.

In year-long courses on our own twenty acres, these stories are so connected to the land, so full of names and adventures of real people, that alumni come back to it feeling it's "a sacred place." That's what always happens when a culture has time to grow up in the same landscape.

ELLEN HAAS,
A Place-Based Story

A Guide for Telling Stories

You might be thinking, "I'm not a storyteller." Hmmm. Try to go a week without telling a story in some form or another. I bet you can't do it. We talk about books we're reading or we explain to someone in detail where we've just been; all of us tell stories all the time. So own it: you **are** a storyteller. You've already got your own style of talking, whether you use crazy hand-gestures like me or speak slowly and calmly like Peter Jennings. We're just asking you to take the storytelling style you already have and apply it towards cultivating nature awareness in those you mentor. Simply be yourself.

To help you to really step into your power as a storyteller and begin to have fun with this old, old practice, here are some tips and tricks we'd like to pass along.

Where Do I Find Stories?

Personal stories: Perhaps *the* most important advice about using storytelling in education uses anecdotes from your own life. You may think, as I once did, that you haven't done anything spectacular enough to be retold in story form.

Have you ever built a tree house, caught a fish, walked with a dog, gotten into poison ivy?

Have you ever looked a wild animal in the eye? Tell what happened.

Have you ever been caught in a storm? How did you handle it?

Have you ever gone out in the darkness before dawn? What did you see?

Have you ever watched a songbird's egg crack open? What came out of it?

Every one of your personal experiences holds potential gold for inspiration, like seeing a deer on the neighbor's lawn. "The forest begins in the crack in my sidewalk," wrote a child in a New Jersey city. That's one reason we've included the "Primer" stories with the activities: so you see how lots of seemingly ordinary events can be made into something extraordinary.

Personal stories are by far the most powerful to hear, because they live so vividly in the person telling the story. And the listener sits right next to the main character!

For examples: scan the "Primer" stories that lead off most of our Activities, browse tales from Wilderness Awareness School role-models in *Exploring Natural Mystery, Kamana One*, find inspiration from Jon Young's audiotapes; *Seeing Through Native Eyes, Advanced Language of Birds*, and *Tracking Pack One*.

Animal feats: Besides accounts of human experiences in nature, any animal—or plant or insect for that matter—can be turned into a fascinating being if you tell (or act out) the story of how it uses its senses and anatomy to navigate its world. Read up on the amazing strategies for survival about bats with their echolocation, beavers with their waterproof eyelids, chickadees who fluff their body-feathers over-top their wing feathers to keep from freezing, grasshoppers who can jump the tallest building. This list is endless and information is easy to find. Check out Lewis Thomas' *Lives of a Cell* or *Medusa and the Snail*, the *ZooBooks* pamphlet series, or DVDs such as David Attenborough's *Life of Mammals*.

Traditional Tales: You can find great nature-based stories in collections of traditional myths or folk tales from different cultures: Native American, Celtic, Polish, Chinese, African, and from your own ancestral lineage. Some forms of these stories are short because they were probably recorded in quantity by anthropologists. Unless specifically asked by your source not to do so, you can use your imagination to fill in the gaps and elaborate on the brilliant images and story lines that have been passed down for thousands of years. You will find rich, deep stuff there and your imagination can bring the characters and scenes back to life and keep them growing.

If you go back far enough in any cultural lineage, you will find stories deeply connected to the natural world. We suggest you do a little research into your own ancestry and find nature-based stories from your own heritage. Whoever you

Find and practice FOUR stories, each of a different type:

❑ Hero Story: An amazing story from the life of naturalist or tracker, a legendary or fictionalized adventure in the natural world.

❑ Personal Story: A story from your own life of an inspiring or fun interaction with nature.

❑ Local Native Lore Story: A story specific to the native culture of your bioregion, such as an "origin" story that provides search images of local flora and fauna like "How Skunk got its Spots," or "How Robin got its Red Breast."

❑ Ancestral Heritage Story: A nature-based traditional myth or folk story from your own ancestry, whatever it may be.

Then, practice, over and over—to a mirror, your dog, your friends, your children—experimenting with different ways of telling them.

JON YOUNG & EVAN MCGOWN, Storytelling 101

are, your ancestors were trackers and naturalists, or else you wouldn't be alive today. So have some fun digging up old stories of *your own* ancestors, and enjoy telling about the same rooted connection to the earth that your distant grandfathers or grandmothers once experienced.

Natural History Literature

Our sidebar provides a list of Ellen's Top Ten extraordinary nature writers who she says should be "required reading!" She reports with vehemence that she reads nature writing for her Sit Spot time, an armchair voyeur's version. American literature offers us some entrancing tales from the lives of explorers like John Muir and Lewis and Clark, and naturalists like Sigurd Olsen, Barry Lopez, Richard Nelson, Terry Tempest Williams, or Annie Dillard. The fiction of John Steinbeck and Wallace Stegner overflow with the feeling of the American landscape and its effect on its human inhabitants. Stories for youth abound, such as Jean Craighead George's *My Side of the Mountain*. Tom Brown, Jr.'s best-selling book, *The Tracker*, captivates imaginations with its stunning tale of a young boy mentored by an aging Apache scout in the Pine Barrens of New Jersey. Dennis Olson's book, *Shared Spirits*, is a fine collection of Native American stories about animals and what they have to teach us. Check out stories based on wildlife, such as *Bobcat Year* by Hope Ryden, or *Buffalo Gals* by Ursula LeGuin. Native American authors have contributed as well, such as M. Scott Momaday and Leslie Marmon Silko. Luther Standing Bear's *My Indian Boyhood* or *Land of the Spotted Eagle* offer a marvelous picture of growing up Sioux.

Seek out powerful classics from India, by the late great tracker, Jim Corbett, famous for his tiger-hunting, or Rudyard Kipling, famous author of the *Jungle Book* and *Other Stories*. Mowgli's life with Baloo the bear and Bagheera the panther are jewels, but read Kipling's *Other Stories* as well, about wise elephants and a brave little mongoose. Read tales from Africa, by Laurens Van der Post, Norman "Ingwe" Powell, or Jane Goodall's intimate relationship with African chimpanzees which still inspires Western science.

How do I Tell a Story?

Once you've found your story, the first step in telling it is to remember it. Generally two schools of thought exist on how to do this.

Memorized Narrative. Many native cultures, such as the Akamba, as our friend Ingwe witnessed, required their storytellers memorize word for word, pause for pause, in order to ensure accurate transmission. However, it didn't come off as rote memorization, for those storytellers empowered the lines with a ritual sense that the story they told was happening here and now. Ingwe often used this kind of storytelling to "bring the house down."

Storyboard Improvisation. In our culture, we recommend remembering the basic set of images as if it were a cartoon strip and then improvising. But the same principle of being totally present to your story also applies.

By using the Core Routine of Mind's Eye Imagining, both storytelling methods can be powerfully delivered. You want to remember the scenes not only by the dominant images and events, but also by all the sensory and emotional nuances and tones. Try listening to stories like this, so you hear more than words, you also see a movie, full of facial expressions, tones of voice, body language, background noises, and experiences of smell and touch—all from your Mind's Eye Imagination. Remember, this "muscle" will get stronger each time you use it.

When you are with an audience of one or more, and it is telling time for a story, simply press *play* on the movie or comic strip in your imagination, and let it roll out of your own imagination. Use the *power-booster* button to *re-live* the story as it plays in your imagination. As its images, sounds, smells, textures, and emotions run through your head, you become like a sports commentator, simply describe to others what you "see" happening.

If you want to watch masters, find videos of stand-up comedians like Robin Williams, Bill Cosby, Eddie Murphy, Margaret Cho, John Stewart, Tina Fey, or Ellen DeGeneres. They have it down—grabbing attention, voice imitation, body gestures, phrase-delivery and timing, and perhaps the most important element: fun and humor. If you want to get really serious about this art, find some Improvisational Theatre classes in your area. They can transform your approach to being in front of an audience. At mentoring workshops, we often do Improv games to get people into the mood: open, in the moment, and able, like Ingwe, to "bring the house down" with a pause, a look, or a few perfectly timed words.

Bring Setting and Character Alive

With any story, first you paint the background setting of place and time and texture, and continually reinforce it using all the senses. Introduce the characters as they show up and bring each one to life. Don't just describe them—*become* them. It can be as small as shifting into a deep voice and slow rhythm of words for Bear then a high chattering squeal for Squirrel, or as large as getting out of your chair and imitating a whole-body movement. Such constant diversity of body language grabs attention. If you are the main character, you can get the listeners into your mood and mindset by exaggerating or making fun of yourself. Always remember to appeal to the Child Passions for things that are funny. A good storyteller is truly a shape-shifter, able to shift into the mind of others and become them. It's just like Animal Forms—you really transform, mentally and physically into that other being.

Keep Listeners Engaged

You can't focus only on your story and forget your audience. You need to be present both with the moment in your story and with the listeners ringed around you. So, as a storyteller, you want to be in two places at once. One place will be in your imagination, watching the video. The other place attends to every nuance from your audience: observe their body language, notice what grabs them, watch out for when they yawn or seem to grow a little bored (it happens to the best of us). The audience's reactions will feed your story and shape how you tell it.

All good storytellers have some common tricks up their sleeves to keep the attention focused. One trick uses refrain and repetition to create an on-going interaction with the audience. A classic example is the "Little Engine That Could," with its repeated refrain of "I Think I Can, I Think I Can, I Think I Can!" each time a new challenge arises. Another way to get the audience responding sets up a game within the story, such as "Whenever I say 'river,' you guys say 'otter' after it, okay? This little awareness game shows how well you're paying attention and how quickly you can respond." Of course when you do say "river," and they do say "otter," it interrupts your story, but it keeps your audience awake, laughing, and engaged. If you can get your listeners laughing, you've got 'em hooked. If you notice lagging attention, here's another good trick. About anything in the story at that time, say, "You know what it looked like? It looked like THIS!" Immediately, heads will jerk up, and if they look up to see you in some funny pose, they'll fall straight into laughter. Boom—they're back in the story, right there with you.

Another device that will catch attention and add intrigue may surprise you: silence. Most people think to catch attention you have to be loud, but many of the best musicians and storytellers know the power of the rest, the "pregnant pause." You may be going along in a consistent rhythm, and abruptly, when you come upon a climactic moment in the story, you drop silent. What will happen? The dreamy listeners will turn their heads up, with searching, captured eye. "What's he waiting for? What is about to happen?" Rests and pauses invite the imagination and let the story breathe.

A great bass-playing friend of mine tells about playing for great jazz trumpeter Dizzy Gillespie. One night he played a virtuoso solo full of so many notes that he thought would knock Dizzy out. After the show, though, when he asked Dizzy what he thought of the solo. Dizzy said, "You need to leave some holes in your playing, because you never know, some music just might fall out." So likewise, leave some holes in your storytelling … and see what falls out.

The Most Important Thing—Have Fun!

Above all, good storytelling that effectively engages Child Passions will invisibly lodge search images into your listeners' brains. Storytelling gives you permission to play and take your imagination to a level of foolishness and outlandishness—we usually aren't allowed such good fun in normal society. Yet all the while, amidst the fun and laughter of it, you walk the edge and grow more serious in your lessons as you advance from Level One to Level Three topics. Eventually, you will

pull the audience deeper and deeper into another world. Aspire to deliver both laughter and profound lessons and overtones—great storytellers are known for their tension of opposites. I recently heard a most serious sermon by Martin Luther King, Jr. in which he quotes a joke from Bob Hope that gets the crowd rolling, saying, "I am trying to laugh a basic fact into all of us ..."

Once again, Coyote sounds the challenge to follow him into his best act: "shape-shifting." So enjoy it! Get loose, feel free, and have fun up there. If you have already faced your nervousness and find yourself standing up in front, why not go all the way? Throw your body into it; forget how silly others might think you look. It's about role modeling child passions, it's about being natural, and it's about meeting people where they are—and if you do it with nature-based stories, you will undoubtedly capture their imaginations to connect in a personal way with all the elements of your story's landscape.

Chapter 7
MUSIC MAKING

Music at the Heart of Community

An African Tale

Under the shade of a large mango tree, children and adults alike were singing, their eyes sparkling, their bodies moving to the sweet pulse of drumming. Along with them, I danced the dance they had taught me—it acted out a traditional story mocking the foolery of pride. I danced and sang, laughing along with them at my mistakes, stewing in the collective, sweaty joy that boiled warmer and higher each moment. Everyone was interacting: the lead drummer cued changing dance moves with his rhythms, the other drummers listened for the signals of change as well, and children, parents, and elders all moved together. On that patch of African sand, I was given permission to feel free, to feel the river of music erupting out of me and every other shining face there.

 This happened when I visited Ghana some years ago to study traditional West African drumming and dance. During this trip I was shaken awake by something I observed. Although without a fraction of the material wealth of America, the children in those mud-hut villages radiated a sense of happiness that I had really never seen in America. These children felt

A bird doesn't sing because it has an answer. It sings because it has a song.

Chinese Proverb

Welcome to our circle, thirsty travelers
Drink of our water, join our song
Bring all your loved ones, we are grateful
That you have chosen to come along

We will travel through the forest
Gathering harvests we can share
Meet with me again in the evening
We'll feast on the stories that we bear

Sol Doran, Welcoming Song

alive. Their happiness shone brightly during the delirious singing and music-making so common there in everyday life.

When I returned home, I searched the eyes around me for that sparkle, that same vitality. But I rarely found it. Just a few months later I moved to Duvall to study nature mentoring. During the first few weeks, I was surprised to discover how often we sang songs, some funny and playful, some more mature. As a trained jazz instrumentalist, too self-conscious to sing in public, I dismissed the songs as "simple" and "amusing." I was a musical prude.

Music as the Trickster/Transformer

This was definitely a Trickster/Transformer experience for me, for after a while I noticed: after singing those simple songs for a while, smiles crept onto faces, bodies started to move. And despite my silly musical arrogance, I couldn't help but move, too. As the year progressed and we spent more time singing those simple songs, I finally noticed it again: the same joy and aliveness as in the African children I had met. Giving permission to play and experiment with music—everyone, including my humbled musician self, responded. Music and singing transform people from stiff, shy individuals into a rocking community.

Music-making is deeply engrained in human nature. Look how prevalent it is in nightclubs and marching bands, iPods and MTV. A friend once told me Bruce Springsteen played Yankee Stadium fifteen nights in a row—to 75,000 people each night—and my friend could not get a ticket to any of the shows. Who else could ever attract such a consistent crowd? A head of state? A movie star? Well, probably the Yankees played to such crowds. Music captivates our souls, and its power moves us to tears and praises.

Music builds community in almost every niche of society. Singing together affirms each individual's voice and expression within the group, and subconsciously reminds everyone of the power of unified community. Christmas songs bring hope on winter nights; football cheers pour out people's loyalty to their team; the folk music of Arlo Guthrie and Joan Baez and the legendary Reggae music of Bob Marley called together whole political movements. National anthems and patriotic battlefield tunes build confidence while bombs burst in the surrounding air.

Making Music as a Mentoring Tool

So why not align our universal Child Passion for music and singing with the study of nature? Tapping into the passion of music-making, singing and dancing opens up a lush realm of possibility. Use music with your participants to center a community based on nature. Music can gather and facilitate the flow of focus and energy as nothing else can. The content of songs also sinks rhythmically and tunefully into their brains.

Using Song and Sound for Gatherings and Transitions

Use songs to start and end each day. Singing the same songs to mark beginnings and endings gives everyone a sense of familiarity, consistency, and belonging. If your group takes a vacation between gatherings, the practiced songs will help them "re-member" their community of peers and instructors.

You can also use music to gather the focus of a group and help transition from one activity or mood to the next. I remember watching a high-energy running-game fizzle down as my fellow instructors began singing a slow, relaxing song everyone knew. Soon, without a word of direction, the kids stood calmly in a circle and sang along, attentive and ready for the upcoming art activity. Songs can be used for the opposite effect when the group needs some lightening up or enthusiasm. Waldorf Schools use songs for just about every transition, such as a "put-on-your-shoes and go-outside" song.

Songs and other sounds wield a gentle and effective force for gathering diffused energy. If people are spread out and unfocused, doing different activities, or taking a lunch break, you can call them back together in a group with music. Play a simple drum beat, sing a chant that rises in volume, start clapping rhythms and ask people to clap them back to you. Or, to call in folks who have gone far astray outdoors, send out loud calls like crow caws or pig squeals, and pass them on in concentric circles. (This is addressed in the Activities section; *Setting up the Learning Culture*.)

CHILD PASSIONS

Comparing the stamping, twirling and hoots of Native American dancers, a biologist was able to accurately predict what species of grouse—sharptail, sage grouse or prairie chicken—lived in a tribe's homeland. Observing the Kalahari Bushman hunters imitate the peculiar gaits and gyrations of ostrich, it is no surprise that dance, music, song, and mime originate from hunting cultures imitating animals they hunt. String instruments like the bass, violin and guitar have their origin in the bow and arrow, and reed instruments may come from hunters using hollow-stem marsh plants to call waterfowl. Likewise, whistling may come from imitating birds to attract them. Language itself may have begun by naming animals by imitation of the sounds they make. The word "wolf" is an obvious example of a noun derived from the sound the wolf makes: woof!

RANDALL L. EATON,
Why Hunters Save the World

Songwriting
Songs are a delightful way to
introduce a subject or help
participants learn more about
their wild neighbors. I created "A
Buzzing We Will Go" to provide
a fun context for introducing bees'
lives. We act out each verse as we
sing. I do recommend singing new
songs as "repeat-after-me" and
then singing the song the whole
way through once the students
or campers have gotten the hang
of it.

A-buzzing we will go
A-buzzing we will go
Search for flowers high and low
A-buzzing we will go.

A-buzzing we will go
A-buzzing we will go
Bring the pollen to our nest
A-buzzing we will go.

A-buzzing we will go
A-buzzing we will go
Make the honey for our family
A-buzzing we will go.

A-buzzing we will go
A-buzzing we will go
Feed the honey to each other
A-buzzing we will go.

"A-Buzzing We Will Go"
to the tune of Farmer in the Dell

Arianna Alexsandra Collins,
School & Camp Programs
Coordinator
Bonnyvale Environmental
Education Center, Brattleboro,
Vermont

Imparting Information with Songs

Many folk songs call our attention to elements of nature. Their words can relay facts, such as names of trees or the lifestyles of animals, and they can also cultivate sentiments, such as respect or gratitude. Traditional cultures around the world abound with songs that "honor" or express thankfulness for elements of nature, such as Native American prayers, Jewish psalms, or Gospel praises. When we sing songs imbedded with names of plants or animals, rocks, rivers, or stars, they become a bodily memory, an emotional memory.

Where do I Find Songs?

You will want to gather a bundle of songs of all types: silly and humorous, respectful and profound, celebratory and joyous. Luckily, there's no shortage of songs you can learn. Lots of resources, written and audio, in libraries, music stores, and the internet will provide words and music specifically for working with kids or relating to nature.

Luckily, the most popular songs—the ones that hang around generation after generation in the oral tradition of every child, like "Row, row, row, your boat"—are always the *simplest*. So start out with the simple classics you already know. You can take these traditional tunes, such as "Happy Birthday," or "Twinkle, Twinkle Little Star," or "Here We Go Round the Mulberry Bush," and trade out the words for nature-based lyrics of your choosing, custom-make songs for your bio-region.

Another wonderful and unexpected source of songs: the people you work with might bring with them songs from their family heritage, from their childhood church, or scout camp, or cheerleading team. Once they see that singing is accepted, folks will share songs that they've learned in other settings that were meaningful for them. You can usually persuade these people not only to teach you, but to lead the whole group. After classes, people often ask me for the words or musical notation of songs we've used and I'm glad to help them out. Test it and see what happens.

Leaders from cultures around the world feel proud and happy to expose others to their cultural heritage. We encourage you to seek out singing sources yourself, and take a recorder along with you to remember and learn them later. However, we should tell you that some cultures are sensitive about the use of their songs outside of their cultures, and you should respect their wishes and provide background on the cultural heritage of the songs you sing.

What if I Can't Sing?

Who told you that? Everybody can sing. It's just that when some people hear they aren't very good, they start believing it. When saxophonist Charlie Parker first started playing as a teenager, people said he sounded like a dying frog. He was laughed off the stage at jam sessions. Years later, every saxophonist tried to imitate his sound. If you didn't know Bob Dylan was famous, would you call his singing voice "good?" So don't worry what other people tell you. You can sing. My best friend and fellow instructor sings off-key, but she still leads songs with groups—and the kids love it.

To work on your voice, sing along with the songs on your car radio with the windows shut so no one will hear. You probably already do it under your breath. Just kick up your volume. Practicing alone will raise your confidence. To get the ball rolling, bring in someone else who loves to sing. If you are really balking, at least do this: get a drum from somewhere, whatever kind you like, and play a simple one-after-another beat to gather people up. Soon, others will start humming or clapping along, and perhaps even break out in their song.

Just Do It

Whatever your comfort level with leading music, just do it. The musicality of humans is so innate that you just have to open your mouth and let the sound out. Start believing that you can sing and discover your own voice and style. You may not become Sinatra or Streisand, but you don't need to be. In fact—regardless of how you sing, you will most likely become a rock star in the eyes of those you work with. They'll be your fan base that propels you to confidence. Don't sweat it. Just have fun. Be a kid again, and sing, Sing, SING. It is very liberating.

My colleagues and I wrote this song during a workshop on songwriting by Sarah Pirtle at the annual Massachusetts Environmental Education Society Conference. This song was then integrated into BEEC's Forest Ecology school program. It's such a catchy tune that I also created another song entitled "Spring Is Here" for our spring school and camp programs.

Somewhere 'tween earth and sky is a promise;
the promise of the acorn —
I will provide.
Food for squirrels. Shelter for birds. Shade for children.
Breath for me.

Precious seeds
a chipmunk cheekful
a yummy treasure
journey with me.
Food for squirrels. Shelter for birds. Shade for children.
Breath for me.

I draw in from thick air and out of nowhere,

I make sweet meat.
Who will eat?
Food for squirrels. Shelter for birds. Shade for children.
Breath for me.

Promise of the Acorn, To the tune of "Wishi Ta Do Ya"
Arianna Alexsandra Collins, Sarah Pirtle, & Katy Trembly

Chapter 8
THE BOOK OF NATURE

Jungle lore is not a science that can be learnt from textbooks; it can, however, be absorbed, a little at a time, and the absorption process can go on indefinitely, for the book of nature has no beginning as it has no end.

JIM CORBETT, *Jungle Lore*

Reading the Book of Nature

If your reading skills are weak, a book might seem like just a lot of letters to decode. But, if your reading skills have become an easy mental habit, then words mean things, and reading shifts to a joy. So it is with the Book of Nature. If your skills are undeveloped, it might seem like just a blur of green. But, steady practice with Core Routines, inspired by Child Passions, in direct contact with plants, animals, and seasons, will develop a huge vocabulary of meaningful search images. With such language skills, you can take delight in reading the Book of Nature through all its dynamic twists of plot.

"The Book of Nature has no beginning, as it has no end," says the late great tracker, Jim Corbett. So now, the question to begin this chapter is, "Where do you *start?*" David Rains Wallace, writing his natural history of the tangled Klamath Knot in southern Oregon, struggled with this same question. He remarked that his subject matter was "less a tidily consecutive array of increasingly advanced organisms than a leap-frogging mob of plants, animals, and dubious beings, such as fungi, all earnestly photosynthesizing, feeding, respiring, and

Language is basically the collection of labels we have for the universe. If our language doesn't contain a word for something, it quite literally doesn't exist in our consciousness. If we don't have a noun, then we won't see something. If we don't have a verb, we can't imagine doing that. The 32 different words for snow in the Inuit language is a classic example. Without those different words for distinction, how closely do we look at snow? How much more closely do the Inuit, without having to try? Their consciousness has built-in search images.

JON YOUNG, Language as Label

reproducing … but considerable action and color tend to compensate for this lack of plot." He concluded, "A story without a plot is not an easy one to tell."

Nature's story *is* infinite, messy, and leapfrogging, but once again Coyote can help us out. Coyote calls us to *start at the edge* in so many ways—the edge of a person's curiosity, the edge between what they know and don't yet know, and the edge between the images of nature and the language of modern science. This chapter emphasizes *starting* with the edge of what your people can personally appreciate and relate to in a memorable way. We call it "meaningful relationship," or in other words, "connection."

Start with Meaningful Relationship

In his book, *The Geography of Childhood*, Gary Paul Nabham describes a trip with his young children into the "geological jumble of northern Arizona" when he realized "how much time adults spend scanning the land for picturesque panoramas and scenic overlooks … while the kids were on their hands and knees, engaged with what was immediately before them." I remember hiking with a young boy to the top of such a scenic peak. We arrived, and I—stunned by the breathtaking view—stood gazing, hypnotized. When I remembered to share this moment with the boy, I looked down to find that he was completely lost in the mesmerizing march of ants on the ground. As much as I wanted him to look at the amazing view, the little one had no interest. After the long hike to the top, the tiniest thing right under his nose most intrigued this child. I took this as a parable: learning depends on what is *meaningful* to each individual, not necessarily what has meaning for a mentor or parent.

I found the same thing with my dad. After studying tracking in Washington, I took him out in the woods of our home in Georgia, hoping to get him interested in the subject that had enthralled me so much. After finding some squirrel tracks in a patch of mud, I wanted him to get down with me and look. But after a glance he didn't care for them at all. Instead, he wandered all around, excitedly tracking beavers, discovering

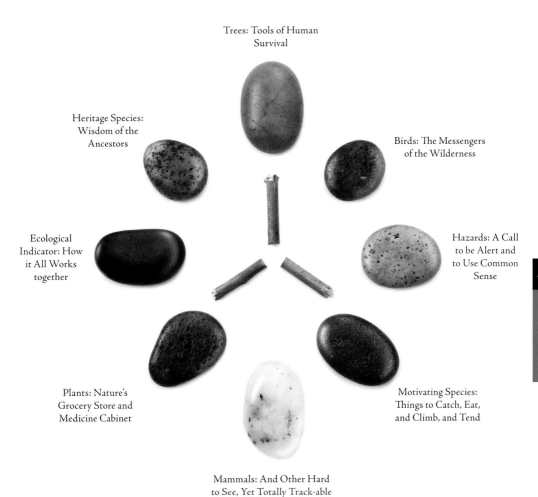

Trees: Tools of Human Survival

Heritage Species: Wisdom of the Ancestors

Birds: The Messengers of the Wilderness

Ecological Indicator: How it All Works together

Hazards: A Call to be Alert and to Use Common Sense

Plants: Nature's Grocery Store and Medicine Cabinet

Motivating Species: Things to Catch, Eat, and Climb, and Tend

Mammals: And Other Hard to See, Yet Totally Track-able Critters

The 8 chapters of the Book of Nature, placed in their natural orientation

BOOK OF NATURE

It is taboo for a biologist to be anthropomorphic, which means to ascribe human qualities to animals. And in this time of environmental crisis, there is growing concern about humans being anthropocentric, which means "human-centered." The New Physics proposes the "observer effect," which means the observer necessarily influences what he/she observes. We humans are "anthro," and it is impossible for us to be unbiased, objective, neutral, or independent of our human-ness in all our relationships. It is also true that the hunting life adapted us to imitate animals to the point of identity, which is why it is possible to say that a naturalist knows their animals so well that they literally "walks in their skin." My own growth as a naturalist has followed this path: "When I say I want to know a tiger I mean that I want to walk in a tiger's skin, flex my tiger body and feel what a tiger feels. If the truth be known, I most want to be a tiger."

RANDALL L. EATON, "Counter–Counter Point" The Human/Animal Connection

the trails they used to get from one piece of water to the other, and intrigued by their dams and their effects on the ecology. As I sat frustrated that he wasn't "tracking" with me, I realized that he actually was tracking, and with more zeal and excitement than I had been. I laughed at myself and joined with him in his connection to the world of beavers, water, and ecology.

In this chapter, we want to help folks find personal relevance in the species and elements of nature so they internalize the information. When you cultivate the same feeling of familial relatedness you share with your friends and family and expand that feeling to include the plants, animals, and even the drainage patterns and forces of weather—your local place suddenly feels neighborly. Think of when you meet strangers. Until you have a personal relationship with them, they are easily forgotten. But when you get to know them, everything builds and grows and becomes memorable.

Reading the Book of Nature *starts* with discovering threads of connection with our natural landscape. Once you have truly connected with one dandelion leaf because you can eat it, then a brain-pattern evolves to absorb more detailed knowledge. Once you begin to wonder how a cottonwood tree lives, you will want to read on about nutrition and soil layers and water cycles and pollination, even local geology. Once you care in a personal way, scientific language and analysis come naturally.

To read the Book of Nature, then, start with experiencing aspects of nature your participants can directly relate to with their physical, sensory, or emotional nerves.

Organizing the Book of Nature

To sort through nature's abundance, Botany and Zoology texts most often use phylogeny—evolutionary family linkages. The scientist's version of the Book of Nature includes chapter titles like Animalia, Plantae, Fungi, Bacteria, Arcaea, and Protista. They call these groupings "Kingdoms." This is useful for their purposes. However, we take a different approach. We base our sequence of sections within this Book of Nature on what people will progressively connect with in our year-long outdoor schools. During our collective years as Coyote Mentors, we have seen this sequence successfully pique curiosity on a continuous, well-rounded journey into nature.

To sequence our Book, you may want to start with the first species group—things that can hurt or kill you—Hazards! Next in the motivating continuum: Things to Catch, Eat, Climb, and Tend, species you can get your hands on. After that, we'll move into Track-able Critters, Elusive Animals whose track and sign can be commonly found and followed. What else can we directly experience in a meaningful way? Plants in Nature's Grocery Store we can eat or use for healing. The next two Book of Nature sections will appeal to those with an ecological and historical imagination: Ecological Indicator Species, How it all Works Together; and Heritage Species, The Wisdom of the Ancestors. This brings us to species that adventurous and sensitive readers will appreciate most of all: Trees, the Tools of Human Survival; and Birds, the Messengers of the Wilderness.

One might imagine each section within this Book of Nature chapter as heralded by a sort of family shield or coat of arms. As you read, you'll get a clear sense that each topic has its own unique flavor, a distinct spirit.

You will find at the beginning of each section descriptions for the Spirit, Learning Objectives, Mentoring Actions, some tips for Related Core Routines and Activities, and a sample List of common species or elements for the area. Our minimal commentary offers details and suggestions for you as a mentor, including professional advice about leading and safety. Finally, we provide a list of Recommended Resources.

All together, these *shield divisions* introduce everything field ecologists need to know to do their jobs. For our purposes, they guide you, the mentor, to find the sticky edge where you can begin to restore the bond between people and the rest of nature.

No One-size-fits-all Curriculum

This Book of Nature works more like a field guide or encyclopedia than a novel. You can open and read anywhere and we encourage you to do exactly that. Develop strong reading "muscles" through full immersion into all the chapters. Balance knowledge and

Approaching the book of nature in terms of what we humans can connect with is a subtle form of "anthropocentrism"—human-centeredness—as if nature has value only when it's useful to us humans. Make an effort to raise consciousness about this fallacy. Remember that "natural resources" belong to the birds and bees as much as they belong to us, and that really, they don't belong to anyone, for even the rocks and the waters are our kindred relations.

EVAN MCGOWN, Counter Point

Washington State Essential
Academic Learning Requirements
for Geography
To understand the complex
physical and human
characteristics of places and
regions, students will

❑ Describe the natural
characteristics of places and
regions and explain the causes
of their characteristics

❑ Describe the patterns
humans make on places and
regions

❑ Identify the characteristics
that define the Pacific
Northwest and the Pacific
Rim as regions

To observe and analyze the
interaction between people,
the environment, and culture,
students will

❑ Identify and examine people's
interaction with and impact
on the environment

❑ Analyze how the environment
and environmental changes
affect people

❑ Examine cultural
characteristics, transmission,
diffusion and interaction

experience of all aspects of nature by cycling through these eight chapters, seizing opportunities as they arise in the moment. This flexible and open-eyed approach not only honors nature's way of organic unfolding, but also honors the varying interests and learning styles of your participants and co-mentors.

With nature, there is no one-size-fits-all curriculum. Your specific mentoring requirements will shape your emphases. What is meaningful for a five-year-old in the Southwest U.S. will be different from what is meaningful for a grown-up in the tundra of Canada. Someone from the heart of a big city will have a different set of interests than someone from a rural landscape. A mother will care about something different than her teenage boy. A classroom science teacher will have different learning objectives than a summer camp counselor. Recognize your people's interests, backgrounds, and stage of life as you browse this guide for what is most useful for you. Developing it into "good science" for every curriculum is beyond the range of this book, although we do give you some helpful references.

We recommend you begin your curriculum planning by creating a Master List of essential species in your area. Our short Lists of common examples cannot include every possible species in each bio-region. We've attempted to select those things just about everywhere as examples of what to get to know. Like everything else in this book, we've done our best to translate the principles into examples that will help you get the feel. Then, the fun of making it work for you, in your area and with your people, will rise up through your own creativity. You'll quickly become the meaningful-relationship-taxonomist for your homeland. Enjoy the dance.

Role Modeling to Start the Fire

Before you jump in, remember what will really prompt and ignite the learning: your own passion and curiosity. You, as role model, will inspire those around you. We want each section of the Book of Nature to be, first and foremost, an invitation to the curious, wide-eyed child inside of you. Let yourself go wild, literally. Fire will not spread except from fire itself.

Hazards: A Call to be Alert and to Use Common Sense

Everyone remembers physical injury in sharp detail. Remember your first bee sting? Your first burn? Your first bout with food poisoning? Did you ever go fishing and sneak up on the edge of the water, observing the fish just below the surface? Can you remember shivering and getting silly in the rain or snow, or feeling suddenly faint and nauseous in the sun? Have you have gone carefully in pursuit of a deer, or a fox to photograph or hunt? Have you ever had a near-death experience?

Where the possibility of injury exists, people pay attention. Hazards in the natural environment provide fertile ground for connections because they appeal to our most basic need for physical safety. Use hazards thoughtfully and strategically to keep everyone alert, present to the moment, and learning. Real alertness is positive and expansive, while over-blown fear can be negative and restrictive.

Some explorers will be gung-ho to run out into the wilds oblivious to danger. More folks, however, are likely to be afraid of some aspects of the wilderness, full of an unrealistic and exaggerated sense about hazards and the dangers they pose. Use hazards to inspire; a little information transforms the fear from intimidating roadblocks into easily navigated, minor speed bumps.

Use hazards with care. If people seem fearful already, tone the hazards awareness down; if they are over-confident and could be a danger to themselves and others, help them to understand and become more aware of hazards. Most of all, remember to keep things fun! That's when learning is at its best.

SPIRIT: To inspire an ever-present need to "be on your toes" in every sense of the word—alert but not intimidated or overly fearful. People trained in this manner will always watch out and look ahead for wildlife and potential dangers. As a result of this common sense introduction, they will manage risk comfortably and wisely wherever they explore.

LEARNING OBJECTIVES: To understand the specific, known dangers and hazards of the local environment, how to avoid them when possible, and how to respond when they are encountered. To dispel "old wives' tales" and other scary misinformation. To learn that birds and animals can be flushed unexpectedly, announcing the arrival of people in the forest—a hazard to the goal of getting closer to wildlife.

MENTORING ACTIONS:

- Create a Master List of local hazards and show how-to respectfully avoid and deal with them.

- Reassure them if they fear harmless things.

- Temper any "fearless" energy in your group.

- Make participants aware of things that can bring harm by looking closely at local Hazard Species, telling stories, and inspiring field-guide research about them.

- Examine the natural history of hazardous tendencies of weather and geology in your area.

RELATED CORE ROUTINES AND ACTIVITIES:

Routines: Expanding Our Senses, Exploring Field Guides, Nature Museum.

Activities: Nature Names, Nature Museum, Sit Spot, Expanding our Senses, Body Radar, Exploring Field Guides (Hazard Scavenger Hunts), Survival Scenario (with Hazards), Meeting Poisonous Plants, The Lost Test, Shelter Building.

Generic List of Hazards

Yellow-jackets, Wasps, Bees (*Walk lightly around ground nests and listen for a "bzzz" sound.*)

Venomous Snakes & Spiders (*Be careful where you put your feet and hands – especially in dark places.*)

Ticks (*Check yourself thoroughly after a walk in the woods. Where on your body will they likely be?*)

Rabid Animals (*Beware of any irregular behaviors in nearby animals.*)

Cougars (*Pound-for-pound the strongest cat on earth, but if you LOOK big, they'll shy away.*)

Bears (*If you find tracks or sign of their presence, do not sleep with food in your tent.*)

Poison Ivy/Oak (*Watch for telltale color and shape in all seasons.*)

Dead-falls from Limbs (*Which trees of your area fall or drop limbs the most?*)

Plants that will Kill/Sicken if you eat them (*LEARN your poisonous plant ID basics and their edible look-a likes.*)

Mushrooms (*Even trained mycologists have died eating what they thought were wild edibles. Don't touch!*)

Temperature Illnesses (*Know the signs of hypothermia and heat stroke as well as the treatment!*)

Trees & Shrubs that Enhance Wildfire Dangers (*What woods make fire in your area?*)

Dehydration (*Always drink PLENTY of water!*)

Severe Weather (*Learn what to do in a lightning storm, tornado or hurricane, how to read weather patterns, and where the closest safety is.*)

Dangerous Humans (*Avoid dangerous parks and hike with a buddy. Get in touch with your "Spidey sense."*)

Drinking Water Hazards (*Giardia or Cryptosporidium have miserable effects. Treat your water effectively.*)

Your local list may differ and go on and on.

Commentary

Alert Awareness. Hazards and the possibility of close proximity to wildlife awaken a curiosity-filled alertness to the world as few other things can. Nothing gets a person really listening to the forest like the possible presence of a nearby cougar or bear—and even deer, rabbits or songbirds when one desires to get closer. When we visit a new area, little kids always show everyone the big spider they found. In a new program, they also show off their nature knowledge by telling about a dangerous snake or animal they know about—and I must add, often with great emphasis and amusing animation. There are always stories about what animals were seen and how close they were. You can engage alertness and excitement around the presence of poison sumac, poison oak, or poison ivy and use this to teach how to identify a plant and distinguish it from others. Leaf shape, growth habit, subtlety of twigs and buds, where it likes to grow—all this initial learning happens because we have a *healthy* fear of things that can hurt or torment us with itching.

Perceived Danger. In Coyote Mentoring, we use "perceived dangers" to enhance awareness, even if no real danger exists. When it comes to getting close to wild animals and birds, the "danger" always exists of scaring them away. This is a very powerful inspiration to become alert and cooperative. These should be presented as challenges, not threats. For instance, if you go into an area to learn the basics of plant ID, then reach for that first berry, you can stop and say, "Wait ... we need to really look at this plant to make sure it's not a poisonous look-a-like." We will stop, because we don't want to get poisoned. Use this opportunity to explore that plant's aroma, to learn about opposite versus alternate leaf patterns—all before they reach for that first berry. Whether or not poisonous look-a-likes actually grow in your area doesn't matter; the "perceived danger" keeps both mentor and learner's alert awareness up. As long as something is perceived as a challenge, the alert state can be a powerful ally to the brain's learning. But once the learner crosses the line and feels threatened, old patterns of preservation behavior kick in, and learning shuts down. In the field, we call such behavior "downshifting"—brain processing literally shifts into the lower, more primitive centers of the brain. So, don't over do it and, you the mentor, must also be alert to this possibility.

Real Danger. There are of course "real dangers." Awareness of real hazards should be one of the very first things you cultivate. Research where and when wasps make their nests. Learn the habitats and daily habits of snakes and spiders, cougars, and bears. Study the weather, and understand what the weather reports mean and what certain cloud-shapes tell you about on-coming storms. When you lead folks out into the wilderness, you should be able to keep everyone safe. Most outdoor schools understandably require staff training in Wilderness First Aid and CPR.

Cultural Attitudes. It really pays to know the cultural background of the folks you work with. Some people have very little experience outdoors and can have very strong reactions to things that don't bother you. Many seem to have deep fears of spiders, snakes, various other wildlife, or the dark. Try to understand where they're coming from, and then guide them through their fears with kindness and reassurance. Help them grow to like nature and to trust you.

Reasoned Respect. Some people won't even walk into the woods on the first day because they have some "urban legend" in their head that poisonous spiders will be hanging from every tree. Or they won't walk off the asphalt because they have a friend who nearly died of Lyme's Disease. Or they won't let their children out the door for fear of predatory strangers. Whether you orient people at the beginning of a one-day program, or gradually teach them about hazards over time, your net goal is this; replace unfounded fear of nature with reasoned respect based on understanding. Once they know how a rattlesnake hunts and lives, they can show the snake its proper respect by not accidentally blundering into its habitat and may even begin to understand and utilize the snake's most powerful survival tactics. Reasoned respect shows up as conduct over time, and folks will become quite skilled at moving in an alert state into any situation—whether in the wilds, or in the town.

Take a Sad Song and Make it Better. In the event of a painful interaction with a hazard, be ready to handle it calmly. These things will happen to all of us, eventually. Carry a first aid kit and know how to use it. Carry a cell phone that works or at least a two-way radio (and remember to put someone with the other radio somewhere helpful). Carry extra water, extra wool, and dry matches to pull out in an emergency. Once you've handled an emergency, try to cast the experience in the positive light of learning and growth, of "rites of passage." Laugh and be proud that you and your dependents came home safe and sound with "a story to tell."

Resources

Remember that the internet is a great resource for looking up things like ticks, hanta virus, and other nature related hazards that might not be gathered together in one definitive resource.

Backcountry First Aid and Extended Care, by Buck Tilton (ISBN 0762722703)

Bay Area Mycological Society's Webpage of Mushroom Poisoning Stories (*http://www.bayareamushrooms.org/poisonings/index.html*)

Bear Attacks: Their Causes and Avoidance, by Stephen Herrero (ISBN 158574557X)

Cougar Attacks: Encounters of the Worst Kind, by Kathy Etling (ISBN 1592282962)

David Fischer's Webpage on America's Poisonous Mushrooms (*http://americanmushrooms.com/toxicms.htm*)

Golden Guide to Venomous Animals, by Edmund Brodie (ISBN 0307240746)

Golden Guides: Weather, by Paul Lehr (ISBN 1582381593)

Kamana One: Exploring Natural Mysteries, by Jon Young (ISBN 1579940080) (*www.WildernessAwareness.org*)

North American Mycological Society's Mushroom Poisoning Case Registry and Volunteer Emergency Mushroom ID (*http://www.sph.umich.edu/~kwcee/mpcr/*)

Peterson Field Guides: Edible Wild Plants, by Lee Peterson & Roger Tory Peterson (ISBN 039592622X)

Peterson Field Guides: Venomous Animals & Poisonous Plants, by Steven Foster & Roger Caras (ISBN 039593608X)

Poison Control Centers: (*http://www.1-800-222-1222.info/poisonhelp.asp*) (1-800-222-1222)

Seeing Through Native Eyes: Understanding the Language of Nature, (Audio) by Jon Young (ISBN 157994017X) (*www.WildernessAwareness.org*)

Tiny Game Hunting: Environmentally Healthy Ways to Trap and Kill the Pests in Your House and Garden New Edition, by Hilary Dole Klein and Adrian M. Wenner (ISBN 0520221079)

Wilderness First Responder (WFR) courses:

Solo (*http://www.soloschools.com/index.html*)

Wilderness Medical Associates (*http://www.wildmed.com/*)

Wilderness Medical Institute (*http://www.nols.edu/wmi/*)

Motivating Species: Things to Catch, Eat, Climb, and Tend

Have you ever seen a child come upon the sudden movement of a frog? Just like any predator, their eyes light up and in a flash—bam!—they're off, bolting after it, trying to catch it before it scampers away. In a moment, their attention focuses, their bodily instincts engage, and they instantly imprint a search image they'll never forget. The same is true for adults and berries—we just move towards them without thinking and our fingers start testing for ripeness. The hunter-gatherer spirit lives in everyone's

DNA. A large part of the nature-deficit disorder phenomena has to do with the modern "hands off" approach to nature. As a nature mentor, you have the power to reverse this trend and the ability to tap into our hunter-gatherer instincts with the touchable elements of nature.

SPIRIT: To physically motivate learners into action, to jump-start passions, to draw out instincts first and information second. To bring out the hunter-gatherer in others.

LEARNING OBJECTIVES: To actually touch "motivating species" by catching, eating, climbing, or tending. To provide small successes in hands-on connection that fuel the hunter-gatherer desire.

MENTORING ACTIONS:

+ Research Motivating Species in Field Guides and make a Master-List to check off when touched.

+ Design field trips, walkabouts, hunts, and errands that include gathering and eating berries, fruits, and vegetables; catch-and-releasing frogs, snakes, fish, insects, and tide-pool critters; climbing trees and rocks; building forts and hideaways; swimming in natural waters; drinking rain from the sky; handling domestic animals; tending terrariums or gardens.

+ Explain principles of respectful and safe plant and animal handling.

+ Clarify ethical hunting and fishing techniques, either by direct experience and/or through stories.

+ Create chances for small, easy successes, then continually up the ante of the challenge.

RELATED CORE ROUTINES AND ACTIVITIES:
Routines: Sit Spot, Story of the Day, Animal Forms, Mapping, Exploring Field Guides, Survival Living, Thanksgiving.

A friendly reminder about caring for our amphibian neighbors. Amphibians, including frogs, toads and salamanders, breathe through their skin. This skin is very sensitive to many things (salt, chemical toxins, soap, bug spray, chlorine in our drinking water, sunscreen, etc.). When handling our wild friends, please remember to create a microhabitat between you and them. Create this layer by putting your hands in a water source—a vernal pool, stream, pond, lake or any kind of wetland—or you could also use soil and leaves. When holding, make sure you keep low to the ground and be mindful that the temperature of your hands can raise theirs, and this can create stress for them.

FRANK GRINDROD,
Founder, EarthWork Programs,
Amphibian Etiquette

TRY THIS after you have prepared yourself by quieting your mind and have wetted your hands with source water. See if you can slowly stalk up on the frog and barely touch it. While stalking you may observe it hunting, basking, being hunted by a snake or other predator, and you may just decide to watch it without touching it. Have Fun!!

Frank Grindrod, Founder, EarthWork Programs, A Frog-Stalking Challenge

Activities: Animal Calls, Deer-Bounding Challenge, Cougar Stalks Deer, Sleeping Fawn, Eating Wild Edibles, Nature Museum, Animal Senses, Fox-walking, Body Radar, The Five Voices of Birds, Otter Steals Fish, Predator-Prey, Plant Concentration, Capture the Flag, Tree Tag.

Generic List of Motivating Species

Frogs and Tadpoles (*Visit vernal pools, neighborhood ponds, or big puddles to watch or catch these amphibians. Careful rearing of certain species can create lifelong memories.*)

Salamanders and Newts (*To find out which salamanders are in your area, carefully walk a stretch of road on a rainy spring night with a flashlight—you might even witness a mass migration of these herps.*)

Lizards and Snakes (*Look in sun-baked areas for these basking reptiles, but don't catch a species of snake unless you're 100% sure of its identity.*)

Crayfish (*You can easily spend an afternoon hunting down these freshwater crustaceans along streams, brooks, and rivers.*)

Tide Pool Animals (*Most kids and some adults can spend hours exploring the intertidal zone, turning up well-known animals such as hermit crabs, anemones, mussels, sea stars, crabs, and odd species such as limpets, nudibranchs and amphipods—and you can eat some of these too.*)

Butterflies, Fireflies, and Moths (*Take one bored kid, add one jar with holes, and a net, to transform an ordinary day into a magical one.*)

Big Crawling Insects (*Get a big clear container and start turning over logs, bricks, and old junk to inventory your local insects—and don't forget to let them go after a good study session.*)

Pets and Farm Animals (*Animals can be extremely fertile mentoring grounds, whether it be tracking your dog on a sandy stretch or slaughtering your pig for family sustenance.*)

Fish (*Fish the easy waters first—those with crappie, bluegill, and other fun fish—then build off the success and tackle your local trout streams or bass ponds.*)

Bird Nests, Wasp Nests, and Beehives the abandoned ones. (*Very few birds re-use nests, so go ahead and make them a part of your nature museum, each with a story of its own.*)

Wild Berries (*As long as you know the dangerous ones, very few moments in life match up to watching a child or adult satisfy their hunger with fresh, wild berries.*)

Wildflowers (*Find seasonal wildflower patches to visit with field guide in hand; gather and display with labeled names their transient beauty.*)

Tree Fruits (*Eat them fresh, collect and can or freeze them for use in baking recipes.*)

Home & Community Gardens (*Gardens are wonderful classrooms for nature awareness—ripe with lessons on biology, natural history, stewardship, life and death.*)

Leaf Piles (*Not only great for jumping in, but they also make a great instant survival sleeping bag.*)

Water Holes & Rain Ditches (*From making rivers in the dirt, to standing in gutters during a downpour, to dunking in the waterfall, H20 is a super play medium for most humans.*)

Natural Forts & Hideouts (*You don't need a fancy tree house, although they're great too—just use branches, grasses, cattails, scrub, etc. for fort-making and when the kids ask "Can we sleep out here?" be ready to say and mean "yes."*)

Climbing Trees & Rocks (*Don't let the fear keep you grounded—climbing is healthy and fun for all ages, just be committed to knowing the comfort zones of the people you work with.*)

Primitive Hunter-Gatherer Weapons (*Learn to make spears, bows and arrows, traps, etc. Begin target practice with nonliving targets. Approach the parents about taking children fishing or hunting. Always be ethical, get permits, and obey the laws.*)

Commentary

Identifying Motivators. Absolutely the best way to learn the motivating species in your area is to watch kids at play. Ask them about natural areas in their lives. Listen to their stories. Watch their body language and cadence. The pitch of their voices will rise up and they will start talking faster and louder over each other to tell you about the crayfish, the snake, or the climbing tree nearby. Pay attention to this "mentor's intelligence network;" these little teachers do a lot of work for you! So, get a grasp on species in your local area and channel the innate motivation they incite into as much learning and connection as possible. Remember to bring that motivating spirit to your work with kids of all ages—sometimes the elderly have the best secrets of all.

Natural Gifts. Certain learners will gravitate to one species or activity more than others. Ask yourself how you can use that natural passion to guide further discovery. Like a fisherman or a hunter you can sneak up on your quarry by knowing its habits. Some like to fish; others like to paddle the canoe for the fisher. Some like to hunt while others hunt with a camera. Some like to climb, to hide, to catch, and others like to cultivate their gardens. Take them to places where you know there's "kid-bait" then watch which bait they take. Offer opportunities to care for living things in classroom, bedroom, basement, or back yard, and see who keeps their domesticated wards thriving. Whatever they move towards instinctively, go with it and fan the flames. The effect of these close encounters will be a firmly established motivation that comes from deep within and is different for each individual.

Rules for Good Behavior. Right away, you'll have to designate firm boundaries for Catching Things. Depending upon the situation, you'll likely want to establish at least these two sets of principles: "Leave No Trace," and "Catch and Release." Demonstrate *how-to:* catch things without harming them or their habitat, handle butterflies and amphibians, tide-pool and plant-picking etiquette, swimming and climbing safety, taking off muddy shoes before going indoors. In some cases, taking the life of animals for food can serve as a simple and powerful lesson. In such cases, always make sure you're following all wildlife laws and have the permission of parents. Although hunting and fishing can be sensitive areas to tread with some adults, most young children innately understand that our survival depends on the death of other life forms. Nonetheless, extra sensitivity to parent and community issues is an absolute must.

Resources

Care of the Wild Feathered and Furred: Treating and Feeding Injured Birds and Animals by Mae Hickman, Maxine Guy and Stephen Levine (ISBN 0935576533)

Golden Guide: Fishing, by George S. Fichter (ISBN 4490300695)

Golden Guide to Pond Life, by George K. Reid (ISBN 0307240177)

Golden Guide to Reptile and Amphibians, by Howard Zim and Hobart Smith (ISBN 6000008481)

Golden Guide to Seashores, by Herbert Zim and Lester Ingle (ASIN B000IXOLOY)

Golden Guide to Spiders and Their Kin, by Herbert and Lorna Levi (ISBN 0307240215)

Golden Guide to Stars, by Herbert Zim and Robert Baker (ASIN B000O6OGYG)

Golden Guide to Venomous Animals, by Edmund Brodie (ISBN 0-307240746)

Hand Taming Wild Birds at the Feeder, by Alfred G Martin (ISBN 0911469047)

Honeysuckle Sipping: The Plant Lore of Childhood, by Jeanne R. Chesanow (ISBN 0892722347)

Seeing Through the Eyes of the Children, (Audio) by Jon Young (ISBN 1579940234) (8shields.org/products)

Talking to Fireflies, Shrinking the Moon: Nature Activities for All Ages, by Edward Duensing (ISBN 1555913105)

The American Boy's Handy Book: What to Do and How to Do It, by Daniel Carter Beard (ISBN 0879234490)

The American Girls Handy Book: Making the Most of Outdoor Fun, by Lina Beard (ISBN 1586670891)

The Field and Forest Handy Book: New Ideas for Out of Doors, by Daniel Carter Beard (ISBN 1567921655)

When Pappy Goes Hunting, by Kurt L. Bonello (ISBN 0964224801)

Mammals: and Other Hard to See, Yet Totally Track-able, Critters

Universally, mammals intrigue humans, and that stands to reason, because we *are* mammals. We aren't rooted in place like plants, we don't fly high in the air like birds, and we don't breathe underwater like fish. Instead, like most other

Let us now examine the tracks of the leopard. The path where it crosses the watercourse runs over red clay, trodden hard by bare human feet. Over this clay is a coating of fine white dust, so the conditions for our purpose are ideal ... The first thing we note is that the pug marks have every appearance of having been newly made, and therefore that they are fresh. We get this impression from the fact that the pile of nap of the dust where it took the weight of the leopard is laid flat and smooth, and that the walls of the dust surrounding the pads and toes are clear cut and more or less perpendicular. Presently under the action of the wind and the rays of the hot sun the nap will stand up again and the walls will begin to crumble. Ants and other insects will cross the tracks; dust will be blown into it; bits of grass and dead leaves will be blown on to, or will fall on it; and in time the pug marks will be obliterated.

Jim Corbett, "Tracks of the Leopard" *Jungle Lore*

mammals, we walk the land, keep our bodies warm, navigate with our five senses, and raise relatively few young that we take time to care for.

Ah, but there's a snag. Wild mammals, with the exception of the ubiquitous squirrel and the occasional house mouse, are almost impossible to see, much less get to know personally. Most mammals highly prize the skill of avoiding such one-on-one time with potential predators—their lifestyle is defined by the tactic of *invisibility*.

If you want to form real relationships with real mammals, tracking provides a doorway. Yes, the red fox may be long gone and tucked away in some mysterious cubbyhole, but it does leave tracks behind. You can touch them. You can lie on your belly and pick out the outline of the hairs on its paws. You can interpret the walking pattern of its tracks. And you can follow it to piles of freshly chewed bones and rabbit fur, maybe even to its secretive hideout near the rocky cliffs.

One of the most effective ways to connect with mammals and other track-able critters is to turn on the power of a tracker's awareness: to teach how to observe the seemingly unobservable, to pull stories from clues—and to see how much fun this can be.

What will be the results of this kind of training with animal tracks? People will practice the Core Routine of Questioning and Tracking. You know they're paying intense attention, because suddenly they ask dynamic questions. By looking for subtle clues in and around the tracks, their ability to focus will be heightened. Details will appear through this intense awareness for all sorts of identification challenges among plants, trees, soils, and weathers. Their deductive powers will be sharpened. Their pattern recognition will deepen and widen. By osmosis, they will just pick up a vibrant vocabulary of search images.

SPIRIT: To enter the world of wild mammals. To sharpen observation, inquiry, and pattern recognition, by noticing subtle clues, asking good questions, and thinking imaginatively. To "see" the "unseen," to "read between the lines."

LEARNING OBJECTIVES: To learn the biology of mammals and other track-able animals. To develop skill in tracking through knowledge of track and sign. Through the experience of tracking, to develop patterns of scientific inquiry that can apply to anything.

MENTORING ACTIONS:

+ Create a Master List of local mammals and check off what you find—footprints, scats, feeding sign, beds/dens/nests, live sightings.

+ Study anatomy and physiology to understand animal body movements and perceptual strategies, and imitate animals through Animal Forms.

+ Identify and interpret track and sign, emphasizing scientific questioning. Study tracks in the field and in tracking field guides.

+ Journal and Map animals' tracks and trails.

+ Take field trips to look for track and sign where you will find good tracking substrate, such as sand, mud, or snow. Follow animals for a long way and play trailing games.

+ Celebrate seasonal events of migration, mating, nesting, and other visible behaviors.

RELATED CORE ROUTINES AND ACTIVITIES:
Routines: Questioning and Tracking, Animal Forms, Exploring Field Guides, Mapping, Mind's Eye Imagining, Journaling, Listening for Bird Language.

Activities: Nature Museum, Sit Spot, Story of the Day, Sharing Circle, The Six Arts of Tracking, Fox-walking, Body Radar, Silent Stalker, Animal Cards, Stick-Drag Game, Tracking Expedition, 100 Tracks in a Row, Track Journaling, Field Guide Research.

Generic List of Track-able Mammals; many might live in your area

Coyote! *(Our namesake. Look for dog-like tracks that move in a straight line for long distances.)*

Squirrels *(Look for their leaf-clump nests, "dreys," in branch crotches. Why did they pick this tree? How many live up there?)*

Rabbits or Hares (*Look for "Cocoa Puffs," roundish, pelleted scats. What have they been eating?*)

Domestic Cats (*How do the neighborhood birds react to them? Where are their hidden hunting spots?*)

Domestic Dogs (*Can you tell the neighborhood dogs apart by their tracks? Where does this one walk everyday?*)

Deer (*Heart-shaped hoof prints are some of the easiest to find. Also look for oval beds in the grasses. Then look for whitish hairs that are hollow like straws. When were they here last?*)

Beaver (*Find trees that look like they were chewed at 45 degree angles. Where did the tree go from here?*)

Bears (*Trash can spilled all over the place? Look for claw scratches and bite-marks on trees and utility poles.*)

Cougars (*Check out sand and mud-patches for large four-toed prints with NO claws. Why don't the tracks have claws in them?*)

Raccoons (*Their tracks look like little human hands. Why do they have such long fingers?*)

Skunks (*Has something been making little digs in the grass? Why do you smell that skunk aroma in the same area all the time?*)

Weasels (*These little guys will kill rabbits twice their size and carry them in their mouths? Where do they leave the bones?*)

Otters (*Find their tracks and slides on the edges of ponds or rivers. Go early and wait until you see them come out.*)

Mice and Rats (*How do they get into the house?*)

Moles (*How do such little creatures make such big clumps of raised earth? How does that happen exactly?*)

Shrews (*Did you see that flash of movement through the leaf litter?*)

Voles (*Often mistakenly called "field mice." Look for small trails above ground, at the base of tall, grassy stems.*)

Other Track-able Critters:

Shorebirds: Killdeer, Sandpiper, Mallard, Canada Goose, Great Blue Heron (*Distinguish waterside birds by size of track, webbing, depth in substrate, and habitat. What do they eat here? Who might want to eat them?*)

Woodpeckers (*Sign includes: Large cavities in trees, sawdust around the tree trunk, elaborate patterns in bark, stores of acorns stuck in bark. What are they seeking in the depths of the standing deadwood?*)

Earthworms (*Piles of their castings, "poop," mark their territory. What do they eat?*)

Slugs and Snails (*Find a slug or snail slime trail. How far can you follow it?*)

Herps (*Frogs, toads, turtles, snakes, lizards, and others all leave scat, tracks, and sign behind. Where can I find toad scat around here?*)

Caterpillar Frass (*Inspect your garden for tiny "grenade-like" structures. How long ago were these made?*)

Fish Beds and Nests (*Mating fish display extravagant behaviors to show their location. Can you find them?*)

Commentary

Tracking Basics. When we say "tracking," we not only mean looking at footprints, but we extend the metaphor to include asking questions about all the "prints" animals leave, including their scats, signs of feeding, and signs of bedding and nesting. And, while usually we focus on mammals, birds leave very telling tracks, especially along shorelines; in the desert, reptiles and large insects can be easily tracked; and you can track anything that touches the surface of fresh snow. (We have in our Mind's Eye a favorite image of mouse tracks on snow, a great dusting of owl wings, a jab of talons, and no more mouse.)

Since tracking may not have been part of your wildlife education, try to keep one step ahead by learning some basics for yourself. In the discussion of Tracking and Questioning in the Core Routines chapter, and in the Six Arts of Tracking Activity, we've developed the classic questions:

Who? Identification
What? Interpretation of behavior and habits
When? Aging tracks
Where? Trailing to home and habitat
Why? Ecological Tracking and prediction
How? Empathy and imagination

Jon Young's book, *Animal Tracking Basics* gives a much richer picture. Tom Brown, Jr.'s book, *The Tracker* tells a very compelling story. Mark Elbroch's guides give wonderfully detailed information about animal tracks and sign. See other Resources below.

Reviving Instinct. If you back-track modern children, you will see what fundamentals they already know for tracking animals. Ask them to name their favorite animal and you'll likely get, "tiger," "monkey," or even "Mickey Mouse." What does this tell us about the extent of their relationship with these animals? Hmmm, movies and cereal boxes. There was once a time when our ancestors' awareness was directed toward life around them for survival purposes. It is natural, and even imperative to human development, that our brains get exercise in this way again. The mysterious nature of mammals makes tracking a particularly powerful opportunity to revive our instincts.

Imagine if every child in America knew about raccoons in their backyards—where they sleep, when they are active, where they get their food, when they have their babies, and how many they raised this year. Children can know about the coyotes on the fringes of town—where they scavenge, how they hunt the mice under the porch at night, or leave their trail in the alley. They can learn about the deer in the greenbelts—where they can be found in each season, whose roses they like to eat, where they bed during the day. Imagine kids knowing the names of animals they recognize by body markings or slight tracks. This and much more is possible. Our kids *can* have direct relationship to their fellow animals and so appreciate other mammals within a local fabric of intelligent life.

Tracks Mean Presence. My friend Laura told me this story after a summer camp. At a local park outside of Seattle, after going a few feet off-trail, Laura's kids found huge tracks in the mud. "Laura! Laura! Look at these? What are they?" It wasn't too hard to guess, and they all came to the conclusion that these tracks were made by none other than a Black Bear. The kids, naturally, thought this was pretty neat. Another five minutes passed, as Laura called attention to the other signs of broken berry branches, scratch marks on stumps, and hairs hanging off low-lying branches. Suddenly, one of the girls stopped dead in her tracks and stared at Laura with huge eyes and a dropped jaw. "You mean the Bear was actually *right here?*" She couldn't believe that a bear had been at the same place she was now standing. Laura said she stood in disbelief for minutes, staring from track to track in a silent daze.

Even though that little girl had understood that the tracks belonged to a bear, the idea that the famous Bear—of whom she had undoubtedly read in books, and seen on TV—actually had been in the same place and time, struck her with force. This is how tracking places us into direct relationship with animals. Once we see the tracks, we are shocked into another reality where human life is only one piece of the picture. In a trackless world, where we see mammals as television fantasies, then anthropocentrism, the tendency to put humans at the center of the universe, is all too easy for the next generation to inherit. But when real relationships enter their experience, their entire world shifts.

Start with Successes. What is the doorway to tracking? Jon Young argues it is a confident start. So, start with fun-da-mentals. Make it fun first, then add the mentals later. With a complex, brain-teasing skill like tracking, find opportunities to see tracks of the species that will give your beginners success. Start with mammals who leave their tracks locally. The really easy, successful ones in nearly ANY environment would be raccoon, opossum, squirrel, domestic cats and dogs—and if you're willing to raise them, small rats and mice. If you have a wooded area, deer still live nearly EVERYWHERE. You can begin by tracking your own footprints on a sandy stretch, or following the track-sets left by local dogs in a muddy spot in the neighborhood. You can call a special field trip the morning after a new snow and find tracks everywhere. Where the landscape lacks sand, mud, or snow, you can recognize the sharp-hoofed imprints of deer, the huge tree-nests of squirrels, or the very visible chew-sticks of beavers.

Of course, the mega-fauna will entice people initially, especially if dangerous—bears, cougars, wolves, even coyotes or bobcats—so find a way to track these too, if only in their books and imaginations. As confidence develops, and the passion for tracking emerges, move to the tougher-to-track mammals, and broaden your scope to the larger ecosystem.

Stay Still and They'll Come to You. Getting to know animals' daily patterns is one of the most potent inspirations for Sit Spot time. Once they know an animal roams or lives in waters nearby, turn that curiosity into Sit Spot time at sunrise or sunset. With enough attempts, such silent sitting will lead to first-hand experiences with animals, eye-to-eye—and the stories of those experiences will stay with people for a life-time. Just as potent, sitting quietly and noticing bird alarms in the same thicket again and again ultimately leads one to crawl in there and to see what's causing the alarm.

Then the bobcat tracks amaze us! Here at our sit spot, Animals, Plants, and Birds merge as they pull our natural curiosity ever more deeply into complex and synergistic relationships.

Practice Animal Forms. An excellent way to understand tracks comes through imitating the movements of animals. By getting down on all fours and practicing dog and cat forms, the body begins to appreciate how four-legged's limbs attach differently than ours. Also, by visualizing how these mammals actually walk on their toes, heels in the air, we realize what a lot of energy it takes to make a direct register trot. By practicing raccoon and bear forms, they'll discover that bears and raccoons, unlike most other animals, put nearly all their weight on their rear legs, just like us. By trying to imitate rabbit, they'll understand why the rear prints always appear in front of the front prints. By being squirrels, they'll feel how to gather and hurl themselves forward, and on and on. This list of descriptors could be as long as your bio-regional Master List of animals.

Resources

Animal Skulls, by Mark Elbroch (ISBN 0811733092)

Animal Tracking Basics, by Jon Young and Tiffany Morgan (ISBN 0811733092)

Animal Tracks and Hunter Signs, by Ernest Thompson Seton (ISBN 23210044301183)

Bird Tracks and Sign: A Guide to North American Species, by Mark Elbroch, Eleanor Marks,

Diane C. Boretos (ISBN 061851743X)

Field Guide to Mammal Tracking in North America, by Jim Halfpenny (ISBN 061851743X)

Field Guide to Tracking Animals in Snow, by Louise Richardson Forrest (ISBN 0811722406)

Jungle Lore, by Jim Corbett (ISBN 0195651855)

Mammal Tracks & Sign: A Guide to North American Species, by Mark Elbroch (ISBN 0811726266)

Peterson Field Guide to Mammals of North America: Fourth Edition, by Fiona Reid (ISBN 0395935962)

Peterson Field Guides: Animal Tracks, by Olaus J. Murie & Mark Elbroch (ISBN 061851743X)

Princeton Field Guides: Mammals of North America, by Roland Kays and Don E. Wilson (ISBN 0691070121)

Stokes Field Guide to Animal Tracking and Behavior, by Donald and Lillian Stokes (ISBN 0316817341)

The Art of Tracking: The Origin of Science, by Louis Liebenberg (ISBN 0864862938)

The Tracker, by Tom Brown, Jr. (ISBN 0425101339)

The World of the White-tailed Deer, by Leonard Lee Rue, III (LOC # 62-11348)

Tracking and the Art of Seeing, by Paul Rezendes (ISBN 0062735241)

Way of the Whitetail, by Leonard Lee Rue, III (ISBN 0896586960)

Wild Animals I Have Known, by Ernest Thompson Seton (LOC# 66-16584)

Audio & Video Resources

Planet Earth - The Complete BBC Series, with David Attenborough

The Life of Mammals, by the BBC with David Attenborough

Tracking Pack One, by Jon Young (ISBN 1579940056) (*www. WildernessAwareness.org*)

Tracking: Mastering the Basics, a four part DVD by James Halfpenny (*www. TrackNature.com*)

The Great Dance, DVD or VHS (*www.sense-africa.com*)

Plants: Nature's Grocery Store and Medicine Cabinet

When you first encounter nature, the realm of plants can be a giant "wall of green"— it all looks the same. No one finds it easy to penetrate the wall and differentiate the plants. To break through this wall, get to know a handful of plants—or even just one plant—like a best friend. What would give you a real need to get to know plants? How about if you could eat them? Or make handy, life-saving and itch-relieving medicines or functioning survival tools from them?

As one of my wild plant teachers once told me, "Plants are fun and easy to connect with, because, unlike mammals, they don't run away from you." Always there, if only as roots in the winter, plants offer abundant potential for relationship as you harvest them, eat them, cure your ills, or fashion them into baskets, throughout the different seasons.

Knowing plants empowers people to walk in the woods and find food for themselves. With this sense of trust in their own—and the earth's—combined ability to provide edibles, wandering in the woods becomes a welcome event. If I can find food around me, it's not as big of a deal if I get lost. With this increased empowerment comes a mentality that doesn't feel the need for mental agendas, but feels rather confident to wander where the body leads.

Through direct experience of gathering edible plants, tasting morsels, and making meals and medicines from wild plants, we learn to listen to the instinctive wisdom of our bodies. We make a direct connection to plants when our instincts become engaged, so each plant can provide a learning experience. Over time, people begin to trust their senses to eat a certain kind of food, or to avoid another. I once heard about a man who had a heart attack. In his recovery, he was seized with the urge to eat carrots, which he ate almost exclusively for two weeks. He healed quickly. No doctor could have prescribed this, but his body somehow knew. We want people to trust their own experience and their own innate, body-based wisdom. This goes beyond health and diet, and includes how we all wander through life. Perhaps most importantly, each of us will know, through such intimate experiences with plants, that nature and the earth we walk on provide our food and our means of health and healing.

SPIRIT: To experience and appreciate, firsthand, how the Earth directly sustains our needs. To slow down. To hold an internal sense of peace, and throughout life, expand one's ability to wander in nature with trust and relaxation. To know how to listen from this place of peace, to the needs, instincts, and intuitions of our body.

LEARNING OBJECTIVES: To identify and make use of local wild plants. To understand and appreciate plant-life through the four seasons, and the contributions plants make to food and medicine. To gain competence and confidence in wandering and foraging through the wilderness.

MENTORING ACTIONS:

+ Create a master list of plants for your area: Poisonous Plants, Edible Plants, Medicinal Plants, Beautiful Flowering Plants, and Plants We Cultivate.

+ Identify and avoid poisonous plants. Find matching plants in Field Guides.

+ Explain methodical plant identification by flower-structure, branch-pattern, and leaf-type.

+ Illustrate life-strategies of plants, such as the functions of roots, leaves, and flowers and how they are adapted to their ecosystems and interact with soils, sun, wind, water, and animals.

+ Research how native people cultivated and used edible and medicinal plants.

+ Cultivate, process, use, and display plants for food, medicine, cordage, and baskets.

+ Practice slowing down and doing activities that turn on bodily touch and feeling and so change the rhythm of normal activities, such as eating at half-speed, or blind-fold exercises.

RELATED CORE ROUTINES AND ACTIVITIES:
Routines: Sit Spot, Expanding our Senses, Wandering, Mapping, Exploring Field Guides, Survival Living, Mind's Eye Imagining, Journaling, Thanksgiving.

Activities: Nature Names, Four Directions, Fox-Walking, Body Radar, Mind's Eye Imagining, Plant Concentration, Eating Wild Edibles, Meeting Poisonous Plants, Songline, Get Lost, The Lost Test, Circle of Thanks, Ideal Ecological Vision.

Common Wild Edible and Medicinal Plant List

(This list only includes herbaceous, or low-growing plants and bushes. Any woody plants are grouped with the trees.)

Common Dandelion (*Claimed to be the highest plant source of Vitamin A; try marinating and stir-frying the roots. Or chop up a few leaves and throw into a salad.*)

Plantain (*Many people claim that the fresh juice from these leaves has healed spider and insect bites.*)

Chickweed (*An abundant, succulent green that can really fill out a salad.*)

Cattail (*In every season, parts of this plant are edible—the roots, roasted, are like buttered mashed potatoes.*)

Dock (*Yummy cooked green, like spinach and used in Asian medicines for centuries.*)

Lamb's Quarter (*One of the tastiest on-the-go snacks.*)

Sheep Sorrell (*Exquisite lemony taste that kids love, just don't eat a pound of it at any one sitting.*)

Miner's Lettuce (*A favorite because of its clean, succulent taste, thus the name given by early gold-mining settlers.*)

Stinging Nettle (*A green "superfood" high in protein and other nutrients, takes skill to pick without getting stung.*)

Local Berries (*Every region has their favorites, along with a culinary history of using them to sweeten the tongue.*)

Yarrow (*Use mashed or chewed leaves as a poultice to stop bleeding in seconds, but always beware of look-a likes.*)

Wild Mustard (*Wonderful spicy taste. Harvest plentifully, a great way to reduce the presence of this invasive species.*)

Common Violet (*Leaves and soft flowers are delightful in the spring.*)

Burdock (*Huge taproot can be cooked like carrots.*)

Seaweeds (*Salty taste is great to add to soups and they contain trace minerals and nutrients only found in the seas.*)

Cleavers/Bedstraw (*Edible leaves, and great fun because they cling to your clothes like Velcro.*)

Jewelweed (*Gorgeous orchid-like flowers with leaves that treat poison ivy rash.*)

Field Mint (*Steep for a fragrant tea that helps your digestion...look for square stems and that minty smell.*)

Horsetails (*Tea from it is high in silica and great for bones and teeth.*)

Thistles (*Inside stalk is moist with water-like juice, "survival celery."*)

Common Poisonous Plant List

Poison/Water Hemlock (*The plant that killed Socrates ... others have died after putting a piece to their lips, or by just licking their hands after touching the plant. Also looks like Wild Carrot.*)

Nightshade (*This creeping vine has shiny red berries that look yummy ... but eating them can pull the shades on your bright life.*)

Buttercups (*Many kids play games with the shiny yellow flowers, but don't let them eat these digestive system trouble-makers.*)

Poison Ivy and Poison Oak (*Not only does the oily compound urishol make you itch like crazy, but ingesting this plant—either directly or via smoke, can be deadly.*)

Foxglove (*Latin name Digitalis, source of a much-valued modern heart medicine. Why? It can slow down your heart ... or make it completely stop.*)

False Hellebore (*Don't mess with this one—its high concentration of alkaloids will eventually kill humans and livestock who ingest it and don't evacuate the poisons.*)

Baneberry (*Another tempting red berry that can quickly be the bane of your life. Not widely common.*)

Death Camas (*The name says it all. There's also a camas that's prized for it edible root bulbs, but they look exactly alike. They only visible difference? The color of the flowers. What if it's not in bloom?*)

Wild Iris/Blue Flag (*This looks like and grows in the same swamps as the delicious Cattail ... but you'll know you messed up when your throat starts stinging like needles on fire. What can you do then?*)

Mushrooms (*Technically, these aren't "plants." They don't photosynthesize. Treat all mushrooms as dangerous Hazards.*)

Commentary

Aren't Trees Plants? Indeed many trees provide food or medicine, but their wood and other characteristics create meaningful relationships to humans in another important area—the survival skills of shelter, fire, and tools—so they have their own section later in this chapter.

Where to Start. We begin with the plants most likely to be found in everyone's backyard, and then we branch out into the more specialized plants of the forests and fields, deserts and mountains. The surprising benefit that comes from searching close to home—people will develop a search image and begin to notice these plants everywhere. Also, the handful of plants they learn first will provide a useful foundation for reaching out to the more subtle and less common species.

Poisons First. For plants, we recommend a three-pronged approach to mentoring: 1) poisonous plants abundant in your area. 2) plants with poisonous look-a likes and 3) plants known to be edible, medicinal, or craftable that have no poisonous look-a likes. We suggest you start with poisonous plants and compare them with edible plants you can harvest and gobble down without concern. Working with hazardous plants will get people to really pay attention. This should be done slowly and thoughtfully. Mix in a poisonous plant or one with a poisonous look-a-like so they can remember to always pay attention. It doesn't help people to only learn the 'bad news" species, as in "this plant can give you a bad rash" or "eat a few of these leaves and you're dead." You want to mix it up. Keep them excited about useful plants for food, medicine, or their fibers for baskets or string. Introduce respect for plants for the extraordinary benefits and for the rare, but present, dangers that they can also pose. Common sense comes through hazard awareness.

Good news, statistically speaking: only a small percentage of plants out there are poisonous. If all the plants were stacked up in a statistical pyramid, then the bottom layer would be harmless plants. That doesn't mean they're edible or yummy, only that they won't hurt you. The next layer up, somewhere in the middle of the abundance of plants, would be the edible or medicinal plant species. At the very tip top of the pyramid, just a handful of species, sit plants that will hurt or poison you.

WARNING!!!—Some wild plants can be dangerous to connect with, so as a mentor you need to really know your stuff. If you don't, you could poison yourself, or worse—someone else. Do your own homework and get several field guides to reference and cross-reference. Remember that plants look different in different seasons, soils, and sun and moisture conditions. Where a cardinal always looks like a cardinal, an evening primrose can look like many other things while it is young, in its rosette stage. Through most of the growth cycle, plants don't have nice flowers we depend on for ease in identification. Prepare yourself and other staff with sound advice, as well as trained emergency response personnel that you can reach quickly. Know the phone number of Poison Control Center and local hospitals.

The Language of Plants. Once you yourself have learned a few common edibles in your area, you should have enough material to begin explaining not only those specific plants, but the *language* of plant biology—how to tell one plant from the next by flower, branch, or leaf structure. For instance, here are some basic questions for plant ID:

1) Flower type. Is the flower "regular," meaning it is symmetrical and with a certain number of petals that you can count? Or is it "irregular" and non-symmetrical? Or is it so small and strange that it's "indistinguishable" when you try to classify it?

2) Branch Pattern. Do the branches and leaves grow in an "opposite pattern," on opposite sides of the main trunk of stem, like two arms on a body? Or do the branches grow all the way around the main trunk or stem, "whorled," like propellers on a helicopter? Or do the branches grow in an "alternate" pattern, uneven on each side like the metal pieces of a zipper?

3) Leaf Type. Is the leaf "entire," made up of one unbroken shape, or is it "compound," made up of several leaf-lets? Does it have lobes or teeth? Are the edges smooth or serrated? What is the shape of the leaf?

The terms of these three basic questions of plant ID will be found in most plant field guides. The leaf branching and shape/types are pretty standard. For flowers, most guides will focus on the color and number of the petals. Training everyone's eyes to look for these key features will make the field guides user friendly. In the Plant and Wandering Activities, you'll find a more detailed explanation where the ID centers around one edible plant. You only really need a few plants to break through the wall of green and get people saying, "Look … this one is different from that one because of how the leaves attach to the stem. I wonder if you can eat *this* one. Do you know what kind of plant it is? Where's that field guide … you know, I think I should draw this one …"

Medicinals. It's exciting to realize almost all modern pharmaceuticals originally derived from wild plants—and so you can imagine the meaningful relationships that humans developed with those plants before the pharmaceutical companies discovered them. Kids and adults alike feel thrilled when they realize they can go straight to the source to gather, prepare, and treat themselves and others with live, effective medicines. They love the idea of nature providing a free "Medicine Cabinet," whose only price is knowledge and curiosity. In particular, kids love to learn about medicinal plants, and will often proudly become the class "doctor," ready to jump in with bracken fern when someone gets stung by a nettle.

Remembering Plants. Using all the senses helps in remembering plants. See them, sketch them, compare them with pictures in Field Guides, but also feel their texture blindfolded, squish them and smell them, taste them on various parts of your tongue. How can you hear them? A wise, spirited, storytelling Elder friend of Ellen's insists you can hear them if you listen. In their own language, they whisper an invitation to you to name their tastes and smells. So much plant lore lives in the stories told about them. People also remember best from not just studying in a book, but using the plant. I never will forget the plants I have gathered to add to a salad, or dried to make cordage for a basket. The ones I have to re-learn over and over every spring are the plants that I have not used. Plants can become dear friends when all ways of learning feed into one's naturalist intelligence.

Giving Weeds a Good Name. Many edible plants that will build relationship and foundational botany skills carry the label "weeds." Think of this sensible definition of a weed—"a plant growing where you don't want it to grow." As humans who cultivate gardens and yards, it's entirely appropriate to make such a distinction. We encourage you, however, to rethink the stereotype. After learning how delicious, healthful, and teachable they are, you might *want* them to grow after all. These so-called "unwanted" species are very much wanted by the local insects, birds, mammals, soil inhabitants and other members of the natural community. Monarch butterflies, for instance, drink from a "weed" called dogbane and milkweed. You could even turn the stereotype upside-down: see landscape plants as "weeds" because they take up space where delicious edibles and useful medicines could be growing.

Sustainable Harvesting & Low Impact Gathering. As a gatherer of wild plants, you'll also need to think like a caretaker of the land. A common sense way approaches harvesting for only what you need and never harvest more than 25% of a group of plants. In order to have little impact on the plants, caretakers leave the larger, more productive plants alone and take some mid-sized and smaller plants (these tend to be tastier as well). This allows the larger plants to go to seed and ensure future generations of sustainable harvesting.

Resources

Botany in a Day, by Tom Elpel (ISBN 1892784157)

Edible Wild Plants & Useful Herbs, by Jim Meuninck (ISBN 0762740868)

Edible Wild Plants: A North American Field Guide, by Thomas Elias and Peter Dykeman (ISBN 0806974885)

From Earth to Herbalist, by Gregory Tilford (ISBN 0878423729)

Identifying and Harvesting Edible & Medicinal Plants in Wild (and Not So Wild) Places, by Steve Brill (ISBN 0688114253)

John Gallagher's herbalist training website (*http://www.HerbMentor.com*)

Newcomb's Wildflower Guide, by Lawrence Newcomb (ISBN 0316604429)

Peterson Field Guide to Edible Wild Plants, by Lee Allen & Roger Tory Peterson (ISBN 039592622X)

Peterson Field Guide to Medicinal Plants and Herbs, by Stephen Foster and James A. Duke (ISBN 0395988144)

Plants of the Pacific Northwest Coast: Washington, Oregon, British Columbia & Alaska, by Jim Pojar & Andy MacKinnon (ISBN 1551055309)

Plants, People, and Culture: The Science of Ethnobotany, by Michael Balick and Paul Alan Cox (ISBN 0716760274)

The Encyclopedia of Edible Plants of North America, by Francois Couplan and James Duke (ISBN 0879838213)

The Forager's Harvest: A Guide to Identifying, Harvesting, and Preparing Edible Wild Plants, by Samuel Thayer (ISBN 0976626608)

Wild Cards, by Linda Runyon (ISBN 0880795158)

Wildcraft! An Herbal Adventure Game, by John and Kimberly Gallagher (*www.learningherbs.com*)

Ecological Indicators: How it All Works Together 🌿

Now everything enters the big picture as we invite the question children love to ask, "Why?" and look to the infinite science of ecology for some answers.

"Why is the sky blue?"

"Why does this tree grow down by the river but not up on the hill?"
"Why are there so many earthworms here?"
"Why does the hawk always sit there?"
Wondering the "why" of any situation is native to all of us, insistently so in kids.

Asking why about something *indicates* we sense something else, something below the surface. The indicator sends us on an errand to find out, making us "ecological trackers." The why questions almost invariably point us to the realm of relationships, of interdependence, of how one aspect of nature affects—and is affected by—another. By asking, guessing, and gathering more data, we discover stories that connect the sky to the blue water and sun rays, the trees to certain types of soil, the earthworms to decaying leaves, or the hawk to the mice in the abandoned field.

The Ecological Indicators shield division offers this goal: to get out of a narrow framework and back into the larger framework, to relate and link everything, including ourselves, to the big picture.

SPIRIT: To understand that everything is an inseparable piece of a greater whole, including our own human community. To realize that our every action leaves a track and to be aware of the tracks we are leaving.

LEARNING OBJECTIVES: To appreciate every element of nature, and the interdependence of its needs and roles with others. To be aware of what conditions local "indicator species" indicate and use this awareness both to track animals and to give early warning of degradation problems. To understand ecological principles and to apply an ecological understanding to our human community. To know that we have can effect positive change for the environment.

MENTORING ACTIONS:

+ Create a Master List of Indicator Species for your area, and allow that list to grow indefinitely. Monitor local "indicator" species, those plants, animals, and living organisms that most strongly suggest ecological conditions, such as the water quality of freshwater wetlands or aquatic systems. Also, pay attention to non-native invasions, and anything else that significantly alters habitat characteristics.

+ Pay attention to sensitive species, such as arthropods, amphibians, and reptiles that give early warning of the declining health of a habitat.

- Organize and/or take part in a local "Bio-Blitz" (one day all-species biological field inventory).

- Develop knowledge and vocabulary of ecological systems, principles, and dynamics.

- Use the principles of "Larders and Lacks" to indicate where to look for plants and animals (see page 162 for explanation).

- Encourage people to look below the surface for hidden yet vital relationships. Constantly ask the questions "How do things connect? How do they live and how do they live together? What gives order and meaning to this web of life?" Stimulate questioning and facilitate finding answers to questions that require scientific research.

- Use simple test kits to further understand the components of your local soils and waters.

+ Make these rich connections meaningful to individuals by relating concepts of ecology back to their lives. Acknowledge and honor the unique talents and gifts of each individual within your community so that a genuine sense of mutual appreciation arises on its own. Use the opportunity that this Chapter of the Book of Nature presents to weave together all other species.

+ Tell stories of ecological heroes who affected positive change for other species. A good example is Rachel Carson who helped save eagles with her book, *Silent Spring.*

RELATED CORE ROUTINES AND ACTIVITIES:
Routines: Sit Spot, Story of the Day, Questioning and Tracking, Mapping, Exploring Field Guides, Journaling.

Activities: Group Sit Spot, Wildlife Survey, Exploration Team, Ideal Ecological Vision, Storyteller's Mind, Thanksgiving.

Commentary

Inspiring Ecological Imagination. The science of Ecology examines the relationships among all living organisms and their environments. It seeks to explain the seemingly miraculous symbiosis between carbon-dioxide-breathing trees and oxygen-breathing humans; or the surprising benefit that predator species offer to prey species by regulating and actually strengthening both populations over time; or the profound way that the nitrogen in salmon finds its way into the trees of the forest for miles and miles around.

To start up your group's ecological imagination, attach it to the plants they eat. "Why is this dandelion over here bigger?" Soon, a wild snack can turn into a full-blown investigation of how rain and soil and sun interact to make that one bigger. Or try, "Let's go sit over there where those dragonflies are flying. There should be fewer mosquitoes there." "Why?" And off they'll go to find out about dragonflies' diet. Or "Let's try to catch butterflies later when its cooler." "Why?" Or, "Why do you think the red fox walks along the edge of meadow, while the gray fox stays in the thickets more?"

As a young science, Ecology benefits from the rise of equipment for gathering precise information and processing extraordinary quantities of data, so it has great promise. Magazines like *Scientific American* and accessible science writing by Edward O. Wilson, Lewis Thomas, and Stephen Jay Gould give a hint of the possibilities. Encourage people to research any topic that captures their interest and then let them report a mystery solved as their Story of the Day. If you have a classroom and equipment, then approach ecological mysteries through science projects, such as monitoring animal tracks, doing bird counts, taking water-quality tests, or doing soil composition studies.

Keep on Wondering Why. Humans are fascinated with interconnectedness. They are driven to understand "the gestalt," or "the big picture," or the "intelligent design" of nature. Adults, however, can fall into a habit of thinking they already know it all and do more pontificating than inquiring. Luckily we have those instinctive power-houses we call kids to keep us humble, with their endless barrages of "why?" or "how come?" One goal of Ecological Indicators for adults could be to reconnect them with their childhood passion. We know our work with adults is successful when their own natural curiosity and instinct fires up and we no longer need to ask questions to get them motivated.

Indicator Species. Indicator species are those specifics in a bioregion that indicate a trait or characteristic of the environment, such as the conditions of the soil, moisture, or sun exposure. Working with indicators, you can analyze the vegetation zones and habitat types of your area.

"At what stage of succession is this forest?" In mature, "old growth" of the Pacific Northwest, you'll find such indicators as understory diversity, tall hemlocks, snags, nurse logs, and maybe a spotted owl or a tree vole. If the forest has been recently logged, perhaps just starting to grow up again, you'll find indicators like alder trees, crowded thickets of sun-loving vegetation, and non-native invasive species such as Scots broom, blackberries, and poison ivy.

"Where can we find water?" In dry climates, look for drainage patterns in the landscape, an oasis of cottonwoods and willows, and a lot of animals and birds. "What are the boundaries of the wetlands on my land so I can site my house without disturbing them?" Dig for telltale soils, insects, and amphibians, and notice how far beyond the obvious wet area horsetails and hardhack grow.

Larders & Lacks: You will find that larders and lacks often go together. For instance, the bear may go to eat apples in the orchard (larder), and then it will retire to the juniper thicket up over the ridge and away from the sight of the farmer, and far from his dogs (lack). The two together often tell one story for whatever animal or bird you want to follow. This dynamic duo approach works easily when you get the hang of it, but first you must identify the extremes and lacks of extremes that affect animal life in your own local zones.

Larders. A larder simply means a "food store." Learn a little about the "food chain" relationships among producers (green plants that use the sun to make energy), consumers (animals that do not make their own energy), and decomposers (life forms that break down matter). Then think about what foods draw concentrations of what predator, or herbivore, or insect, or fish. For instance, a sudden hatch of water-born insects such as mayflies will become a larder for both the trout in the stream, the frogs on the bank, and the flycatchers on the willows above the stream. In turn, you will see the trout as a larder for the hovering osprey above. Down the food chain, trout to osprey links become "secondary" larders. Bears' tracks may point you straight to another larder—an abundance of salmon or berries. Deer tracks might indicate abundance of fresh blackberry greens in the spring. New spring grass growing above the ankles, becomes a most potent larder for voles, who in turn become a larder for bobcats, foxes, coyotes, weasels, snakes, hawks and owls. Get the idea?

Larders tend to be seasonal in nature. They tend to be abundant, yet short-lasting. They migrate with seasons, and happen at different times in different climates. Many northern forest-dwelling species venture onto roadways in the spring to lick the build-up of road salt. Or, for instance, in early spring, the wetlands will shoot up with high-protein vegetation. Bears move in for the feed. Then the next place where plants spring up with high-protein shoots is in the areas just above the wetlands. That larder of shoots migrates up the hills as spring advances. You guessed it, so do the bears.

What happens next? Well, then the fawns start arriving. The bears move to these areas next. As the season advances, the berries bloom, form, and ripen. Now guess where the bears will be found? Then the later berries, then the acorns? Well, what a wonderful dance!

We can use Larders and Lacks as a fun and accessible principle of ecology to track fish, birds, and animals. Larders and Lacks represent conditions of geography, climate, and weather, and therefore conditions of vegetation that are important when you want to know what your quarry is likely to be up to. This can be a really fun game to play with folks. Look at the lay of the land, and ask yourself things like "Given today's wind, sun, and temperature patterns, and given the exposure of these hills and forests, let's try and figure out where the animals will be resting today." Then go tracking!

Lacks. "Lacks" just sounds good after "larders!" Larders & Lacks. Lacks means the absence of larder, but with lacks, we include more than food. Where the wind blows hard from the northwest in winter—causing anyone in its path to feel the freeze to his or her very bones—there will be a lack of wind blowing on the southeast exposure of a thicket or rock outcropping. Where would you want to be? When the hot sun shines for long periods, look for the animals, birds, and invertebrates in the shady places. When it has been raining, raining, and raining, look to the drier sheltered areas for the concentration of living things. All life depends on nutrients, from calcium to selenium, and these can be missing in certain habitats or at certain times of year.

Generic List of Larders

Fresh Greens

Berries

Nut Trees

Garden, Farm & Orchard Crops

Compost, Leaf, Wood Piles

Garbage Dumps

Bird Feeders

Hatches of Insects; Fish, Frogs, Reptiles, Amphibians

Bird Eggs & Nestlings

Fungi

Newborn Mammals

Salt and other Vital Nutrients

Generic List of Lacks

Warm sun spots when there is a general lack of light in dark times of year.

Shady spots when there is a general lack of coolness in sunny times of year.

Cool northern exposures in summer.

Warm southern exposures in winter.

Hiding spaces in wide open places.

Open spaces in thick forest.

Wetlands in dry seasons.

Dry places in wet seasons.

Endangered Species. When the indicator species is listed as "threatened or endangered," this designation often indicates the precarious nature of its habitat. Field sightings recorded over time for certain indicator plant and animal species help scientists determine if a species and its habitat are endangered. Frogs and other amphibians with their thin skin have proven particularly susceptible to changes in the chemistry of the air and water. If you find them with deformities, or you hear fewer and fewer of their calls at night, such clues may indicate poor ecological health of the area studied. Why are there no fish left in your fishing hole? Check the aquatic invertebrate (bug) population. Perhaps the bugs that indicate good oxygen and cool temperatures are no longer abundant? Then something upstream, maybe fertilizer, maybe loss of shading vegetation, has changed the water quality. Maybe the migratory birds that used to stop at your feeder in April no longer come by? What habitat on their route has been lost or degraded?

Bio-Blitz. A Bio-Blitz, a full day all-species inventory, offers an excellent way to determine the presence or absence of species in your area. Done in a consistent manner, repeated Bio-Blitzes can serve as a database of local species. You may realize that the decline of species diversity, and the presence of invasive non-native species—like blackberries, starlings, or even coyotes who take advantage of degraded habitats starved off by their competitors—often indicates environmental ill-health. On the other hand, you may determine that the rare species everyone thought was locally extinct has simply changed its core area and, in fact, is doing quite well.

Grief and Empowerment. One vitally important thing leaders and mentors must realize, is that this ecological approach holds enormous potential to generate sadness or anger. People will bristle upon realizing the terrible impact humans have on the natural landscape. All the issues and emotions about natural imbalances filling the news each day can hurt. Seeing your Sit Spot destroyed can destroy you. Recall our original goals of love and connection to both nature and the human community, and be careful not to breed disdain of humans. We do not want to deny the truth, but when people get near such thresholds of pain and grief, it calls us as mentors to be mature counselors and guides.

We've got to have the presence of mind to help people process and express their emotions in ways that cause unity and positive action, rather than division and misguided acts of rebellion. Guide those you mentor toward understanding all perspectives on an issue of degradation, toward respectful communication, and toward active solutions. Many wonderful stories can be found where people have turned the tide in a million small ways. Help your people toward actions that give them a success story to tell.

Human Ecology. The Ecological Indicators approach means not only intricate knowledge of ecology and the relationships among wild beings, but an appreciation of human community and one's self within that community. To be a mentor to others requires we become mentors to ourselves, and seek out elders, mentors, or counselors for *us*. We need people who have been down a similar road before and can help us along, so we can help others. Cultivate a community of support behind you, and ask for help when you need it. Everyone has an exquisite and irreplaceable place in the whole that is needed for overall health. Therefore, the ultimate expression of this shield division is contributing one's unique talents and gifts to the community and appreciating others, different from you, who do so too. Nothing inspires the development of an individual's gifts more than having a community of friends, each standing powerfully in his or her own natural gifts.

Resources

Volumes of books touch on ecological themes, with wonderful curriculum activities for relationship-based science. We list some wonderful books here and in the Suggested Reading section, that explain many things about the solar system, climate, geology, biology, and habitat niches. If they seem useful, even intriguing, let them inspire your innate curiosity to find the link between things. A pure diet of ecological principles without positive felt interaction can dull interest, though. The trick is to always keep ecological understanding vivid, personal, and meaningful.

American Wildlife & Plants: A Guide to Wildlife Food Habits, by Martin, Zim and Nelson (ISBN 0486207935)

Autumn: A Season of Change, by Peter J. Marchand (ISBN 0874518709)

Biophilia, by Edward O. Wilson (ISBN 0674074424)

Bumblebee Economics, by Bernd Heinrich (ISBN 0674016394)

Dinosaur in a Haystack: Reflections in Natural History, by Stephen Jay Gould (ISBN 0517888246)

Fish Watching: An Outdoor Guide to Freshwater Fishes, by C. Lavett Smith (ISBN 0801480841)

Golden Guide to Pond Life, By George K. Reid (ISBN 0307240177)

Keepers of the Animals: Native American Stories and Wildlife Activities for Children, by Michael J. Caduto and Joseph Bruchac (ISBN 1555913865)

Life in the Cold: An Introduction to Winter Ecology, by Peter J. Marchand and Libby Walker (ISBN 0874517850)

Lives of a Cell: Notes of a Biology Watcher, by Lewis Thomas (ISBN 0140047433)

Mind of the Raven: Investigations and Adventures with Wolf-Birds, by Bernd Heinrich (ISBN 0061136050)

Naturalist, by Edward O. Wilson (ISBN 1597260886)

Peterson's Field Guides: Eastern Forests, by John Kricher, Roger Tory Peterson and Gordon Morrison (ISBN 0395479533)

Peterson's Field Guides: Ecology of Western Forests, by John Kricher and Gordon Morrison (ISBN 039546742X)

Project WET K-12 Curriculum & Activity Guide 2007, by Project WET (ASIN: B00134ZAHK) (*http://www.ProjectWet.org*)

Project WILD K-12 Curriculum & Activity Guide 2004, by Council for Environmental Education and Project WILD (ASIN: B000F9HJ96) (*http://www.ProjectWild.org*)

Reading the Forested Landscape, by Tom Wessels (ISBN 0881504203)

Sand County Almanac (Outdoor Essays & Reflections), by Aldo Leopold (ISBN 0345345053)

Stokes Nature Guides: Observing Insect Lives, by Donald and Lillian Stokes (ISBN 0316817279)

The Medusa and the Snail: More Notes of a Biology Watcher, by Lewis Thomas (ISBN 0140243194)

The Panda's Thumb: More Reflections in Natural History, by Stephen Jay Gould (ISBN 0393308197)

The Richness of Life: The Essential Stephen Jay Gould, by Stephen Jay Gould, Oliver Sacks, and Stephen Rose (ISBN 0393064980)

Winter: An Ecological Handbook, by James C. Halfpenny and Roy Douglas Ozanne (ISBN 1555660363)

Winter World: The Ingenuity of Animal Survival, by Bernd Heinrich (ISBN 0060957379)

Heritage Species: Wisdom of the Ancestors

Heritage species are present in every human culture. They are living testaments to our irrevocable connection with nature. These are the species that grandparents tell stories about around the fire. At the heart of ceremonies woven into lore, they create a fabric of local lessons and teachings about the land and culture. Heritage species are the plants that are seeded, the animals that have become our companions, and the staple of the local diet and economy. The heritage species of a culture may go so far back into our ancestry that our connection to them has become an inherent aspect of our daily human experiences. Our ancestors have proclaimed to us: "*These* are important to know and to honor."

We have the capability to deeply connect to our own culture's heritage species. They remind us of our connection to our natural environment. Throughout history our ancestors have lived within nature and tended to the lands. Thinking of our ancestors reminds us that we still have that capability to *know, honor, and tend* to the land as our home. In turn, we may then pass on this knowledge—of how to increase the Earth's health and vibrancy—to the next generation. Look for inspiration from the heritage species—they inspire us to contribute to the regeneration of the land, its natural systems, and *all* its inhabitants.

The Permaculture movements, and the related off-shoot called "Regenerative Design," have developed skills, processes, and models that offer people world-wide the tools they need to heal and tend the land. Permaculture honors humans as a keystone species, a species essential to the healthy balance of life. Its principles create the framework for highly productive environments beneficial to all life, offering great hope for a network of regenerative human communities living in harmony with nature. Rooted in careful observations of natural patterns, permaculture leads people to awareness of the heritage species and their role in the ecosystem.

SPIRIT: To awaken an ancestral knowledge of place that bridges nature and culture and encourages caring for and tending of the land. To inspire a sense of reverence for the past and a sense of responsibility to tend to its future. To model skills of tending the wild and human habitats through deep nature connection, awareness, and regenerative design.

LEARNING OBJECTIVES: To appreciate what human ancestors of an area depended on and often included in their cultural lives. To discover the intricate knowledge and rich lore they have accumulated in your region. To revitalize and restore a healthy landscape and place-based culture over time.

MENTORING ACTIONS:

+ Research what species and other natural elements local residents have depended on and honored throughout history. Include those elements vital to the current economy or central to regional celebrations. Create a Master List of these Heritage Species.

+ Find ways to study and deepen appreciation of them. Tell traditional stories from the people of your place. Interview elders who carry these stories and skills in their memories. Visit places of historical significance.

+ Create or renew seasonal celebrations. Were there gatherings to celebrate the harvest or to honor the quiet space of the winter?

+ Conduct art projects that connect nature with culture, such as decorations, place-based songs, masks, replicas, or public murals.

+ Repopulate your family or community culture with traditional stories, symbols, songs, and sayings.

+ Coordinate projects that renew use of the land tender's historic skills. Include Permaculture, composting, wild-crafting, organic gardening, sustainable forestry, and ecological building.

+ Encourage volunteering, political action, and charitable giving in service of transmitting our heritage, in health, to the future.

+ Ground all your research efforts, your cultural creativity, and land tending in the awareness of being an important link in a great chain of life.

RELATED CORE ROUTINES AND ACTIVITIES:
Routines: Thanksgiving, Exploring Field Guides (especially those that include ancestral lore and uses), Storytelling, Mapping.

Activities: Thanksgiving, Nature Names, Nature Museum, Group Sit Spot, Songline, Exploration Team, Ideal Ecological Vision.

Worldwide List of Exemplary Heritage Species and Elements

Aquatic/ Marine Heritage Species

Salmon & Steelhead (*For many river and sea cultures, including the Celts of Ireland and England, salmon hold a sacred, cultural position with many legends and stories abounding along with their importance as a food source.*)

Shad (*In older times, in some places still, the shad run offers an important opportunity to gather a staple food.*)

Whales & Seals (*Whales are animals of mythic dimensions that along with seals have been vital to Arctic peoples.*)

Lobster (*In modern times, the American Lobster is a classic heritage species—an entire region of North America, New England, is famous for this species.*)

Oysters, Clams, & Mussels (*For numerous coastal and migratory indigenous and modern people, these shellfish have dominated their menus and seasonal economies.*)

Washington State Essential Academic Learning Requirement for History

To understand the origin and impact of ideas and technological developments on history, students will

❑ Compare and contrast ideas in different places, time periods, and cultures, and examine the interrelationships between ideas, change, and conflict

❑ Understand how ideas and technological developments influence people, culture, and environment

BOOK OF NATURE

Herbaceous Heritage Species

Sage and Sweet-grass (*Common smudge-plants for ceremonies and daily customs in the Great Plains.*)

Bunch-grass (*The generator of springs, seeps and small streams, this important grass used to grow on the coastal hills of California with 20 foot deep roots keeping the hills green later, and the springs flowing longer.*)

Corn (*The fruiting ears, the pollen, and the leaves and stalks of the plant are central parts of the survival and cultural vibrancy of many Central American and Native American cultures. See the Omnivore's Dilemma by Michael Pollan for its current cultural legacy.*)

Rice (*A food staple in nearly every Asian county as well as North-Central North America, branching into many elements of culture.*)

Strawberries (*The Haudenosaunee hold a Strawberry Festival each spring because it is the first plant to herald the season with their ripe and delicious fruit.*)

Bamboo (*A vital and sacred part of most Asian cultures.*)

Mistletoe (*There's more to this plant than the kissing custom. Look into how this modern ritual originated.*)

Tobacco & Cotton (*Long before cigarettes and T-shirts, many North American native tribes used these plants extensively for medicine, ceremony, and lore.*)

Woody Heritage Species

Apple Trees (*Tell the story of Johnny Appleseed. There are festivals centered on these trees all over North America.*)

Cedar (*Legendary but now extinct in Lebanon; the "Tree of Life" for Northwest Coastal Peoples for whom they provided clothes, canoes, long-houses, diapers, baskets, totem poles, and much more.*)

Redwood (*Tall trees with legend-inspiring presence, they pull down the fog to keep the forest moist and cool, their thick bark resists burning, their wood resists rot, splits and planks well.*)

Oaks (*Acorns, a food staple for many native cultures, come from oak groves tended over generations. Also, many oak groves are sacred to traditions of Old Europe.*)

Pinon Pines (*Pine-nuts were a staple of Native Americans of the Southwest.*)

Olive Trees (*Their oil is at the base of all meals in Italy and Greece, and the ancient symbol of Peace.*)

Grape Vines (*Cultivated prehistorically for wine, a symbol of insight and ecstasy.*)

Cherry Trees (*In Japan, the blossoming of the Cherry and Plum trees are very special parts of their culture and very special times of year. Cherry trees celebrations occur in Washington, D.C. and many other places around the U.S.*)

Sugar Maple (*Continues to serve as a species that gives regional identity, food, and trade value for North Americans.*)

Western Redbud (*This species is a favorite basketry plant of the native peoples throughout the Pacific Northwest.*)

Avian and Mammalian Heritage Species

Beaver & Marten (*Natives and voyageurs were heavily dependent upon this aquatic mammal and arboreal weasel for their pelts, which served as currencies long ago.*)

Wolf & Bear (*Lots of native lore surrounding these wondrous animals all over the Northern hemisphere, with bears' mysterious hibernation tied to the mythic ideas of rebirth and the unconscious.*)

Bison (*Native Plains cultures such as the Lakota revolved around this animal for food, clothing, housing, and myth.*)

Reindeer & Caribou (*Nomadic people of the north travel with the migrations of these species.*)

Coyote (*This book, for instance, helps to keep Coyote part of our on-going cultural heritage.*)

Tiger (*If you live in Asia, stories of this figure weave all through your upbringing.*)

Bald & Golden Eagles (*Often touted as the bird that flies the highest, and therefore often seen as having connection with the heavenly or spirit realms ... think about where angels get their large wings.*)

Raven (*A marvelous trickster-figure that is highly revered throughout the Pacific Northwest.*)

Passenger Pigeon (*Now extinct, this sky-darkening gregarious species was integral to pre- and early colonial inhabitants of North America.*)

Heritage Landscape Features

Natural Springs & Wells (*The central meeting places. Many cultures honor these with songs, stories, and guards!*)

Distinctive Rocks (*The Mesas of the Southwest, the Uluru monolith of Australia.*)

Distinctive groves & gardens (*Hanging Gardens of Babylon, Sacred groves of Greece, Taoist gardens of China, and any still living old giant tree—all are power places in the landscape, often held as sacred.*)

Places whose names suggest they have a sacred story (*Look into place names and ask good questions of local elders ... refer to the book Home Ground by Barry Lopez.*)

Research. You've got to do a little detective work to discover the plants, animals, trees, birds, and special places that have ancestral significance in your bio-region. Such information may come easily, but that depends on the regional collection of your local library, the cleverness of your internet skills, and the presence of surviving natives or elders in your neighborhood. Field Guides with an ethnic perspective will show the native uses of plants and trees. Place names and street names like "Death Valley," "Eureka," "Bryn Mawr," or "Angel Oak Lane" can start you on a trail of discovery. Relics of old mills, wells, goldmines, graveyards, and stone piles tell of earlier inhabitants and their livelihoods. Christmas Trees, Mistletoe, Jack-'O-Lanterns, Easter Rabbits—all these seasonal celebratory symbols came from some ancestral heritage.

Best of all, find and invite elderly inhabitants of your place to come and tell their stories, or arrange to send your people to interview them. Befriend the old farmers down the road and learn from them. You'll be humbled by what people have already figured out. The *Foxfire* Books have recorded an amazing amount of regional lore this way, and in the process, have enriched the lives of interviewers and storytellers, alike.

Story and Legend. For reasons both obvious and mysterious, human cultures, fermenting for generations in the unique brew of a certain place, arrive at a group of revered species. They regale these species in lore and legend and feature them in song and dance. To become heritage, a culture celebrates their own unique species in seasonal festivals or daily rituals through hunting and farming, gathering and sowing. Because of their traditional power and accumulated lore, heritage species offer a fantastic mythology and folklore which taunt and tug at our heartstrings. Young and old will listen amazedly to how the cedar tree first grew from the grave of the most generous woman the village had ever known; or how—marvelous wonder!—the hazelnut tree holds wisdom, so if you drink from a bit of stream where hazelnuts drop, you will be wise; or—can it be?—a bear kidnapped and married a human wife, on the top of that very hill over there, and legend claims we all come from that very wife. However hidden or buried in your area, find stories that trigger collective memory and cultural imagination. Tell the stories of your land, sing the songs of mammals and mountains, and make yourself at home.

Reverence and Ceremony. With sensitivity to the culture of the people you borrow from and the culture of the people you now mentor, you can reenact ancestral ceremonies, including those of welcome, farewell, celebration, thanksgiving, forgiveness, or grieving. Ritual and ceremony have a deep place in human culture, belonging to a time before science and secularity removed or marginalized them in public education. As Richard Louv documents in his book, children seem to be born with a natural spirituality that recognizes the sacred power inherent in natural things like birth, death, and the turning of the seasons. Really, awe and reverence are universal spiritual experiences and they need to be allowed, encouraged, and dramatized in community. So, please, do what you can in your place with your people to revive these crucial life-enhancing celebrations that bring forth depths of feeling and caring for the communities of the natural world.

Starting a New Heritage. Heritage Species do not come solely from the past. As the current generation, we live as ancestors to the people of the future, the current link in the chain determining the heritage of following generations. As salmon or acorn oaks diminish, apple trees and sweet potatoes, llamas and ranch buffalo may be on the rise. You can make up silly songs about your local Banana Slugs, or create Songlines about seasonal celebrations based around the local flora and fauna that show you the way. You can even be so bold as to begin your own festivals based on what seems most meaningful. Create stories and lore now so you and your children may return to the site years later for the retelling: spend time salvaging and replanting vegetation; help kids raise salmon fry in an incubator and later, release the little fish into the local creek; or make your mark by restoring and maintaining a trail system for people to enjoy.

Caring and Tending. Perhaps the greatest tribute we can pay to our heritage species is to honor the people of long ago who tended this land for us so we can enjoy it today. Find ways to directly connect with this legacy by actually tending the land and its inhabitants yourself. For some this may be gardening. Some may work to rehabilitate wildlife or watersheds. Some will delve into local political action—writing letters, attending hearings, organizing coalitions in defense of endangered sites and species of vital importance to the future of their heritage. Some people will offer charitable donations. For some, it may mean taking up a profession in Permaculture or Ecological Design. For all of us who care, our efforts should be something hands-on and personal, something that connects us as a part of the living heritage of our place. Tend your land and your culture to leave it that much better for your grandchildren and their grandchildren after them.

Resources

Look for resources under the Ethnography, Anthropology, and Archaeology of your region.

Biodiversity & Native America, by Paul Minnis and Wayne Elisens (ISBN 0806132329)

Changes in the Land, Revised Edition: Indians, Colonists, and the Ecology of New England, by William Cronon (ISBN 0809016346)

Cultures of Habitat: On Nature, Culture, and Story, by Gary Paul Nabhan (ISBN 1887178961)

Edible Forest Gardens: Ecological Design and Practice for Temperate-Climate Permaculture, by Dave Jacke and Eric Toensmeier (ISBN 1931498806)

Good Rain: Across Time and Terrain in the Pacific Northwest, by Timothy Egan (ASIN: B000RQHAV4)

In Search of New England's Native Past, by Gordon M. Michael K. Foster and William Cowan (ASIN: B000NJY0UY)

A New Earth: Awakening to your Life's Purpose, by Eckhart Tolle (ISBN 0452289963)

Gaia's Garden: A Guide to Home-scale Permaculture, by Toby Hemminway (ISBN 1890132527)

Keeping It Living: Traditions of Plant Use and Cultivation on the Northwest Coast of North America, by Douglas Deur and Nancy J. Turner (ISBN 0295985658)

Natural Grace: The Charm, Wonder, and Lessons of Pacific Northwest Animals and Plants, by William Dietrich (ISBN 0295982934)

Open Horizons, by Sigurd F. Olson (ISBN 0816630372)

Permaculture: A Designers Manual, by Bill Mollison and Reny Mia Sley (ISBN 0908228015)

Reading the Forested Landscape: A Natural History of New England, by Tom Wessels, Brian D. Cohen, and Ann H. Zwinger (ISBN 0881504203)

Reclaiming Our Natural Connection, (Audio) by Jon Young (ISBN 1579940242) *(8shields.org/products)*

Reflections from the North Country, by Sigurd F Olson and Illustrated by Leslie Kouba (ASIN: B000R3A3K2)

Sand County Almanac (Outdoor Essays & Reflections), by Aldo Leopold (ISBN 0345345053)

Seeing Through the Eyes of the Ancestors, (Audio) By Jon Young (ISBN 1579940226) *(8shields.org/products)*

Tending the Wild: Native American Knowledge and the Management of California's Natural Resources, by M. Kat Anderson (ISBN 0520248511)

The Archetype of Initiation, by Max J. Havlick Jr. and Robert L. Moore (ISBN 073884764X)

The Foxfire Book: Hog Dressing, Log Cabin Building, Mountain Crafts and Foods, Planting by the Signs, Snake Lore, Hunting Tales, Faith Healing, Moonshining, by Inc. Foxfire Fund and Eliot Wigginton (ISBN 0385073534)

The Ohlone Way: Indian Life in the San Francisco- Monterey Bay Area, by Malcolm Margolin (ISBN 0930588010)

The Woodland Way: A Permaculture Approach to Sustainable Woodland Management, by Ben Law (ISBN 1856230090)

Wildlife in America, by Peter Matthiessen (ASIN B000OSTV58)

Wintergreen: Listening to the Land's Heart, by Robert Michael Pyle (ISBN 0395465591)

Trees: Tools of Human Survival

If you grew up in an area with trees, you probably can remember these mammoths are important to play and imagination. Most children instantly gravitate towards trees. Some feel called to climb into their crowns; others search the ground for sticks, and it is almost always the biggest tree in an area that is instantly named "base" in games of tag or hide-and-go-seek. Most children will instinctively "set up camp" around trees. They build stick forts, make imaginary fires by piling sticks, gather acorns and other nuts, and stir puddles gathered in tree roots with stick-spoons. The children seem to know trees are important to living and they are always keen to interact with them.

We connect instantly with trees because they are important to survival. Even today most of the items that make up our homes are made of trees; the walls, the roofs, the floors, even the furniture, all trees. Other than food and water, trees (and their woody substitutes where no big trees live) provide everything we need to stay alive: shelter to stay warm and dry and keep out life-threatening elements; fire to warm the body, purify the water, cook the food, and dispel the dark; and tools with which to dig, hunt, travel, make music, etc. There are hundreds of ways in which we relate to trees to survive: think of a primitive hand-drill set made of tulip poplar branches, or the supportive wood-beams of modern homes made of laminated lumber, or the paper behind the words you are reading right now. We use trees everyday and we wouldn't want to lose them, so appreciation of these life-sustaining beings grows more critical as development overtakes more and more forests. Fortunately most of us are born loving trees and are just waiting for someone to guide us to a better understanding of their value.

SPIRIT: To grow confident in directly experiencing dependence on natural elements for survival. To cultivate the attitudes of self-reliance, teamwork, improvisation, and positive-thinking. The ultimate expression of this shield division is the "scout mentality"—an ability to ensure the survival of one's people for many generations to come.

LEARNING OBJECTIVES: To acquire experiential knowledge of trees and their survival uses. To learn "primitive" techniques to make fire, purify water, make tools, and build shelters. To successfully experience edgy environmental challenges such as cold, wet, dark, and being lost, stressed, and lonely, and to see the effects of attitude on how well one survives. To be comfortable and at home in the woods.

MENTORING ACTIONS:
- ✦ Create a Master List of Trees-important-to-survival in your area, and keep notes on their uses.
- ✦ Identify trees by growth habit, by leaf/bud/flower/seed, and by wood characteristics. Journal trees and play ID games.
- ✦ Relate to trees through survival skills, making fire, purifying water, building shelter, hunting, and crafting tools, weapons, baskets, ropes etc. Discover the useful characteristics of wood-types.
- ✦ Lead projects that involve using wood. Inform about fire-safety. Sit by fires as often as possible, and notice how wood, weather, and structure affect the way they burn. Explain the basics of knife safety and usage and techniques of wood-carving.
- ✦ Demonstrate, manufacture and use stone-tools.
- ✦ Create "rites of passage" situations, such as solo-sits, night hikes, immersion in cold water, survival trips, or "walkabouts."
- ✦ Role-model and inspire attitudes of self reliance, teamwork, group survival—and techniques of cooperation—including peacemaking skills!

RELATED CORE ROUTINES AND ACTIVITIES:
Routines: Survival Living, Exploring Field Guides, Mapping, Thanksgiving.

Activities: Survival Priorities, Shelter-Building, Meet-A-Tree, Tree Tag, Five-Minute Fire, Group Sit Spot, Sharing Circle.

Generic List of Useful Trees and Shrubs

White Oaks (*Acorns have fewer tannins and are more edible than those from red and black oaks.*)

Red & Black Oaks (*Wood burns long and hot, with almost no sparks.*)

Pines (*Needles make tea high in Vitamin C. Also, can yield "pitch sticks" which are highly flammable.*)

Firs (*Sap/Pitch lights on fire and can be made into candles or fire-starter.*)

Maples (*Strong wood for carving and tools, and of course, if you know how to tap and process it, sugar maple sap makes maple syrup!*)

Cedars (*Outer bark can be shredded for tinder; inner bark for cordage, or clothing;*

For a decade, I lead whole eighth grades into late October storms on the far coast of the Northwest. We did it in the name of Lord of the Flies, to understand viscerally what strains fall on a group when there are no grownups to guide. We prepared hard and long, but once we got out there, in the wind and tides, the kids were on their own. They had agreements they'd signed—no litter, stay together, get to destination—but they had to carry, travel, camp, cook, and cope without us. We teachers trailed them.

What happened? They survived, and they each brought home a story to tell. They met weather eye to eye. They shivered with a sense of wildness. They forged a sense of community. And in every trip, their teen culture turned topsy-turvey. Roles were reinvented. The Cool lost their cool and the unnoticed kids displayed wonderful gifts of courage, leadership and ingenuity. A whole new set of heroes and embarrassed, a re-cast of "Jacks" and "Piggys" and "Ralphs," and "Littluns" and "Beasties" entered their cultural fabric and our English class vernacular.

Ellen Haas, Eighth Grade Survival

rootlets can be used as string, and the wood itself resists rot.)

Hemlocks (*Dead twigs make great kindling; good shelter in rain or snow but NOT in a wind storm.*)

Birches (*Bark has flammable compound inside, perfect for starting fires; bark slabs also fold into quick containers.*)

Willows (*Branches are very pliable and great for baskets.*)

Cottonwoods (*Find water nearby or underground where the cottonwood grows, buds contain Balm of Gilead.*)

Spruces (*Pitch can be chewed as gum; rootlets strong and pliable; also make fine guitar and other instruments.*)

Cherries (*Beautiful heralds of spring; hard wood burns well and makes strong tools.*)

Red Alder (*Very carveable wood; inner bark makes a nice brown dye.*)

Hickory (*Great wood for making flexible yet sturdy hunting bows.*)

Ash (*Burns great even when green; is used in bow-making and splint baskets; and it's easy to carve.*)

Beech (*Dead leaves hang on branches throughout winter; produces tough leaves for shelter material.*)

Shrubs

The Rubus Clan (*the "brambles" – e.g. blackberry, raspberry, salmonberry, cloudberry, loganberry, dewberry, thimbleberry, etc.*)

Vines (*Many vines can be quite useful for basket-making, cordage-making, as well as other survival skills. But beware of vines with any hairs on them. Remember "hairy rope – don't be a dope!"*)

Arrowood Viburnum (*If you live nearby this species, you are lucky, as it lives up to its name as a great arrow shaft plant.*)

Commentary

Starting. Our objective is connection to trees. Approach the study of trees through the window of wilderness survival. Again, start with the most abundant trees in your area, most useful in terms of survival, and thus most available for connection. After you learn the answers to these research questions, you could pass them on to your beginners. Every area has different answers to these questions.

- Which trees provide dry shelter in a rainstorm?
- Which trees regularly snap during winds?
- Which trees attract lightning the most? And, which trees do not get hit by lightning?
- Which leaves or needles make good bedding, and which don't?
- Which woods catch fire quickly? Which burn cleanest? Which burn longest?
- Which trees have the strongest, sturdiest branches for building shelters?
- Which have the best leaves for insulation?
- Which trees are flexible and good for crafting?
- Which woods should not be burned in an enclosed space due to toxic smoke?
- Which woods are great for smoking and preserving meat?
- Why would you <u>not</u> want to burn poison oak or poison ivy in a fire?

Experience with the qualities of trees deepens our appreciation of familiar ones and stretches awareness into discovering new ones. Learn to recognize trees at a distance by their growth habit, and you will know which ones to run for in a rainstorm. Identify trees close up by their bark, leaves, flowers, fruits, and cones, and you will know which ones to rely on for food and shelter materials. Then, as you gather wood for fire, you begin to notice the details of their broken limbs and twigs littering the ground: how the leaf-scars locate opposite or alternate along the branch and have a distinctive shape to them, how the bark feels rough or smooth and changes colors as it dries, and how pithy the very core appears.

Constructing Shelters. Making forts and survival shelters from branches and leaves offers one way to connect with the trees, physically experience how trees give us our homes, learn which woods prove sturdiest for load-bearing, which leaves are the most abundant for weather-insulating debris. Appreciate the strongly-built, and often taken for granted, homes we live in. Let folks spend the night in one of the shelters they build. Juvenile squirrels make practice nests that they spend a night or two in before going back to the family drey. Let your people do this and then make improvements on their fort so it will be more comfortable for the next overnight. Better yet, if you have the opportunity, make a shelter at the center of a "village" in your local woods, with surrounding areas for cooking fires, logs to sit or drum on with sticks, and nearby trees as climbing lookouts. Then everyone camping out together will ease the edge of loneliness for their first overnight.

Crafting with Wood. Also, explore trees by using their diverse woods to manufacture any number of tools. Use the beautiful branches of foliage to decorate your mentoring spaces, classrooms, and homes. Make rope or baskets out of tree-bark, fine branches, or rootlets. Demonstrate how to carve safely and soon your participants will begin to tell woods apart by their ease for carving, by the flexible or brittle quality, and how well the scrap heap will burn. Carve spoons and forks, walking sticks, hunting bows, bow-drill fire making sets, wooden toys, flutes, drums, or whatever else you can imagine. And as you work on such minutely-focused projects, play games and tell stories that fill imaginations with pictures of the living trees themselves.

Building Fire. Of course, use wood for making fire. If you know how to use bow-drill or hand-drill to make fire by friction, participants will eat it up. But even if you just start fires with matches, that opens the door for direct connection to trees and their varying woods. Igniting a fire with nothing but matches and the natural materials around you is not as easy as you might think. Together with those you're mentoring, figure out which kindling woods start fires the best, and gather bundles of various sizes. Then naturally you'll want to figure out which trees have tinder for starting fire, where dry wood can be found in a wet climate, or how to tell apart the twigs and branches of a maple from those of a willow. A craft leading to deep learning about what burns and what just smolders is "long-matches," the age old art of carrying coals from one fire to start a fire in another place.

Tending Fire. Fire-tending could well be another Core Routine. In fact, for some of our participants at certain periods along their learning journeys, it is *the* Core Routine. Humans have tended fires for thousands of years and it seems to have a permanent home within our psyches. Think of the thousands of metaphors common in our languages, "I suddenly got this spark of creativity." "Her face lit up." "I'm all fired up about it!" "Her anger flared," "My wound is inflamed," "He showed a flicker of interest." "I need to tend to my inner fire." "Our love burns like an ember." "The fire has gone out." "My hopes were reduced to ashes." "Goodness, Gracious, Great balls of fire!" Fire is simply one of the most magical and metaphorical elements on earth.

Humans of all ages—but especially those connected to their childlike wonder—are easily mesmerized by fire. I've watched kids spend entire days doing nothing but sitting by a campfire—as happy and content as pigs in a mud-bath. Staring into a fire puts you into a trance, practically hypnotized by the continually changing flickers and flames. Some people call it "Survival TV."

However, unlike most TV, staring at fire for hours will do wonders for the brain patterns of those you mentor. As logs collapse and burn and shift around, people overcome fears of fire and learn to trust the process. They learn how things cook, both in pots and at the end of sticks. They practice sitting still. They move into storytelling mode around a fire. They learn to listen to other people with silence and thoughtfulness. Tending the dynamic process of a Central Fire seems to translate to moving through life with confidence, patience, and wonder. You can see it in their eyes. So if you have the opportunity in your program, invite fire-tending as a central part of your learning community.

Fire Safety. As magical as we find fire, we must respect the inherent, potential hazard that requires training in the basics of fire safety. We list some hazardous aspects of fire and our tips for prevention:

1) Forest Fires. Whenever you create a fire, clear away any nearby flammable materials, such as leaves, grasses, or branches, and tarps. To prevent toppling a tower of fire onto someone's feet or igniting overhead branches, keep your fire-wood cut short in length, and your fires small,. For repeated use, establish a pit and routinely clean and monitor it. Be mindful that fires can spread through the inter-linked roots of trees underneath the ground. Also be aware of local laws and fire bans.

2) Bodily Burns. Take a good First Aid course and study up on how to treat burns, if they should occur. Plunge burned flesh into cold water and carry burn salve in your first aid kit. Rather than using your hands, tend your fires using a pair of fire-tending sticks, as if they were tongs. Two to three feet

long and as thick as a small wrist, these can be a lot of fun for everyone to make. They often like to carve designs in them, admired until they get burnt enough to become firewood. Then another pair emerges.

3) Smoke Asphyxiation. Be careful with smoke. Unventilated wood smoke in the lungs can be hazardous to health. Be especially considerate of varieties of allergic response to smoke. Round shelters should include smoke-holes or windows on the roofs.

4) Parent Concerns. If you work with the children of others, you will need to consider the concerns of parents who may not be familiar with fire. This will encourage you to lay out clear fire safety rules and make sure everyone stays safe, all the time. Fire safety also offers an opportunity to bring the family into the fold of a child's education, by inviting them to a class-day about fire, or by encouraging them to make a fire-pit at home.

Resources

Tree and shrub identification guides are abundant. Pick a local one that works for you and use it.

A Natural History of North American Trees, by Donald Culross Peattie and Verlyn Klinkenborg (ISBN 0618799044)

Animal Architects: How Animals Weave, Tunnel, and Build Their Remarkable Homes, by Wanda Shipman and Marna Grove (ISBN 0811724042)

Participating in Nature: Thomas J. Elpel's Field Guide to Primitive Living Skills, by Thomas J. Elpel (ISBN 1892784122)

Peterson's Field Guide to Western Trees, by George and Olivia Petrides (ISBN 0395904544)

Primitive Technology, by David Wescott (ISBN 0879059117)

The Foxfire Book: Hog Dressing, Log Cabin Building, Mountain Crafts and Foods, Planting by the Signs, Snake Lore, Hunting Tales, Faith Healing, Moonshining, by Inc. Foxfire Fund and Eliot Wigginton (ISBN 0385073534)

The Tree: A Natural History of What Trees Are, How They Live, and Why They Matter, by Colin Tudge (ISBN 0307395391)

The Trees in My Forest, by Bernd Heinrich (ISBN 0060929421)

Tom Brown's Field Guide to Living with the Earth, by Tom Brown, Jr. (ISBN 9992335025)

Tom Brown's Field Guide to Wilderness Survival, by Tom Brown, Jr. (ISBN 0425105725)

Trees of North America, a Golden Field Guide, by Brockman, Zim, and Merrilees (ISBN 6823523)

Hidden Forest: Biography of an Ecosystem, by Jon R. Luoma (see Amazon books)

Birds: Messengers of the Wilderness

Because birds are the most abundant and visible wildlife, many people are drawn into the natural world by birds. The beauty of their song and plumage instantly captures our attention to provide us a powerful hook into nature. They are easy to observe and entire industries have grown up around the observation and feeding of wild birds. Our interest in birds, however, may be more deeply rooted in survival than aesthetics. The birds tell us secrets and we mean that quite literally. Most of us are aware that a bird frantically calling from six or so feet off the ground alerts us to the neighborhood cat who has unpleasant intentions towards its nestlings. Possibly, we may be less aware of their more subtle communications such as birds also reporting back to the natural world about us. Imagine how important this knowledge was to our ancestors. Not only do the birds communicate to us about potential dangers and prey but they also have the power to spoil a hunt. Our ancestors had to be deeply aware and respectful of the birds. Perhaps this is why we have such a powerful interest in birds.

Birds and their vocalizations and behaviors constantly radiate information—about predators, skirmishes, or other dramas around them. This is amazing to realize. By gaining knowledge of bird language, we tap into a network of alarms and news reports of events in the landscape right now and we also become the news. So, except for those birds who capture attention simply by being so visible—such as eagles, herons, or swooping swallows—bird language provides the most fertile field for planting seeds of connection with birds and their lives.

Many times I've been on a back porch of my home in the forest, chatting with friends, and suddenly a bird call gets us all to listen. We put conversation on pause as we set off into the yard or the surrounding woods to find the source of the alarm. Many adventures have come about because of simple listening. I've been able to see countless owls, foxes, hawks, and weasels this way. Some of my strongest bonding moments with friends have happened because we followed bird-reported mysteries together, and surrounded by tense bird alarms right over our heads or at our ankles—until look—from a hidden spot, something swooped or sprang into view.

Bird language not only gives reason to connect with birds, it also continually calls us to expansive awareness and vigilant listening to the sounds and moods of nature and how we affect them. "Did you hear that?" will bring people into a state of dynamic alertness.

Quieting down, listening intently, and looking widely can break us out of the patterns of our own behavior and wake us up to a world most modern humans miss out on.

SPIRIT: To see the invisible. To inspire a mental state of extra-ordinary attentiveness and the practice of moving without creating a disturbance. The ultimate expression of this shield division is the "Quiet Mind"—an ability to listen with an inner calm that allows us to track subtle energetic patterns, to increase our intuition.

LEARNING OBJECTIVES: To listen for and understand the language of birds and to appreciate the multitude of lessons that this awareness offers. To notice the impact on bird activity with the appearance of predators—in the air and on the ground—and how changes in wind, weather, and light influence them. To be aware of how our human movements and intentions impact everything around us in a similar way. To practice strategies for movement through the landscape that require careful attention, listening, observation, and empathy.

MENTORING ACTIONS:

- Create an on-going Master List of common birds of your area, with those most useful for bird language study at the top. Check off well known birds, and write in new ones.

- Inspire the research and observation of local birds whose vocalizations we can hear and whose behavior we can witness.

- Utilize "The Five Voices of the Birds" as a means of simplifying the overwhelming diversity of bird vocalization.

- Carefully identify birds' every detail: key field marks such as size, wingbars, flash patterns, flight patterns, beak color and type, plumage traits, and eye-rings, as well as body language, songs, calls, and habitat.

- Locate and identify bird nests. Find night roosts for the birds at one's Sit Spot.

- Conduct Bird Language Sits followed up by debriefs, including mapping and discussing vocalizations and behaviors. Sit at different times of day, in different wind and weather patterns, and at different times of year, and call attention to how the patterns of animal and bird behavior differ in each condition.

- Pull and sort out the "shapes" of animal and bird behavior from different kinds of disturbance. Bring about awareness that behavior and attitude create "concentric rings" of disturbance on birds and animals, and also on ourselves and other people.

- Practice "routines of invisibility:" walk among wild things without creating a human disturbance.

- Physically react to bird alarms or changes in baseline behavior of birds. If you turn your head toward the scolding of a sparrow so will everyone.

RELATED CORE ROUTINES:
Routines: Sit Spot, Story of the Day, Expanding Our Senses, Questioning and Tracking, Mapping, Exploring Field Guides, Journaling, Mind's Eye Imagining, Listening for Bird Language, Thanksgiving.

Activities: Four Directions, Bird Language Sits, The Wildlife is Watching, Silent Stalker, Bird Language Scenarios, Akamba Tracker Form, Fox-Walking, Owl Eyes, Owl Approaches the Forest.

Generic List of Birds

American Robins (*These birds have a "cheery-up" song and a distinctive alarm call that has given many—including me—our first bird language success. They are abundant and watchable, with a wide vocabulary. Spend five minutes a day watching robins and you will understand bird language.*)

Dark-Eyed Juncos (*Alarm call sounds like a smacking kiss or two rocks being tapped together. Masters of etiquette and subtlety, they are not loud—but the animals are paying attention to them.*)

Wrens (*Stick up their tails like stiff paddles. All wrens sound very indignant when alarmed.*)

Song Sparrows (*Each song sparrow's repertoire is different, so you can even identify individuals by ear.*)

Towhees (*Ground feeders, one of their contact calls is produced by their feet scraping the ground as they search for food.*)

Canada Geese (*Sudden take-off filled with honks ... what caused that? V-shaped flights in spring and fall.*)

Jays (*Corvids with personality. They make a sharp "tattle-tale" cry over any animal "sneaking" around.*)

House Sparrows (*Prominent in cities. See their dust-baths and territorial fights in parking lots. Nests on store signs.*)

Common Yellowthroats (*An abundant low-nesting warbler you're likely to see if birding, females use alarm calls when nest is threatened.*)

Red-Winged Blackbirds (*Loud whistling songs. A common bird of cattail swamps with fascinating territorial dynamics.*)

Sharp-shinned or Cooper's Hawks (*These both hunt birds, even "on-the-fly," so birds go absolutely silent when they fly over.*)

Owls and Large Hawks (*Songbirds will consistently alarm at these adept predators, often mobbing them in broad daylight and chasing them about the landscape.*)

Eagles (*Majestic and always awe-inspiring, their flight patterns appear as distinctive large soaring circles and slides, and their chattery screeches belie their beauty.*)

Commentary

Start with the Ground Feeders. You may want to start with the birds whose body language you can see—those little birds who spend a lot of time near the ground—ground-feeders. Fortunately, these birds are also some of the most common ones, robins, towhees, juncos, and sparrows. They have reason to care about critters that move over ground. Your first experience with these ground-feeding birds can easily cascade into learning about habitats, foods, nesting sites, migration schedules, natural history, biology, and lore.

Stop and Listen. Imagine if every child on the block could identify the local birds by sight or sound, keep tabs on nest locations, and make daily reports on how their chicks were doing. Imagine kids stopping at play for a moment,

falling silent and all turning to look in the same direction at the same time—not because someone shouted from that direction, but because a song sparrow began its subtle alarm. One of the children says, "Hey I think the fox is coming." The others agree and wait with anticipation. Then the fox appears on the edge of the yard, emerging from behind the bush that hid her.

Such a vibrant awareness of birds and animals is possible, totally possible. We see this sort of thing happening over time in communities who mentor people in bird language. Once, such awareness passed from parent to child, as a natural part of our ancestral legacy. But how do you make bird-study have meaning to noisy, active youngsters, whose attention constantly gets courted by a great host of other things?

Simply tune into the phenomena of bird language. "Shhhh! What's that alarm? Is there a cougar on the ridge again?" If you just tell someone that the flute-like song they hear comes from a Hermit Thrush, they may not care. But if you tell them that the incessant calling of that bird in the bushes may mean there's a weasel or an owl trying to eat the bird's babies—practically no one can refuse that bait. Eyes plume wide, bodies wake up: "No way! Let's go see!"

The Five Voices of Birds. We mentioned "the Five Voices of Birds" in the Listening for Bird Language Core Routine, and you'll see it again in the Bird Language Skits Activity. Here's the whole story:

We use birds' five "voices" to group categories of their sounds. These categories define the birds' vocabularies, just as we use verbs, nouns, and pronouns for our language. We use the categories of song, companion or contact calls, juvenile begging, aggression, and alarm. As you'll discover in more detail below, you only need to remember birds play the first four as baseline voices—so when you hear them, you understand the vocalist is not in mortal peril. The last one, ALARM, indicates something is amiss. It might be a big something or a small something, but the bird alters its routine.

1. **Song** is easy to hear and a good way to identify birds. You usually hear the song on bird identification tapes. Birds probably have many reasons to sing, from attracting a mate, to heralding the dawn, to defending territory, or perhaps simply to express the joy of being alive. In our latitude, primarily the males sing, and their song varies in intensity and frequency throughout the year. Usually a bird's song lasts the longest of any other sounds that bird makes. Listen and learn the most complex and melodious songs.

2. **Companion or contact calls** used by birds keeps them in touch with their families, flocks, and mates. A group of kinglets or geese will call to each other in a conversational tone. They play a call-and-response rhythm. Usually short and sharp sounds, some species also use these calls—at a more intense volume and increased frequency—as alarms. Also the sudden cessation of these companion calls can indicate alarm.

3. **Juvenile begging** sounds happen when baby birds ask for food, or when parent birds hand off food to their mates. You will hear wheezy, repetitive calls, coupled with wing fluttering and a hunched-over body. This can be as subtle as the whisper-like calls of baby savannah sparrows, or as obnoxious as baby crows screaming for "more, more, more."

4. **Aggression** calls, still considered baseline, can often be heard. They usually involve two males, but females will also loudly chase intruding females out of their territories. Folks, in dramatic detail, learning bird-language provides a peek into nature's soap opera. While aggression will be a big deal for the few birds involved—and usually this just means one species reacting to each other—it does not indicate a threat to others, so we don't call it an alarm. Male robins can be pulling each other's feathers out while the song sparrows and towhees still sing from the fence or the ground.

5. **Alarm alerts us to birds' perceived danger.** If baseline is a still pond, alarm is a stone thrown into the pond. It could be a boulder or a pebble disturbing the singing-begging-flock-calling fabric of bird life.

To convey the range of alarm, we offer a helpful human analogy. Imagine sitting at your naturalist desk on a warm summer day. The front door is open and your neighbor's dog wanders in. You know this animal is not dangerous, but it doesn't belong in your house, so you get up and escort the dog back out the door. Maybe there was a little mild concern, and an altering of your plans for the moment. That's the low end of the alarm scale. Now you are back at your desk, except this time a large and unknown dog comes through your door. You might be a little more cautious! At the extreme end, imagine a rampaging Bengal tiger leaping into your living room. Birds show all these responses, from mild concern to screeching panic.

When we spend time outside, we enter birds' homes. How could they not notice us or anything else moving through their living rooms? Alarm vocalizations tend to be like call notes, but with more intensity. They might be higher-pitched to indicate a hawk or harsh and buzzy as when mobbing an owl or cat. An alarm might also be an absence of sound. In some cases, silence can be the indicator of danger in the area; I have heard a huge flock of pine siskins fall silent, only to look up and see a Cooper's Hawk flying overhead.

Corvid Disclaimer. The vocalizations we have described work best when applied to the passerines, also known as the perching birds, a group of 4,600 species which include our own robins, sparrows, juncos, towhees, and wrens. Other birds, such as owls, herons, and hawks, also use vocalizations to help them get by in the world, but for our purpose of discovering predators around, passerines provide clear assistance.

HOWEVER, one family of passerines has a definite trickster quality. Beginners beware! It's not always easy to understand the language of the corvids. This very intelligent crow tribe, full of wily jays, ravens, magpies, and crows, communicate extensively among themselves and resist our attempts to eavesdrop on their conversations. Marvelous birds to observe, these corvid species do not use the five voices clearly or reliably. When a song sparrow alarms, there is something threatening it. When a jay alarms, it could be for a number of reasons, including deceiving you.

Disturbance and Invisibility. In Resources below, we refer you to Jon Young's audiotapes for a more luscious, full-sound description of "Alarm Calls," "Concentric Rings" of disturbance, and "the Routine of Invisibility." Concentric rings emanate from all disturbances. If the forest at peace is like a still pond, concentric rings roll out like ripples coming off a rock thrown into the pond, disturbing everything in the circle around it, with those disturbances affecting, in lesser degree, a series of rings reaching further and further away. Like buoys on the water, birds indicate alarm as the ripples wash past them. If you tune into the right frequencies, you can pick up on amazingly subtle ripples. How do you know an owl has perched in the hemlock tree? The birds have been shrieking at it for the past twenty minutes. How do you know a coyote approaches down the ridge? You have heard the winter wren off to your left and the song sparrows across from you jump up to the top of their thickets and give a brief note of annoyance.

You too give off concentric rings as unavoidable as breathing. Once you become aware of the ripples you give off, you will feel surrounded by unforgiving motion detectors.

Thankfulness. We learn this from Mohawk legend: At the beginning of time, the Birds were given a very special duty to perform. They were instructed to use their song to help lift the minds of the Human Family. Naturalists and bird-watchers everywhere understand this: listening to birdsong is transforming. It quiets the mind, helping us break patterns of negative, worried, chattering thinking, and restore base patterns of peace, hope, and gratefulness. Regular listening for the birds' messages helps us to become aware of our mental state, reduces our ring of disturbance, and raises our spirits in respect and Thanksgiving.

Resources: Bird Field Guides are abundant. Pick one for your area.

Advanced Bird Language: Reading the Concentric Rings of Nature, (CD) by Jon Young (ISBN 1579940188) (*www.WildernessAwareness.org*)

Birds, Birds, Birds! An Indoor Birdwatching Field Trip (DVD) by John Feith

Bird Tracks & Sign: A Guide to North American Species, by Mark Elbroch and Eleanor Marks (ISBN 0811726967)

Cornell Lab of Ornithology, Macaulay Library (Free Bird Sounds Archive) (*http://www.animalbehaviorarchive.org*)

Courtship in the Animal Kingdom, by Mark Jerome Walters (ISBN 0385263384)

Echoes of Kenya & Other Poems, by Ingwe (ISBN 1579940145)

Folklore & Legends of the Akamba, Volume 1 (CD) by Ingwe and narrated by Victor Wooten (ISBN 1579940161) (*www.WildernessAwareness.org*)

Giving Thanks: A Native American Good Morning Message, (Reading Rainbow Book) by Jake Swamp and Erwin, Jr. Printup (ISBN 1880000547)

Ingwe, by Norman "Ingwe" Powell (ISBN 1579940137) (*www. WildernessAwareness.org*)

Jungle Lore, by Jim Corbett (ISBN 0195651855)

Learning the Language of Birds, (Audio) by Jon Young (ISBN 157994003X) (*www.WildernessAwareness.org*)

Peterson's Field Guides: Bird's Nests, by Hal Harrison (ISBN 0395483662)

Peterson Field Guide(R) to More Eastern/Central Birding, by Ear (Peterson Field Guide Series) by Richard K. Walton, Robert W. Lawson, and

Roger Tory Peterson (Audiobook) (ISBN 0395712602)

Sibley's Birding Basics, by David Allen Sibley (ISBN 0375709665)

Sibley Field Guide to Birds, (Eastern and Western), by David Allen Sibley (ISBN 067945120X and 0679451218)

Spirit of the Leopard, stories & narration by Ingwe (CD) (*www. WildernessAwareness.org*)

Stokes Nature Guides: A Guide to Bird Behavior Volume 1, by Donald and Lillian Stokes (ISBN 0316817252)

Thanksgiving Address: Greetings to the Natural World, by John Stokes (ISBN 0964321408)

The Birder's Handbook: A Field Guide to the Natural History of North American Birds, by Paul Ehrlich, David S. Dobkin, and Darryl Wheye (ISBN 0671659898)

The Life of Birds, (DVD) with David Attenborough. BBC Video. 2002.

The Other Way to Listen, by Byrd Baylor and Peter Parnall (ISBN 0689810539)

The Singing Life of Birds: The Art and Science of Listening to Birdsong, by Donald Kroodsma (ISBN 0618405682)

Thayer Birding Software (by Region) (*http://www.thayerbirding.com*)

Tom Brown's Field Guide to Nature Observation and Tracking, by Tom Brown,Jr. (ISBN 0425099660)

Western Birding by Ear, a Guide to Bird-Song Identification (Audiobook) (Peterson Field Guides) (ASIN: B000EOBEDY)

Conclusion

As we said in the beginning, "Nature has no beginning as it has no end." So, for these eight sections of the Book of Nature, we do not suggest they be taken one at a time in sequence or in isolation from each other. Rather, approach them collectively and holistically, so they all may dance together, feeding and playing off of each other.

Cycle through these topics again and again. The simple but important dynamic we offer is to cultivate these eight topics, *as a whole*, to truly transform awareness of and connection to the natural world. As time allows, with beginners, take a very 'shallow' first cut through all eight areas, hoping at least one area will 'capture' each person. Then continue to cycle and dip through again and again, taking a deeper cut each time, so a participant, sustained by his or her personal interest in one or another area, will grow to understand how everything connects to everything else. Even if you ONLY find interest in mammals and tracking, you still quickly reach a point where the answers to your mammal questions cause you to learn about a neighboring or downstream being. Your connections with nature will continue to go deeper and deeper as you ask questions and follow your heart's curiosity to where it wants to take you.

The deep connection will sprout in each person differently, but it will originate from a heartfelt enthusiasm, a passionate engagement with some aspect of the natural world. As mentors, we sustain and encourage personal connections throughout our time with people. For some it will be the mystery of tracking. For others it will be interpreting bird language. For others, the sense of connection will come from learning to live outside in the woods with nothing but their wits to keep them alive.

It doesn't matter what avenue brings people to this heartfelt connection, it only matters that they find it. This connection is what brings about a sense of meaning in our lives—it deepens in each one of us a sense that we have a special place in this precious world.

Chapter 9

ORIENTING TO THE NATURAL CYCLE

Orienting to the Natural Cycle

We hold a beautiful vision: a whole culture of naturalists practicing habits of awareness, bright with passion, and literate in the Book of Nature. By now, you've got the picture and you've got the bag of tricks.

When you lead a group of people over a period of time, you awaken that sparkle in their eyes—outside, with no walls to corral their energy—then you might be wondering, "Coyote Mentoring makes exciting sense, but how do I plan my day? How do I take this bundle of ideas and organize them into a lesson plan? How do I orient and guide all that Child Passion?" In this chapter and the next we suggest bringing our innate consciousness of the Natural Cycle to the surface to help design the learning experience.

We already know the Natural Cycle intimately. Since you live on planet Earth, then you are quite familiar with the sun's path through our lives. You know it in your bones, in your wardrobe, and in your daily schedule. Round and round

The Bagua, a model which is still used today in Chinese medicine, martial arts, feng shui, and traditional customs. Many people still hang a rendering of the Bagua, with a mirror in the middle, by the entry doors to their houses.

the sun goes, beginning in the East, wrapping around to the South, then tucking in to the West, and resting in the North before emerging in the East once again. The same thing goes for the seasons. We're all subject to these cycles as Earth turns and tilts and spins around the sun.

A Worldwide Sense of Direction

I remember the first Art of Mentoring class I attended years ago. First, they asked me to choose a twig from a pile resting on one of eight differently colored cloths and remember the color of the cloth. "What kind of phooey is this?" I wondered. Well, I took one, and the next morning I learned my twig from the green cloth meant I was "Southwest" for the week. "What the heck is this about?" I wondered again, looking around at the others, every one of us puzzled at being named a different "direction."

That question stayed with me that entire week and for a long time after. This chapter integrates you into a worldwide, on-going conversation based on the complexities of that simple question, "What are these directions all about?" Orienting to the four directions of the Natural Cycle indicated by the compass we see on the corner of our maps—the one with its needles pointing E, S, W, and N—started a long time ago.

Many cultures across the world use a common tool to orient themselves to life. You'll find the directions noted in most traditional cultures, especially those that live a fair distance north or south of the equator. Those cultures, therefore, have four distinct seasons. The seasonal orientations are central to Native American cultures on both sides of the Equator.

Farther afield, the Chinese have an ancient and intricate model of the eight directions (the four cardinal plus the four intermediate) called the Baqua. European descendents may be surprised to know that the four or eight directions have also been prominent in the lifestyles of their own cultures. The Celtic traditions celebrate seasonal turning points eight times a year. Caves found in France were ancient burial sites where archaeologists found bodies lying exactly in east-west or north-south orientation. The cross symbolizes the directions for myriad Christian cultures. Cross-shaped churches in

Distillation and Integration

Release and Reflection

End and Beginning

Harvest and
Celebration

Excitement and
Inspiration

Relaxation and
Internalization

Orientation and
Motivation

Focus and Perspiration

The qualities of the Eight Directions

Ethiopia have been spectacularly carved out of stone and hollowed into the earth. Westminster Abbey, home of Christian ceremonies and royal British coronations, was built in four long aisles set in the four directions.

Of course many more examples of orienting to the Natural Cycle exist around the globe: the pyramid builders of Egypt oriented precisely to the four directions; the Hawaiians and Pacific Islanders depended on directional knowledge for sea navigation; San Bushmen of southern Africa live by the time of sun and rain; the Aborigines of Australia, with timeless spirits, reportedly break wristwatches when they wear them! Whether for practical purposes like the design of Dutch colonial homes to maximize sunlight distribution, or as functional customs that channel the entrance and exit from ceremonial space, the directions have long been core to cultures everywhere.

A Natural Cycle of Meanings

We find even deeper meaning when we look at the symbolic associations of each of the directions. Each carries common archetypal characteristics and energies. For instance, in Chinese tradition, one direction may stand for fire, another for water, another for metal. One direction may be seen as beneficial to face when meditating, while another may be good to face when training for a martial art. Clearly observable in worldwide cultures, the four or eight directions are aligned with times of day and seasons of the year and are permeated with symbolic power to guide us.

The Natural Cycle is an Orienter, for its directional arrows tell you both literally and metaphorically where you are, not only in geographic space and in time, but also in terms of cultural identity and life wisdom.

The common thread derives not from the specific content of the directions, but from the context, how they are used. We want to call attention to this context. Cultures everywhere observe a distinct and recurring cycle, which always has the compass directions as its units of measurement and whose vectors have meanings drawn from the influences of the sun on life. Both the dynamic turn and the directional meanings of the Natural Cycle orient the people to the great processes and energies that thread through their lives.

The Natural Cycle as an Organizer

You already have—at the least—an unconscious awareness of the influences of the compass directions on your life. Now it's time to really look and feel deeply into them. For is it not possible that they affect more than just how we dress and plan our days? Do you experience different feelings and emotions watching a sunrise than you do watching a sunset? Or sitting in the dark of night? It could be that these direction-based cycles affect us more than we realize.

Perhaps once we tune into these natural cycles with our conscious awareness, we will see—just like watching a magic trick with wiser eyes—subtle happenings that we've been subject to all along but never fully appreciated. Perhaps then we can say, "Hey, let me see that deck of cards ..." and perform magic ourselves.

So here we are, setting up a nature-based program, creating a learning culture to immerse people in the language of nature. Why not follow in the footsteps of every other nature-based culture? What if we orient our educational model to the four and eight directions? What if we align our program with the Natural Cycle of the sun, seasons, and our own human lives?

The Natural Cycle provides mentors with a sense of direction and an orientation for designing and facilitating learning experiences. The next chapter presents three ways to use the Natural Cycle as an Organizer for Educators. Initially, use it as a baseline for mentoring—what you do all the time—designing the flow of learning. The second way offers a perspective to notice emerging edges; it profiles the stages of the natural learning journey. The third way uses the Natural Cycle as a guideline for coordinating mentoring teams, learning groups, and program logistics when your program grows too big for one person to handle.

I didn't know it at the time, but there was quite a bit of research and intention behind that little twig I picked up off a colored cloth that represented the Southwest. Building a culture based on the eight directions puts us in sync with the moods of nature. And this, when you stop to think about it, provides a profound model for "nature education." What is more "nature" than the sun, the seasons, or the eternal processes of time, growth, and decline?

But first, let's take a swing through the Natural Cycle itself.

We are accustomed to thinking that the sun rises and sets, but in reality, wherever we are on the earth turns into the sun in the morning, faces it roundly at noon, and turns away from it at sunset. It is wonderful to realize that always there is a band of sunrise somewhere, moving slowly westward around the earth. Always accompanying this rim of light is a moving horizon of birdsong to greet it, the "dawn chorus." It's like a sonic version of "The Wave" that goes round the stadium with fans at a ball-game, but this wave takes twenty four hours to make a full circle and never stops going!

Ellen Haas, Dawn Chorus

Think of alfalfa, the plant grown in the fields to make hay for horses and cattle. Begin with the alfalfa sprout that we sometimes find on our sandwiches, those little wiry, thin, white, rooted things with the tiny green leaves. Hold one in your hand in your imagination, and stare at the palm of your hand. Notice the little seed coat that once held in the alfalfa sprout. Let that alfalfa sprout shrink back in your mind to when it was just a seed.

Now, imagine a fifty-five gallon drum filled with those seeds. By spring imagine all those seeds have been planted and sprouted. Between early spring and mid-summer's day, there is a revolution of growth and change on the surface of the earth, which is called "rapid, explosive growth." Imagine the field that would be big enough for each alfalfa plant to grow to its fullest expression, perhaps four or five feet tall, and maybe three or four feet in diameter. The field stretches on towards the horizon in all directions as far as your eyes can see.

By midsummer, the alfalfa has filled the field. The bees are visiting and beginning to pollinate the flowers. It is midsummer's day and the plants know, "It's time for us to change our focus. Now it is time to turn all that solar energy from now to the end of the warm season into preparation for winter." The same amount of solar energy still goes into the plants but now it's concentrated in causing them to become strong, to be filled with wood. Wood is the manifestation of new growth into hardness, which will allow the plant to spread its seeds.

continued...

The Natural Cycle

Welcome to the Natural Cycle of the Eight Directions. We want to start by feeling the moods of each direction. We'll look first where the sun begins our day—in the eastern sky. As we follow the sun, we also venture into parallel seasons of year and life-stages of every growing thing.

As you read, let yourself experience each direction like a distinct pool of water, and swim not only through what we've written, but also through whatever thoughts and images come to you from your life, your experience. Enjoy.

East

Each day begins at **dawn**, when the radiance of the great fire of the sun glows over the eastern horizon then breaks into sunrise, pouring its light over the land like warm water. Birds lift their voices, heralding the fresh light, the new day. Humans rise from their dreams and plants lean sunward. All visible creation expectantly turns to a new beginning, suddenly renewed with energy.

The season paralleling the time of sunrise is **Spring**. The wet, swelling soil blushes with sprouts of grass and fragile leaves bud like green mist in the trees. Wet little babies stumble into the excitement of life. Daylight lengthens, the air warms, and humans look ahead with energetic plans. Everything in the natural world reaches towards the returning light with enthusiasm, inspiration, and a sense of renewal or rebirth.

If there is parallel time in the journey of a human life, it's the moment of **birth**: when a baby cries into the world of light and oxygen for the first time. Suddenly the horizon looms limitless with possibility: who knows who this little human will become?

The general energy of these times, of the East, is that of tenderness and excited beginnings. The feeling is of renewal, fresh possibilities, and glad welcome; of Excitement and Inspiration.

Southeast

As the sun rises, it arcs, sweeping and climbing southward. By **mid-morning,** the golden ball is in the Southeast of the sky, in mid-climb. Life warms up and kicks into gear, jump-starting into action. The day-light creatures begin the work of the day, the robins establish their worm-hunting grounds or search out the best twigs for nest-building, the humans sharpen their tools, turn on the computers, and motivate themselves into the work du jour.

The parallel season is **late Spring**, when the young plants burst with green growth, rapidly building bodies of foliage that orient to the light, winds, and walls of their environments. Plant energy, devoted to abundant external growth, develops its physical form and orients to its world.

The parallel time in human life is **childhood**, when we measure a child's rapid growth with pencil marks on the walls and bills for ever-new shoes and clothes. Children instinctively follow urges to test out, experiment with, and orient to the surrounding world. They play (watch out!) with the forces of gravity and fire, and they learn so much, becoming sturdily prepared for full lives as adults.

The dominant energy of the Southeast is that of movement, jump-starting into action, rapid external growth; so we focus on Orientation and Motivation.

South

The sun reaches its zenith when it sits enthroned in full glory in the South at **mid-day**, noon solar time. Around this time, the birds immerse themselves in the full-throttled work of feeding and building, while humans are in the full swing of their day—focusing, sweating, out in the fields, inside business meetings, taking classes, working hard. Inertia has been overcome and everyone and everything is in the groove.

The parallel season is **Summer.** Through long days with hot temperatures, the tall, green grasses and other plants flower in bold reds and yellows, enticing shapes, and alluring smells of rose or lavender. At this zenith, the flowers attract

That time between the south and the west, between summer and autumn, is the time of making fruits and seeds and storing energy in roots for other plants. It's a time of internal development, internal preparation. And it is just as profound and powerful as the time of explosive growth.

Jon Young, "Alfalfa"
Seeing Through Native Eyes,
audiotape

NATURAL CYCLE

busy pollinators and provide sensual delight. Humans labor hard to take advantage of the long daylight.

In terms of our human lives, **adolescence** parallels this pinnacle when external growth matches internal development. It is time to center on self, to question and search. If *inspiration* is an in-breath, *perspiration* filters that input into building an identity. Devoting furious energy to "flowering," dressing in name-brand shoes and hip clothes, at this time every action attracts attention. Focus is narrowed and sharpened, and most everything else outside of that focus becomes "uncool." Notice the singularity of vision and action.

The general energy of these times, of the South, is that of hard work and busyness; so we key on Focus and Perspiration.

Southwest

After reaching its peak, the sun lowers itself down into the Southwest at mid-afternoon, but its heat lingers. The plants droop, and the birds and mammals mostly lie silent and still, as they feel the urge to rest and nap. This is **"Siesta."** The insects stay busy, giving voice to this time of day through their buzzing and throbbing tones and rhythms. Lizards move about quickly if they have the shade they need, or take refuge in intense heat. At this time, when the school day ends, work loses productivity, and everyone just wants to take a break, a nap, or a dip.

In terms of the seasons, this is **Late Summer**. The birds' work of nesting and feeding comes to an end and they drift off to get some time alone. The plants dry into shades of gold. Now, fully pollinated, they focus their energy on hardening stems, on producing the internal woody strength that will support the coming fruit.

In terms of a human life, this is the **transition from adolescence to adulthood**, the time to find oneself apart from parents, to develop inner strength for independent adulthood. Nowadays, this could mean college, or perhaps youthful travels, when young leave the protective care of their parents and experience things never before possible. In the midst of this transition comes, hopefully, internalization of identity and ownership of personal gifts. Among cultures whose ancient routines are intact, this is an intense time of training, rites of passage, and initiation into the roles, responsibilities, and spiritual challenges facing adulthood.

Southwest energy is that of internal growth and of taking care of the physical need for rest from the hard work; Relaxation and Internalization.

West

Finally, the **sun sets** more or less in the West—depending on the time of year—signaling the **end of the day**, throwing oranges and pinks from the horizon out over the sky. At this time of day, birds like the squawking geese congregate in flocks to fly to their roost for the night. At this time, humans arrive back home and sit down together to eat dinner and share their exploits. Completion and celebration fill the air.

In terms of seasons, this is the **Autumn**, or the harvest season, when everyone gathers together to reap and celebrate the bounty of the year. Singing and dancing, storing up and giving thanks—the community comes alive. The reds, golds, and crimsons of the autumn leaves reflect the sunset's vibrant colors. In the life-cycle of the plant, this time bears ripe fruit—nuts and squash, corn and apples—finally achieving their fullness to make a contribution to the community.

The parallel stage in a human life, young **adulthood**, one bears fruit that nourishes everyone—either literally in the form of children, or metaphorically in the maturation of vision, role, and identity. Often demonstrated as the abundant productivity of a career, or masterful honing of a set of skills, adulthood marks the time to be of service to the greater whole. The mutual celebration arrives when parents really see their children develop into comrades, friends, and peers.

The essential energy of the West, is that of gathering together, in community, to share our bounty; of Harvest and Celebration.

Northwest

When the sun goes out of sight, light still lingers and slowly fades away into the darkness of night. The true transition to night-time happens at **twilight**, when the sun is in the Northwest, out of sight and behind the Earth. Birds settle in their roosts, and humans prepare for sleep, giving up this day and turning towards the next.

In terms of the seasons, this **Late Autumn** time causes leaves and annual plants to decay back into the earth. Unused crop plants turn back into the ground, as the work of the whole year resigns to the growing darkness. The feeling is of letting go and death. Interestingly, all across the globe, human holidays reflect on death and the passing of ancestors—Halloween, All Soul's Day, Day of the Dead, Shamhain, Ghost Supper.

In terms of a human life, at this time, energetic **adulthood** winds down because children have reached adulthood and age begins to show. Development and attention turn from personal accomplishments to one's place and role in the community as a **teacher or leader**. At this time, one surrenders the past and gleans wisdom from experience. Facing unfinished inner work, at this time we ask, "What did Grandmother or Grandfather do in times like this?" "What will I leave for the next generation?" This is a time of **transition into the role of an elder.**

The energy of the Northwest is that of letting go, of looking back on what has been, and preparing for a role of leadership as an Elder in the community; the growing darkness generates Reflection and Release.

North

The sun sits in the north, firmly on the other side of the Earth, at **midnight**. In this time of deepest darkness, the song birds sleep soundly, so do the humans.

The season is **Winter**. Days are short and nights are cold. Humans seek warmth indoors. They work on crafts, listen to stories, sleep, and dream. The seeds of the plants lie dormant in the ground. The whole year's cycle—and all of the hope for continuation of that species—now lives in a tiny seed.

In human life, this time of **elderhood**, turns hair white like snow, and one becomes less active physically. During this time, patience and wisdom seem fully realized, and the mothering and fathering instincts turn toward the entire community. In a healthy society, Elders take on the subtle and gentle role of passing on culture and values to their many "grandchildren" through storytelling, providing a patient and non-judging ear, and guiding the processes that take children into adolescence, adolescents into adulthood, and adults into the roles and responsibilities of leadership.

The reflection of the Northwest has sifted through all past-experience, and now in the North, essential nuggets of wisdom filter back into community life, just as the work of a plant's life distills into a tiny seed, waiting to integrate back into the next cycle of life.

The general energy of these times, of the North, is that of dormancy, the culmination of experience, of wisdom; of Distillation and Integration.

Northeast

Still out of sight, the sun now moves towards the East, into the Northeast, **pre-dawn**. Light gently seeps into the world, muted and gradual, and yet the stars still twinkle, so one wonders: is this still the night of the previous day or morning of the next? This time holds mystery and uncertainty. The humans are deep in the dream-time of sleep. For many monks, yogis, martial arts masters, and holy men and women, this also happens to be when they wake up to do their practice of prayer and meditation.

In terms of the seasons, the nebulous time when Winter lingers and Spring hesitates, we call the **"Thaw."** In the life cycle of a plant, this time of miraculous spark back to life, the seed mysteriously awakens and secretly germinates, so life begins anew. Maybe this actually marks the "death" of the seed? Perhaps the event marks both new life and the seed's death?

In terms of human life, the Elder gracefully breathes his or her last breath: **death**. But one wonders: Maybe this end begins some other life? The Northeast is a mysterious, or some would say "spiritual" time, when the death of the old twinkles and transforms into rebirth of the new. Some people take note of a special bond between the very old and the very young. Perhaps they each touch this place of mystery.

For in addition to being the place of death, the Northeast undergoes **conception**, a sperm unpredictably gets through to a certain egg, or a dormant seed at last finds all the conditions perfect for germination, suddenly sparking into underground movement. And soon enough, after gestation time—be it a day or so for a plant or nine months for a human baby—a seed shoots its eager head above soil, a baby cries its first breath, the sun returns.

The energy of this Northeast time, therefore, is that of transition from one cycle to the next, of being near the mysterious source of creativity; of the invisible connection between End and the Beginning.

NATURAL CYCLE

Chapter 10
THE NATURAL CYCLE OF LEARNING

We've been with wild kids in the woods without designing ways of orienting to the Natural Cycle, and we've seen disaster. Those colorful cloths linked to directions at The Art of Mentoring program seemed hokey at first, but they turned out to be an incomparably helpful way to shift our mentoring consciousness from crowd control to orchestrating a learning experience.

How to Use this Chapter

This chapter offers detail and flow-charts for using the Natural Cycle to orient Learning:

Orientation for Flow Learning — Use the Flow Learning Cycle as a guide to planning the dynamic flow of an educational experience whether you call it a lesson, activity, outing, course, program, or walk in the woods.

Some Representative Models — Apply the Cycle in a variety of situations. Read through a detailed narrative showing how it works with a "Tracking Club," then study a set of charts showing models of short and long nature courses.

Shifting Direction: Adaptation — Once acting within a planned design, use the Fifty-fifty Principle and Improvisation to observe energy patterns and adjust as needed.

Profiling the Learning Journey — Over time, watch for the cues that help determine the Profile of the Learning Journey with the folks you serve with mentoring to anticipate growth phases and be prepared for passages.

Orientation for Larger Groups and Complex Programs — Mentoring needs low ratios of mentors to participants and outdoor education requires attention to program logistics. The Natural Cycle offers tips for coordinating mentoring teams, grouping participants, and managing programs.

Orientation for Flow Learning

Two decades ago, Joseph Cornell, in his well-loved book *Sharing the Joy of Nature*, developed the idea of a natural rhythm that he named "Flow Learning" for outdoor education. Introducing it, he said, "In leading nature activities over the years, I gradually realized that there was a sequence for using games and activities that always seemed to work best, regardless of a group's age, its mood, or the physical setting. I became convinced that the reason people responded so well to this particular sequence was that it's in harmony with certain subtle aspects of human nature."

Teachers, parents, and outdoor educators have long agreed, and so do we: Cornell's Flow Learning uses a time-honored notion to follow the Natural Cycle:

1) Start by creating **enthusiasm**

2) Move into focusing **attention**

3) Concentrate on direct **experience** of nature

4) Gather and share the **inspiration.**

Cornell's model is brilliant. The Natural Cycle we present is very similar, but more detailed. The Natural Cycle has eight aspects to it rather than four, it develops more subtle energies that are experienced during the learning process, and we apply it not only to educational design but to the entire workings of nature. Many people take away the Natural Cycle as the tool from our workshops, because they can apply it in so many ways: from organizing their lives, to strengthening organizations, to writing songs or papers or books.

Both the Natural Cycle and Flow Learning share one primary assumption: people aren't necessarily ready for focused learning when they show up, such as at the start of a day. So if your teacher routine always begins with instruction, you'll be happier if you climb out of that box. When you begin in the Northeast, listen and watch very carefully to meet the people you mentor where they are at. Take into account what mental and emotional state they will be in when they arrive, and how you can inspire and motivate them into following your lead around the cycle.

The *context* and *timing* of learning is equally, if not more, important than the *content*. A Coyote Mentor always has his or her eyes on both—presenting good information and lessons and activities, but doing so in contexts timed and set up for success. Going with the flow of the Natural Cycle of Learning is critical.

Designing the Flow

Northeast—Open the Learning Experience

Create a ceremonial opening that "shakes off the road dust" and brings everyone to the current time and place. Depending on age and circumstance, this can be anything from a long deep breath, to a "pop-corn" thanksgiving, to a regalia-filled invocation, or a simple song.

East—Inspire

A good way to start is by inspiring, pumping up, filling with enthusiasm (notice the Latin roots, *En + Theo = God inside*). Tell fresh personal stories or rousing hero stories and demonstrate an impressive skill for your listeners. Raise a powerful question in their minds. Create a vacuum within them ready to suck in learning. Look for wide eyes shining with excitement and body language showing eagerness and curiosity.

Southeast—Activate

Activate people into learning. Activate Child Passions to kick them into action. Bridge the gap between excited inspiration and focused learning by being an encouraging coach and an action-based role-model.

This may include getting their bodies moving and ready to pounce with Animal Forms, or getting the group mind chattering to figure out what must be done to track the mystery. This may also include orienting them with clear instructions—explaining ground rules, or creating community agreements. For this phase of transition, from Inspiration to Focused Learning, role-modeling is key.

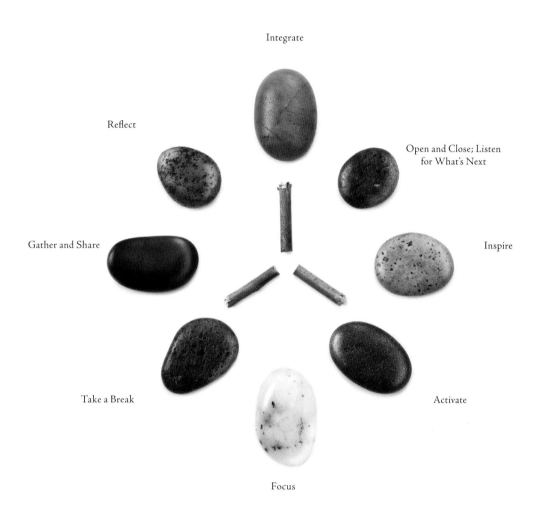

Integrate

Reflect

Open and Close; Listen
for What's Next

Gather and Share

Inspire

Take a Break

Activate

Focus

The moods of the Flow Learning Cycle

NATURAL CYCLE

South—Focus

Channel energy into first-hand experience and focused learning.
Use the Art of Questioning to prolong inspiration and curiosity
as long as you can. During this time "the lesson" shows up.

Plan an activity that may include scientific investigation,
researching field guides, journaling and sketching, mapping
the territory, gathering and counting, building a structure,
making a fire, cooking a meal, or tracking an animal. The lesson can definitely be disguised as a game, but its key ingredient involves mental focus and eventually arrives at "learning
something" whether or not they realize it.

Southwest—Take a Break

After working hard, rest easy. Plan time to allow different
people to finish up the lesson at different paces, to have a
snack, drink some water, or play a casual game while a few
take a nap under an old tree or by a warm rock. This offers
the perfect time to wander around, walking with no agenda or
destination, just flowing like water. Let the efforts of work be
forgotten for a time and take care of your hard-working body
and mind. Be timeless. Think fun games, think laughter, think
afternoon naps.

West—Gather and Share

Using crow calls, drumbeats, or a Song Circle, gather the
refreshed group together to harvest the learning. In community, invite them to show and tell their Story of the Day, adding everyone's contribution to the Map.

From your circle platform, use this time for Mind's Eye
Imagining. Celebrate and be proud of what you've done and
appreciate each other's accomplishments as well. Ask, "What
did we each learn? What was your favorite moment? What
are you thankful for from the day?" Sing songs, break out the
instruments, get happy.

NOTE: In short programs with younger kids, the contact time
with instructors might actually end in the West. But you can

certainly include a quick homework challenge (Northwest), or a short wisdom story, nugget, poem, or reading. (North), and then be sure to end with a closing, however brief (Northeast). Even if your intentional learning program ends in the West, be assured that reflection, integration, and new interest will happen naturally within the home community. When you meet them again, you might check in to see what happened in the night.

Northwest—Reflect

Reflect, look back on the process, ask introspective questions, do some "inner tracking." Go deeper into the story of the day to reflect on its lessons, both natural and human. What do the strewn bones and fur of the rabbit tell us about the nature of survival? Why did I get scared like that? What is that telling me?

For younger kids reflection most often happens on the trail walking back with the instructor to the pickup point, or back at home as they report their news to the family who knows their history. With older kids and adults, suggest talking in small groups, solo journaling, or reflective homework.

North—Integrate

In the North, we now have some nuggets of wisdom that the sifting reflection of the Northwest helped us to find. The thing to do in the North is to take those insights—about ourselves and about the learning process—and integrate them into the rest of our lives. Maybe someone felt extremely helpless during a night-hike with no flashlights. What else in that person's life makes them sometimes feel helpless? Could the strategies used to get them through the night-hike be applied to these other areas of life as well? What are those strategies? When other similar situations arise, exactly what actions will they take in order to create change?

This application of lessons to the big-picture of life could be done around the camp-fire at night, in more intimate one-on-one sessions, or through journaling. They could even take it home. The goal is to offer questions or assignments that turn seemingly isolated, life-specific and short-term learning into long-term wisdom.

Northeast—Close and Listen for what's Next

The Northeast of your lesson plan really begins the next lesson; the northeast prepares the ground for new inspiration. Ceremonially close the past "cycle" and get ready for the next. As the mentor or instructing team, get a cup of tea, slow down, come to your senses, and be receptive to what wants to be the subject of the next Natural Cycle of Learning.

Recall or observe the body-language of the people you mentor to tell you what inspires them, listen to what the weather and the season offer, and notice what surfaces in your own creativity. Like scouts, walk around noticing everything from the front and the back. When the spark of creativity for the next round comes, go with it. Be open to the moment.

Northeast Addendum – Open and Close

Everything begins and ends in the mysterious Northeast. Educationally, this means marking the beginning and ending in a conscious way, so that your teaching time becomes sandwiched between two ceremonial markings, like book-ends. Think, for instance, of the opening and closing ceremony of the Olympics. A ceremonial "opening" shakes off the road-dust or the sleep-crust and brings everyone to the current time and place. A ceremonial "closing" wraps up the experience. When you do this, you allow for transformative growth.

This three-part process is commonly acknowledged and practiced in *Rite of Passage* education:

1) Separation — Do something ceremonially to separate your learning community from the normal, day-to-day tasks so immediate dramas and concerns fall away.

2) Learning/Growth Experiences — Enjoy and take advantage of this "sacred space" you have created, in which the duties and roles of mundane life remain suspended, where you will shape opportunities for transformation and lasting learning.

3) Re-Incorporation — Mark the end of the time with a closing ceremony that re-incorporates everyone, along with the boons and learning gained, back into their day-to-day lives.

Openings and Closings don't have to be elaborate. For a day-long program, the opening can be as simple as singing a song or having a go-round of sharing what each participant feels thankful for. The end may be a mirror reflection of the beginning. Just doing **something** at beginning and end, defines the time of learning. Even at staff meetings, try doing this in order to create a clear space for optimal communication and planning.

However, marking the beginning and end of longer programs—one year or multiple years—can be elaborate. Think of the hoopla, the invisible rituals beginning each school year: back-to-school shopping, parent-teacher socials, opening ceremonies with the principal. Of course, we also remember more about the commotion made at the end of the year: tests, final grades, yearbook signings, and the Big Boom—graduation.

At Yale University, a ceremonial gate marks a sacred place on the land where students may walk through only twice: once when they step onto campus, their first official act as freshmen, and the second time, four years later at graduation, when they walk off the campus. We often invite Elders to sit with the folks we are mentoring through programs, to witness beginning-of-program commitments and goals, and hear end-of-program stories (of course, with acute listening and pointed questioning). You can create your own Rite of Passage traditions and use little ceremonies that open and close them, but remember, always devise ceremonial bookends for even the shortest of times with your learning community.

Applying the Model

Another time-honored tenet of good teaching: theory should be followed up with examples. So, following you will find a set of examples. The Tracking Club Model provides a narrative, showing how mentors organize the event in their minds throughout a half-day tracking adventure with adults on a beach near Santa Cruz, California. This is followed by a set of charts:

+ A generic One-Hour Period with Kids of All Ages

+ A representative Day-Long Outing on Plants

+ A summary of a Five-Day Summer Camp sequence

+ An ambitious School-Year course plan for a Grade Four Science Class working with support from the NatureMapping Program of the University of Washington (with a website inviting you to take on something like this with your classroom www.depts.washington.edu/natmap).

These examples flesh out the theory. Study the ones that approximate your situation and imagine them with your people in your bio-region. We hope they help.

Tips & Thoughts from a Tracking Club

For this edition of *Coyote's Guide to Connecting with Nature*, we want to provide a deeper framework for our readers, and especially for the folks who are out there using this guide as their guide. We have had many conversations about this section, and its importance to this work. This led to discussing the section with some veterans of one Tracking Club. After reviewing the first edition, we edited the older version, and added some feedback for our readers—we hope this will help you in thinking about this model, or similar models in your region.

Our friends from this particular Tracking Club were concerned that readers might get the idea that in order to start a tracking club on their own; they would have to have an infrastructure and a lot of skilled volunteers. They want you to know that this is not the case. This model can work for just a few folks starting out, or a larger group who've been together for ten years. The more seasoned trackers offered some ideas and feedback on this section for us. In the beginning, they assure you, they were not very good at tracking, and had never done this before. With training in the Art of Questioning, humility and openness to feedback from participants and one another, they grew as mentors, trackers, and people. This has been a great experience. The tracking club model is wholly scaleable, and if only a few people show up (besides your volunteer facilitators), then you can just wander from station to station together as a small group. When a lot of people show up, break into groups and circulate through stations. Try to keep your group size small (three to four is ideal, six gets too big), and at least twenty minutes to a station (so it is not too rushed). Less is more in tracking. Offering fewer well-studied stations is preferable to many superficial visits—which can serve to frustrate participants beyond necessity.

For developing new station facilitators it works best to have people who have been to a few Tracking Clubs, experiencing how it works. When they are getting ready to move into the position of station facilitator, it is good to train them (using this book!) on the Art of Questioning. Have them shadow a station facilitator for a few rounds. It's also good for them to see a couple of different experienced people in action—and in between groups at stations—to discuss things with the experienced facilitators. When it is time to become a station facilitator for the first time, have a veteran shadow them for a few groups to help them get started.

In between Tracking Clubs, try to stay in touch by sharing nature stories with one another (by phone, in person, or on internet forums) and work on your own tracking skills (the *Kamana Naturalist Training Program* is great for this, as is the *Shikari Tracker Training Program* available through the Shikari Tracking Guild).

Here's a bit of history and perspective on one local model. It helps to know what others have gone through to get started so that you can learn from the example.

Tracking Club Beginning

This particular Tracking Club started sometime around 1997 with a group of people taking workshops with Jon Young. This group of attendees wanted to push their tracking skills further. They complained that the only time they got together with others who loved tracking as much as they did was when Jon visited their area every few months offering workshops—everyone agreed this was not frequent enough. Jon suggested the group begin a tracking club; similar to the one Jon had started along the Skykomish River in Washington State.

The next time Jon came there was still no tracking club—and the same complaints. Jon reiterated, "Start a tracking club and you can get together every month and track together. This will keep things going for you to learn together as a community." Jon visited once again to conduct a workshop with still no tracking club. It was during his next visit in 1998, that Jon ran a workshop on The Art of Questioning. The day after this workshop the attendees went to a local state park, and "served up a Tracking Club experience." Secretly enrolled local docent volunteers were sent to 'test' the tracking club model. The tracking workshop participants were paired up and placed at stations as tracking club station facilitators for their first Tracking Club gathering. As the "test participants" moved from station to station the docents offered great feedback to help refine the model. With Jon along as the time-keeper they were able to find red-legged frog tracks on the sand dunes—indeed an amazing experience.

That was the first day. Now, ten years later, this particular Tracking Club still persists as a monthly, volunteer-run event. If you would like to read more about Tracking Club models, find help or discuss this more, visit the Shikari Tracking Guild's website (www.shikari.org) and enter the discussion forum for Tracking Clubs.

The Tracking Club Model

The model of the Tracking Club is good to look at as an example of how the Natural Learning Cycle may be applied. Notice small cycles within a larger cycle nested within a still larger cycle. Like the old nesting dolls from Russia, each track and sign station is a small cycle, on a good day; the stations will each be based upon the Natural Cycle. This circle of cycles is the "public" part of the experience nesting within the larger and longer time cycle of the volunteer staff that are lead facilitators, scouts, station facilitators, lead trackers, time keeper, and other support. The staff holding the event come in service to the larger community of participants, while serving their own desire to learn and grow in their skills of nature connection.

Staff and volunteers arrive at 7 AM and stay after participants have departed to debrief the entire experience. Adults, teens, and family participants arrive at 7:45 AM, the program runs from 8 AM to around 11:30 AM depending on the weather, the group's interest level, and the tracks themselves.

Northeast for Staff – Minds Together & Service Intentions Set 7:00 AM

The volunteer scouts and staff facilitators arrive at the tracking site, grateful to be together so early in the morning. This is the best time to track since everything is pristine; the ground still holds moisture, and most of the year the sun comes across the tracks at a great angle. Everything in the early morning sun is beautiful. The lead facilitator usually acknowledges the beauty and reminds everyone of the need to be in service to participants arriving later that morning. Someone will offer a brief kick-off to start a Thanksgiving circle. Others may contribute with a quick Northeast round of gratitude. This creates a space for everyone to set aside their "grocery lists" enabling them to "see" this place and each other. The birds' alarms speak of hawks and coyotes. This magical time for volunteers and staff establishes anticipation as everyone excitedly begins to relish the stories left by the tracks from the night.

East for Staff – Inspiration & Goals 7:15 AM

One of the lead facilitators of the scout team will help set the tone for the team by bringing to mind what phase the moon was in last night, what the weather is doing or has done recently. Usually seasonal ecology is discussed and predictions made about sign and track to be found, anticipating some interesting stories. The group may have a quick discussion about projected attendance for the day to plot out routes and goals. Much may be gleaned at this time, scouts and staff break off individually to search out all the likely places.

Southeast for Staff – Track Station Errands at 7:25 AM

The volunteer scouts head out looking for "berries for Grandma's pie"—in this case the berries are really fun and engaging sites where tracks have been found called "tracking stations"; the pie is the Tracking Club. After scouting, they gather up and begin to share their findings. Noticeably animated, they distill the best things they have found:

"There's a badger trail across the sand between the dunes, it's so clear, it's so perfect!"

"Whoa. I found some great coyote tracks where the male and female tracks braid down the beach. I think they're licking the kelp!"

"I found some really tricky mouse tracks that obliterate partially at least, the front foot of a brush rabbit. The other foot is visible and the nails are clear in the damp earth. This will be a great station to build mystery …"

South for Staff – Tracking Club Focus Begins 7:45 AM

The team of staff, scouts, and volunteers are about to become interpreters at each station of track and sign, and selected individuals will remain at each station until the last group of participants moves by. One will become a time-keeper, and any remaining others will rove to "trouble shoot," helping with questions. The South truly kicks in as the team reviews their stations deciding on an order and a flow for the participant groups. They set up between three and six stations, or mentoring locations, and will rotate small groups from the badger through the coyotes. Decided in a hurry, the stations arise from: 1) the pick of the tracks; and then 2) ease of location; 3) proximity to one another (a time-keeper keeps folks moving); and 4) varied landscapes (to examine different substrates with tracks).

Now it is time to turn attention to the arriving group. Brace yourself, for the South mind does not dissipate for three hours to come! It requires focus on the part of the staff to hold the intention of the day, to represent the stations for the lessons they present—both intended and unintended, and for the station facilitators to facilitate.

Northeast for Participants Begins – Team Transitions from Staff Cycle to Participant Cycle 7:45 AM

During this time, cars start to pull into the parking lot near the tracking site. Some of the volunteers are there—greeting new folks, welcoming veterans, and orienting people. Some are down near the tracking site, collecting arrivals into a group and sharing general conversation—dropping hints of the finds of the day. Still other volunteers are out at the site, making last minute preparations, and keeping the delicate substrate situations safe from accidental erasure by passing feet. Everyone is told by email or on the website to arrive at 8 AM, though often there are stragglers until 8:30 or beyond—it is best to start at 8 AM for whomever is there.

As people gather, rumors circulate about the really cool stuff on the beach this morning. No one knows the details of the cool stuff except the scouts, but awesome mysteries await. A special visitor we haven't seen in a while too, the badger! People who arrive early move around a bit more quickly and finish their to-go cups of steaming beverages. They also act, unwittingly perhaps, as the "east network" helping us build the charge for the day by talking to each other and guessing who the special visitor might be. Someone always guesses cougar.

Northeast for Participants – Opening Words 8:00 AM

The group gathers in a circle, away from the street noise, but not yet near the tracks. One volunteer begins the circle with a brief thankful welcoming greeting to bring everyone to the present. Smell the scent of the season. Listen to the wind. Feel the sun peaking over the ridge and the gentle air. Look at those beautiful, puffy clouds, Ahhh. Watch as the birds settle back into song. Wow.

East for Participants – Welcome, Introductions & Overview 8:10 AM

The chosen facilitator gives a quick overview of the day after sharing Thanksgiving words. Hints are given and stories told. Staff offer suggestions for group selection and organization. After staff and volunteers are introduced the group process begins with people sharing their names, where they are from, how many times they've been to the Tracking Club, and often a short, but cool nature story—especially a recent one, or something they are thankful for.

Southeast for Participants – Facilitate Group Flow 8:25 AM

The learning elements are explained: stations, small groups, time keeping, moving between stations, and call-outs. The timekeeper demonstrates the "crow call" that will be used to move groups when it is time to move. Next, the big group is divided into manageable, evenly sized small groups. The number of groups is the number of stations. We try to divide up by skill level, so the station guide can focus on everyone. The large group is directed to follow the staff volunteers at varying experience levels who have their hands raised, thus self-selecting into today's work groups. Each group is given a number matching the station number, and goes with that numbered station facilitator to the track stations, i.e. Group 1 follows station facilitator 1 to the badger tracks; Group 2 follows station facilitator 2 to the coyote tracks; Group 3 lines up with their leader, and so on.

South for Participants – Focus on Track & Sign 8:30 to 10:30 AM

Here's where the real work begins for the participants and station facilitators alike. All groups move to the stations and some of them already go deeply into the Art of Questioning. Each station facilitator has a method of bringing the participants into the lesson, but they all agree to keep everyone wondering. Through the Art of Questioning, the stories at each station build with every observation—intensified by the many eyes, minds, and perspectives on the track, sign, and surrounding ecology.

Cycles within a Cycle – Stations as Mini Cycles

A skilled station facilitator with some training, modeling, a bit of time and experience can increase both the learning experience and fun for participants, while honing deep tracking and nature connection into their own learning. This is the reward for serving as a volunteer at the Tracking Club. To provide the experience of the Natural Cycle, the Art of Questioning, and other Core Routines as a method for bringing participants into a nature connection experience within the context of Tracking.

Each tracking station cycle can employ a brief Northeast moment to open the learning experience offered at that station, helping people feel present and ready. The East begins when the station facilitator shares stories of the track and sign discovered during the morning scout, throwing in some natural history, and building each new group's perspective to inspire. The Southeast begins by activating the group's engagement with the track, sign, and landscape, maybe even using some imitation. The South kicks in by sharing questions, offering perspectives, and adding more field ecology and science. When foreheads wrinkle, and in the context of the time allotted, the station facilitator senses it is time to take a break. At this point the Southwest kicks in; perhaps folks drink some water, share a snack, a body stretch, or even do a quick sensory check-in. The West follows with a "gather & share" recapitulation of the station, making observations with new perspectives celebrated, and individuals honored for their contributions.

"Two minutes … almost time to move …" the call out is given …

A quick point of reflection is offered, the Northwest, wrapping thoughts and observations, trailing questions offered over shoulders. On a good day, a station facilitator can offer a bit of wisdom from the North just before the group disperses to the next station—an integrating principle offered from the context of track and sign knowledge, of group experience, and ecological awareness. The group goes away with some parting words, a thank you, and a reminder to pay attention to the birds, wind, and landscape along the way— back to the Northeast on their way to the next mystery.

Back to the Participant Cycle – A Larger Perspective

Hours pass as groups shift from focusing on each set of tracks. Watching from a distance an observer will see participants laughing, straining, literally running their fingers through their hair in frustration and intent study. This is a South kind of day!

It's like watching trackers take a test and play a game at the same time. No one ducks the Art of Questioning and everyone has a blast. Time passes very quickly. The groups each begin to lag and straggle. The timekeeper and coordinator help move things along between stations because even facilitators lose track of time when the mystery is good—which it always is.

Usually, the staff group aims to wrap up stations by 10 to 10:30 AM; this always depends on the weather, the tracks, the number and interest of participants and staff, which varies each time.

Southwest for Participants – Take a Break 10:30 AM

After completing their investigations for all stations, trackers disappear to the bio-break facilities. Some sip from water bottles and eat their snacks while watching the birds while others continue to focus on mouse tracks. Some imitate the bobcat tracks to know which way it was looking. Over all, blessed and relaxed chaos reigns. Most of the station facilitators gather up with the coordinator to discuss what information was processed and how the stories changed and deepened. They quickly agree on how the debrief should proceed; in which order the station facilitators will speak, and how much time there is for each of their reports. They will also discuss opportunities for participants to interject their thoughts, deciding when the most experienced trackers should share, and to what level of detail. Most everyone is mentally tired by now, and it's good to be clear and succinct at this point in the day.

West for Participants – Gather & Share 10:40 AM

Everyone anxiously gathers together, anticipating solutions to their puzzles. Shooting each other glances, everyone fidgets, moving from foot to foot. Now, together they harvest the stations with the station facilitators summarizing the trends of questions and theories that came from the different groups. Honor goes to those who made great guesses or demonstrated some special zeal. Laughter always accompanies this part of

the day. Each station facilitator will ask what was learned or enjoyed by the group. The facilitators often have to prompt discussion and touch on highlights that were missed, and ask for feedback. Finally, the volunteers reveal the Mystery Answers—or sometimes not. Even the station facilitator admits absence of scientific proof.

Northwest for Participants – Reflections on the Day 11:10 AM
The most experienced trackers speak up now and share the trends that tie all the stories together. How the two coyotes come here every day for the last several months. They descend from the hills on the other side of the highway and use the culvert to cross through the willows. For the first time, some of these people look up and around again. They look back over the parking lot with searching and questioning expressions. They feel the intrigue build as the tracks come to life. Movies are playing in their heads.

North for Participants – Integration until Next Time 11:20 AM
The leader of the team makes quick announcements for next time or other related activities, and the senior member of the team shares some nugget of wisdom about badgers and tracking and how this can really help our local conservation community monitor the rare, threatened, and endangered species. The summary reveals wisdom about tracking's time-honored role to serve the people and gives thanks that it still does. Everyone breathes differently. Their body language shifts yet again as their eyes now indicate self-reflection. They begin to see their own lives weave with other people and with the animals themselves.

Northeast for Participants – Gratitude & Closing 11:25 AM
The person who opened the circle steps up again. She or he says, "Remember how happy and grateful we felt for all the things of this world when we first gathered this morning?" The group voices agreement woven through interlocking sounds and gestures. "Do we still feel this? I know I do!" The agreement deepens. Thanks go to the volunteers and participants for driving safely and bringing friends and families. Everyone is asked to bring good stories home to our loved ones. We all disperse from the circle; some wander to revisit the stations they are most interested in.

Back to the Staff Cycle, Southwest for Staff – Break 11:30 AM
Now it's time for the staff and volunteers to take a short break. During break time they will wander with participants to wrap up conversations perhaps

visit with friends or hang out by the vehicles for a bit. This is also a good time to grab a snack, get a drink or satisfy other needs.

West for Staff – Debrief Circle 11:45 AM

The station facilitators often get together for a few minutes afterwards to discuss how things went:

* Did everyone have a good experience?

* Did things run smoothly?

* Did it feel good?

* What could be better?

* Do we want to do something special next time?

* How do we get more people to come out?

Northwest for Staff – Experience & Mentoring 12:15 PM

Ideally the more experienced trackers help mentor the station facilitators on their journey by providing tips, helpful information, and skills in tracking or natural history. The mentors can also offer "homework" to follow up on for those inclined to take things a bit further. Natural history journals are often filled in at this time; logging weather specifics, listing species seen through track and sign, recording which birds were observed. The mentoring approach offers a core group of people the benefit of learning on their own during recreational journeys. Coordination of this team ensures that someone will always be there to run the Tracking Club if others cannot attend.

North for Staff – The Fabric of a Learning Community 12:30 PM

Now the "elders" of the staff community speak to the overall experience of the Tracking Club. How does this community of staff best support the larger community of interested participants? How does this work fit into the larger network of community-based learning in the region, in the country, and internationally? There are affiliates all over the world learning and developing models like Tracking Club and sharing with one another through a variety of means. Discussions about community development initiatives take place between staff, volunteers and experienced participants. At this point we review what will happen during the time between the next Tracking Club.

Northeast for staff – Until Next Time… 12:45 PM

A quick renewal of thankfulness for a good day of fun and learning, and away we all go. Tired, but very, very satisfied, we know people will dream of animals tonight and will look with new eyes at the forests and fields surrounding their own homes and families.

The Tracking Club in Conclusion

Over time we learn from this experience how to facilitate a better experience for participants and ourselves. The questions that come up from participants shape our approach, as we follow their interests and direct them with questions. Their questions often lead us to look at the tracks and their interpretation in a new way. Each group coming through a station adds something to the story and we end up with a fuller understanding of the tracks. Between stations, we usually have a couple of minutes to contemplate the bigger story around the tracks, investigate unresolved questions, or find new directions to lead the next group.

We typically run through some or all of the "who, what, when, where, why, and how" questions. New station facilitators needn't be intimidated by trying to remember all of this, just go with what you know. If you haven't had training in the cycles, it may take a while to get into rhythm. We suggest that the six questions be used for the initial framework. They are easy to remember, and the investigation of just these questions is broad and endlessly deep.

Although you may not run your Tracking Club exactly like this, work to hit all of the elements in your own way. We feel it is essential in mentoring to make it your own, delivering it in an authentic way. It is important to remember the model it comes from and to constantly refer back making sure not to miss anything. As time goes by we anticipate some people will not have all of this explained to them, it may even get watered down a bit, or not used wisely. Having Tracking Club referenced in *Coyote's Guide* is a valuable tool, even for those of us who have been participating for a long while.

Representative Models

One-Hour Period with Kids of All Ages, any topic

Cycle	Amount of Time	Activity
Northeast - Open	5 min	Circle up, give a yip of thanksgiving.
East - Inspire	10 min	Inspire with a story or demonstration.
Southeast - Activate	5 min	Break into small groups and move outside with crisp instructions and clear boundaries.
South - Focus	20 min	Coach each group to do a twenty-minute game or project.
Southwest - Take a Break	5 min	Relax, fool around, and finish up. Water break.
West - Gather and Share	10 min	Circle up for map or story of the day with a few folks reporting for their comrades.
Northwest - Reflect	3 min	Keep the embers burning with a follow-up activity—a challenge or "super-secret mission" to do at home.
North - Integrate	1 min	Leave a question or weave a story to leave them thinking.
Northeast - Close	1 min	End with a renewed yip of thanks for the time of fun and learning.

Day-long Outing (9am-3:00pm) in Late Spring, topic Edible Plants

Cycle	Time of Day	Activity
Northeast - Open	9:00 am	Gather in community. Play a plant-focused circle name game, go-round sharing what they feel thankful for in the moment.
East - Inspire	9:15 am	Tell a story like "Surviving on Greens" and announce our activities for the day—to make a wild edible meal!
Southeast- Activate	10:00 am	Play "Plant Concentration" game. Take a peek at a selection of plants you've hidden under a bandana, then run out to find their matches and share their larder locations. Give instructions and rules for a Plant Scavenger Hunt, and then give small groups a pouch for gathering wild edibles.
South - Focus	11:00 am	Go out in groups and gather in the field. The goal: collect, identify, and draw as many edible plants as you can. Use field guides and journal sketching to identify and imprint finds, teaching and tasting safe plants as you go.
Southwest - Take a Break	12:30 pm	Gather back together in big group for lunch. Each group lays out its plants and sketches around the circle. Break. Play some fun games, "Eagle Eye" or "Sleeping Fawn."
West - Gather and Share	1:30 pm	Call in a Sharing Circle: Each person shows one plant he/she gathered and sketched and puts it in the bowl in the middle. Each group tells their story. Sing a happy song!
Northwest - Reflect	2:30 pm	Assemble all gathered plants into one big salad. Pretty up with wild flowers, add some dressing, and pass around to taste in silence.
North - Integrate	2:45 pm	Give out homework challenge of finding one edible plant around home that we learned today and teach it to their parents.
Northeast - Close	2:50 pm	Close with a child-friendly song of thanks for plants or a sharing of one thing each person feels thankful for from their day of learning.

5-Day Summer Camp Program, topic *The Book of Nature*

Each of the five days follows a complete cycle, but without the North or Northwest directions (which we hope they'll do at home with parents). Days focus on chapters of the Book of Nature.

Cycle	Day and Chapter	Activity
	Pre-program	The site is permitted and prepared. Resources and nature tables are set up, equipment is checked and ready. 40 kids age 6-12 show up and are organized by age into 4 groups of 10 with 2 instructors for each group. Sign in, capture the last medical forms, and touch in with families.
Northeast and East – Open and Inspire	Day 1 Awareness and Hazards	NE Welcome with appreciation, jump start with easy active icebreaker games. E Tell "Founder Story" – (we tell of Jon Young, Tom Brown, Ingwe) to inspire Core Routines and set tone. SE Play name games and build group identity. Create common sense ground rules – respect self, others, and Earth. S Play Awareness games centered on using all the senses, exploring hazards, and expanding comfort zones, like Eagle Eye, Fire Keeper, etc. SW Wander back, lunch, and check-ins. W Story of the Day around real and perceived dangers, mention the alarm calls of birds. NE End with a group callout of thanksgiving.
Southeast and South - Activate and Focus	Day 2 Motivating Species, Mammals and Tracking	NE Excite with running, jumping, body-flexing games. Get happy. E Tell a hero story to inspire excitement around Motivating Species, Mammals, and Tracking. Suggest the Six Arts of Tracking. SE Practice Animal Forms that involve catching, eating, climbing, and hiding. Play Animal Forms games such as Otter Steals Fish, Run Rabbit Run! or Cougar Stalks Deer. S Play Tracking games with Animal Cards. Ask Who, What, When, Where, Why? SW Lunch and Explore Field Guides. Questioning and Answering. W Story of the Day makes a group map that marks where you found animal tracks. Go back and show it to other participants, instructors, or parents. NE Wrap with a thankful song and a challenge.

Southwest - Take a Break	Day 3 Plants and Wandering	NE Wake up the senses with games that tap into Child Passions. Invite each to share what they love in nature. E Tell your own story to encourage awareness of plants and aidless navigation. SE Play "Plant Concentration." S Take a Big Long Wander. Practice Body Radar and go on a Plant scavenger hunt. Hide and Seek. Gather for Mapping. SW Long lunch and time for Exploring Field Guides and Journaling. Notice the baseline twitter of birds. Play games like Get Lost or Sleeping Fawn. W Scavenger hunt check-in as Story of the Day and eating Wild Edibles. NE Wrap with singing a plant song and an Errand.
West - Gather and Share	Day 4 Community and Ecology	NE Gather with active cooperative games. Be thankful for each other and all our natural relations. E Tell any story or legend about teamwork, community cooperation, or peaceable kingdoms. SE Play Exploration Team or Wildlife Survey, find the connections between things. S Do a team challenge, like Shelter Building, Blindfold Caterpillar, or Group Sit Spot. SW Lunch and Capture the Flag or other big group game (you might combine small groups for this). NE Wrap with a Sharing Circle, appreciate everything from the earth to the stars, the ancestors and the children of the next generations.
Northwest and North - Reflect and Integrate Northeast - Close	Day 5 Trees and Survival	NE Gather with active games E Do a Bow-drill fire demo or inspire with Survival stories. (Mention how the language of Birds helps hunters.) SE Play Tree-Tag S Play Survival Scenario, 5-Minute Fire, or Meet-a-Tree SW Lunch, check-ins, Exploring Field Guides and Journaling to finish up sketches, or note things to remember. W Story of the Day. Survival Priorities reflection. NE Ceremonial Potluck with parents, giving thanks and honoring each group's participants and instructors, marking the end of the week.

NATURAL CYCLE

The Natural Cycle of Learning | 231

School-Year course in a Grade Four science classroom with 30 students, topic NatureMapping.

Each unit follows one complete cycle and it installs and practices core routines. Remember to begin and end with gathering up and giving thanks.

The Classroom teacher, supported by the NatureMapping Program of the University of Washington, maintains the goal to "keep common animals common" and to preserve biodiversity. This approach trains individuals to know what's on their land by providing the tools to inventory and monitor their resources and to encourage land management decisions that sustain and restore.

To gather your own support, please address our friend Karen Dvornich: vicon@u.washington.edu, http://depts.washington.edu/natmap/

Cycle	Unit	Activity
Northeast -Open	Set-Up	Set-up. Recruit, schedule, and train teaching team. Set parameters for study; design the year curriculum. Your classroom's goal: to inventory and monitor 30 species of flora and fauna that are indicators of your area's 6 habitat types and provide scientific data to NatureMapping Program. Identify your habitats and species lists. Set-up nature tables oriented to 8 directions; set up gathering circle. Have a kick-off celebration with staff and students (and maybe your local mayor or other dignitaries) to begin ceremonially, showing the community importance of the task that lies ahead.
East- Inspire	Late summer	Excite them with big picture of the year ahead. Start with field trips to a NatureMapping Center and to your school site with a NatureMapping leader. Take nature names by 6 habitat types and 30 species, and establish 6 habitat clans and 5 species societies (animal, plant, tree, bird, and other). Establish Sit Spots by habitat and begin sitting, journaling, and inventorying species in your range. End with a guided tour of all Sit Spots. Work in clans to produce a group wall mural of landscape habitat types. Introduce routines of Thanksgiving and Expanding our Senses – through Owl Eyes and blindfold games. Teach leave-no-trace etiquette and hazards.
Southeast- Activate	Fall	How to spot wildlife on the move. Visit Sit Spots regularly. Pace 100 feet out from center and map features of topography, soil, plants, water, trails. Keep inventory of all wildlife observations. Introduce awareness and invisibility through the five voices of birds. Introduce animal empathy through animal forms and the five arts of tracking. Go on tracking expeditions and set out soot traps. Explore field guides and understand range maps. Study use of plants for food and shelter and create plant-animal habitat terrain. End with a Thanksgiving show-n-tell day for parents.

South-Focus	Early Winter	Monitoring and tracking methods: Demonstrate NatureMapping NatureTracker software at the NatureMapping Center. Learn the scientific requirements for mapping habitat types, for how to locate longitude/latitude, and how to keep data on Excel spreadsheets. Plot everyone's Sit Spot on the wall mural by latitude/longitude from GPS equipment. Download aerial photo and plot Spots on it. On PowerPoint, show layers of overlay on your site maps. Make a group plan. Set up teams. Start gathering scientific data. Solve problems.
Southwest-Take a Break	Midwinter	Take a midwinter break. Change the scene. Stay warm inside! Do a short unit on crazy animal perception strategies! Play some games!
West-Gather and Share	Early Spring	Monitor and report in earnest in a sense of service to the community. Start with a Bio-blitz, a twelve hour Rapid Assessment for as many taxa as possible; then compare data with predictions. NatureMapping professional naturalists support Bio-blitzes. What's gone? What's new? Continue to monitor daily weather, plant growth, bird migration, and mammal sign. Routinely come together to pool findings and troubleshoot problems. Move Sit Spot journals into spread sheets using codes and upload to NatureMapping website.
Northwest-Reflect	Mid Spring	Native American natural history in your area: Begin with Spring Equinox Celebration (March 21). Repeat Bio-blitzes as season progresses. Distinguish residents from visitors. Continue through end of year. Invite extension of this to individuals' sites outside of school. Research natural history topics of your area. Interview community elders. How were plants used? What stories did locals tell about wildlife and human development?
North-Integrate	Late Spring	Individual projects: Excite with a twenty-four hour overnight Bio-blitz to visit the nightlife. Coordinate students and other participants to follow up on personal passions. Wrap the learning up. Demonstrate individual Sit Spots. Tell stories of natural history research. Create a portfolio of the whole project. Find permanent homes for the terrariums. Complete the wall mural replete with all species.
Northeast-Close	June	Finale and Rite of Passage. Send your final info to NatureMapping. Hold ceremony with parents to tell your Story of the Year, and to receive award for good work from NatureMapping or other community leaders.

NATURAL CYCLE

The Natural Cycle of Learning | 233

Shifting Direction: Adaptation

The Flow Learning design sets you up for success. However, good design takes not only forethought, but also experimentation. You try things out and you learn what works—and what doesn't. There are no mistakes, just learning experiences. Flexibility and spontaneity are essential to success. There are going to be a lot of times when you'll need to adapt your plans to fit opportunities that fly in from left field. You'll go through the Natural Cycle yourself as you plan, implement, reflect, and reintegrate ideas to make the learning flow.

Once in the throes of acting out a plan, you can use the Natural Cycle to adapt to whatever energy actually shows up. Carry the qualities of the Eight Directions drawn on the palm of your hand and continually check-in with the mood of the moment. Make attitude adjustments!

When folks don't respond to your plan, ask yourself, "What energy are they manifesting instead?" What does their body language tell you? Are you trying to begin on the Eastern Plains of Inspiration but it feels like a late Southwest afternoon in the Wetland of Weariness? Maybe you feel determined to climb up the Steep Mountains of South Focus but your people are in a private reflective mood that feels much like an Ancient Forest of Northwest Stories? Were you just settling into a fine West sense of group unity when an eagle screeched in overhead with a shot of East excitement?

What energy do your people really exhibit? What energy flows from the season? Check yourself for the time of day and the birds' behavior right now? Is the sun or wind too much right at this moment? How has a sudden emergency or opportunity shifted the group awareness? How will you shift direction?

The 50-50 Principle

Coyote offers a principle giving you permission to "go with the flow" and adapt your plans as necessary. Spontaneity is essential and attentiveness to this necessity has given rise to a guiding tenet we call the **50-50 Principle**.

Plan all your allotted time, with half of it structured and half **unstructured**. It can mean this: after you plan everything out for a program, you go into that time expecting only about 50% of what you plan will actually happen, and the other 50% will consist of unplanned improvisation playing off of what nature provides that day. This could be a long Wander that you plan for 50% of your time. Or, it could be that you plan less, knowing that up to 50% of the time will get unexpectedly filled with in-the-moment opportunity.

Scenarios

Following a Frog

Let's say, in leading your group you have their attention and curiosity for teaching about a tree; you move them toward a game where they smell it and touch it and compare its leaves with the other nearby plants. Your plan is working beautifully into the South. Then suddenly—a frog jumps onto the path. All the participants instantly forget about the tree. Their bodies take over and they chase into the bushes after the frog. What would you do?

The 50-50 Principle suggests mentally checking in with the Natural Cycle. What just happened? You were in a South moment when that frog brought a huge dose of Southeast motivation. (How do I know this? Well they actually MOVED into a new formation all on their own. They were self-motivated).

After the frog disappears into the brush, ask some quick questions. How high is the level of inspiration over the frog? Are they more excited about the frog than the tree game? If so, can you shift your plans and make the frog the beginning of a new, albeit unplanned, Flow Learning mini-lesson? How can the East/Southeast opportunity from the frog be converted in-to the South for study? Could frog biology, or frog handling, become the lesson of the day?

"Hey, you want to try to catch it? Oh, cool, you got it, Sarah…Now look, let's make sure we don't hurt it…Yeah, get some water on your hands and hold it gently just like that, and let's not hold it too long because its skin could be hurt from the salt on our hands. But—wooww!—check out these colorful little spots right under its chin! What is this, anyway? Yeah, I think it's a frog, too. But what if it's a toad? How do you tell the difference? Oh, I see, cool, where'd you learn that? Does it look like it has a full belly? What do these guys eat anyways? Flying insects, eh? Remember that place with all those flies? What if we went there to look for more frogs? Do you know where frogs like to hang out? No? Well, check it out. There's a cool section in this field guide about where to find frogs. Here, find the picture of this frog in the book, and see if we can figure out what kind of frog it is. What color is it? Does it have ridges on the side of its body? Wow! Look at this other crazy-colored frog. What is that?" It wasn't in the plans, but if you can adapt, suddenly nature has offered you a whole new lesson.

Warren and the Skull

Warren was leading a group of ten kids on a Wander through the woods. He had them in a "super-sneak scout formation," all fox-walking in a line, with front and back scouts, and everyone stretching their senses for

My first period 8th grade English class was reading Ken Kesey's One Flew Over the Cuckoo's Nest, the part where McMurphy crows about the dangers of being "hypnotized by habit." After class, Jimmy—ordinarily a punctual straight-A student—didn't leave his chair. .

"Why are you staying here?" I asked, "You're going to get into trouble for cutting second period History."

When he did get in trouble with my team teacher in History and explained he was practicing "not being hypnotized by habit," his consequence was an assignment to write a paper about the value of his experience. The next day he returned with his paper titled "Cultural Education."

He made five points about how Period 1 and Period 2 English, although taught by the same teacher with the same lesson plan, differed. The group of students was different. They brought in a whole different set of group dynamics and learning styles. The time of day was different. They were still sleepy in first period, more awake in second. English came before History first period, and after it second period, so the first students were imprinting the concept for the first time, the second group was fitting new information into an existing pattern. The teaching was different—first period the teacher was trying her lesson the first time, some pieces were full of excitement, some were blurry; by the second time around, the

continued...

sight or sound of any animals that might be lying in wait to "ambush" them. (**Northeast**) In this heightened mode of sensory input, the kids suddenly noticed lots of animal holes in the ground, and scat that they hadn't seen before. Then, one of the kids spotted a bone just off the trail. They were psyched! (**East**) They excitedly searched around and then, after digging after a few bones lodged in the dirt, they found the prize of prizes: a skull! (**Southeast**)

Now Warren pulled a **Southeast-to-South** Coyote Judo move: he pulled out a field guide. He saw a path of action for their excitement to travel down. He also role-modeled enthusiasm about this cool book and what opportunity lay in looking through it. "Let's figure out what this is! Want to?" All the kids shouted their reply, "Yeah!!!"

Kids gathered around him as he held the field guide so everyone could see into it. (**South**) Warren wanted to prolong the inspiration of the skull to yield as much learning as possible. So in looking through the field guide, he began with the pictures of the skulls least likely to be this particular skull. He started with deer skulls, asking them questions to get them comparing and therefore taking the skull in their hands: "What are the eye-sockets like? Oh, they actually look more of an oval-shape and not as big. Hmmm … Well, what about the teeth? Do the teeth look alike? No, huh? Yeah, they *are* sharper. What do you think these teeth are designed to eat? Yeah, meat, you're probably right …"

During this series of questions, Warren noticed by watching body language that focus was waning. They lost their original inspiration, started to change the subject or stare off into space. So he flipped the page to a picture of another type of animal skull …"Maybe this is it!" The kids who had been fading—bam!—they came back inspired again. (**East**) Looking at this new possible match, Warren asked them new questions, slyly teaching them the basics of skull ID: (**South**) "What's this dilly-wack on the top of their head? Oh, look, the book calls that "an occipital ridge." What a strange name! Oh, and this tells how many teeth this animal has in its skull. How many does our skull have?" And then when the energy waned again, he would flip again ... and then again ... and again.

By now the kids had imprinted "search images" that they instantly looked for in each picture: overall shape of skull, teeth type and number, shape and relative size of eye sockets, occipital ridge vs. no occipital ridge. They were now dialed into the process of skull identification. And finally, after looking at almost every other possible animal in the book, (**East to South to East to South**) they came upon the matching picture—they instantly *knew* it, beyond a doubt—an opossum skull! They yipped and high-fived. (**Blast of West Celebration**)

After such an awesome learning experience, they deserved a break. So Warren led them to an open field where they happily played a game of tag. (**Southwest**) Then they tiredly slumped into a circle and shared about the day, almost everyone saying that the coolest part was finding the skull and then figuring out what it was. (**West, Story of the Day**) By then, their parents arrived and boy were they excited to tell what they found that day. (**North**)

Improvisation

The 50-50 Principle gets a whole lot easier when, as the instructor, you accumulate a large tool box complete with a wide variety of knowledge you can draw from anytime. Your teaching will relax because of your toolbox full of techniques and you will feel ample space to perceive people's passions so you can change on the fly.

The 50-50 Principle balances your intentions with spontaneity. So, it calls for Improvisation. Musician, teacher, and writer, Stephen Nachmanovich, says it well when he writes that improvisation entails "a delicate balance of sticking to your guns and remaining open to change." Improvisation involves a genuine sense of play, the same sense that Coyote models for us. Improvisation expects risks: go out-on-a-limb, be willing to fall and ready to get back up, laugh, and keep your eyes open for the next turn. Improvisation is quintessential edge-walking.

Forget the modern image of the teacher as some authoritarian armored tank without a weakness or flaw. Get into the mud and muck, slip into the learning of the moment

excited pieces were dulled, the blurry pieces sharpened. And finally, in second period, there was a new fish in the school so the swimming patterns were both excited and disrupted by Jimmy's odd presence.

This amazingly insightful paper got him out of trouble!

So, even in our modern classroom, the lesson plan is not the lesson. Everything in the culture contributes to what each student takes away as "learning."

ELLEN HAAS, Cultural Education

with everyone else, be vulnerable and human and authentically in awe of life's surprises. Art creates a fine balance between dedicated study (planning) and in-the-moment creativity (improvisation).

Adaptation and Improvisation mix to make mentoring an art, a spiritual practice that connects you to the source of creativity, that forces you to surrender to and work with the process of unfolding life, that aligns you with the Tao, that lets you in on the magic behind the trick, that floats you in mid-current of the Natural Cycle.

Profiling the Learning Journey

We also want to give you insight about how the Natural Cycle profiles a person's learning journey through long-term mentoring. Of course, the model we present here is NOT black and white. To begin with, everyone arrives at a different level of learning. Every single person takes unpredictable routes and detours on their journeys. This Profile of the Learning Journey describes patterns and tendencies we've observed to fit both the sequence and the archetypal energies of the eight directions. Knowing about the potential of Profiling will help you anticipate and visualize people's learning edges at any given time, and so, serve them better.

Even though Nature Connection best describes our learning objective in this book, the natural progression of the Profile Journey could be used to track the progress of anyone learning anything: marketing, medicine, martial arts, music, or magic tricks. Whatever the "platform" for those you mentor, using this Profile keeps you thinking one step ahead, anticipating their next phase. When the time comes for the actual phase-shift, you will be prepared and ready to provide wise guidance.

Mentoring

According to the original meaning of the word, a "mentor" guides the learning journey for another. In Homer's ancient Greek epic, *The Odyssey*, Mentor, an old "helmsman," sits at the back and steers the boat and takes a searching young prince to sea to find his father, the King. But really, Mentor guides so the weak-kneed prince will find his own "inner King" and step into his rightful role. Who hides behind the form of this old man, Mentor? None other than Athena, the Goddess of Wisdom, who carries an owl on her shoulder. Athena, through Mentor, arms young Telemachus, awakens him to his own inner wisdom, and sends him on his way full of strength and pride.

The awareness of the profile journey will orient your navigation. Sitting in the back of the boat, anonymous and unassuming, you always look well ahead towards the horizon for the people you mentor, and think of making subtle tacks and maneuvers for the changing winds. With the sea and the weather, it's up to your own keen eyes and your sea-salt-smelling nose to guess where they might be going next.

Although not a strictly linear pathway, profiling *can* track the learning journey sequentially; both the positive and negative aspects of each profile stage can be used to understand a set of behaviors to match the mood of any one of the eight directions. In the process of learning, we can hop from one profile to another; we can go backwards; we can have "transcendent" leaps to a profile farther around the cycle, if for only a moment.

Also, you'll notice that for each profile of developmental phase there is a potential shadow-side, or what we call a "negative propensity." Expressed at a particular phase, negative energy can be adolescent and ego-focused, arising from fear, needing approval, addicted to perfection, wanting to stagnantly remain in one phase, or many other sources. This can and does happen when people take this journey, needing mentors and elders to guide them along and keep their ego in check. An ego is a necessary and good thing: if we train our mentoring eyes to be keen, we will see these negative propensities for what they are, and hopefully before they take over and run away with hard-won, personal development.

In no way should this Profile of the Learning Journey be used to judge people or raise some people up while looking down on others. We are all at different points on the journey depending on different areas or disciplines of life. I am further along the journey of nature awareness than my father, but when it comes

We are all improvisers. The most common form of improvisation is ordinary speech. As we talk and listen, we are drawing on a set of building blocks (vocabulary) and rules for combining them (grammar). These have been given to us by our culture. But the sentences we make with them may never have been said before and may never be said again. Every conversation is a form of jazz. The activity of instantaneous creation is as ordinary to us as breathing.

Steven Nachmonovich,
Free Play: Improvisation in Life and Art

NATURAL CYCLE

to religious studies or fatherhood or a multitude of other things, he would blow me off the charts. No one is complete and perfect with regard to anything. We are all *in process*, and therefore can all support and learn from each other.

Northeast — Ready

Every journey really starts in the Northeast, where we feel openness and receptivity for something new to enter. Sometimes a major life crisis strips us down and humbles us to look for change. Or, maybe we just have a playful willingness to experiment with what shows up. Or maybe by uncanny synchronicity, we meet someone, we wander into a strange store, we receive a book about a subject, or we watch an Oprah episode, we find just exactly what we feel we need.

East — Set

Boom! The journey begins now, birthing the "baby" of a new path. Someone reads a book that blows their mind open, and suddenly they are talking to all their friends about it, looking online for related classes and dreaming of what might lie ahead. When they show up at classes, all their light bulbs are flashing. They talk a lot, wave their hands around to ask their questions and tell their stories. Without a lot of direction and little *experience*, they don't really know a whole lot about the subject.

A negative propensity of this phase could be all talk without listening or progressing. When you see someone in this state, give them clear directions to begin movement. Better still, take their hand and lead the way at first, making their transition onto the new path as unintimidating as possible. This will naturally lead to the Southeast.

Southeast — Moving

Folks in the Southeast profile actually move. After a teenager talks and talks about getting a guitar, he finally gets it, and starts strumming, doing something, even though he doesn't know how to make music yet. When someone arrives at the Southeast profile, the mentor becomes a "coach." Time to step in and teach them how to learn. Ask questions and give them simple errands. Give them concrete and achievable tasks that keep them excited. Give them success, encouraging them to keep moving.

A negative version of the Southeast profile shows up when people "flail" or "flinch" or "don't get it" so they give up in frustration. Review their basic skill toolboxes and your learning objectives, so folks visualize where they want to go next and ultimately how to get there.

South — Learning

People in the South profile narrow in and focus on a particular thing to pursue. Perhaps at first all of nature thrilled them. But after orienting and sampling the broad field in the Southeast, they feel sure they want to study tracking, perhaps, or fire-making. They pour themselves into that one area of study, almost to the complete neglect of everything else. Their focus is incredible, their dedication admirable, their learning great.

One negative tendency of the South focus is that learners go so hard and fast in their own ways that they teach themselves bad habits or somewhere down the road they may have to "unlearn" them. This is the phase where discipline and techniques gained from an experienced teacher or mentor clearly show their value.

Another negative aspect, arrogance, commonly appears in the South. In this profile participants will have plenty of opinions for everyone else: the best way to learn, what others should or shouldn't be doing, who is the best within the field and why. Their focus may be intense and their technical ability advanced, but their learning journey is not complete, even if they might think so. As a mentor, use the Third Level questions that keep them humble, listening to others, and pursuing their focus with a healthy modesty.

Southwest — Resting

Folks in the Southwest of their Learning Journey simply need a break. They reach a plateau in their learning and relax. To a mentor, this might seem like they're getting lazy and you may want to "crack the whip," but this is actually a natural and necessary phase in the learning process. At this point in the process of learning, people let go of attachments to techniques and discipline, and start to play like kids again.

Just like the time of "Indian Summer" on a farm—when you tire of working, allow yourself rest, enjoy the time to breathe. But as you rest, you remember the coming winter and the work left to do. In this spirit of the Southwest profile, honoring rest as part of the cycle, yet don't forget much still lies ahead.

Internalization often comes through rest, your conscious mind takes a break while your unconscious mind works below-the-surface to solidify your progress so far. I noticed this learning a song on the piano. I would work and work at it, and then, often frustrated at not being able to nail it, I would walk

The great sitar master Ravi Shankar was gifted as a child both in classical Indian dancing and classical Indian music. Uncertain as to which direction to take, he was tempted to pursue both. But one of his teachers told him, "Choose one and pursue it fully, until you master it. If you master one thing, you will be able to master anything else you desire after that." If we go through the process of any one discipline long enough, then we not only gain a high level of expertise, but also great wisdom about how to process towards mastery. This can then be turned towards any direction we wish.

Evan McGown, Ravi Shankar

I have discovered I am not alone in my listening, that almost everyone is listening for something, that the search for places where the singing may be heard goes on everywhere. It is part of the hunger all of us have for a time when we were closer to nature than we are today.

Sigurd Olson, *Open Horizons*

away for a few hours or even a day or two. But when I returned to it, I would sit down and be able to play the song perfectly. I just needed rest to internalize all my hard work. Learning transforms from being intellectual to being embodied right here in the Southwest "resting" stage.

A negative propensity of this profile is staying stuck in rebellion. At this point there may be rejection of imposed responsibility and structure—even at the cost of others' learning experiences in group settings. Learners don't want to come back to finish the work, nor do they see why they should. If this happens, give them some space before you call them back to the center to remind them why they started in the first place. Paint the picture of where they could go. Or, maybe they truly see themselves pursuing another focus. Simply bring consciousness to their choices. Help them go down each possible road in their imagination, vividly, and thereby help them find what they most truly want to choose for themselves.

West — Arrived

Once the learners arrive in the West, mentors can smile, breathe deep, and say, "Yes! They've arrived!" For instance, at this point, I'm no longer thinking about "notes" or "techniques" to play a piece on the piano, but I am relating to the joy or "soul" of the music. In the West profile, learners can now look back and tell the story of their whole learning journey, even if it took five years. When they reach this phase, suggest they celebrate their accomplishment by telling their story in front of you or their community in some meaningful form, even to a small group.

In this phase, they feel proud and confident in themselves, and will eagerly share their experience, including laughing at all their mistakes and bogus attitudes along the way. Ideally, this profile marks an authentic maturity and a healthy humility.

A negative propensity to this profile sounds like just plain bragging. If they blow their own horn too loudly, just try to keep them humble by showing them what lies beyond the next mountain!

The West, marking arrival, also marks maturity and self-sufficiency for learners. For many, the mentoring relationship will end here with a fond farewell and the learner will depart for new terrain. At this point, learners and mentors may begin anew on a different area of interest, a new project. However, if you are both a mentor and a master of the art, you may be able to accompany them deeper into the Northwest, North, and Northeast phases of the process.

Northwest — Historian

In the Northwest profile, learners who have "arrived," now may become historians of their subject. The "hero stories" that inspired their journey at the start now take on new meaning. They reveal layers of wisdom and fascinating details previously clouded in awe and mystery. Historians hear with different ears.

They begin to look for others who reached similar achievements: "Ancestors" of their tradition. They ask, "How did they do it?" to guide their path even further. For instance, once I am able to play in a jazz quartet on piano, I then start to study others who have reached this level of proficiency. I'll start comparing myself to other greats that I've always listened to. Now I want to know about their process, how they lived and learned. I pick up biographies written about them to glean insight. How did they get to this point? Did they take a different approach that might offer an important lesson I missed? What mistakes did they make that I could avoid and learn from? And where did they go from here? Where will I go from here? Mature artists of all traditions do this: they look back and around for others with similar expertise and honor them; they make the inroads necessary to meet previous masters or those who knew them intimately; they link into the community of masters.

As a mentor, you can easily facilitate this process by referral. Suggest biographies to them, introduce them to kindred elders, then ask them what they think about the particular way they've found.

One negative propensity of the Northwest profile might be a sense of "indispensability," a burdensome belief that no one else can fill their shoes. If, for example, the learner becomes the program expert, they may not be willing to move on and let others step into that role.

North – Mentor

The North heralds arrival at a place of integrated wisdom beyond technical and intellectual accomplishment. After research and comparison of themselves with other great practitioners (in the Northwest), the North profile expresses confidence in one's own unique style. Whatever art

NATURAL CYCLE

or discipline is studied, it is now their own. Grounded firmly in personal experience, the mentor uses his or her own language and insight to communicate with learners. In the North profile, masters become master mentors. They see through the surface to the universal lessons; they see the big picture rather than merely the techniques and details. This perspective may be found in *Zen in the Art of Archery*, by Eugene Herrigel, or *Sacred Hoops: Spiritual Lessons of a Hardwood Warrior*, by Phil Jackson, the multi-championship-winning coach of Michael Jordan and the Chicago Bulls. Their mentoring and teaching styles rose from surprising originality because they saw the deeper ground beneath—the potential in their art form for human or even spiritual development—and operated from there.

A negative propensity of the North profile withholds the wisdom because it's simply too subtle to pass on, fearful of "casting pearls before swine." Or a potential teacher might be unwilling to let others in on such hard-fought-for and proprietary knowledge. A third negative propensity of the North is to micromanage the learning journey of another.

Northeast — Cultural Creative

This profile prompts us to say of a person, "He's a natural," or "She broke the mold." Their ability seems completely effortless, as if they were born to do the task they mastered, more like an instinctive act. As a very accomplished and scientific-minded tracker once said to me out in the field, "I don't normally go in for the 'spiritual' or intuitive perspective on tracking ... but right now, even though I can't physically see any tracks, I know these are wolf tracks. I can't explain how I know, but I'm sure of it."

If the "natural" also has maturity, he or she may become a "cultural creative," a front-line leader described by Ray and Anderson in their book, *Cultural Creatives*. The Northeast profile embodies the culture-driving Trickster, the one who bares the cutting edge, expands possibilities, invents new approaches, and finds a way out.

A negative propensity of the Northeast profile may turn out to be one who gets so caught up in vision and dreams that the groundedness to actually mentor, lead, and make a difference in the physical world doesn't happen. The heroic "natural" may live in an ivory tower; revising and refining the vision to such an edge that no one can follow.

Appreciating Every Step

As a mentor at the helm of another person's learning journey, take time to acknowledge and appreciate steps of progress as they move around the wheel. Such acknowledgment affirms and completes passages of the journey, allowing a person to keep moving with a feeling of freedom on their path. For smaller-scale endeavors, such as constructing a rain-proof shelter, you might celebrate by sleeping overnight in it. For longer learning curves, stage completion offers opportunity to contribute skills to the community or throw a party of thanksgiving for mentors, supportive parents, and friends. To celebrate the end of a long and intentional learning journey, it can be deeply integrating to support a learner on a solo vigil or retreat where he or she can let go and open up to whatever might be next.

Orientation for Larger Groups and Complex Programs

You now have a lot to work with, using the Natural Cycle to design Flow Learning experiences and to profile the Learning Journey. For mentoring just a few learners casually, that's all you need to know. But, if you are working with ongoing programs, or more than a dozen participants, or complicated expeditions, we strongly recommend you don't go it alone. "It takes a village to raise a child," and it takes at least a small community of mentors to manage larger groups and complex programs. To complete this chapter, we'll just take a glimpse at how the directions of the Natural Cycle can help coordinate a team of educators, organize small groups of learners, and spread out the responsibilities of program management. We won't take you around all eight directions here, but only suggest how to supply your nature education program with balance and diversity by orienting to the qualities of the eight directions.

Team Teaching

A deliberate ratio of more teachers to few learners may be bad for the budget, but it's great for the learners. This low ratio plays an essential role if you're tapping into the Child Passions of more than a dozen people out in the boundless field. Be warned: it's impossible for one lone teacher to mentor thirty folks outdoors. We recommend making the effort to assemble a team that will keep your mentor-to-learner ratio within range of the ideal 1:6. It may be you and one other person, or a core few that meet regularly to design, facilitate, and debrief the program.

Teaching in a team enables mentors to circle around the edges of a group. It provides more eyes to watch the energy flow and the learning profile and more time for one-on-one contact. It exposes participants to a variety of role-models, and it exposes mentors to a variety of approaches.

One person can only know or offer so much. We each lean in different directions, bring unique gifts, and specialize in certain areas. Some will bring gifts in speaking in front of the group, while others will have one-on-one magic. Different people approach planning and strategizing differently, and this—although it may frustrate you at times—turns out to be a really good thing. What results from team teaching is creative tension. If honored and worked through, this tension produces ideas, approaches, and relationships that one person could never come up with alone (like this book for instance).

Recruiting a Teaching Team

Initially, recruiting volunteers and training apprentices may present a challenge; it might push your edge. But the truth is, many people feel the importance of this kind of nature-based education in their bones; they want to be helpful to a program that makes so much sense. The people who will make up your mentoring community are out there waiting right now. They drink coffee next to you at the local café, shop at the wild bird feed stores, help out at local elementary schools, and volunteer at parks and nature centers. If you dream the dream, take the first step, gather the learners, build the fire circle, and put out the call, they will come. One volunteer will bring in another, who will introduce you to another, who will bring in his or her cousin …

The qualifications for recruits can be fun to imagine and they parallel the qualities of the Natural Cycle. You don't need experienced trackers, Coyote Mentoring specialists, or talented teachers. You need a balanced combination of committed mentors who can inspire, activate, focus attention, apply the 50-50 principle, gather stories, and offer good listening. You need mentors who can ask good questions, hikers who know a few things, and personalities who can work magic with other people.

Where do you go to find these people?

+ Definitely recruit **your friends** and your younger participants' **parents**.

+ Recruit local **naturalists**, adventurers, trackers, fishers, or hunters. Talk to volunteer docents or rangers at local parks and nature centers.

Visit parks regularly and notice the people who come all the time to watch the hawks or pick berries. Pull them in.

+ **Run an apprenticeship program** alongside your regular programs. Offer your nature knowledge or mentoring wisdom in exchange for their volunteer time. Train your alums to become your instructors.

+ Look around for **grandparents**, retired people, anyone with wisdom on their backs and the sparkle still in their eyes. They have time and experience to offer, and can connect with folks—especially the children—in ways younger adults cannot.

After you have your core teaching team in place, try to expand it to include occasional guest mentors. Consider the stages of life in the Natural Cycle and look for representatives:

+ **Children.** Invite younger siblings to give your participants opportunities to be caretakers and mentors to younger kids. Give your caretakers clear responsibilities.

+ **Teenagers.** Invite an apprentice young person, a good role model, maybe a scout or fisherman. Find people who can work with another person who needs mentoring one-on-one in a project. Take time before and after to give him or her guidance.

+ **Young and older Adults.** Invite experienced young adults, or even older adults (who love the chance to play), as invisible scouts. You can have a lot of fun with this. In hunter-gatherer cultures, "scouts" are the accomplished naturalists who go out looking for plant forage, game, or enemies. They were superb at invisibility. The educational use of the scout boosts awareness and constantly keeps people awake in their senses. Unbeknownst to your participants, you can place an invisible scout a distance away and have them alarm the birds, or leave odd tracks and trails, or hide in trees dropping twigs to see if folks are paying attention.

+ **Experts.** Invite in guest experts for a session, give them a grand introduction, a seat and fresh water, then let them tell their story. Write a thank you note.

+ **Elders.** You may not realize it now, but you need the presence of elders to make moments special, especially ceremonial openings and closings. You also need their counsel. They can stand in the wings, advise you along the

At the height of the early 70's, I was part of a teaching team in a private school in Manhattan whose mandate was to team-invent and team-teach ancient World History, matched up with something in Science and English. "Religion, Law, and Ethics" was a knock-out program at the brain-and-energy level of 12- and 13-year old kids: Magnificent kids, late nights, road shows, special projects, and wilderness trips.

Our team of three were quite the crew to behold: a tough New Yorker with a thick accent, a proper Australian with an even stronger Aussie drawl, and me—a Philadelphia debutante turned California hippie. We were young, free, and married to our program.

We were classically different types of people and teachers, and at first we tangled. Early in the first year, running a retreat out in the New York countryside, very late on the second night as the kids still raced around, Robert and I found Suellyn out on the gravel road in the dark with her suitcases packed, waiting for a taxi. We had to beg her to stay and pay off the taxi driver. But after that, we were a team, and nothing could undo us.

We forged goals together, taught each other our boundaries, circled around the kids in a tag team to draw out their individual geniuses, and we spun a tapestry of communal learning that still binds those students (and the three of us teachers) today.

This experience convinced me of the necessity of team-teaching.

continued...

way, help mediate conflicts with parents, and otherwise catch you when you fall. More likely than not nowadays, elders may feel they need you, too; all people need to feel they have a place in community, to feel appreciated and helpful and honored for their counsel and presence.

Training Your Recruits

Give your core teaching team plenty of advance time for training. Assess your combined skills, fill in the blanks, design the learning experience together, and then practice Coyote Mentoring with each other before you meet the participants.

+ **If you've recruited Naturalists**, train them to mentor, lead and teach with Coyote. Give them feedback and spend time debriefing and evaluating the team's design of the learning experience. (Give them this book)

+ **If you've recruited Teachers**, train them in naturalist basics. (See the *Kamana Naturalist Training Program*)

+ **If you've recruited Parents**, train them to step out of the box into Coyote Mentoring. (Study this Manual)

+ **If you've recruited potential Elders**, find guidance for them from other experienced elders and community facilitators; then support them to step into their natural role-modeling with confidence. (One resource recommended by numerous people is *From Aging to Saging: A Profound New Vision for Growing Older*, by Zalman Schachter-Shalomi, creating a world-wide network of "Spiritual Eldering.")

Certify your team. About one out of every dozen parents who sign up their kids for our summer camp programs checks before registering that our instructors have First Aid certification and have been screened through the government files for any criminal records. You can find regional venues for certification and background checks on the internet.

Growing into a Mentoring Team

Bringing your core people together in the first place can be a delicate thing, like planting seeds. Growing them into a team takes some intentional cultivation. Definitely involve your team in the planning process as well as in the actual mentoring so they feel empowered and responsible. Classroom teachers know to expect this sequence as a profile for team development: Forming, Storming, Norming, Performing. It's an old classic, look how it follows the Natural Cycle:

1. **East: Forming** – Morning and intention. Begin with appreciation for one another, and good communication. Hello, who are you? Are we willing to work together? What's our intention?

2. **South: Storming** – Noon and hard work. The heat sets in, the thunderstorms come, and the going gets tough. How can our skills, our personalities, and our roles combine to do the work? What limits and limitations do we have? Some conflict. Ouch. Bounce back. Reorganize.

3. **West: Norming** – Evening and harvest. The group gels, delegates responsibilities and appreciates differences of personality and expertise. We turn our full attention to leading the participants. We improvise and it's just like playing jazz.

4. **North: Performing** – Night and wisdom. We've merged our differences into a unified direction. We've learned to swim together like a school of dolphins. We stand back and watch with our hands on our hips and a sparkle in our eyes like wise elders.

Briefing, Teaching, and Debriefing with your Team

Briefing. Half an hour or more before the participants arrive, carve out "sacred time" for your team to gather—time fully committed to centering body, mind and soul in unity of intention. We call this "Bringing Our Minds Together." You will see this routine everywhere— the orchestra tuning up, the football team stretching and huddling up, the family praying

Having watched the same process and its miraculous boons emerge from dozens of teaching-teams since, I am sure that teaching done with a team multiplies the effects of education exponentially.

Ellen Haas, Teaching Teams

I mentored groups of 25 people by myself in the wilderness on Orca expeditions, but these were adult volunteers, and I split them into teams, which led to lots of friendly competitions among them. Within a team, the structure was strictly horizontal, i.e., management by consensus. Man, that was fun and boy do I miss the people, the place, the creatures and the spirits.

RANDALL EATON, Team Sailing

NATURAL CYCLE

A few weeks into my first summer of summer camps, I had an experience with this model of team-teaching—by myself. I was alone with a group of 12 kids in the woods. I was still cutting my teeth, stumbling a lot. As an apprentice, I had been working with the directional model of team-teaching duties for the past year. I was tired, at my wits end. So at lunch I set the kids to playing a game, sat under a tree, and pulled my hat brim down to just breathe for a minute.

I was startled out of my rest by a joyful yelp! I stood up, and suddenly I scanned the situation with startling clarity, checking off the list inside my head: is everyone feeling included? Yep, but Ben seems to be feeling a little alone. Are they able to focus on the game? Yep, but they'll need a change soon. Has everyone been drinking water? Hmm. Not sure. Is there a sense of community developing, and are they learning to cooperate as a team? Yep, except maybe for Ben, who seems a little left behind. What is the group needing now?

"Hey, everybody," I yelled, "Let's play a water drinking game. Grab your water bottles. Ben, you get to go first!"

I couldn't believe how all this had been programmed deep into me—like there was a team of teachers on my shoulder conferring with each other. Add to that the elements of the Book of Nature I was juggling and all the other layers that played in at different times, and I realized that I bring the team-teaching perspective with me, even when I'm alone.

EVAN McGOWN, A Team of One

before meals. Gather. Share thankfulness for life and the opportunity in front of you. Sing. Appreciate one another. Remember why you want to do this work. Speak aloud your highest intentions for the day or the week.

Teaching. During the time you teach together, each mentor will perform a planned role that fits his or her skills. In addition, you might assign a direction or two of the Flow Learning cycle for each team member to keep an eye on, just as we described under the 50-50 principle.

Awareness yields connection.

+ It's critical for someone to remember to keep the group in their senses and in their gratitude—this is the **Northeast** of your team.

+ Someone keeps watch on Inspiration: What perks up the group and each individual in it? Is the body language sagging? Has unexpected inspiration just flown in? This person takes the title of **East**.

+ Someone else watches the **Southeast** energy, making sure everyone is activated and engaged: Maybe one person needs some coaching; another needs to be reminded of instructions for the game; or the whole group needs moving along.

+ Someone else attends to the **South** focus: Have they paid close attention and actually learned something to take home? Would that one participant with a passion for birds want help finding that thrush in a field guide?

+ Someone else claims the **Southwest** and signals "Break time," or "Let's pause for a sip of water."

+ Someone watches over community dynamics in the **West**.

+ Someone makes sure Third Level questions appear for **Northwest** Reflection.

+ Someone suggests a follow-up project for Integration at home tonight, taking on the **North**.

If your team consciously covers the qualities of all the eight directions, a sense of balance and harmony will make your teaching day feel easy and whole.

Debriefing: After the program participants have left, gather again for at least half an hour. Settle down, put on something warm and dry, share a snack, and let each team mentor tell the story of their day. Aid the process with focused questions.

+ When were the high-points, the magic moments?
+ What were the low-points, the areas for growth?
+ What gifts and passions do we see in individuals (both participants and staff)?
+ Were there any group conflicts?
+ How did our plan work?
+ How did we work as a team? Did we take care of our responsibilities?
+ Are there any bad feelings that need to be cleared up?
+ Based on what happened today, what are the next steps?

Then end this debriefing with words that celebrate the day. Recap successes, give appreciations to each other, and give thanks for the lessons of the day and the support of the natural world and everything that contributes to the process of personal growth, connection and education. Officially separate the team so that each person can be free to turn their attention and whole selves to other parts of their lives.

Cooperative Learning Groups

Your mentoring team and your extended community will bring diversity to the learning experience, to circle around the edges, but be sure to put your attention to the community of participants. If you have more than the optimal 1:6 ratio of mentor for each small band of learners, if you have a group too big for a circle so every individual feels engaged, then take time to subdivide your participants into little learning communities. This model shows how you can design multiple groups where everyone can feel a part of each— comprised of different people with varying opinions, passions, and gifts.

At the core of this, you create a setting so people mentor each other, with Mother Nature as their book. You send them down children's trails in small cooperative learning groups to discover for themselves, run errands, and report back what they've scouted up. This mutual mentoring is pure magic.

Three Time-Proven Groupings

The root words we use for these groupings can be found in many traditional cultures. For instance, you belong to clans or family groups, but there might also be other groups, like the Masons who focus on certain collective purposes, or guilds formed around the practice of different skills, like blacksmithing, arrow-making, or silversmithing. In the context of nature studies, we offer these groupings because they have worked very well over the years for our larger tribes and we recommend you try.

Clans. You could also call these "family groups" or "home-groups." With kids, we usually make these groups according to age, by looking at the roster and putting numerical ages together. Clans usually become the default grouping as it gets reinforced the most. In clans, people get to know each other best, just like they were indeed a family. Whatever the length of your program, have one instructor stay with the same clan to maintain the feeling of family. So if you have 24 participants and one volunteer, you could have 2 clans of 12. Even better, if you had two volunteers, you could have 3 clans of 8. Give clans a "Nature Name" so each group forms an identity.

Societies. Societies, smaller but more numerous than clans, have diversity in ways the clans have uniformity. Having societies breaks up clans and puts clan members with members of different clans. For instance if you have 3 clans of 8 participants, you could then have 8 societies with 3 people each, so all three participants belong to and represent all 3 clans. Definitely, some activities you will want to do with smaller groups of threes, such as blindfold games or scavenger hunts.

For naming the societies, with older people you can use the Natural Cycle as they did for me with my stick on a colored cloth. You can make societies by directions, so one group will be name the Easts, one the Wests, etc. Ask clans to regroup into societies and stand in their direction. Ask societies to regroup into clans, each member reporting back from the caucus of their direction.

With advanced or older learners, you can also apply the Program Management model (coming next) to them, asking the Souths of each clan to help you keep the time and pay attention to details, or the Wests to help make sure people in their clans appreciate each other and work together. Lots of possibilities for application come with the Natural Cycle.

Guilds. Guilds arrange themselves based on the personal passions of the participants and the individual teachers who lead the guilds. With your team of teachers, present the participants with options and let people go where they want to go. Try basing your guild options by Core Routines, such as the Mapping Guild or the Journaling Guild, or from the Book of Nature, such as the Critter-Catching Guild or the Edible Plants Guild.

By using them regularly, the Clans, Societies and Guilds begin to work cooperatively together making one big weave. People of all ages participating will appreciate the rich diversity within community. They feel honored in their personal choices, as in Guilds, and yet also feel belonging within an intricately woven social order, as in Clans and Societies. Thus they experience the individual freedom so valued in our Western culture with group affiliation so prevalent in Eastern and Middle Eastern cultures.

Listen Up and Go West!

"Hey Listen up. Everybody get into your Clans," and twenty-four people scatter in three ways. "Now, quick, everybody get into Societies and stand in your Direction." Twenty-four people stand around for long moments looking at the sky, and then run to stand in their direction, veering as they watch others decide ahead of them.

Whether in Clans, Societies, or Guilds, you can group them for the day—to wander around the woods, to build shelters, or to play games. Then you come back together at the end of the day, as a Tribe once again, and tell the stories to each other about what happened.

In many traditional cultures, someone refers to someone as "my grandmother." Immediately you think of your blood grandmother and assume that this person must be talking about their blood grandmother. You meet another grandmother, then another. You meet a fourth grandmother and you say, "Wait a minute, who's this person and what's their name? How many grandmothers do you have?"

JON YOUNG, Grandmothers

Groupings can help the flow of sharing stories of the day, because you can ask each Clan or Guild to select one or two storytellers to tell about their day. People have so much fun representing the experience of their group or likewise listening with glee to someone tell what they themselves did. Society and Guild stories include bouts of laughter, seeds of inspiration, and great swellings of excitement.

Orientation for Program Management

Outdoor education is a program more than a class. Students don't come into the classroom and sit down at their desks and then you teach them things. No, in most outdoor education experiences, logistics must be planned: signup, facilities, transportation, communication, equipment, timekeeping, safety, payments. And to run an extended overnight expedition, these logistics only multiply.

Delegate your team of instructors, apprentices, and volunteers to be responsible for one of the eight aspects of the Natural Cycle, so you need not worry, everything receives attention, all the time.

It may help to establish among your group the roles designated in the summary chart below by the eight directions. With only two instructors, each of you takes a set of the cardinal responsibilities. If you currently lead alone, keep your owl eyes open and keep all of these needs in mind.

Direction & Archetypal Role	Pre-Program Activities & Planning	During-Program Logistics & Teaching	Actions
East Inspire, Invite & Welcome Participation	Outreach & Marketing	Welcoming & Communications	Marketing & outreach for program with a sense of inspiration & invitation. Initiates & oversees clear & positive communication among all stakeholders—staff, participants, families. Makes sure everyone feels invited, welcome, & included.
Southeast Activate, Orient & Facilitate Flow	Site Preparation & Planning	Facilitating Arrival & Flow Into Registration & Activities	Checks out site ahead of time, prepares the site, reservations & permitting. Handles transportation, travel permissions, parking logistics. Makes & posts signs. Orients for low-impact site use & easy clean-up. Keeps participants motivated & offers voluntary Child Passion games, etc.

South **Commit To,** **Participate** **In & Track** **Agreements**	Registration & Roster	Tracking of Agreements, Time & Attendance	Handles registration & payments; medical, dietary needs & release forms. Makes schedules & rosters. Watches the clock & group attendance. Reminds everyone of agreements & commitments.
Southwest **Tend,** **Maintain** **& Improve** **Environments**	Facilities, Grounds, Meals & Refreshments	Oversight of Physical Needs of Participants; Tending of Grounds & Facilities	Hires & supports kitchen crew; engages volunteers in providing refreshments. Provides for health & First Aid station(s); reviews medical & dietary needs. Encourages breaks & rest. Oversees tending of all facilities. Facilitates end-of-program site clean-up & restoration.
West **Gather, Lead** **& Facilitate** **Community**	Planning, Organizing & Celebrating Teachings	Oversight of Learning Activities, Supporting Keynote & Guest Instructors, MC of Group Sessions.	Organizes teaching team to design &/or implement curriculum. Gathers whiteboards/ flipcharts, markers, field guides, nature museum, handouts, other learning resources. Lectures, tells stories, runs games, leads songs, facilitates cultural mentoring, hosts community moments, provides information, facilitates sensory engagement & story of the day.
Northwest **Honor, Uphold** **& Regenerate** **Lineage**	Staff Training & Renewal; Research & Consultation With Cultural Elders, Resources & Other Lineage Holders	Three Pathways: 1) Providing Cultural Context for Teachings & Lineage; 2) Integration, Support & Meaningful Participation of Elders; 3) Counseling	Three Pathways: 1) Shares & celebrates lineage of all songs, stories, teachings & techniques. 2) Recruits, orients &/or trains Elders for program participation. 3) Mediates conflicts & offers personal coaching.
North **Develop,** **Coordinate &** **Lead Team &** **Big Picture**	Team Development, Budget Oversight, & Community Relations	Behind-The- Scenes Support of Teaching Team(s); Community Relations.	Keeps a pulse on the vision & mission of the program. Identifies recruits, provides training for, & delegates needed roles & skills. Facilitates team meetings & team- building. Checks in at beginning & end of program. Manages any challenges that arise among teaching team, participants, & families. Represents team to wider community.
Northeast **Facilitate** **Peace of Mind,** **Awareness &** **Creativity**	Assessment Opportunities & Facilitation of Northeast Goals	Three Pathways: 1) Quiet Mind Exercises; 2) Coyote Actions to Train Sensory Awareness; 3) Facilitates Creative Expression	Leads thanksgiving circles, sense meditations, & other Quiet Mind activities. Tells jokes, uses hiding games & other scout techniques. Draws attention to bird language. Encourages & models use of Mind's Eye Imagining & dynamic storytelling.

Chapter 11

INDICATORS OF AWARENESS

Radical Assessment

Radical—*root, foundation, bottom, essence; egregious and exuberant*

Assessment— *evaluation, inventory, measurement, appraisal, review, consideration*

Indicator — *symptom, pointer, characteristic, quality*

We knew we wanted a chapter about "assessment of learning" in this mentoring guide, so we started our writing process by looking at the Washington State Essential Academic Learning Requirements to design a curriculum that addressed them. But in the end, we chose to focus on qualities of personal development rather than academic outcomes, as our criteria for measuring success. After twenty-five years of working with people in both public and private education, we see this over and over again: when human development is put first, academic, artistic and vocational successes arise seemingly without effort.

We've decided to make a statement declaring what we're really aiming for and offering assessment criteria that fit. As Gandhi and Martin Luther King so potently proved to us through non-violent revolution, the means must be aligned with the ends. If our end is restoring healthy connection between humans and the rest of nature, then our means of assessing success must use natural, vibrant, vital, and sustainable criteria.

Standards for Nature Education

In most current assessment systems, Environmental Education takes a back seat to the traditional disciplines like Reading, Writing, or Mathematics. Nature education, although recognized by many as "an integrating context for learning," and elevated by Howard Gardner's recognition of "the naturalist intelligence," is still marginalized. It is added on in bits to the traditional academic disciplines but not honored in its own right. The kind of mentoring we describe in this guide intends different benchmarks than such standard education.

Coyote Mentoring awakens people to be alive in their connection with the natural world. Our Field of Learning, as Coyote showed us in the first chapter, includes

Awakening Sensory Awareness

Cultivating Knowledge of Place

Restoring the Bond between People and Nature

This all involves primary learning, learning that uses our "mammalian brain," the one underneath the neocortex, the one responsible for sensory awareness, emotion, and relationship. Our foundational goal is to awaken and hone this native wilderness awareness, our birthright of "naturalist intelligence." Since the blueprint for all these primary skills and abilities was laid in the DNA of the human being a long, long time ago, you won't be teaching so much as awakening them.

So, while we teach measurable skills in this guide—such as scientific identification of flora and fauna, critical thinking, wildlife biology, tracking techniques, and the ability to glean field guides for pertinent information—we emphasize the healthy roots at the foundation of these measurable skills.

Self-Sufficiency

Awe and Reverence

Quiet Mind

Service to the
Community

Common Sense

Caring and Tending

Aliveness and Agility

Inquisitive Focus

Indicators of Awarenes

These roots are qualities of *being* that lead to productive *doing*. For instance, the quality of Inquisitive Focus gives learners a powerful edge for life-long learning in all disciplines, academic, vocational, social, and spiritual.

Standards for learning within the nature education movement must honor not only knowledge, but also the learners' expressed happiness and energy as individuals, and the qualities of their relationships with their natural world. So, our criteria for success expressed by these Indicators of Awareness may seem more qualitative than quantitative. We agree with Ellen's son's first grade teacher who once said in a PTA meeting on assessment criteria, "Sometimes evaluation of students' success is spiritual and intuitive; the most important learning can't be measured in numbers."

Sparkle in the Eye

We're aiming for sparkle in the eye. When adults in their fifties look so youthful and excited about life that their friends ask, "What are you doing these days that makes you so happy?" Or, when a child comes home after summer camp full of excitement, happy to tell the family what he did and to show them what he knows, when such a child keeps that sparkle into the next weeks, jumping into alertness with every track and bird call she sees, when that sparkle extends into awareness of self and community, and ultimately extends into a lifelong commitment to caring for the whole natural world—*that's* what we value, and *that's* what we consider a successful outcome.

We believe—and Richard Louv's research supports our belief—connection to nature creates a foundation from which healthy human functioning and learning flows. Time in nature proves essential to our health as humans because it impacts our psychological, mental, emotional, and physical well being. So as mentors to adults, children, and perhaps most importantly, to ourselves, we must realize that this work is nothing less than healing.

What Coyote does is transformative. As people grow in their connection with nature and their awareness expands to the greater sphere of life, they begin to change from the inside out in the way they perceive and express themselves. Kids and adults alike feel freer and more supported to express who they really are and what they really feel, and they discover what they most deeply desire in their lives. Especially for adults, the journey may arouse emotions of sadness or anger—people often say things like, "Why haven't I had this connection before now?" Thoughts and feelings expressed along these lines are the beginning of healing.

Over the last twenty-five years watching people come into our nature-based learning communities and then leave transformed, we've witnessed the emergence of common primary learning qualities that we call the Indicators of Awareness.

Indicators of Awareness

The Indicators of Awareness are both symptoms of successful learning and learning goals. Here, we'll organize them through association with the directions of the Natural Cycle. We'll also point out Core Routines and aspects of the Book of Nature that help produce them. So this chapter pulls together all the threads already laid out and weaves them into a vision of holistic human health. If "Nature Deficit Disorder" demonstrates one possible set of symptoms as a result of modern cultural influences and lifestyle, the Indicators of Awareness demonstrate the opposite—symptoms of *health*.

See these Indicators as *symptoms* to keep a pulse on your own personal development. Be conscious of the Indicators as you wander, track, play games, tell stories, and role-model habits of awareness and inquiry. Although Mother Nature does a lot of the work for you, you must learn to cultivate these innate skill sets by adding conscious intention to each person's progress on the learning journey.

By understanding these Indicators, they then become conscious *learning goals*. They emerge naturally, but it helps if you model them yourself, find teachable moments that explain them, and emphasize their value. In organizations like the Boy Scouts, martial arts, or gatherings of traditional communities, cultural virtues are routinely recited in opening ceremonies so they become ingrained in the communities' awareness. How you introduce these values and bring them to consciousness will be up to you. Here, we turn your consideration to the Indicators of Awareness at the roots of learning and focus your intention on nourishing their power.

East: Common Sense

The East marks the beginning, of the day, the year, and human life, so here we place the foundational quality we want to see emerge: Common Sense.

Common Sense is a wonderful phrase we all understand. The origin of this quality rises from the practical use of the physical senses. Taught by experience, Common Sense uses good judgment about how to respond to situations. In the city, we call it "street-smarts," in the country; we know it as "good sense." Common Sense emerges from a basic habit of paying attention with all senses alert.

You'll notice how Common Sense shows up in people when they understand how to dress for rain or safely step out into the darkness without a flashlight. People who keep a distance from known dangers in their territory use Common Sense and so do those who wield a carving knife in a sensible way—pushing the knife away from their body and not using their leg as a backstop for the sharp blade! You will see it in the way they approach a new situation—pausing, observing patterns and behaviors of others. Often, people with this indicator will approach the door slowly and listen for a moment before knocking so as not to disturb folks inside.

Common Sense often has to do with physical safety. Studying Hazards teaches Common Sense as few other things do. We learn where to stand (and not to stand) in a lightning storm by understanding the nature of lighting. We learn not to go carelessly into a warm pile of rocks in the desert by understanding the ways of venomous reptiles. We learn not to stick our hand under an old table by knowing where black widows might be lurking. We learn to be respectful as a palpable characteristic of our being.

By understanding the whole truth, Common Sense debunks myths that cause people fear or panic. As you study hazards and get to know and understand them, you'll surely notice an easing of tension in yourself. Understanding creates a relaxed sense of "it's not time to worry yet," making Common Sense a casual intelligence in the face of a potential crisis. When I was in West Africa, I watched my group of American adults cower and shriek as huge insects flew in around us. Meanwhile, a native African boy about five years old stood bored and relaxed. When one of the huge bugs landed on his head, he simply smacked it with his hand and threw it aside.

Experience with the forces of life gives rise to Common Sense and it shows up as skill in maneuvering through these forces with relaxed, stress-less intelligence. People who live close to wild nature develop Common Sense partly through their community's stories and wisdom sayings, but more through personal experience about the truth of those sayings. Hunter-gathers and farmers grow up feeling the cycle of the seasons and learn the workings of hazards in their environments. So, as a mentor using this model: let people get wet and dirty, let them feel cold, feel discomfort, so they can discover what brings natural relief and benefit.

Ingwe always used to say, "Common Sense is not so bloody common these days." And he was right. When we understand that Common Sense only comes from experience, you can understand why. Instead of watching over their every step and insulating them from the forces of nature, guide people to learn for themselves: often the most miserable "story of the day" holds an experience of a "mistake" they never make again.

Common Sense, therefore, means that, over time and with experience, people grow more and more comfortable in nature. They won't mind sitting on the ground, or getting twigs in their hair, because they know it won't hurt them. Likewise, they acquire the knowledge of real hazards and learn how to avoid them or deal with them. When people know what can and can't hurt them, they flow through the woods with confidence and ease. Soon they will be covering themselves in mud and charcoal for camouflage, lying in huge piles of leaves while bugs crawl over them, moving stealthily through ponds of muck with just their eyes sticking out, and catching the safe snakes and bugs. Many natural health practitioners have even observed that experiencing things in this way improves our immune systems.

So keep an eye out for this Indicator of Awareness, use awareness of Hazards to bring it out, provide experiences for sensible choice-making, and then watch thankfully as Common Sense becomes more and more common in our villages.

Southeast: Aliveness and Agility

Without a doubt, you'll hear about Aliveness and Agility from the parents of the children you mentor. "I've never seen my children so alive before!" or "When I pick my child up from your programs, she's just bursting with enthusiasm!" or "I can't get them to stop talking about everything they did." Adults might say, "Hey, I think tracking might be the 'fountain of youth'." Or, "I am picking up where I left off when I was eight years old!" "I haven't felt this agile in years." Or you yourself will get direct feedback from long-time friends: "There's just some light about you now, some glow." Even dogs and small children will gravitate naturally toward that power of aliveness.

The Southeast direction provides all the practices responsible for enthusiastic motivation and excitement in action.

As you tap into Child Passions, people will come alive. Be ready. The fire will come into their eyes, a glint of mischief, a spark of daring, a flare of excitement, a flame of fascination—and they will begin to seize opportunities with boundless enthusiasm. Coming out of the indoor culture which promotes convenience and inactivity, they will burst alive with zest and glee for raw life. More than anything, we aim for this pure child-like happiness. Aliveness could also be characterized by what my football coaches used to tell me, "Whatever you do, really do it! Don't just half do it—do it with everything you've got." Gilbert Walking Bull used to tell all of us, "Being truly alive is like that feeling you get when you jump into frigid cold water." Ingwe once told me, "If you see a mountain and you say to yourself you want to climb that mountain, don't wait or put it off—do it now. Climb the mountain *now!*"

When people's spirits come alive, their physical reflexes come alive too. In the excitement their bodies awaken, their steps lighten, they twist and squirm and jump with grace, their eyes scan, their fingers catch—all with increased quickness. We call this agility. People will begin to amaze themselves at how quickly their bodies move, children running up to tell you their surprising feats—how they can catch things before they hit the ground, jump logs higher than their waists. Adults will walk with spring in their steps; their eyes will flash with youthful mischief. This Indicator taps into something ancient and wild in their bodies, their "animal memory" and spiritual vitality return as neuromuscular and perceptual powers grow stronger.

Once you awaken their bodies, channel that aliveness into meaningful connections. You can take this opportunity to stretch their muscle-imagination: "Jump like a grasshopper, run like a deer, land like an owl." Use Animal Forms as great teachers of agility; they enhance quick-jerk reflexes and deft movements and encourage full abandonment into the art of acting.

Of course, Motivating Species are perfect for cultivating Aliveness and Agility. What brings us more alive in enthusiasm and reflexes than a mountain lion track, a frog, or a snake that begs to be caught? All through human history, those species reappear again and again to encourage humans to come alive in their bodies. If you haven't spent time catching frogs or lizards or butterflies, give yourself a day to go out and try it for yourself. Your body will remember.

So watch for Aliveness and Agility, the sparkle in the eye, the quick reflexes. Listen to the comments of the youth, the adults, and especially the parents and spouses. And, be ready to join people when they move into action. You might just have to get in shape yourself.

South: Inquisitive Focus

Another Indicator to watch for is a brightening of curiosity. Invited to grow, this curiosity becomes Inquisitive Focus. Inquisitive Focus holds the tracking instinct, the natural drive to follow mysteries and search for answers with hunger and determination. The quality of perseverance lives in Inquisitive Focus, a lasting willingness to keep following the trail of mysteries wherever they lead.

Washington State Essential
Academic Learning Requirement
for Scientific Inquiry:
The student will

❑ Understand how to generate
and evaluate questions that can
be answered through scientific
investigations.

❑ Synthesize a revised scientific
explanation using evidence,
data, and inferential logic.

❑ Analyze why curiosity, honesty,
cooperation, openness, and
skepticism are important to
scientific explanations and
investigations.

❑ Analyze scientific theories for
logic, consistency, historical
and current evidence,
limitations, and capacity to be
investigated and modified.

❑ Evaluate inconsistent or
unexpected results from
scientific investigations using
scientific explanations.

This indicator is tied to the wholly absorbed, hard-working energy of the South. It is intense curiosity.

You will notice this in people as they pull on you to go back to an area so they can see if an animal has returned, eagerly tear into a field guide to look for information, barrage you with question after question, or refuse to leave the woods until they figure out what animal left this track!

Inquisitive Focus lies at the root of scientific thinking, the deductive and the inductive kinds. Albert Einstein saw in primitive hunting the origin of the scientific method. It is the ability to used by scientific icons and native scouts to hypothesize and test, to seek clues and investigate. Thomas Edison possessed Inquisitive Focus during his thousands of attempts until he finally got a working light-bulb. This willingness to live within a mystery, to gather facts, to use the powers of reason and intuition, to compile the results into theories, then test them out in comparable situations to see if they hold up-all these practices add up to Inquisitive Focus.

Inquisitive Focus is at the heart of what Howard Gardner identifies as the "naturalist intelligence." Some people just seem born with a propensity to pay attention to natural information: they discern patterns, they imprint and use these as "search images," and they love to inquire into the natural relationships among rocks, plants, animals, and humans. All of us are born with this latent potential; it is simply an under-worked muscle in some of us.

I'll never forget tracking a cougar in the snow: it stepped inside the deep holes of elk-tracks and made it very hard to make out the four toes and "m-shaped" heel-pad of the big cat's prints. My group had been following on snowshoes for hours, but we lost the trail as the elk trails split off into many directions. Using both logic and intuition, I followed down one trail, while others went down other trails. When I was nearing defeat, our tracking leader found me, saw the dimming spark in my eyes, and said, "You're close, but you have to get down on your belly to find the clues." So I did, and just a few elk tracks further, I saw an M-shaped print with sharp retracted claws registering high above its toes in the snow on the side of the elk track: mountain lion, without a doubt. I gave out a barbarian, "Yowp!" and the group gathered behind me to follow the freshly found trail. Relentless Inquisitive Focus will take us to those amazing moments in life. Doggedly following our curiosity, we each will get wherever we need to go.

Watch this Indicator of Awareness as it emerges, and fan its flames as high as you can. Nothing draws out and trains in the brain's deep-set ability to inquire more than exploring the mysteries of Mammals and Other Trackable Critters, wisely guided by the endless questions they evoke. Pursuing tracking mysteries challenges all the faculties of human inquiry and intuition—drawing on the power of mental focus, imaginal resources, and all of the senses at once.

Every person's Inquisitive Focus will reflect a unique direction. Follow some people and their fascination into mammal tracking expertise; note that others will be charmed by plants, or lizards, or weather, or erosion patterns, or pollination systems. Some will become academics, while others might be healers or musicians. Whether they grow into biologists, accountants, teachers, or business leaders, their powerfully trained Inquisitive Focus will help them succeed in their life's path.

Southwest: Caring and Tending

Everyone needs time for rest and relaxation, and the Southwest offers just the place for physical and emotional recovery from the hard work of the South.

Caring and Tending is natural—we all possess instincts to wisely care for ourselves, others, and the natural world. However, due to suppressive influences of our modern culture this attribute teeters on the edge of extinction, just like the many wild, but endangered species. Therefore it's vital that we consciously cultivate this innate sense within our communities.

Odawa Peacemaker, Paul Raphael uses the expression, "Lay low and tend your fire." This image describes the essence of the Caring and Tending spirit. We choose the word 'tend' as in *tend your fire* because we need to remember to look after ourselves in a good way. The Earth itself exemplifies this nurturing spirit by continually providing for and supporting our lives. Tending for the land and people in a caring way causes conscious awareness of physical, emotional and community well-being. As Indicators of Awareness, Tending and Caring embody nourishment and nurture, empathy and protection.

You will notice this natural development in people when they begin to recognize and express their own needs. One might tap you on the shoulder during a hike to say, "I need to drink some water," or, "I need to rest for a minute." Over time and with your encouragement, people will go beyond asserting their needs into taking responsibility for them and being proactive about them. You might hear, "I better bring my coat with me because I know I usually get cold on cloud-covered days like today." You might notice Caring and Tending as they become proactive around camp or on an outdoor project and begin to look after the needs of others.

Caring and Tending will show in behavior that cares for others. People may notice someone's thirst and respond by offering water. They may ask others who seem cold if they want an extra coat or blanket, or they'll find the coziest logs for you and the others to sit on. Sometimes the Caring Tender of the group becomes the protector who speaks out against violations of common decency or acts as a mediator in conflicts.

Of course, this same tending sensibility will also show itself as care for the natural world—and especially one's own native romping grounds. Your people will develop a sense of protectiveness for plants, animals, and fragile areas. When a new member of the learning community comes on the scene who thoughtlessly whacks plants with a stick, the Caring and Tending person will unreservedly speak up in defense.

The Core Routine of Wandering encourages people to attend to the messages of their bodies, to rest or eat when needed, to get physically active when that urge comes up, to follow a curiosity or intuition when it tickles. In many ways, the experience of Wandering without a destination, or practicing "body radar," opens the door to listening to the wisdom of the body. This innate sense of physical care will eventually translate into emotional care, as people grow able to articulate emotions and discover what they need in order to care for their own and others' emotional well-being.

Connection with Nature's Medicine Cabinet, edible and medicinal plants, ties in with this indicator, supporting its emergence. As people experience how to directly nourish themselves and tend to basic first-aid needs by picking plants out of the ground with their own two hands, they gain an appreciation of nature's power to nourish and heal. You will see harvesters and gardeners carry a pouch so they can gather plant medicines and wild edible plants—being ever ready to come to the rescue of a cut, bee-sting, nettle-sting, or satisfy a hunger for sweet berries. Also, as many game-hunters will testify, getting your food directly from nature evokes a natural desire to care for those species and the ecological fabric that nourishes them.

The Caring and Tending Indicator naturally emerges as people grow in connection and empathy for the world around them. You may be surprised by the degree of compassion and concern that some will demonstrate for the well-being of others. So watch for and cultivate this Indicator of Awareness as people grow more aware of simple needs and begin to act—as caring tenders of themselves, of others, and of the earth.

The most important point to hold about this indicator is that we must start by taking care of ourselves first. As I work on taking care of myself as a priority in my own life, I am rewarded with greater health and happiness, and this modeling becomes a gift to all those around me. If you are reading this book, then like me, it's possible that you too have a natural tendency to give, give, and give away your energy in favor of others. But if we don't tend our own fires, what are we teaching by our example? May we each learn to tend our own fire first, for then we can—with skill, centeredness, and endurance—tend to other and bigger fires.

West: Service to the Community

In the West, we move from self-centered activities to the circle of the community that congregates for the harvest. So here is the place in the Natural Cycle for mentors to look for the desire to play the meaningful role of Service to Community.

It is no surprise that being in nature with peers and mentors naturally gives rise to an awareness that we are threads in the community fabric. It is the Story of the Day core routine that develops that awareness by weaving everyone's unique stories, experiences, and personalities together.

When we experience ecology, we quickly realize that our ecosystem is a functioning community. Every member plays a pivotal part—no matter how small or big that part may be—within the entire network of interdependent relationships, lending vital support to the whole. Shrubs stabilize soils, while fish feed the bears who fertilize the forest. Spiders keep down the insect populations, and even mosquitoes help feed birds. Bees pollinate flowers to make honey. On and on and on it all goes—every little thing contributes according

Learn to hear voices in the wind
Music in mountain streams and bird songs
Fall asleep under the stars listening to the call of the owl and the whippoorwill
And dream dreams with the animals as your dream companions
Dreams so vivid, so real they will not be dreams my friends
They'll be visions

NORMAN "INGWE" POWELL,
Lean to Hear Voices in the Wind

Indicators of Awareness | 269

to its gifts. Learning directly from nature that we play a part in the bigger story, we learn Service to the Community.

People of all ages always feel eager to figure out where they fit in and how their gifts can contribute. When our community appreciates us, we feel good and begin to appreciate ourselves on a rather profound level. Competitive folks whose identity originally formed around being "better than" will even shift their approach to group situations when they discover the pleasure of being "helpful to." Traditional cultures around the world recognize this dynamic, holding the belief that each human born into this world brings a unique gift for the well-being of the community. Naming ceremonies often reflect the unique talents and tendencies of a person; quests and initiations help humans get in touch with their gift, their truest, most helpful self. We call this the "Gift Concept," and we think it explains why adolescents act so self-centered—it's necessary! Only by finding one's inner gifts can one truly and powerfully be helpful to the community. We think Lao Tzu, the ancient Chinese author of the *Tao Te Ching*, meant community service when he wrote, "the greatest gift we can give to the world is our own self-transformation." It is the mentor's job, and the role of the elders, to help this transformation along. Ultimately, the process is one of discovery, of alchemy: finding in the raw material of a human being some unique golden gift that makes the entire community richer.

As time goes on, you will see this Indicator of Awareness evolve into everyday forms: people serving whenever possible and proactively seeing what they can do to help out. They'll see that the firewood stash is low and refill it when no one's looking. They'll run out to help Mom or Dad bring in the groceries. They'll see that more seats are needed for everyone and disappear, then return with chairs or stumps for all. People will begin to realize they have gifts that others don't, and they will cultivate these, not with a sense of superiority, but with a sense of humility. Once they discover what their community appreciates about them, they won't need to be asked to express it. The ancient Hindu writings of the Vedas call this instinctive service to the community, "dharma," one of the three basic drives that motivate humans.

As people grow to appreciate their niche in the community, they notice others who fill different niches. Self-confidence leads to generosity and encouragement toward others. When this attitude reaches a critical mass in the community, you will know it. The group swims through the day like a school of dolphins or a formation of geese, trading off the lead, resting in the wakes of others. An immense appreciation for community unifies them. Just imagine a world in which the humans live out their gifts and unique talents in a great symbiosis of sustainability—a veritable "ecology of gifts."

Obviously, awareness of Ecological Indicators fosters the awareness about how every little thing connects to everything else. Attentiveness to inter-connections and mutual dependence naturally builds desire for sustainable living. So watch for and nurture this Indicator of Service to the Community as everyone you mentor comes to appreciate how they fit into the bigger ecology.

Northwest: Awe and Reverence

In the Northwest, day dissolves into night, autumn sinks into winter, and the individual human life slows toward taking on the role of Elder, willingly relinquishing its youth to history, reflecting on the death and continuity of life processes. This is the time of awe and reverence.

An experience of being "awestruck" translates into being humbled by something bigger than yourself, or stunned into silence, or quieted down. We see in almost all nature-based cultures a respect for elders and a reverence for ancestors. This willingness to lay aside one's personal wants and needs in the presence of something bigger, older, wiser, more timeworn, more powerful describes both Awe and Reverence.

The well-known permaculture teacher, Penny Livingston-Stark often says, 'the key for establishing a regenerative, sustainable culture lies in understanding that we are not only a part of nature, but that we are a keystone species within the larger pattern of evolution.' That is to say, we are not here to be observers, but active participants in determining what the world will be for at least the next seven generations to come. This understanding naturally accompanies the sense of Awe and Reverence. Over time it evolves into a deep, spiritual acceptance of our responsibility for the health of the children and their environment two hundred years in the future.

I walked outside for a cigarette,
but what I found was the universe
in dark trees and gravel hard to
the feet and
stars that trembled. In that cool
night, I trembled,
not from the cold but from the
facing of my life,
of my pained and joyous stay upon
this spinning earth.
EVAN McGOWN, A Moment

Sometimes, when a bird cries out,
Or the wind sweeps through a
tree,
Or a dog howls in a far-off farm,
I hold still and listen a long time.

My world turns and goes back to
the place
Where, a thousand forgotten
years ago
The bird and the blowing wind
Were like me, and were my
brothers.

My soul turns into a tree,
And an animal, and a cloudbank.
Then, changed and odd, it comes
home
And asks me questions. What
should I reply?

HERMANN HESSE, "Sometimes"

I revere
The explosive song of birds
that welcome the blush of dawn.

The sacred voice of the wind
that stirs my searching soul.

The music of mountain streams
that fall in crystal showers.

The flaming torrent of color
that pours from the evening skies.

The call of the whip-poor-will
that takes me to my dreams.

These my gifts from Mother
Earth
I revere.

Norman "Ingwe" Powell,
"I Revere" *Echoes of Kenya and
Other Poems*

The gale increased, the great trees
bent to and fro and the earth
trembled beneath them. There
was a tremendous crash as one
of the largest lost hold and fell,
the ground shuddering with its
impact. Then another leaned
nearby and I watched as it slowly
moved downward, bringing with
it a shower of bark and branches.
At that moment I knew fear and
wonder and an inner exaltation,
… a sense compounded of being
one with the elements, the trees,
and the wild forces they bow to.

Sigurd Olson, *Open Horizons*

Awe

You will see Awe in people when you climb the mountain and
they gaze out in silent wonder, or when you find the bright
purple salamander that leaves them speechless. You will see it
when you tell them an old mythic story and they listen with
unblinking eyes and profound stillness, visibly touched by the
ancient images and motifs. You will see it when folks assimi-
late over time how one tree might provide edible foods, survival tools, shade, root-stabilization, and legendary characteristics of life-guidance. If the West is where we find our role in
the here-and-now community, the Northwest is where we see
our place in the community across time: the community of
ancestors and future generations. This is the meta-story of the
evolving universe where we live. With a little contemplation,
we feel Awe and Reverence for the immensity and majesty that
lie beneath "the face of the deep."

Awe comes first and always gives us pause. We find many
things "awesome," a dewdrop dangling off the tip of a leaf, a
loud bolt of lightning quickly followed by thunder, the first
lightning bug, a glowworm in the path at night. "All things
wise and wonderful" have a power to stun and make us "lose
our mind and come to our senses." They leave us speechless
and fully engaged in the moment. Whenever nature hands out
an awe-inspiring "magic moment," people naturally stop everything to absorb it. A powerful elder who shares deep wisdom
from connection to the land and ancestors' teachings inspire
awe naturally. Whether you and your participants experience
extraordinary moments or moments of seeing the extraordinary in the ordinary, always let them know such miracles are
more important than "the lesson plan."

Reverence

During my first season leading summer camps in the Pacific
Northwest, I was leaving an area in the forest with my group
when I caught a scent of what smelled like a dead animal.
Following my nose into a patch of bushes, I discovered something that few people ever find—the body of a Bald Eagle.

For a very long moment, I was seized with a sense of Awe and Reverence for this creature, famous not only for its natural history but also as a central symbol in Native American traditions and the symbolic essence of the United States, engraved on every quarter and dollar bill. I wondered how the kids would respond to the sight of this eagle, or to the sight of me in such an awed state.

I expected the kids to yell in excitement, but instead they were silent and big-eyed—for five long minutes we all crouched around in a state of deep reverence, respectfully admiring and contemplating this great bird. After most of the kids left to play a game, one child, who had been in those nature programs for years, stayed behind. In silence he knelt down next to the three-foot long body and gently picked up the huge, curved, sword-like talons in his hand. For minutes he sat quietly, just holding that Eagle's hand, in a state of complete reverence.

Even young children experience reverence in response to powerful glimpses of nature, and being in the presence of dying or dead animals evokes a deep sense of mystery and compassion for living things. Learning to gather our own food from nature—be it plant or animal—really brings this home.

Respect and reverence radiate from young people in the presence of a powerful elder or grandparent who draws from the land and its ancestral teachings. It just seems to be a natural thing for young children—and even adults—to listen to their stories in rapt amazement. Grandpa can get them to listen to things parents never could. Elders can get through to adults like no one else. No wonder, then, sustainable communities place the Elders in charge!

Respect for Heritage

Eventually, Reverence leads to what some nature-based cultures call "a sense of the sacred." One is struck with how precious life is, and how the continuity of life from generation to generation is sustained by a unifying force. There is a feeling of being caught up in a much larger story rooted in thousands of years of history, and continuing through our lives and through the lives of our children.

"Reverence for life," as Dr. Albert Schweitzer called the philosophy that led him to dedicate his life to healing people and animals in Africa, leads to a lifelong commitment to hold the fabric of life sacred—to care for the earth to "leave it better than we found it" for our grandchildren. In this way, the concepts of permaculture and sustainability make sense; people gladly contribute to endeavors that cannot be completed in one lifetime. My horticulture teacher in college once told me, "A man knows the true meaning of life, who plants a shade tree that he'll never feel the shade of." Ingwe always said, "If you believe in the future, plant an oak tree."

Whenever possible, find ways to link people's experience and practical understanding to myth and lore of the Heritage Species and the ways of the ancestors in your area. Learn how nature-based cultures revered certain species or elements of nature—through ceremonies, stories, art, or life-styles built around such icons as salmon, eagles, oak trees, or natural springs—people can't help but resonate with Awe and Reverence. Guided reflection often leads people to reverent revelations about themselves, seeing their own life-story reflected in the folk-myths, metaphors, and hero stories of the larger culture. In this way, you may lead children and adults, and yourself, through the realm of mystery and into reverence.

So continually lead people into wonder-filled experiences in nature. Watch for those big eyes, that gaping mouth and silent reverence. Help them channel those feelings into skills for lifelong concern for the health of the natural world. Equip them to pass it on to the children of the future, and above all, inspire them with knowledge that they are indeed a keystone species on this earth with an important role to play in protecting earth for the future generations, seven generations to come.

North: Self-Sufficiency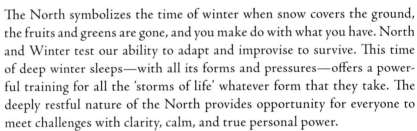

The North symbolizes the time of winter when snow covers the ground, the fruits and greens are gone, and you make do with what you have. North and Winter test our ability to adapt and improvise to survive. This time of deep winter sleeps—with all its forms and pressures—offers a powerful training for all the 'storms of life' whatever form that they take. The deeply restful nature of the North provides opportunity for everyone to meet challenges with clarity, calm, and true personal power.

The Indicator of Self-Sufficiency is all about calm, flexible wisdom. Rather than complaining or wishing things were different, you take what you have in front of you and improvise to solve the problem at hand. Self-Sufficiency adapts to the flow of life, instead of futilely struggling against it. Remembering North is the place of the mature and seasoned Elder, this makes even more sense. The more you experience, the more trials you endure, the less things seem scary. "I've been there, done that. I know I can take care of myself." A sense of Self-Sufficiency integrates one's life wisdom into every task and situation through a deep sense of trust in the process of things and in one's ability to ride the waves.

Ingenuity: *Cleverness, resourcefulness, initiative, creativity, inventiveness, originality, skill, cunning*

Self-Sufficiency also means problem-solving. Practicing survival skills fosters this indicator better than anything, constantly presenting "problems" to be figured out. "So you need a shelter … what are you going to do?" You may observe at first people will feel helpless, wanting to lean on you for answers to each "situation" (a good substitute for "problem"). Initially they might whine, "I don't knooooow!" But have the courage to lead self-sufficiency out of them. Ask questions to get them thinking for themselves. Have them experiment and show them that mistakes hold the keys to learning and growth.

Over time, they will learn to say, "Okay, I need a shelter and what I've got in front of me is sticks and leaves. Look … there's a fork in a tree that will hold up the main beam of our roof. That's how we'll do it!" As they build the shelter, many more little decisions and choices force them to solve their own problems by negotiating with natural forces and with other human beings in the group. The skill to assess needs and creatively address them, serves children and adults in every other area of their lives. Met with challenging situations, we learn to trade in fear for "real hope," action-based hope just like Derrick Jensen writes about in his *Orion Magazine* essay, "Beyond Hope." "When we realize the degree of agency we actually do have, we no longer have to 'hope' at all. We simply do the work. We make sure salmon survive. We make sure prairie dogs survive. We make sure grizzlies survive. We do whatever it takes."

Trees: Tools of Survival, are our best teachers of Self-Sufficiency. We learn which trees have the hardest and sturdiest woods and how to recognize those limbs. Over time, we learn which wood burns without sending off sparks and which has a nice texture for carving. Many of the Survival Activities in this book, such as Five-Minute-Fire, create situations where people need to be Self-Sufficient, to recognize what they have to work with, and to make quick and intelligent choices. You can imagine the incredible value of this life-skill. This Indicator begins to show up in creative choices people make,

The student will think analytically, logically, and creatively, and integrate experience and knowledge to form reasoned judgments and solve problems.

Washington State Essential Academic Learning Requirement; Goal for Critical Thinking

True survival will be measured in whether the archeologists find ruins or continuing oral traditions.

Jon Young

INDICATORS OF AWARENESS

such as how to lean against their backpack to comfortably take a nap or how to make a bridge for others to cross on.

Notice this indicator in people as they grow self-confident in all areas of life. They'll become more easy-going with changes of plans and able to "go with the flow" of the day. They'll stop watching the clock and relax into the moment. Beginning to trust themselves, they step right into the natural flow of things. Also, notice it in yourself when you no longer feel anxious or stay up late to plan out every detail of your mentoring experience, your lecture, your job, or whatever you spend your time doing. Over time, and through meaningful, survival-based connection with nature, you discover yourself trusting more and more in the process, in the moment, and in your own ingenuity and creativity rather than spending hours worrying and planning.

Watch for this indicator of Self-Sufficiency and foster it through activities that provoke improvisation. Help facilitate the group to work with the power of creativity and unity, and help everyone see possibilities on both small and grand scales. As those you mentor become much more comfortable with change, and much more confident in their abilities to maneuver through seemingly tough situations, those "dark winters" of life seem more inviting. This profound and gentle force of the North inspires true leadership of the archetypal Elder: piercing the future with a powerful vision for real hope that comes from the knowledge we can and will do whatever is necessary to make it through.

Northeast: Quiet Mind

Imagine that moment in the wee hours of the morning, just before the soft pink light of the dawn starts to chase away the stars. As it is said, 'the darkest hour is just before the dawn.' There is a stillness, a mystery, a pregnant calm …

When the indicator of Quiet Mind begins to show, you will be looking at a well-rounded success of connecting with nature. The whole of this approach has been about coming alive, feeling passionate and healthy, and about awakening the

Sparkle in the Eye! The peak of it all appears as the Quiet Mind, an intensely alert ability to be still, peaceful, present in the moment, and listen. We notice an active, unobtrusive receptivity to what is happening everywhere at all times.

And yet, the Quiet Mind also signifies the beginning, the place you want to start, with every person, the quality to invisibly and deftly cultivate from the beginning. Our Elder, Gilbert Walking Bull, always said, "Start with the Quiet Mind and through this, all the other sacred attributes will emerge." Tom Brown calls this the "sacred silence." Athletes call it "the zone." Brain-wave scientists call it "theta." Various meditative or religious traditions name it yet differently. Quiet Mind represents a state of alert attention and complete presence that accompanies our daily activities. It's not religious, only natural. People immediately reach their Quiet Minds in nature through hiding games where they sit up and listen up.

Notice this Indicator emerging when sitting-still becomes natural and easy. Up until then, your participants might have fidgeted a lot, but now you see them grow relaxed as their Quiet Mind strengthens. Eventually, this translates into Sit Spot time they take for themselves during lunch or other breaks. Or, you might hear about it from parents who tell you their children can sit under a tree for hours. Sneaking also helps to induce the Quiet Mind. At first people tend to be loud, dependent on speed or strength in moments of stealth. Time with nature brings a very natural ability to move with stillness, patience, and ever-present listening. A sneaking scout—whether playing a game or stalking a wild animal—no longer darts mindlessly from bush to bush in spurts of noise and movement, but waits for a gust of wind to rustle the leaves and cover up other sounds. The scout then moves in a way that blends into the overall patterns already present in an environment. The Quiet Mind—uncluttered, calm, observant—begins to reveal the "art of invisibility."

Listening to the Language of Birds supports this emerging quality of Quiet Mind. Midst the screaming of children or thunder of traffic, listening to the birds' voices causes people to reach out with their ears to discern "the still small voice midst the storm." Also, as we often hear rather than see birds,

My father could hear a little animal step,
Or a moth in the dark against the screen,
And every far sound called the listening out
Into places where the rest of us had never been.

More spoke to him from the soft wild night
Than came to our porch for us on the wind;
We would watch him look up and his face go keen
Til the walls of the world flared, widened.

My father heard so much that we still stand
Inviting the quiet by turning the face,
Waiting for a time when something in the night
Will touch us too from that other place.

WILLIAM STAFFORD, "Listening"

INDICATORS OF AWARENESS

we can often be inspired to stop in our tracks, look around, or even sit down, to see the bird making such sounds. To encourage development of the Quiet Mind, send people out into the woods to sit and LISTEN—for birds, planes, wind, and people's voices—as intently and widely as they possibly can.

Having a Quiet Mind, however, doesn't just mean stillness alone in nature. You will also notice an internal peacefulness that prevails even when a person mingles with a large group of people. This is "peace of mind." Those you mentor will really listen when you share a story or a teaching, and they will also listen to each other without needing to interrupt. They won't have to fidget. They will grow peaceful with stillness. As a long-practicing Buddhist elder and jazz pianist once told me when I asked if he had a meditation room in his house, "No... Every room is my meditation room!" Ultimately, our quiet mind creates "the zone" that we walk with, where being fully present and alive to our senses becomes our default mode. The thinking, analytical, and "to-do" list mind becomes more like a pocket-knife that we keep on our belt. When we need it to fix a computer glitch or solve a math problem, we simply pull it out. Otherwise, we feel alert and alive to the moment, while our mind rests in quiet, attentive peace.

When people discover this ability to be still and peaceful, notice how they develop a more insightful sense of thankfulness. Their thankfulness reaches to new depths. When people first take part in a Thanksgiving Circle they might say nothing or say too much. As they grow in peacefulness, all their jumping up and down impatience falls away and transforms into a serene listening for what they feel truly thankful for, and they speak from that feeling.

So watch for stillness and emerging patience, attentive listening to bird calls and others' stories, peaceful presence, genuine thankfulness, and long sits in silent awareness. Use hiding, sneaking, bird language, long pauses in stories, and role-modeling to cultivate and lead out the apex of all the Indicators of Awareness, the Quiet Mind.

Reviving the Original Blueprint

These Indicators of Awareness offer the final layer of intention for you to be conscious of for guiding your people back into their most natural and powerful selves connected with their place. Wonderfully, the Core Routines and species in the Book of Nature match up with the Indicators of Awareness. Eventually, everything interweaves with the integrity of a basket which, woven green, tightens into place as it matures into a woody and lasting container.

Chapter 12
WRAPPING THE BUNDLE

From Theory to Practice

If you have made it this far in reading Coyote's Guide, you're at the end of a long walk through a landscape of many ideas. We could call this the Land of Theory. At the end of this journey is a gate—the land beyond we could call the Land of Practice. Before we take this metaphor any further, we have to stop and think about something: to the people from whom we have received this style of mentoring, this stuff is not theory, *it's life*. Their wisdom flows in their bones. Native people's knowledge is truly embodied, passed through generations of personal experience from people who had to be connected with nature or they would have died. These are our ancestors. Their lives—and our future lives—depended on their knowledge of place. It's time-proven stuff and your living hands holding this very book demonstrate the connection between theory and practice.

However, for many who have not had nature connection as a sacred part of life, we have to re-train ourselves in this old method, and wake up the ancient memory in our bones. We've laid it out as well as we could in the form of this book, and now it's time to

Who are elders? Paul Raphael has some criteria. You get butterflies in your stomach when you are about to go visit elders, because you know they will be able to look right through you.

JON YOUNG

bring it to life. For as martial arts legend Bruce Lee once said, "Knowing is not enough, we must apply. Willing is not enough, we must do." This chapter is the gate, a few short pages that lead from the Mentor's Manual—with its theory and philosophy—to the Activities—with their application and practice.

We want to acknowledge the "ancestors" of this Coyote Mentoring lineage, the elders of indigenous cultures from around the world, Gilbert Walking Bull of the Lakota of the Great Plains and Ingwe of the Akamba in East Africa. To these mentors, this was not about "ideas" or "theory" at all—they lived this way of life. Practicing these old ways will get you so comfortable with the application of these ideas that you gain a new fluent "language"— one you can speak when you need it and lay aside when you don't.

Let's recap the "Story of the Day"—your reading journey through this Mentor's Manual. In wrapping these core ideas into a bundle, we create what primitive fire-makers call a "tinder bundle"—a bundle of fine, shredded materials, often inner bark or fluffy seed-heads, with a consistency like a tender handful of dryer lint. The tinder bundle only awaits the spark, the little embryonic coal with some air blown into it, to become a blazing fire. That spark, that coal—is you.

For we want nature connection to be alive within our children and our communities, with a life of its own, just like fire. Right now, all over the world, small fires are blazing strong in the form of schools and communities, and they grow steadily through personal experience, inspiring and starting other fires along the way. Following the Activities, you will find "Coyote in Context: Weaving the Web" written by Jon Young. Through his storytelling, we visit the realm of future possibility and what is possible when nature connection is taken seriously. Beautiful and amazing, the vision Jon paints is a mosaic of stories and images from real-life communities around the world where the fire of nature mentoring already blazes.

A Tinder Bundle of Ideas

Ready to make some fire? Alright, then. Let's bundle-up the tinder of this Mentor's Manual.

We can remember back to that first story of mine, that day in Redmond, the home of Microsoft, when a Coyote led me from my car and my errand-busy mind, and through the clear-cuts of new development, edge-by-edge, until I came to a relationship with a wild patch of woods, with its trees, and birds, and bones. The first idea of this book is that Coyote Mentoring is about constantly straddling, stretching, and pulling edges. It's about leading people from edge to further edge, not by coercion or force-feeding, but by subtle cues and mysterious hints that wake up human curiosity and empower it into self-led action. It is about starting where people are at. Nowadays this means concrete roads, houses and cars, computer-based technologies, fears and misconceptions about nature, and internalized patterns of disconnection from nature, others, and our selves. We must accept the reality of what is and begin there. Our imagination of what else is possible—fresh ways of learning and shifted routines of connection—takes us from edge of possibility into new reality, which shows us the next edge, and so on. Coyote leads exactly in this way. Our goal is to entice the people we mentor through personal experience and meaningful connection with nature toward a more natural conception of reality.

The Core Routines of Nature Connection—proven over thousands of years—lead humans to deep and personal learning. They are not ideas that we teach, but practices we instill in their everyday lives. As mentors, we encourage the "dirt time," of personal experience through practice of the Core Routines, while engaging dialogue and reflection about those experiences. Through this dynamic process, our personal edges get revealed, our curiosity is stoked, and we feel inspired for yet more experiences. Back and forth the dance goes—experience, reflect, question, experience, reflect, question. Find the edge and go into it. It's a dance that awakens self-challenge, self-propelled learning. The Core Routines are the foundational dance steps.

But we can't force people into doing the Core Routines; we must lead with artful, almost mischievous guidance, employing the phenomenon of Child Passions. By tapping into what all humans get excited about and love doing, we sneak the Core Routines in so that they become default behaviors associated with fun and exhilaration. Through the doorway of Child Passions, the Core Routines are invisibly woven into the fabric of people's lives. Core Routines just feel natural, because they cause everyone to feel happy and alive. Playing games, taking adventures, exploring landscapes, asking questions, telling stories, singing songs—Core Routines enter into peoples' routines through these avenues of fun.

The central idea in the Book of Nature presents learning through relationships: meaningful relationships and real connections. We recommend making connection one of the fundamental intentions in your mentoring. That's why we included "connecting" in the title of the book. We emphasize real relationships with real animals, real plants, real clouds, real mountains, and real people. This emphasis brings us back to the personal experience behind Core Routines. We encourage field guides with mud-stained pages, eating the things we study, touching them, feeling them, wearing them … and through these experiences, learning to love them. The Book of Nature points out to us as mentors the most fertile places to start growing nature connections.

Yet when we invoke such aliveness and close connection, we had better have an awareness of how to handle all that energy and direct it in positive ways. That's where the Natural Cycle shows us a framework of energy-flows—for an hour, a day, or a year—grounding our plans (and improvisations) in common sense and observation. Ultimately, the Natural Cycle gets us to the question: "What is really needed right now for learning or for integration of learning?" Our imaginations leap forward to plan for success based on orientation to the Natural Cycle; it can save mentors a lot of hit-or-miss. Because we're not always in control, it teaches us to look for optimal contexts and conditions for learning so we continually adjust our timing and settings. Even in teaching about nature, we are nature, and subject to the whole flowing equilibrium.

The big idea behind Indicators of Awareness admittedly rests upon an assumption on our part—the assumption that connecting with nature is a natural thing for human beings to do. If this is true, then certain outcomes and qualities will emerge within the nature of people themselves. That's exactly what all of our founders, elders, and instructors have observed over a long time of watching. Qualities like Common Sense, Inquisitive Focus, and Quiet Mind are the fertile soil from which all learning naturally grows, according to the seeds of curiosity in a person's mind and heart. These ways of being indicate both successful learning and learning goals. We think it's the job of the mentor to take care of the soil and to leave it up to the seed to determine the shape of the plant. We also think a similar re-visioning of the outcomes that measure success in education is needed in our modern world, and we offer the Indicators of Awareness as one way to begin doing just that.

Bursting into Action

See these elements—Core Routines, Child Passions, Book of Nature, Natural Cycle, and Indicators of Awareness—as layers of intention that lie behind Coyote Mentoring. To continue the fire metaphor, these layers may behave as the starter materials—the shredded bark and thistle fluff—for wrapping into a nice, tight tinder-bundle. All that's needed is the coal of action. That's where you come in and that's what the rest of this book is about. Each Activity combines specific layers of intention meant to produce specific results of nature connection (of course they'll also generate a lot of opportunity for connection we could never predict).

You can pick and choose among the eight sets of activities in the following Activities Guide. They are organized so you can select your best tinder to Introduce the Core Routines, Set up the Learning Landscape, then engage people with Plants and Wandering or Mammals and Tracking or other chapters of the Book of Nature. We divided each of the activities into four sections—Primer, How-To, Inside the Mind of the Mentor, and Alternatives and Extensions—to enable you to shred out the bits most likely to catch fire in your situation.

These activities spark into flame with the "Key" that introduces each activity. This five-idea Key reveals how the big ideas of the Mentor's Manual are invisibly inserted into learning situations. It de-constructs each tinder-bundle of an Activity, showing the separate threads of intention that underlie the fire-making. It helps put you inside the Mind of the Mentor, asking:

When you have something to offer, you have to keep offering it until somebody comes up behind. When we recognize what needs to be done, then we should roll up our sleeves and get to work. [That's] the way life is. What you are doing is you're teaching a different way of looking at things.

Jake Swamp, *Art of Mentoring and Coyote Teaching* audio

1. What Core Routines are being invisibly practiced through this activity?

2. What Child Passions are being invoked to make this activity a fun and engaging experience?

3. What species/elements of the natural world, as organized in the Book of Nature, are being connected with?

4. What's the general energy of this activity? Where might it likely fit in the Natural Cycle of your program?

5. What Indicators of Awareness are being cultivated in participants through this activity?

The intention and attention that mentors use to design and facilitate learning can shift a "simple game" into a transformational learning event. The clearer our intentions behind a story, a lesson, or a game, the more potent the opportunity will be for teaching and learning.

Making It Your Own

Of course, there are many more possible layers of intention. Don't feel you have to limit yourself to our layers of intention. Right now, ask yourself: What are my most vital intentions in education? What do I care about? What do I stand for in the world? How can I integrate these intentions into educational activities? Rather than give out recipes for you to follow, the intention of this book is to unveil the principles behind the recipes so you can create recipes yourself.

A music mentor once told me that he had a collection of the very first recordings of the Beatles. Every one of the forty tunes was a cover-song—written by other bands. His metaphoric point: first we get really good at playing the creations of other people; then as we internalize the principles behind the songs—or the Activities—we begin to write our own. Now think of the huge plethora of original songs that the Beatles eventually wrote. You are capable of doing the same in nature mentoring. Start with the bundle of Activities here, but let them eventually launch you into your own creative scene. When you become strongly centered in your own intentions as an educator and or mentor, and artfully weave these intentions into the experiences you facilitate, to the point that your intentions are invisible, then you are dancing Coyote.

At this point, we should know that the nature of Coyote Mentoring will be invisible to other people. It's meant to wake up curiosities so that your learners feel like they did it all by themselves (because really, they did). You may get people who say, "The instructors didn't teach anything." You may get supervisors who wonder if you're doing your job. Finally, you may grow frustrated, deciding you'll just have to explain it, and start teaching workshops on mentoring (that's how our mentoring workshops got started). Even if you never explain it, people will start to see it. The results will speak for themselves. You'll get invitations from the parents of children you mentor, or your adult participants will bring you hand-made baskets as gifts or show up to do spontaneous repairs on your house. Trust us: Coyote Mentoring works.

The Coyote Mentoring journey is like the growth of an old oak tree. It will take a while for it to grow, and even longer to bear fruit, but it will grow strong and sturdy and productive, and stand firm over hundreds of years. And when it meets the fire, it will burn long, slow, and hot. The outcomes and relationships that result from this mentoring journey will be rich and rewarding. But, at first, it might be hard.

Therefore, as fellow mentors, let us begin by appreciating each other. Thank you, whoever you are with this book in your hands, thank you for taking this journey. Thank you for the work it's taken to get through this Manual. Thank you for following your curiosity this far and for your desire to empower others' curiosities. Thank you for the mentoring you are doing and intend to do. Thank you for tending the earth and its many-life forms … whatever direction you may go. Jon, Ellen, and I sincerely look forward to meeting you and hearing your stories.

Sparking the Bundle

In closing: this book isn't much without action. It is a tinder bundle, just sitting and waiting. The spark of fire exists in you as your creativity. Each time you step outside now with someone and ask a question—or tell a story, or play a game—each action, big or little, is a breath blown into the tinder bundle. Eventually, momentum builds, the ideas actualize into your own brilliant, unique mentoring style—and the fire burns into magnificent shapes no one could predict. Ever-changing, yet always dancing with universal elements and principles of nature, the flame goes on. Humans grow. Evolution moves forward with greased wheels. And Coyote, looking back at us from that next edge of dark woods—wags the tip of a tail—and vanishes again.

ACTIVITY GUIDE

Introducing Core Routines
ACTIVITIES

Stories and Activities that
set up and inspire continual practice and
create life-long learning habits

The activities in this section introduce the Core Routines of Nature Connection. By *core*, we mean they are starting places, foundations, to be continually practiced over time in as many ways as possible. You can add stories, songs, and your own adaptations to fit your people and place. Activities introduce you to the magic of each Core Routine. After participants have done them once, repeat and interweave in an infinite number of ways. Never let them become boring chores or disciplines—in fact, younger children should never even be told they are practicing "Core Routines." Always keep their magic alive.

In this section, we preface each activity with a personal story that could be told to inspire others and set-up the activity. Feel free to re-tell these if you like them, or use them as triggers that evoke stories from your own life. In the Suggested Reading, you will find a multitude of stories from natural history writers that you could read or adapt to inspire the practice of Core Routines of Nature Connection.

Sit Spot

CORE ROUTINES	Sit Spot, Expanding Our Senses, Mapping, Questioning and Tracking, Listening for Bird Language, plus all other Core Routines.
CHILD'S PASSIONS	Hiding, Spying, Discovering, Seeing Animals Close Up
BOOK OF NATURE	The whole Book of Nature
NATURAL CYCLE	Northeast: Open and Listen, Southwest: Take a Break
INDICATROS OF AWARENESS	Inquisitive Focus, Caring and Tending, Quiet Mind, and all other Indicators of Awareness.

Story: *A Whole Different World, by Evan McGown*

Do any of you have a special place you like to go in nature, maybe in your backyard or a park near your house? Some of you might already have a Sit Spot, a special place somewhere in nature that you visit all the time, a place that's just yours, a place that you know better than anyone else, a place where you know wild animals as your friends.

I have a Sit Spot in my backyard. When I go there, I enter a secret world most adults don't know about. I want to tell you a story about this other world, the world of nature, always around and waiting for us. I once lived in a house on the busiest street of a small town. Cars would drive by all day and I could hear them from my house. But this house backed up to a park, and that's where I had my Sit Spot. To go to my Sit Spot I slid down a steep bank at the end of my backyard. Here my neighbor always dumped his grass clipping and leaves, and no one else ever went down there, or probably even thought of going down there! But me—I would leave my shoes in the house, walk across the nicely-cut lawn, nice and cool on my bare feet, and slide down that hill on my butt, sometimes getting good and muddy.

Down that hill, I entered a whole different world. Everything was wild, cottonwood trees and snowberry bushes. The muddy-ground was often full of tracks from all kinds of animals—deer, raccoons, feral cats. It took me a while to tell who left what tracks, but after a while I could read the tracks pretty well. The muddy ground became a storybook that told me about my animal neighbors and what they had been up to the night before.

This place down the hill was so special to me that I explored it as much as I could. There was one particular area I loved the most. I called this my Sit Spot, and even though I would tell my friends stories about it no one knew the exact location. The park had a nice big stream flowing through it, and the spot where I loved to sit was right on the bank of the stream. I would sit there for hours, especially at sunrise and sunset, because that was when the magic would happen … just like it did on a day I'll never forget.

On this day, I woke up very early, before the sun rose, when it was still dark and little chilly. I slowly Fox-Walked out into my backyard careful not to alarm any sleeping birds, and then I otter-slid down the hill. Everything was quiet, the air was cool. I Fox-Walked out to my Sit Spot and sat down by the stream. After 20 minutes, the eastern sky started to turn light pink, and I was basking in the beauty of the first rays of sunlight, when suddenly—SPLASH!—a sound came from the creek right behind me. It was behind my back where I couldn't see, and it seemed to be only two or three feet away. I heard other smaller splashes, and decided to sit as still as I could and hold my breath.

I waited, my heart pumping, when out of the corner of my eye I saw a large animal walking in the stream. My heart beat faster and faster, and soon that critter ambled out of the stream right in front of me: it was a big, beautiful raccoon. It waddled toward me and then came right in front of me without reacting to me. Then my owl eyes picked up another movement, and then another, three baby raccoons paraded in a straight line right in front of me. Following their mom they looked so cute! I could have reached out and petted them. Still none of them seemed to ever see me, hear me, or smell me. Then the last little baby raccoon suddenly stopped right in front of my lap, stood up on his hind feet with his front paws dangling in the air, and turned towards me and sniffed the air. It must have been wondering, "What the heck is that?" That moment seemed to last forever as we stared at each other, but in a flash it turned and loped playfully back to its family.

Sitting at that one spot, I watched those baby raccoons grow up, finding crayfish to eat and playing with each other in the stream. I also got to know other wild friends that lived there: deer sniffed me and stared at me before crossing the stream, beavers carried sticks up and down the stream, eagles swooped right over my head, great blue heron stalked up behind me silently and scared the heck out of me, and even a little springy jumping mouse once jumped right into my lap!

I spent a lot of time sitting at that one special spot, and it seemed the animals accepted me as a natural part of that place. Going there felt like going home. Even the song sparrow who hung out in a nearby patch of knotweed eventually stopped chipping its alarms at me; instead while I sat, it would come to the bush behind me and sing its beautiful song right over my head. I named it Singer. I had so many amazing, unforgettable experiences, just sitting quietly in this place until I became part of the other world of wild animals and nature. You can do the same thing. All you need to do is find a special place, a Sit Spot where you can go to explore, sit still, and watch and wait for that world to welcome you.

How-To

Inspire. First, make sure to inspire people. Tell a story like the one above or ask them if they'd like to be able to see or touch a wild animal.

Find a Spot. Wherever you are, ask the participants to go out and find a Sit Spot where they will sit still and be silent and wait to see what they notice. Ask them to Fox-Walk to find a spot that calls to them in the nearby area. You can take a group along a path and let individuals veer off one by one. Keep everyone at least in earshot. Once they find a spot, they will sit as still and quiet as they can, and turn on their Owl Eyes and Deer Ears to see what comes.

Give a Time Limit. Tell them you will call them back in a few minutes, and ask them not to come back until they hear your call. The amount of time you have them sit will depend on your group. Start with an awesome 5 minutes for five- or six-year-olds; older people might find their initial capacity for sitting still at around 15 minutes. Adults completely vary, but some can easily sit for hours. Expect a wide range of reactions. No matter how long they sit, some will want more, others less.

Return with Story of the Day. Call them back in and ask them what they noticed. Participants will often come back with excited tales to tell of animals they think they heard or butterflies or birds they saw. If the inspiration is alive and flowing in the group, encourage them to find a Sit Spot at home and come back next time to share their stories. Making time for telling personal Sit Spot stories from home is a great way to start a day. Use this opportunity to role model your own Sit Spot practice. This also helps us mentors stay grounded in our own Sits Spots and learning journeys.

Inside the Mind of the Mentor

Wait until they seem ready. Your goal includes everyone adopting a Sit Spot at home, and visiting it daily, even before sun-up and after dark. But we want it to flow naturally from a love for nature—**never a forced or boring activity**. Therefore, before you introduce the conscious routine of Sit Spot, we suggest you wait until your people feel comfortable enough in nature to accept the idea of sitting alone. Games such as Eagle Eye or Sleeping Fawn help increase their comfort level. Introduce Sit Spot at the right moment; otherwise it may be a Nervous and Uncomfortable Spot, or an idea they'll rebel against. After only a day or two of playing hiding games to invisibly expand their comfort zone, and after hearing their friends tell Sit Spot stories, even fearful people will spontaneously want to find a Sit Spot.

Love the One You're With. As we said in the Mentor's Manual, the search for the perfect Sit Spot might entangle some people in frustration and competition. So, show them how to use their Body Radar (See Wandering activity) to sense out a spot that attracts them, but encourage them to enjoy whatever place they land. Once the stories come home, everyone will realize sitting reveals the perfection, because every spot is perfect.

Alternatives and Extensions

Go Often. Incorporate the Core Routine of Sit Spot into your ongoing program, so participants get to visit the same spot in different times of day and weather.

Equipment. We do not recommend taking equipment, lunch, pets, or friends to the Sit Spot, because the whole idea is to be private, fully attentive, and make no disturbance—to "lose your mind and come to your senses." However, certainly exceptions to this rule include: binoculars help near-sighted bird-watchers; jeweler's loupes reveal amazing detail in mosses and leaves; sketching in a journal can help quiet down a fidgety body; and mapping the surrounding terrain can focus Mind's Eye Imagining. If your program calls for keeping good scientific records of life around your Sit Spot, then by all means, include equipment. But just remember that any kind of secondary activity can detract from the purity of the Sit Spot experience.

Pine Cone Bird-Feeder. For a more immediately engaging introduction to Sit Spot, have everyone make a home-made bird feeder: take a pine cone, spread peanut butter over it, and then roll it in birdseed. Attach a string and go find a Sit Spot and hang the bird feeder in front of them and observe the birds that come to feast. Great for younger people.

Group Sit Spot. Find under Community and Ecology Activities

Story of the Day: Sharing Circle

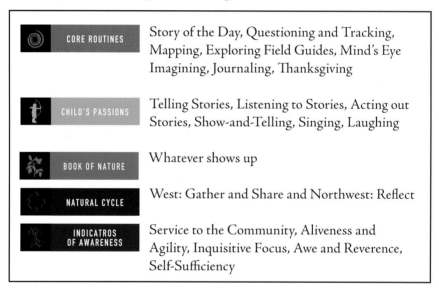

CORE ROUTINES	Story of the Day, Questioning and Tracking, Mapping, Exploring Field Guides, Mind's Eye Imagining, Journaling, Thanksgiving	
CHILD'S PASSIONS	Telling Stories, Listening to Stories, Acting out Stories, Show-and-Telling, Singing, Laughing	
BOOK OF NATURE	Whatever shows up	
NATURAL CYCLE	West: Gather and Share and Northwest: Reflect	
INDICATROS OF AWARENESS	Service to the Community, Aliveness and Agility, Inquisitive Focus, Awe and Reverence, Self-Sufficiency	

Story: *The San Bushmen of the Kalahari, by Evan McGown*

The San Bushmen of the Kalahari Desert in southern Africa live as one of the last remaining groups of hunter-gatherers on the earth: some of them still get all their food from hunting and harvesting wild roots and plants. Their hunting success comes from their incredible knowledge of nature and especially the art of animal tracking. Just by looking at tracks in the sand, they can tell you whether a leopard is a male or female, what state of health it is in, or when it made the trail. Such skill comes from long hours of tracking, and ultimately from hunger—if you can't track, then no meat for you.

Now imagine: you are a Bushmen and you go out for a day of hunting with your bow and arrows. You pick up the fresh trail of a steenbok, a slender

African antelope, and you start tracking it. You jog along, silently following its trail, looking ahead to predict where it will go. Always listening for birds, you know they will warn you of the lions, water-ox, or other dangerous animals. Eventually you catch up with the steenbok, but it is full of energy and easily bounds away, out of sight. The day grows late, and you know you must turn back to the village before the night comes because lions and leopards and hyenas take over the dark landscape of the night.

When you get back to the village, you sit around the fire with all your friends and relatives, and you tell the story of your day of tracking and unsuccessful hunting. As you tell the story, you mention all the tracks you found—porcupine, leopard, rhino, eagle, owl—telling the whole day like reliving it. When you finish your story, another hunter tells about his day hunting in a different part of the land, and he tells of all the tracks and plants he came across, describing his day in detail. He was unlucky, too, no meat. Some tell about the patch of root-plants they found where they played, and hand some to you to eat. They tell you the story of the tracks they found on the way there, and ask you about them. Think about how much people learn from each other.

Then, just as the sun sets, another hunter returns with a small deer-like animal slung over his shoulder. Because of a good hunt, he has brought back meat. He shares the meat and everyone is happy. Then comes the time for him to tell about his hunt; everyone listens intently. He explains how the tracks changed as he went along, how the deer tried to hide, what the deer ate, and finally how he snuck up on it, shot it with his bow then followed its tracks until it lay down for the last time. The videos I have seen of these hunters show them dancing the movements of the animals as they tell about them, and dancing their own hunting steps; the story comes alive in their body as they act it out.

This happens over and over: tracking, exploring, hunting, and harvesting plants during the day, and then returning to tell stories around the fire. Some storytellers love to act out their story, while others tell it more calmly, but usually everyone laughs and eats and share stories until sleep time. Telling each other stories of what happened at the end of every day means everyone benefits from each person's adventure.

I like that. That's my idea of a good time: have crazy-fun adventures during the day and then come back at the end and trade stories.

How-To

Formal or Informal. Make The Story of the Day a conscious routine every time you gather. It can happen as formally or informally as you want. The above story clearly sets it up as a more formal thing, around a fire, with the whole community. In your program, everyone could gather after a dispersed adventure, sit in a Sharing Circle at lunchtime, or circle up before heading home. But it can also be casual, a few people talking on the way. In fact, sometimes this works a lot better, as participants feel less pressure to speak and stories come naturally. Try to keep these casual chats from straying back into the world of human gossip or TV shows.

Sharing Circle. Generally, an effective way to share Stories of the Day comes through a Sharing Circle where everyone can see and hear everyone else. People can share their stories one by one around the circle, or "pop-corn" style when they have something bright to say. For large groups subdivided into smaller groups, one person can represent the group story—with other group members invited to add on.

Talking Stick. Sometimes, it helps to have a physical object to pass around, signifying whose turn it is to talk. It can be anything, a pine-cone, a stick, or a rock just found for the occasion, or a decorated and honored "talking-stick" kept in the Nature Museum and brought out for the Sharing Circle. You could call it a "talking stone," or better still, a "listening stone." Whoever holds it becomes the one listened to by everyone else.

Telling and Listening. Be sure to role-model dramatic, colorful, five-sensory Storytelling, not only to expand your skills but to draw out the more confident, expressive people in the group. (See Storytelling in the Mentor's Manual for lots of advice.) Remember, though, good listening complements good storytelling. So role model and coach for attentive listening that values everyone's voice.

Focal Questions. To help the sharing flow more easily and mitigate the overwhelming feeling of, "I don't know what to share," narrow things down with a specific question: "What was your favorite part of the day?" "What one thing did you learn today?" "What bird did you hear alarming today?" "What funny thing happened today?" "What made you laugh the hardest today?"

Inside the Mind of the Mentor

When people share personal stories from the day, they express themselves, their creativity, and their own experience of life. They affirm the validity of their experience, they gain confidence, they find their own voice, and they also find the edge of their knowledge and become inspired to go back out and learn more.

Sharing Circles for Story of the Day create opportune times for mentors to listen, watch, and artfully question the people we mentor, so we can lead them from one edge of knowing to a farther edge.

Celebrate. Just as important, through Story of the Day, each person's experience and learning gets celebrated by the community. People feel pride in what they've seen, learned, and felt; they also have their passions and gifts seen and acknowledged by others. A little "performance" in front of a community raises awareness and imprints nature in their memory.

Be Creative. The Story of the Day can happen in a lot of ways. Do not shut people down; let the excitement and aliveness get expressed and celebrated. Bless it, and do what you need to in order to keep the cycle going: have adventures, and then come back and tell stories that inspire more adventures. So it goes on, without end, a perpetual round.

Alternatives and Extensions

Mapping. Mapping is a perfect thing to combine with the telling of the Story of the Day. Draw a big map on the board or large paper, and mark on it the location of each story-event. This can engage all the scouts in refining their Mind's Eye Imagination of the whole landscape and seeing their own story in context.

Journaling. With teenagers and adults, written journals of the Story of the Day grow into awesome collections. With younger kids, this can be dictating or drawing.

Beyond Story. If you have a more expressive group, try to help them create a song or rhyming poem that tells about their day. You can also act out stories in skits which can be quite hilarious. Ask people to collect or create something to Show-and-Tell and then add their artifacts to the Nature Museum.

Field Guides. Story of the Day also generates the perfect time to Explore Field Guides, identify things you found, pursue questions, and inevitably find new things to look for when you go out again.

Short Version. When running low on time, go around in a circle and ask people to share one word (or two or three or four) of what they learned or feel thankful for from the day.

Expanding Our Senses: Animal Senses

CORE ROUTINES		Expanding Our Senses, Animal Forms, Mind's Eye Imagining, Exploring Field Guides
CHILD'S PASSIONS		Running, Jumping, Catching, Sneaking, Imitating, Pretending, Being Animals, Making up Characters, Playing House
BOOK OF NATURE		Birds and Mammals
NATURAL CYCLE		Northeast: Open and Listen, South: Focus
INDICATROS OF AWARENESS		Quiet Mind, Aliveness and Agility

Story: *Evan's OWLs, by Evan McGown*

One day I had an unforgettable experience with one of the most elusive and most beautiful of birds. Leaving my Sit Spot just as the sun started to set, I decided to jog on the trail back to my car.

Jogging, I used my peripheral vision, what we call Owl Eyes, intentionally causing my eyes to see more than normal. I also used all of my senses, sniffing the earthy air, listening to the last bird-songs of the day, and feeling the breeze on my skin. Suddenly I heard a great big "whoosh!" right behind me, stopping me in my tracks. It's a good thing I ducked, because a bird about as big as a cat swooped right over my head. It landed on a tree branch about three feet away from me, settled its wings, and just stared at me. Can anyone guess what flew at me? It was a Barred Owl.

Standing there, my heart beating fast, I thought, "Owl ... if I want to learn to use Owl Eyes, here is the greatest teacher I'll ever meet." So I stared back at the owl with its huge eyes and imitated the way it perched on the branch, completely calm and quiet, blending into the woods around it. My whole body relaxed like Owl's, and I slipped back into Owl Eyes, allowing my eyes to go soft and wide. As I did, my body relaxed.

I became Owl: when he turned his head slightly to follow the sound of leaves rustling on the ground, I also turned my head, feeling my neck as a well-greased machine, turning on bearings. Rotating my head and using my Owl Eyes, I could see almost the entire landscape around me.

I'm not sure how long I stood there. Time didn't matter, maybe only fifteen minutes passed. Suddenly I saw a movement ahead of me. I quickly turned my owl-head to focus: a pair wings thirty feet away, opened up and sailed into the air … and came straight towards me. In a moment, this second bird landed three feet away on the other side of the trail … another owl!

So now, one owl perched three feet to my left, and another one perched three feet to my right. Can you imagine my excitement at being so close to these two wild animals of the night? I returned to my Owl Eyes so I could see both owls in my peripheral vision. I looked at their beautiful, long, sharp talons, but didn't feel fear. Instead, I imagined I was just another owl, sitting with my relatives. I felt the fluff of feathers all over my body. I gripped my toes and imagined talons clutching the branch. Moving my shoulders ever so slightly, I felt great wings resting at my side.

The sun sank below the horizon, and the woods around me grew darker and colder. I listened, and smelled, feeling the wind blow against my skin. Then I heard a sound down the trail. In the exact same moment, all three heads turned … mine and two Owls'. Using Owl Eyes, I recognize a joggers' shape through the trees. We heard footfalls and heavy breathing. When that jogger was still down the trail, Owls and I made eye contact one last time, then they lifted silently, and flew about twenty feet into the woods where they perched a bit higher. They dissolved into the darkening web of tree branches silhouetted against the sky.

I took a cue from the Owls and took just one step off the trail, next to a tree, then relaxed back into being an owl, blending into the leaves around me. Watching, my Owl Eyes detected the swooping flight of bats. I could still make out the lump-shapes of the two owls. I wondered if they watched to see to see if my owl disguise would hide me from the jogger.

As the jogger approached, he ran with his head down, huffing and puffing away. I kept being an owl as the man ran by … and didn't notice. Whew, he didn't even see me. But the instant I thought this, he must have seen a glimpse of my bright yellow shorts, because he suddenly screamed, tripped, and fell on the trail, looking up at me as if I were a ghost.

"What … wha … what are you doing? You scared me to death!" He was shocked, not understanding why I would just be standing on the side of the trail like that.

"Sorry, I didn't mean to scare you … I am watching and imitating Owls, see up there in the trees?" He didn't even look where I pointed, but just got up, turned around, and ran off, running more quickly this time.

I had to let out a giggle … so this is what it's like to be an owl. Silent, catching every single movement with their eyes and ears, hiding just enough so that people can't see them … except; it seemed I still had some work to do on my hiding skills. I thanked the Owls for the lesson they gave me and walked the rest of the way in the dark, my senses drinking in the landscape.

The Owls taught me about using my senses to notice everything happening around me and how to stretch those senses far out into the distance. By doing this, we can see others before they see us. Since then, I've used Owl Eyes and my other senses to see animals before they see me: I have stalked herons, and leaping frogs, massive bears, and tiny shrews.

How-To

After inspiring people with a personal story about using all your senses, such as the one above, have everyone stand in a circle outdoors. Then invite the group to expand their senses by imitating the following set of animals. You can adapt these however you see fit. If you have an attentive group, you can do them all together. Or, you might break them up over a series of days, practicing a new sense each day.

Owl Eyes. This is a way of using peripheral vision. Pick a single point somewhere straight ahead of you, glue your eyes on it, and imagine that your eyeballs can't move, just like an owl's eyes. Owl's big eyes are literally stuck in place, so they turn their heads all around when they want to focus. They spend most of their hunting time open eyed and gazing widely, waiting to notice the tiniest movement in the field that would be their food. Imagine and become an owl perched on a tree; feel the wind ruffle your feathers, feel your sharp talons and the strength in your wings.

Still anchored on that single point, let your eyes go soft into peripheral vision, and notice that without moving your eyes, you can actually see in all directions for 180 degrees. You naturally use this type of vision when you look at the night sky hoping to catch a shooting star, or when you want to catch the hiders in hide and seek.

Now stretch your peripheral vision: hold your hands straight out in front of you and wiggle your fingers. Notice that you can see the wiggling movement. Now move your arms slowly out towards your sides while your eyes still look absolutely straight ahead; stretch the edges of your vision sideways as far as you can to still notice the wiggling. Bring your wiggling hands back in front of you, then stretch one up and one down. Widen your vision again, this time vertically.

Relax your arms and now notice with your Owl Eyes if you can see tiny movements of leaves when the breeze lifts them and all the people in the circle, even the ones next to you. Notice all the different colors you can see, the different shapes, the shades of light and dark—all without moving your eyes even once.

Deer Ears. Let your ears become the huge ears of a deer. Deer ears have huge bulging muscles that can turn about like satellite dishes to focus on different sounds. To put on deer ears, cup your hands behind your ears and turn your head to focus on certain sounds. Do you notice that the sounds become louder? Now cup your hands and put them in front of your ears, so you can hear behind you without turning around? Does it make a difference? Wow, you can hear twice as much as your eyes can see because your hearing picks up a full 360 degree sphere of sound.

While also keeping your vision wide, pay attention to all the sounds around you. What do you hear in front of you? From your sides? Behind you? Are there constant sounds, like wind or running water, car traffic, or maybe your own breath? Listen for soft sudden sounds like little birds or buzzes. Where are they coming from? What is the closest sound? What is the farthest sound?

Raccoon Touch. Now, use the touch of raccoons. Raccoons practically feel their way through the world. They don't have good vision or great hearing, but they have long and amazingly sensitive fingers. They can use them to break into our garbage cans and then feel for the food they want. So, while keeping your Owl Eyes stretched and your hearing tuned, feel with your skin.

Feel the clothes on your body. Feel your feet touching the ground. Do you feel heavy? Light? Do some parts of your body feel cold and some warm? Feel the sun on your skin. Feel the wind on your skin; which way does the wind blow? Feel your heart beating.

Dog Nose. Think of dogs you have seen walking down the street, with their noses to the ground, or sniffing around every bush, smelling every thing as they go. Turn into a dog and pay attention to your sense of smell. Take quick sniffs of the air around you like a dog. What do you smell? Smoke from a fire? The grass or the flowers? Yourself?

Can you smell differently with a long breath than with quick sniffs? Try taking a long slow breath in through your nose. Try sucking in a tiny bit of air through just parted lips. Get down on all fours like a dog, or pick up a leaf or handful of dirt and hold it close to your nose. If it's safe, taste your leaf. What do you smell? Does it smell like it tastes? How would you describe it? What smells hit your nose the strongest? Still keep your Owl Eyes wide and your Deer Ears perked and your Raccoon Touch sensitive.

Synthesis. Now turn on all your senses together. Let your eyes be soft and stretched, listen with your ears to the little sounds around you, feel the wind on your face, smell the air with long breaths. Hold this whole, wide-open awareness for as long as you can stand it. How long can you simply pay attention like a wild animal? Some animals do this all day long, that's why we never see them. By expanding your senses, you too can have the awareness of a wild animal.

Inside the Mind of the Mentor

Feed them bit-by-bit. With young children, or people new to the nature experience, you usually can't hold their attention and take them through every aspect of all five senses at once. For them, make it fun and introduce it bit-by-bit in bundles of story, games, and sensory practice over the time you have with them. Continually follow-up and reinforce these ways of using the senses through role-modeling, games, and storytelling. Seize sensory opportunities. You don't need a formal lesson to introduce or practice any of the senses: an aromatic morning may mean you invite everyone to smell for a minute in silence before you tell your morning story; a blustery wind invites everyone to roll up their sleeves to feel all they can.

Pay Attention. We want to awaken the senses at every opportunity by creating a need to pay attention. By introducing hazards, heroics, and hunts, you can bring your learners' senses to life. Maybe the poisonous plant smells really bad? Was that an alarm call? Who can hear the furthest away sound? How many spider webs can you count without moving from your spot? Which berry tastes sweeter, the blue ones or the red ones? Was that a bear outside my tent?

Alternatives and Extensions

Seeing Games. As humans, vision easily dominates our senses, so play one of the many games or use tools to inspire looking more widely or closely or colorfully. Pick ones that guide attention toward natural patterns and processes and that keep their eyes open wide. Coach them to look for subtle quick movements, shifting patches of brightness, the shadow of wings on the ground, dark areas where light should be … And, since seeing dominates, blindfolding the eyes for any number of games reminds us of our visual orientation, and awakens all the other senses.

Cornell's Listening Game. Joseph Cornell has a simple and wonderful game to help people get into listening. Simply have them close their eyes for a few minutes and count on their hands how many different sources of sound they can detect.

Raccoon Touch Game. Beforehand, gather a handful of natural objects that each have unique textures, such as pine cones, fern fronds, or rocks. Stand in a circle or a line blindfolded or with eyes closed. Pass each item, one at a time, around to the next person in the circle or the line. Ask them to feel each object, name it, and give it a number (the first one, third one, fifth one …). After all the objects have been touched by everyone, hold them behind your back and discuss, as a group, what they thought each one was, finally revealing the objects and letting them see them and handle them. This can range from basic to advanced, i.e. "What kind of tree grows this kind of leaf?" or "Do you think this rock has basalt, quartz or composite qualities?"

Scent Trails. Prepare a patch of ground ahead of time by using essential oils or air freshener sprays to lay out a trail of scent about twenty feet along, and mark the end of it in a hidden way with a stick or a small prize. If you have a big group, you can create three or four separate trails, each with a different smell. Take a few participants to the beginning of each trail and ask them to sniff out the trail and follow it to the end. They will be crawling on the ground, sniffing everywhere—the ultimate dog-nose experience. Beware, though, some people could be allergic to artificial odors.

See Sensory Awareness Activities for more games.

Questioning and Tracking: The Six Arts of Tracking

◎ CORE ROUTINES		Questioning and Tracking, Expanding Our Senses, Animal Forms, Exploring Field Guides, Listening for Bird Language
CHILD'S PASSIONS		Detecting Clues, Pursuing Mysteries, Asking Questions, Being Asked Questions, Exploring
BOOK OF NATURE		Mammals, Birds, Ecological Indicators
NATURAL CYCLE		South: Focus
INDICATROS OF AWARENESS		Inquisitive Focus, Common Sense, Aliveness and Agility

Story: *Giant Tracks by Daniel Evans*

If you're anything like me, you love to solve mysteries like a detective; tracking wild animals makes some of the juiciest mysteries. Once I was lucky to find some giant tracks of one of the largest animals in North America. I learned a lesson I'll never forget.

I wandered in and out of some forested sand dunes with friends, and came across some messy, sand-blown tracks. The sand was so dry and loose we couldn't tell what kind of animal had been there, but we wanted to figure it out. We didn't think it was a person with large boots on: the pattern looked like it moved on four legs, not two. We first guessed elk, cow, or bear.

Following the tracks, we thought, "Maybe if we found more clues, we could determine what this animal was doing, helping us discover who made the tracks." The trail led behind a hedge of hairy manzanita and evergreen huckleberry. In the shade of the shrubs, the wind and sun hadn't crumbled the tracks; the sand was firmer and moist. Looking at those tracks, we could clearly see five toes with claws, the shape and size of a wide human footprint. Who do *you* think had made those tracks? Yep—we knew it had to be none other than a black bear!

The tracks led to the huckleberry bushes. Noticeably, the upper branches were broken and the berries and leaves had been stripped off. I think that bear just put the branch in its mouth and pulled with its teeth. We had found one of its feeding areas!

We could see how it wandered from bush to bush, eating here and there; we stopped following when we saw the tracks led down a steep ravine into some thick rhododendron. We felt more than a little scared to go down there. "Where is the bear now?" we wondered. "Was it still napping down there, in the cool shade? Does it sleep in the same place every evening?" We were full of questions about where that particular bear went, and when.

Since we still felt a little scared about encountering a bear in the ravine, we decided to figure out how long ago the bear came by. We returned to where we saw those first, clear tracks in moist sand protected by the bushes from the sunshine and wind, and they still looked fresh to us. Not much sand had fallen into the tracks, so we could see the claw marks clearly. But where the sun blazed down and the wind blew, the tracks were almost flat sand, barely recognizable. They looked more like sunken bowls in the sand. "How could the same set of tracks look like they had been made *both* yesterday and moments ago?"

A friend asked the question, "Does anyone remember when the wind started to blow?" That was it! We used that clue because we had paid attention to the weather all day. It had been windy when we went to bed last night, but there was no wind when we woke up that morning. Between breakfast and lunch, the wind returned to blowing hard for the last three hours. So when do you think the bear had been there?

Looking back at the clear tracks, I suddenly noticed a bizarre detail. On all of the hind feet, where the big toe should be, there was a pinky toe! On our own feet, the big toe sits on the inside of the foot, and the pinky sits on the outside. But, here, it was reversed on the bear! I thought, "What in the world?" Maybe the bear crisscrossed its feet as it walked? To figure it out, we took off our shoes, got down on all fours, and walked like bears in the sand. Believe me, if you crisscross your legs while walking on all fours, you end up with a face full of sand. Back at camp, we looked in our Tracking Field Guide and it showed us that bears actually are opposite from humans—their big toes are located on the outside of their feet, where our pinky toes sit. Can you guess why?

When I first learned to track I would have been happy just to see some tracks and say "Wow, that's a bear," then just walk away. Now if I act like a detective, and ask lots of questions, I find out so much more. Sometimes I don't want the mystery to end. It's more fun to be on the hunt, talking with your friends as you try to figure out your mystery.

How-To

We like to approach tracking through the "Six Arts of Tracking," based on the most basic questions answered by any mystery novel or piece of journalism: Who? What? When? Where? Why? and How?

You only need a situation allowing you to use these questions: tracks or sign you find in the field, or indoors with an interesting object from nature. Once you find a mystery, have your group gather around making sure everyone can see and no one damages it by stepping on it.

The Six Arts of Tracking. Remember the Art of Questioning through the Six Arts of Tracking. Small groups work well because questioning becomes an interactive dialogue between all involved. Use the Three Levels of Questioning (Listed below in the Mind of the Mentor. For full discussion, refer to Chapter 5, Questioning and Answering) and carry a tracking field guide to help find some answers. The questioning tactics begin with looking at tracks, but fan out into everything about the animal. We list the questions only in the rhythmic order people learn them, and although many have no right or wrong answer, most inspire questions specific to your own situation.

Who? – Identification

Who made the track? Look at size, weight, shape, number of toes, claw marks, tail drags? Can you identify its species? Can you find its Latin name? What else can you tell about this individual animal?

What? – Interpretation of Behavior and Habits

What do the tracks indicate about behavior and habits? Explore the vicinity of the tracks. What direction did they come from? What direction are they going? What gait is the animal in? Did it stop or turn? What was it doing? What do these tracks suggest about the animal's common activities, habits, and behaviors? What does it eat? What eats it? What do you need to know if you encounter this animal?

When? – Track Aging

Look for evidence of the effects of sun, moisture, and wind on various substrates. When did it leave this track? When is it most active? When does it sleep? When does it mate? When does it have babies?

Where? – Trailing for Home and Habitat

Follow the tracks to find out about home and habitat. Where does it live, feed, and sleep? Where are its sources for food and water? During different seasons, where does it move? Where does it raise its young? Where is it right now? Where in the world can it be found?

Why? – Ecological Tracking and Prediction

Look around for Larders and Lacks. Of all the places it could have been, why was it here? Why does it want to be here? Why is this animal running? Ask *why* about the *who, what, where,* and *when* questions.

How? – Empathy

Imitate the way the animal moves. How does it move its body? How does it feel to be this animal? How big, little, or muscular is it? How does it perceive the world—Sight? Smell? Hearing? Touch? Radar? A combination of these? Pretend to be the animal and make a track pattern in the same way it did.

Inside the Mind of the Mentor

When people exhibit curiosity around found objects or tracks, this activity almost plays itself. Ask questions that prolong their questioning (and thus "questing") state. It doesn't matter if you don't know the answers yourself, because what's being learned is how to ask good questions. The feeling of being on a quest excites the mind, awakens the senses, and creates life-long learners.

Remember the Three Levels of Questioning strategy: 1) questions you know they know the answer to, 2) questions that they'll have to put effort into solving, and 3) an inspirational one, a bit beyond their league, that will give them a satisfying "A-ha!" when they close in on it at a later date. (For full discussion, refer to Chapter 5, Questioning and Answering.)

For people who feel apprehensive about tracking, discomfort outdoors, or shy about sharing their opinion, questioning works best when it plays to strengths they already have. Those who love wandering, and not standing-in-one-place focusing, often engage when a question allows them to follow the tracks. Along the way, as you lose the trail and find it again, everyone asks questions that open up an expanded awareness and knowledge.

Remember, Tracking isn't limited to mammals. Apply the principles of the Six Arts of Tracking for anything that interests your group while out in nature—plants, insects, fish, geology, weather, or whatever.

Alternatives and Extensions

Carry Field Guides. Generally, in small groups, it helps if everyone can gather around the book. In larger groups, a few people may be excited to be designated researchers who help spotlight questions onto particular species, habits, and habitats as they discover and answer the clues.

Don't Carry Field Guides. Record measurements, draw tracks and jot sign-clues into journals for later research in field guides. Perhaps after research time, a Story of the Day session can report the answers.

Inclement Weather? Stuck Indoors? Challenge your participants to come up with twenty questions of who, what, where, when, why, and how about a nature object that captures their fascination. Field guide or drawing time follows as they research the questions most interesting to them.

Tracking Games. See under Tracking Activities.

Animal Forms: Fox-Walking

◎ CORE ROUTINES	Animal Forms, Mind's Eye Imagining
🏹 CHILD'S PASSIONS	Imitating Animals, Acting Out Stories, Running, Jumping, Crawling, Chasing,
🌿 BOOK OF NATURE	Hazards and Mammals
NATURAL CYCLE	East: Inspire and Southeast: Activate
INDICATROS OF AWARENESS	Aliveness and Agility, Common Sense, and Quiet Mind

Story: Straight from the Fox's Mouth, by Nate Summers

Any number of people who have tried out this Core Routine can probably share stories about how practicing Fox-Walking, an Animal Form, has enabled them to see wildlife or get close to wildlife. Of course, very few of those stories actually involve a fox.

Late in the fall, a couple of naturalist friends and I went hiking in the Cascade Mountains. In the middle of the afternoon, light snow was falling. As perfect light dust, we actually followed very, very fresh rabbit tracks through the snow.

The characteristic "Y-shaped gait pattern" clued us in; we followed a rabbit on the side of the mountain, probably a snowshoe hare. Hoping we might spot the animal making the tracks, I decided to try to impress my friends by demonstrating an Animal Form I had learned, Fox-Walking.

Soon, all three of us slowly tried to imitate the movements of a fox with careful, delicately placed deliberate steps. We held our heads steady, all our senses alert, followed the trail of rabbit tracks through the snow. We must have made quite a sight.

Only a few minutes later, we noticed another set of tracks following the rabbit tracks ... The tracks were small, just a little bit bigger than cat tracks but not quite big enough to be coyote tracks. Sometimes the tracks had claw marks and other times it appeared obscured by fur so we couldn't be sure. After a bit of head-scratching and trailing, we finally realized we tracked a fox. Our Fox-Walking had led us to something very interesting indeed!

Now, here's the best part of the story: not too long after we discovered the fox tracks, they peeled off to the left and disappeared into the brush. We decided we should probably head back to the cars since it was getting late and the snow was falling harder. On the way back, following our own trail through the snow, we had an interesting discovery that had not been there on the way in. Right on top of our tracks, someone had deposited a fresh scat and yellow snow nearby indicated a urine marking as well. None of us felt all that surprised when we all caught a whiff of the characteristic musky smell of fox urine! We had been out-foxed by a fox while Fox-Walking!

How-To

Inspire. Fox-Walking can be inspired by the hope of being so invisible that you can actually sneak up on an animal. Just ask, "How many of you like to see wildlife? Who would like to learn how to get close to wild animals?"

Demonstrate. Next, demonstrate how to Fox-Walk. Bend the knees a little, relax your body, and then gently step forward with one foot, toes first. If, as you begin to set your foot down, it seems like you might make noise, simply lift the foot and place it elsewhere. Once the foot rests quietly on the ground, shift your weight into that foot, and repeat with the other foot. Imagine with each step, you check out the ground like a fox to see if you can step quietly.

Also with Fox-walking, make sure to hold your head nice and steady (not bobbing up and down like most people when they walk). Make sure you look up, and not down at your feet. One of the main reasons we use Fox-Walking: it frees up our dominant sense of sight so that we can tune in to the whole world—not just our feet! You should start out nice and slow, but over time you can walk at almost a normal walking pace. Also, it helps greatly to picture in your Mind's Eye a fox walking carefully through the forest. (Additional resources can be found including more detailed descriptions of Fox-Walking like Tom Brown's Field Guide to Nature Observation and Tracking for Children).

Try it Out. After demonstrating, have the people you're working with try Fox-Walking. It might be best to walk around in a circle to slow the pace. See if the participants can Fox-Walk and not talk. Make sure they keep their eyes up and use Owl Eyes.

Take it on the Trail. After several minutes of practice, see if they can take their Fox-Walking out on the trail. Check to see how animals respond to your group now that you can all Fox-Walk. A great thing to do from here would be to have each person Fox-walk to their Sit-Spots, and notice how it feels compared to other times they've gone there.

Inside the Mind of the Mentor

There are two main aims in Fox-Walking. One: to free up the eyes and other senses from focusing on the ground and broaden awareness and brain-patterning. Two: to get people into a conscious relationship with their bodies and the way they move through the world. Ultimately, there no "right" or "wrong" way to do Fox-Walking. There's only your own way. Whatever works for you, works, as long as it's quiet, smooth, and empowering to all of one's senses and faculties of awareness

Realistically, many people you work with will not be able to *suddenly* become Fox-Walking experts. However, anything that can slow them and quiet them down will enhance their experience with each other, with wildlife, and with the landscape around them.

Notice which people do Fox-Walk slowly and quietly. Maybe they can role-model for others. Also, this exercise gets increasingly better with time so we use it in several of our other Animal Forms games like Firekeeper. Perhaps people need to demonstrate their Fox-Walking prowess just before they play one of these games.

Alternatives and Extensions:

Have a Fox-Walking Competition. Who moves the quietest? Who goes the slowest? Who moves quickly but still remains quiet?

Use a Variety of Surfaces. Try Fox-Walking on dirt, pavement, logs, grass, or whatever presents itself.

Do the Opposite of Fox-Walking first. Try to stomp around and be monstrously loud and noisy. Then compare that with the feel of Fox-Walking.

See Animal Form Activities for more games.

Wandering: Body Radar

CORE ROUTINES	Wandering, Expanding the Senses, Story of the Day
CHILD'S PASSIONS	Exploring, Being Animals, Surprising, Wondering, Following Intuition
BOOK OF NATURE	Everything
NATURAL CYCLE	Southwest: Take a Break, Northeast: Open and Listen
INDICATROS OF AWARENESS	Self-Sufficiency, Aliveness and Agility, Inquisitive Focus, Caring and Tending, Quiet Mind.

Story: *Another Sense, by Daniel Evans*

It's easy to remember how the forest felt the day I went looking for cougar. My friends and I wandered into a deep section of old trees, Douglas fir, cedar, and hemlock. An amazingly happy little brook babbled away and even though clouds covered the sky, the dawn light slipped in underneath them and lit the place up. Even as we searched for evidence of the mysterious, powerful, and elusive cougar, our hearts felt light and happy.

Actually, we were on a tracking expedition in a nice sized patch of mature forest. For two whole days, we had combed the area, made maps, and noted all the areas where we found signs of deer and elk. We hoped to find an area that didn't have deer or elk because they were afraid to go there. That would be where the cougar's trails would go.

On our last day of tracking, we felt excited to once again find cougar sign, although we all noticed a feeling between us: we felt kind of lazy. Our laziness turned into a buzz of excitement once we found something! When a tracker finds scat, we use it to tell us what kind of animal we have discovered and what it's been eating. This great big pile up of elk scat told us we were just minutes behind the animal. I know this may sound gross—but the pellets were steaming and stuck all together with strands of what looked like mucous.

I felt both scared and excited as we followed the trail of crushed vegetation. What would the elk do if we got too close? Is it possible to run away from a charging elk? Would we be able to get close enough to see it without scaring it? These questions and more bounded through my head as we followed the trail. Soon though, the questions disappeared. We trackers had our eyes to the ground, to the trees in front of us, what lay beyond, and we longingly watched the sun disappear up into the clouds.

An elk trail is both easy and difficult to follow. Following through thickets, we could see tender branch tips were broken by 800 lb. bodies moving past and in a sea of ferns, we saw fronds stepped on, pushed down, but hadn't sprung back up. I felt a little like a bloodhound dog. With the rest of the pack behind me, my eyes picked up important clues to lead us to the Elk.

Walking through a section of ground covered with just pine needles, we felt we had lost them. We rested for a while, because following tracks can be intense work, and we felt really tired. After we ate a snack, we decided, since we couldn't find the trail of tracks, we would just wander wherever we felt curious to go. Maybe then we would find more tracks.

We entered a zone of sword ferns again, and the trail seemed to lead right through it. Walking through those ferns, something strange happened: I felt my body being pulled in a certain direction, and I found myself walking towards a group of bent over trees, shaped like an open umbrella. "Odd," I thought, "Why am I going down here where there aren't any elk tracks around? Why do I want to go this way?" As I took a few more steps, something even stranger happened: I felt a weird sensation in my body, like walking through an invisible wall of molasses mixed with tiny prickles and air. If the invisible wall could have talked it would have growled deeply, but with a voice far away and distant, "Go away." My body almost listened. Without even thinking about, I started to turn and form the words to tell my friends I had gone the wrong way. But, I wrenched back. There was something irresistibly drawing me forward to explore. My curiosity felt stronger than the "Go away" threat.

I'm glad I continued on. At the very edge of the umbrella vine maple lay the biggest vertebrae bone I had ever seen. A tingle of the excitement of discovery shot up my spine. More bones came into view, a giant leg bone, some more vertebrae, even the atlas joint. Then wonder of wonders, I found my first elk skull.

We dropped to our knees as if we had been blessed by a buried treasure. We passed the bones from hand to hand. They were clean, completely white, and moss already started to grow in places. We tried to assemble the vertebrae together, and fit the atlas joint into the skull. Then

I noticed some marks on the back of the skull. I had heard about little forest rodents gnawing on bones for their mineral content, but these seemed different. Deep gouges seemed like they had been scratched into the skull. I didn't think they were rodents. We sat under that umbrella tree for a long while, we made up stories of what we thought had happened. What do you think?

After that day, I would always remember what mysteries and magic treasures you can find when you let your body and your curiosity lead you where it will.

How-To

Introduce Body Radar. Try introducing the Core Routine of Wandering by inspiring others with the possibilities of what we call Body Radar. Body Radar encourages us to let go of our plans and agendas and listen to the unconscious knowledge and guidance of our body. Notice dogs that wander and sniff, or cats that walk a little way, stop, look and listen to the left, to the right, ahead, behind, and above. Like dogs and cats, people intentionally using Body Radar seem to find things that others usually miss—feathers, bones, tracks, hideouts. So, encourage your people to be conscious of the way their bodies can intuitively lead the way to amazing discoveries and experiences.

Just before you enter a natural area, ask everyone to pause for a moment, to be still and silent, and to use their senses. Maybe even have them close their eyes. Then ask them to physically turn their bodies until they *feel* a direction calling them. That *feeling* comes differently for everyone—tingling, warmth, solidness in their gut, just some unexplainable knowing, or maybe nothing at all. For some it helps to stick their hands out in front of them to sense with Body Radar. Some will dismiss all this as unscientific and decide to just wander without such silliness.

Practice Body Radar. After each person feels which way they'd like to go, help the group negotiate which way they'll go first, assuring them that others will get to go in their direction later. Begin wandering in the chosen direction and stop periodically to let the group check into their Body Radar. Go again wherever their body curiosity leads. Sometimes you may want to loosely set a group focus—find a skull, catch a frog, or find a neat place to have lunch. Continue your Body Radar wandering for as long as you wish or until you "find where you need to be." Often some place out there waits for you to enchant the whole group: a pile of bones, a group of fallen trees that serves as a climbing gym, or a patch of delicious flowers.

Story of the Day. At the end of a wandering experience, form a sharing circle and ask everyone to share their Body Radar experience. How did this differ from the usual way of just walking along a trail? What did they like about it? Was there anything uncomfortable about this new way of wandering? What do you think might happen if you applied this same approach not just to walking through the woods, but to other life choices as well?

Inside the Mind of the Mentor

The main goal in Wandering is to change agenda-driven habits and develop confidence in participants' own sense of curiosity and inner direction in the moment. Pausing to check into Body Radar encourages this. Allowing them to take turns being the leader of the group can be a huge confidence builder, as well as excellent training in leadership.

Wandering regularly with Body Radar, over a period of time, in groups or with more experienced mentors, people gain enough confidence that they feel comfortable wandering off-trail to follow their curiosity at their own Sit Spots, in their backyards, or at local parks or wilderness areas. This confident relationship to the innate wandering spirit creates children's trails so local landscapes everywhere become joyful romping grounds. In such places, mystery and discovery will soon outshine the thrills of indoor video games.

Alternatives and Extensions

Short Body Radar Activities. Place a stone in one hand and a grass blade in another. Have people feel, not guess, which hand holds the stone. Place a nature museum artifact outside. Ask the participants to find it using Body Radar. If someone loses their keys or glasses, have the group locate the lost item using Body Radar. Note the million variations here.

Extend the Analogy. Teens and adults can use wandering quite effectively to reflect, think about, and gain insight into all the challenges in their life. Encourage the habit of pausing to intuitively feel which way to go in moments of choice.

See Plants and Wandering Activities for more games associated with Wandering.

Mapping

CORE ROUTINES	Mapping, Mind's Eye Imagining, Story of the Day, Wandering
CHILD'S PASSIONS	Drawing, Hide and Seek, Scavenger Hunt, Creating Stories, Telling Stories, Show-and-Telling, Keeping a Diary, Helping Each Other
BOOK OF NATURE	Ecological Indicators
NATURAL CYCLE	Southwest: Take a Break/Wander, West: Gather and Share, Northwest: Reflect and Home-based Challenge
INDICATROS OF AWARENESS	Common Sense, Inquisitive Focus, Service to the Community

Story: *Scout Camp Blows My Mind, by Evan McGown*

Every year at Wilderness Awareness School—after a year of developing naturalist skills in interpreting bird language, tracking, and imitating animal forms—a group of thirty teenagers and adults go to a weeklong camp: Scout Camp. Basically, with four or five teams, Scout Camp means five days of one big Capture-the-Flag game. You better be on your game if you don't want to get caught during this week.

When it was my year, I felt both excited and a little nervous about going. I've never been the most graceful and athletic person, and so I figured I needed to rely on other things to help me out. My strength came from visiting my Sit Spot everyday that whole year, and from drawing weekly maps of my Sit Spot area. I drew everything I observed. On my maps, I included what animals and plants I saw, tracks I found in this or that place, trees and bushes and what kind of bird nests they held, the kinds of birds living where, and how much each bird tended to alarm. I had wandered around my Sit Spot area and drawn so many maps of it—probably close to a hundred—that I felt like I knew how to keep from getting lost and could navigate a landscape with the skill of a sea captain.

At the beginning of the week, I donned the dark green suit of clothes I would wear during the whole week, and I completely covered my clothes and skin in natural camouflage, using mud, charcoal, leaves, and dirt, anything to help me blend into those woods. Rest assured, I smelled really terrible by the end of that week.

When the week officially started, and the game was simple: don't be seen. I had to see everyone first, before they saw me. The place differed completely from my Sit Spot, with different trees, plants, and animals, so I began to get to know it as well as I could. As the hours and days went by, with me sneaking from place to place through bushes, groves of trees, and rock-piles, a map formed in my head of the whole place and the location of all the elements: where the rock-slides were that made a lot of noise, where the yarrow plants grew on the hillside that would stop my bleeding when I got small cuts, and which holes and rock ledges had rattlesnakes in them. The coolest thing I learned and put into my mental map was where the killdeer, a ground-nesting bird, had its nest. Killdeer loudly alarmed at anyone who traveled on what I called "the beach." Thanks to the killdeer's alarms, I could tell exactly when anyone was sneaking through near the beach.

On the final day I lay on the ground by a lodge-pole pine; I had a scenic view of everyone as they left base camp after a meal to return to their secret territories. While I memorized each person's trail and added that to the map in my mind, suddenly something happened—the whole map clearly appeared in front of me in my mind, a three-dimensional image of hills and trees and animals. I was blown away by how much information I had taken in about this landscape in just four days. This place was hundreds of square miles, and now my mind-image formed as clear as if I had a map sitting right in front of me revealing precise detail: where the alarm birds lived, where the deer trails cut through the thickets, where the best travel routes were, which trees were easiest to climb, where the best and most invisible look-out points were, and of course the location of all the best hiding spots. I so amazed myself by what I imagined in my Mind's Eye, I forgot everything else and shouted, "Wow!" Just then, someone walking by heard me and turned to look uphill, but they couldn't see me. I laughed and laughed, trying not to be heard … but it's hard to laugh and hide at the same time.

The next morning, as the sun dawned, signaling an end to the five-day game, our team had the most flags and we celebrated our victory. Driving home, I still felt dumbstruck by how my brain had been re-wired to soak up so much information about an unknown landscape and turn it into a

Introducing Core Routines | 319

detailed map in a matter of a few days. From then on, I get excited whenever I have the chance to draw a map or look at a map … and the next time I go to Scout Camp, I'll be even more ready.

How-To

Link with Story of Day. Start with one big piece of paper or a dry-erase board mounted on the wall. Set up the paper or board beforehand by drawing the most basic, bare-bones frame of a map of the area you want to explore that day. Later, as people tell their Story of the Day, simply fill in the map, asking questions to guide your drawing and get participants building a mental map inside of their own minds. Be sure to mark North and ask about the exact shape of the pond? Where did that path get really steep? Mapping can go hand-in-hand with telling the Stories of the Day, or it can be done by individuals in their journals.

Process More Important than Product. Map accuracy or the right scales do not matter. More important are the questions that get asked, causing people to go back in their minds and think of the landscape from a bird's-eye view. Then they tell their story in mapping terms: directions, landmarks, noting relationships between habitats and animals, linking places and trails together, and so on. If they are visual learners and get a lot from seeing the map, then all the better.

Inside the Mind of the Mentor

Learning to think from a mapping perspective prepares younger people to grow into their developing intellects and become eager to work out their own maps. But while they are young, your worthy accomplishment will be to get them thinking from this perspective—build a Mind's Eye map of the place and make connections about things in the landscape. And of course, Mapping also establishes brain patterns and creates relationships with the larger ecology of a landscape. Whether navigating in a big-city or a vast wilderness, the forming of those patterns and ecological relationships will serve them for life.

Ultimately, your goal will be for every person to have a map-based knowledge of the land similar to the story above. I've observed people who develop deep knowledge of place—they feel confident and at home in nature, they know really valuable information like how not to get lost, where certain plants grow, where to seek shelter from the rain, and where to find tracks or nests or certain animals. Mapping brings all their knowledge together into a three-dimensional image in their mind. These confidence and belonging indicators mean they are becoming "native" to their place.

Alternatives and Extension

Map Your Home. Challenge yourself and others to draw maps from memory of their room, their house, their yards, and the routes they take to get places.

Puzzle. Make copies of a contour map with roads left off the area around your meeting place. Let them figure out how contour maps show steep and flat places, and then challenge them to fill in the missing landmarks.

Map your Sit Spot. Challenge yourself and others to keep a map of an area—maybe 100 feet—all around your Sit Spots. Note the compass directions, and draw out features of geography, waterways, vegetation, and trails. Redraw the map every once in a while as people get to know their Sit Spots better. As experience grows, add animals' trails, birds' nesting and perching sites, and changing larders.

Play at Map-Making. Hand out paper and markers and art materials and invite each person to make a map of a Make-Believe place. Inspire imagination of wonderful places they dream about. Ask how its peaks and valleys, caves and meadows, rivers and seas, would be connected in their perfect Make-Believe World. Let them draw, and ask questions to pull out more information or get their brains processing in new ways. For an inspiring example, check out the maps from Tolkien's *Lord of the Rings*.

Exploring Field Guides: Field Guide Treasure Hunt

CORE ROUTINES	Exploring Field Guides, Questioning and Tracking, Mind's Eye Imagining
CHILD'S PASSIONS	Reading Picture Books, Solving Riddles, Running Errands, Hunting, Finding, Collecting
BOOK OF NATURE	All
NATURAL CYCLE	East: Inspire, Southeast: Activate, South: Focus, North: Integrate
INDICATROS OF AWARENESS	Self-Sufficiency, Inquisitive Focus, Common Sense

Story: *Murie, by Evan McGown*

Imagine spending six years in the heart of Alaska ice and snow, doing nothing but tracking and studying one species of animal—Caribou. You know these animals from our imagination—Santa's Reindeer, those members of the deer family with stately, beautiful antlers. Imagine tracking and watching these animals every day for six years. One man did that, Olaus Murie. He saw them slide out onto ice, like they had roller-skates on their hooves. He heard them bugle for their mates. He saw the little babies grow and find their way in the world. Following all along their route, Murie watched the magnificent Caribou herd migrate, coming and going with the seasons.

He didn't just watch, oh, no. He loved tracking animals so much that wherever he went, he sketched any and all tracks he didn't know. He did this for many years beyond his Alaska experience. Murie continued to track until he was an old man, tracking almost every mammal in North America. He used his tracking abilities to help create the boundaries of National Parks so they preserved the land where wolves, cougars, elk, bears, wolverines, and other animals actually spent their time. With all this knowledge and experience, he did something no one else had ever done before: Olaus Murie wrote a book about Animal Tracks.

He filled it with thousands of drawings he had made over the years of every kind of animal, from tiny shrews to huge buffalo. He told wonderful stories about these animals. Imagine how many years of experience, how many hours of tracking and animal-watching have gone into this one book. To learn the most important lessons he learned about tracking and animals … we only need to open THIS book.

This is the story of just one book. Looking at our shelf of field guides over there, imagine how many people's lives have been spent gathering all that knowledge. How many hours of time in the field went into making each page so we can simply pick up and read? We've got it so easy.

Think about this too: whether studying caribou for six years with other biologists, or learning the names and edible properties of every local wildflower, every author started out learning from another person who had knowledge. Who were the knowledge-carriers those people learned from? The knowledge contained in these books doesn't just equal one person's life, but the lives of dozens or maybe hundreds or thousands of people who came before them. These books contain ancient magic, the best trackers' hard-won wisdom, the most clever scouts and observers. Now it's all gathered in one place: a field guide.

But it doesn't stop here. The author of the next field guide might be sitting right here with us: YOU.

How-To

To introduce a group to using field guides, custom design a Field Guide Treasure Hunt for your bioregion and your particular group of people.

Build a Library. First, you'll need to buy or get from the library a set of field guides for your area By set, we mean a field guide each for tracking, trees, flowers, birds, and mammals; these would be the minimum requirements for a Treasure Hunt. Of course, there are many more, like butterflies, spiders, fish, and so on; the list is quite extensive (check out our recommended reading and resources lists in the Book of Nature chapter and the Suggested Reading).

Create a Treasure Hunt. Devise a series of challenges, framed in riddles and word puzzles, that involve using the index, comparing the field marks from pictures with those found in the field, finding differences between like species, finding common names and Latin names. You have infinite possibilities, like these samples:

+ "A boy's name and an animal's source of warmth." Answer: Douglas fir (Have them bring you a few needles).

- "The top of an emperor's head and a baby king." Answer: Golden-crowned Kinglet (Have them show you the picture in a book)
- "Bring back and identify a fern frond cut by an aplodontia." Proof requires finding out where aplodontia live.
- "Find pictures of two birds with white rings around their eyes." Answer: Well, for this one, how about you grab a bird field guide and see for yourself?

The Game. Using field guides, they must figure out the name of the species that the clue refers to, and then go out and bring back a sample from the field or provide evidence of its passing (take you to an actual track … even if it is pigeon poop on a railing). You can verify the answer and give out a new clue, or you might hide an envelope with a new clue in the place where the answer can be found.

Inside the Mind of the Mentor

Our goal is to turn field guides, usually a bit on the dry side, into exciting resources. The Treasure Hunt format invisibly excites participants into discovering indexes, comparison charts, range maps, various ways of categorizing plants and animals, common and Latin names, and all the species differences. So, without knowing it, they become adept at researching and finding answers to questions.

As they flip through field guides in search of information, a wonderful thing almost always happens: their innate curiosity takes them down side-paths of learning. They see a bird with weird red feet they've never heard of—completely unrelated to the challenge/clue at hand and say, "Wow! Check this out!" Or maybe they see the picture of a bird they see a lot, but never knew the name of, so they learn the name and begin to read about other birds of its kind.

Once people have been drawn into comfort with field guides, the pictures and bits of surprising information grab their curiosity and lead them to lots of learning that we couldn't have planned and that we'll never be able to document. Field guides offer information tailored to an individual's curiosity and personal experience. It is amazing what search images and vocabulary can sneak in and how powerfully it can stick.

Alternatives and Extensions

Go as complex as you want. You can put envelopes inside of envelopes inside of envelopes as clues. Once each clue is solved, the next envelope can be opened. Each clue could indicate characteristics of an important twig to be gathered for use in fire making. Then the last clue challenges: make a fire in five minutes!

Inside Only. On days when you just can't go outside, field guide Treasure Hunts can be can be played with sketches replacing the "go out and find" part.

Warm-Up. These Treasure Hunts eventually set people up to generate their own research questions and warm them up nicely for a Tracking Expedition.

The Core Routine, Mind's Eye Imagining, is a natural partner, leader, or follower of this activity.

Journaling: From the Ground Up

CORE ROUTINES	Journaling, Thanksgiving, Mapping, Story of the Day
CHILD'S PASSIONS	Keeping a Diary, Drawing, Wordplay
BOOK OF NATURE	Animals, Plants, Trees, Birds, Ecological Indicators
NATURAL CYCLE	South: Focus, West: Gather and Share, Northwest: Reflect and Home-based Challenge
INDICATROS OF AWARENESS	Inquisitive Focus, Awe and Reverence, Quiet Mind

Story: *Making the Ordinary Extraordinary, by Ellen Haas*

As an elementary school child, I lived in Pennsylvania in a rolling, hilly neighborhood with creeks running through all the connected backyards. In summer, with nothing to do and the air muggy, I would gather up my sketchpad and soft-lead pencil (I didn't like those hard-lead school ones), a big thermos of lemonade, and wander off toward the creek, checking on things as I went—the waterfall, the old stone springhouse nearly buried by time in the neighbor's yard, the dam I'd built to make a swimming hole—and find my way to the little meadow where the trees thinned out and the creek-cooled breezes made a fan of fresh air.

Each time, I settled into a comfy place, opened my journal, and began. I always started by recording the weather of the moment and my exact location. Since it was usually hot, I made fun searching for words describing the hot—"sticky hot, muggy hot, dry hot, eye-stinging hot, dirty-sweat hot." And it was always easy to look around and picture where I was sitting. I had names for favorite places and used people's houses as location landmarks—so I might write "On the root sofa, facing Hughes house."

Then I'd decide what to write about. At home, my father loved big words and used them in funny ways all the time. He'd come in for breakfast, look out the window and say, "What a pregnant day!" meaning it was full of promise. He gave our pets and my friends long funny nicknames, changing all the time when he noticed silly things they did. So I too loved finding words for things that made them seem special, just like he did.

I had games I'd play with words in my journal. Sometimes I'd write down the alphabet in a list and find something that began with each letter. "Ant, Beetle, Cerulean blue sky, Dogwood, Easy going grass." I knew a few poem forms that required exactly so many syllables in a line, or certain rhyme schemes, and I'd pick something that caught my eye as worthy of a poem, and ponder it until I found the perfect words to fit the rules. Or I might do just the opposite, write what they called "stream of consciousness," just write everything that came to mind without ever stopping to think. Sometimes I'd talk to a tree, have a little conversation in my journal, which was a good way to find out how it feels to be a tree.

Hours could go by on these summer days until my lemonade was gone, and all the while my brain felt happy making small everyday wildflowers or leaves into something extraordinary by clothing them with delightful words. And, of course, hunting for words made me look, and feel, and touch tree bark or water flows or vine tendrils really close and long until the right word came. It felt almost as if they spoke to me and the word popped into my head.

Sometimes back home at dinner, I'd read my day's journal. I remember pretty clearly what usually happened. My Mother said, "Oh Honey, that's just beautiful. You're going to grow up to be a writer." And my Dad would say, "Let's try to improve on that third line," and then we'd spend the rest of dinner hilariously finding new and different words.

So, because I grew up loving words, keeping a journal was fun. And because I kept a journal, words came easily. Maybe you already like words, or maybe you feel a little clumsy with them. Either way, go outside, look around until something speaks to you; then listen for good words to pop into your mind—this brings nature alive in your mind's eye. Maybe nature wants you to tell its story. Try it. It's fun.

How-To

First, get equipped. Everyone needs a journal and a pencil, a way to make color, to sharpen, and erase. The journal can be a portable sketchpad, or a journal at the desk—or both. You'll also want an accessible set of field guides.

Heading. The first lesson creates the heading box. This should be put on every single journal page of an ongoing journal. Somewhere on the page, wrapped in a box,

- Day, date—*Monday, June 6, 2006*
- Time, weather—*late morning, light rain, no breeze*
- Place and Compass direction—*facing east toward the sun from a hill*

The Journal Page. Then find a good time to settle down and draw and/or write everything happening in this moment's window of the natural world. Most people journal more easily when you provide some instructions or limits, rather than "just go find something to write and draw." So, you can propose things to focus on.

- Describe what the weather's doing.
- Spot a bird and describe what it's doing.
- Write down Who, What, When, Where, and Why about a plant at your Sit Spot.
- Sit in one place and find something that interests you. Draw and label it.
- Write about what something looks like close-up. Now write about what's going on behind it. Then write how you feel about this thing you've just witnessed.

Inventory from the Ground Up. Writing an inventory works well for one time-tested journaling framework. Challenge yourself and others to keep a field inventory journal of one, or all, of the following things drawn from the traditional Thanksgiving address of the Mohawk. This full inventory calls attention to all niches of nature, from the ground up.

1. The People in our lives
2. Earth and its under-soil beings
3. Waters and their beings
4. Low lying herbaceous vegetation and bushes
5. Animals
6. Trees and their beings
7. Birds in song and flight
8. Air and wind, clouds and rain, and the weather they make
9. Sun, Moon, and Stars, their force, beauty, and stories
10. The qualities of the East, South, West, and North
11. The Creative Force that Moves Through All Things

In their journals, older folks can do what our Kamana participants do—keep a running inventory of things happening in the ten layers (check out the Kamana program to see a good example of a structure). Start with a pad of "templates" with all layers indicated, then jot down notes on it every day for a week until it seems pretty full. Start a new one with a new heading box the next week. If you inspire them to journal a different layer of the Thanksgiving Address each day, in ten days they'll have a beautiful little ecology journal to display. If each of ten participants journaled a different layer for ten days, then you would have a group book.

Inside the Mind of the Mentor

This initial exercise just emphasizes how to *set up* the journaling experience. But of course, *keeping it up* anchors their brain patterns to creativity and to learning. Repeated frequently, the heading box itself becomes a story. In the end, journalers seem most captivated after the fact, when their journal grows into a thick wad of pages chronicling the whole Natural Cycle and Book of Nature, as discovered in their place, through their eyes.

Above all, encourage everyone to find his or her journaling gifts. Many people seem to fear the idea of writing or drawing, and say, "I can't, I won't, and you can't make me." This resistance probably harkens back to some unfortunate schooling. Talking and writing come from different brain areas. Some people talk with complete comfort, but the words get stilted and formal when they write them. And the reverse will be true of others. Do your best to pull them through that edge, looking for their writing and drawing gifts, and appreciating whatever they do. For younger kids or folks who can't write, you can take dictation and show them what their words look like in print. This can be very exciting.

Sharing Journals. All their hard focus and good art deserves to go public. So, create ceremonial performances of their journaling work. They can break into small groups and share what they've worked on, they can put their journals out for everyone to see, and they can have a big deal finale where they display their books to their parents.

Applications and Extensions

Journaling from Field Guides. Kamana participants draw journal pages for one specific plant, tree, animal, or bird. Such a page includes many variations, but generally, a heading box which gives common and Latin name, taxonomy, a range map, and field guide source(s). Then, using the Mind's Eye technique of looking at the field guide picture, then drawing from memory, next looking again and improving. The subject sketch contains labels pointing to key field marks. Words below may note information about habitat and habits, mating, nesting, tracks, voice, perceptive strategies, comparison with similar species, and personal encounters.

Maps. Another variation on journaling—after the ever present heading box—participants draw maps in their journals, with themselves at the center, and notable trees, hills, waterways, roads, and paths to show the orientation. On this map, they can make notes about compelling events that happened as they sat and watched or wandered. Some note the two birds that landed and companion-called, the dog that ran through off-leash, or tracks discovered.

Writing Starters

- Write a haiku that puts in a few words a perfect little picture—a seventeen syllable poem in three lines of 5, 7, and 5 syllables.

- Pick a great sentence from a naturalist writer and imitate its basic structure, but change the situation.
- Think by analogy. If this were bigger, if this were harder, if this had a smell, what would it be?

Drawing Starters
- Sketch three contrasting leaves at your feet
- Sketch three views: ground level, eye level, sky level
- Draw from a field guide using the Mind's Eye Imagining technique. Draw a wrapper sketch—what it looks like from the outside. Draw a skeletal sketch—the veins of the leaf, the bones of the body. Draw a spirit sketch—the gist of its movement, a typical pose in just a quick line or two.
- Cut pictures from old magazines (National Geographics work great, cheap at used book stores). Collage the qualities of each of the four directions into a circular picture (some call this a mandala).

Resource. For a wonderful inspiration, check out: *Keeping a Nature Journal: Discover a Whole New Way of Seeing the World Around You*, by Clare Walker Leslie and Charles E. Roth. Foreword by Edward O. Wilson.

Survival Living: Survival Scenario

CORE ROUTINES	Survival Living, Mind's Eye Imagining, Thanksgiving
CHILD'S PASSIONS	Creating Stories, Taking Challenges
BOOK OF NATURE	Plants and Trees
NATURAL CYCLE	East: Inspire and North: Integrate
INDICATROS OF AWARENESS	Self-Sufficiency, Common Sense, Awe and Reverence, Quiet Mind

Story: *Practicing Survival, by Nate Summers*

I still remember the first time I tried to practice my survival skills on my own on an over-night outing. I went out in the late summer to a sandbar on a river near where I lived. I took lots of camping equipment with me just in case I needed it: a sleeping bag, a pot, water filter, a knife, a lighter, a little food, and some warm clothes. This might seem like a lot of stuff for a "survival" trip, but I was going to try not to have to use any of it.

The day was beautiful: sunny and dry with blackberries still on the bushes. I found my campsite pretty quickly and started building my debris shelter. Since it was mid-morning, I figured I'd have plenty of time to work on it. I picked a nice place under a hemlock tree, but it took me a long time to finish. Alone was a lot harder than when I had practiced with a group. I felt hungry and thirsty, and the sky looked well past noon.

I drank the last of my water, and decided I had better make a fire so I could boil some water and then go look for some food. Of course, being dehydrated and hungry makes it kind of hard to make a bow-drill kit from scratch. In fact, before I knew it the afternoon sun was fading, and I didn't have a fire or water or food.

I ran out and grabbed a handful of berries to help with the dehydration and hunger. Then I started to get a bow-drill fire going. I had kindling, a tinder bundle, some bigger pieces of wood and a fire site all set up, but I could not get a coal. It was sure a lot harder on survival than when I practiced at home. I tried and tried, until it grew dark. Finally, with it almost too dark for me to see, I grabbed my lighter to light my fire. It was either that or no fire at all.

I lay down next to the fire feeling very thankful for lighters. I poured some water I had gathered into my pot and boiled it on the coals. Thank goodness for pots. After drinking some and burning my tongue a little, I crawled into my debris hut and collapsed. I was tired, hungry and thirsty, but at least I was warm and alive.

The next morning I awoke at sunrise, it dawned misty, cool, and unbelievably beautiful. I breakfasted on blackberries and water. I only had a couple of hours out on the sandbar before I had to leave, but I had a great time tracking, wandering, and snacking on dandelion leaves.

As I packed up my equipment, I realized how thankful I felt for bringing it all with me and how lucky we were to have things like lighters, knives, and pans. Later, at the grocery store I drooled over all the food and wondered about the sheer quantity of it.

There's nothing like a little survival trip to make us appreciate what we have.

How-To

Inspire. To introduce the Core Routine of Survival Living, participants might imagine themselves in a scenario where they would have to use their skills to help themselves out. It might be nice to set up the scenario by first reading a survival story like, *My Side of the Mountain* by Jean Craighead George or *The Tracker* by Tom Brown, Jr. These will really help participants realize possibilities in a survival situation.

Create a Scenario. Once the tone has been set, take the participants on an imaginary journey. A plane crash scenario always works, but it could also be a trip back in time or an imaginary trip to an existing hunter-gatherer village in a remote setting. Let them really get into the feel of the situation of not having any of the comforts of modern civilization. You might find this movie, *Into the Wild* with Emile Hirsch based on a book by Jon Krakauer; or best yet, read the book: it brings survival skills to a new level of importance.

Art of Questioning. Next, ask them some questions about what they would do. What would be most important for them and why? How long do they think they could survive? How did other people do it in the past? How do they do it now in remote parts of the world? Let the participants explore their answers and develop their own survival scenarios.

Pass an Item. You can also take a simple item, such as a pocket-knife, a t-shirt, or a shoe-lace and pass it around the circle, asking everyone to volunteer a different task that they could use it for in the survival situation. Could we carve a fire-making set with the knife? Would we use a shoelace to lash together branches for a shelter? How creative can we get? What would our needs be?

Imaginary. It can work to end the experience by just letting the participants imagine this experience. This can also be a jumping off point for all of the other survival activities in the Trees and Survival Activities section.

Inside the Mind of the Mentor

Definitely use Survival Living to "push the edges" of your people some. Make the scenario realistic and at least a little frightening. How do they react? Who thinks they know what to do? Who really knows what to do? How many of them have actually thought about this before or have had an adult introduce these ideas before?

Watch the level of excitement with the participants. When they have reached a high level of excitement about the imaginary scenario can be a good time to propose or announce an upcoming survival adventure.

Alternatives and Extensions

Play the Lifeboat Game. Provide a list of possible things they could take into their lifeboat from a sinking ship and have a small group decide on the top ten things they'd take. Alternatively give them a list of types of people (skills, professions, character types) and have the group pick the ten invited into the lifeboat to live together on an island until rescue (which, of course, will take 20 years). Or, instead of a list, you could give each participant a slip of paper with an item or character type on it, and invite them to make an argument for their worthiness to get on the lifeboat.

Research. Give participants scenarios in different settings (arctic, desert, mountain) and have them do some **research** into how natives of those regions survived.

Natural History Museum. Take them to study indigenous survival tools in your area and then play this game asking what raw materials they'll need to make their tools and clothing and shelters. Or research a field guide that shows indigenous uses of plants and trees for food and medicine and ask them to pack up a larder of plants they'd want for survival.

Real Life. Have the participants spend time during one day noticing everything they use that enables them to survive comfortably. Then pare it down. This can be pretty funny when they want to keep the TV but have nothing to run it on.

Mind's Eye Imagining: Talbott's Game

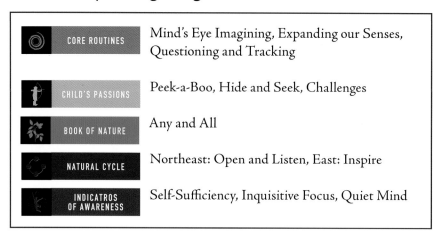

◎	CORE ROUTINES	Mind's Eye Imagining, Expanding our Senses, Questioning and Tracking
	CHILD'S PASSIONS	Peek-a-Boo, Hide and Seek, Challenges
	BOOK OF NATURE	Any and All
	NATURAL CYCLE	Northeast: Open and Listen, East: Inspire
	INDICATROS OF AWARENESS	Self-Sufficiency, Inquisitive Focus, Quiet Mind

Story: *Surviving Talbott's Game, by Nate Summers*

I remember it all so clearly. I was about to be put on the spot at a class where I was training a large group of instructors to mentor others in nature skills. The speaker at the front of the room was talking about the importance of always paying attention to our surroundings.

He had just asked one of my friends what was on the wall behind him, and we could all see that he desperately wanted to turn and look but couldn't. That was the whole point of Talbott's Game which we'd been playing for a few days. How much were we really paying attention to your surroundings?

My friend had to admit that he didn't know. Just as he was doing that, I snuck a quick glance at the walls all around me and noticed above the back door, a bright painting with a circular face in many different colors. Not hesitating a moment, the speaker turned to me and asked me what was behind me. I paused for a moment, "A painting with a circular face in many different colors."

"Not bad," the speaker said after a pause.

How-To

Talbott's Game is utterly simple, but, thrown into the lesson aptly and often, it works effectively to get everyone (including mentors and parents) to pay more attention to their surroundings. The simplest form goes like this: when you see your group getting slack in their awareness, announce to everyone, "Alright, folks, close your eyes." Soon, this simple phrase will produce a multitude of groans as everyone realizes their awareness will be challenged. You might ask:

+ Who is sitting next to you on your right?
+ The person across from you wears what color of shoes?
+ What direction are the clouds moving?
+ Were there any birds in the tree we just passed?
+ Where is north?
+ What flowers are blooming right now?

Be sure to ask questions that at least a few people will get right. Try to vary your questions to emphasize different skills. Make sure to include all of the senses in your questions—not all of your questions should revolve around sight. The possible questions, even the answers, will prove hilarious.

Once you have asked a question, give everyone a moment to imagine in their Mind's Eye what they remember. You can put individuals on the spot on purpose to wake them up, or you can let those who do know the answer show off, or just invite everyone to call out what they remember. Then they can all open their eyes and check to see if they were right.

Once everyone knows the routine, you can ask multiple questions each time you have them close their eyes. Perhaps the questions get harder and harder each time! This will definitely get your group in the habit of paying more attention to their surroundings.

Inside the Mind of the Mentor

The purpose of this exercise motivates more awareness and increases and enhances Mind's Eye Imagination. The blind challenge gets the adrenaline going, and then the act of checking imprints the image in memory.

Alternatives and Extensions

After introducing the game, encourage all your participants to call the game and ask the questions whenever they see group attention slacking. This will keep you, the instructor, on your role modeling toes!

During breaks in an indoor day, quietly move a picture from one wall to another, change your shirt, or shift around the furniture, then when the group gathers again, ask, "What changed?"

Before beginning an outdoor session, plant some bright unnatural litter on the edge of a field, or move a log into the path, or hang a flower in a tree, then wait to see who notices.

Listening for Bird Language: Bird Language Skits

◎	CORE ROUTINES	Listening for Bird Language, Expanding Our Senses, Animal Forms, Thanksgiving
	CHILD'S PASSIONS	Acting out Stories, Performing, Dressing Up, Singing, Whistling, Clapping, Stomping, Shouting, Throwing, Pushing, Racing, Chasing, Playing Tag, Imitating, Laughing
	BOOK OF NATURE	Birds
	NATURAL CYCLE	East: Inspire, Southeast: Activate, West: Gather and Share, Northeast: Open and Listen
	INDICATROS OF AWARENESS	Common Sense, Aliveness and Agility, Quiet Mind, Questioning and Tracking

Story: *Animal Communication, by Daniel Evans*

If you've ever known a dog, you will know exactly what I'm about to tell you. Even if Snoopy is the only dog you've ever seen, you'll still know what I mean. People CAN understand animal communication. Dogs communicate with us in dog language, cats in cat language, and of course, gerbils use gerbil language. Their language isn't something they do with words of course, but they do communicate.

Let's go back to the dogs. When Snoopy feels frustrated with Charlie Brown, he raises his eyebrows and without any words, his face says, "You're ridiculous." When he feels excited, his tail wags all over the place while he bounces around the room. Have you noticed what dogs do if they feel scared? If they're hungry? If they want to go outside?

For the cat lovers out there, you know your cat feels happy when it purrs. What if your cat flattens its ears and hisses at you? Animals that I really admire, all the wild ones, also communicate all the time, just like our pets. They use their ears, tails, bodies, wings, scents, and of course their voices to communicate their feelings and needs.

One special group of wild animals uses language so important to survival that all the other animals have learned to listen to them. These critters act as the alarm system of the forest. We can listen in and hear the alarm, too, if we pay attention. These animals tell you when hungry intruders sneak around, or they alarm whenever some human being jogs through the forest. They'll tell you when they see a deer hiding in the woods, and if you're fox-walk and stalking-skills are good enough, you can use this information to sneak up on them! These scouts are posted around the clock—so, all you and I need to do is hook into their system of communication.

I remember pulling into a parking lot early one morning with my friend, Evan. The air was still chilly as we opened our car doors. Immediately Evan said, "Hey, what's that thing making so much noise about? I've been studying that bird … it's called a Dark-Eyed Junco and that sound is its alarm call, easy to remember, because it sounds like a kiss." The bird was flying around a ditch, clearly aiming its kiss-smack calls at something down in the ditch. While other people just walked on by, wondering what we could possibly be so fascinated about in a ditch, we peeked over the edge. Suddenly, we saw it: a long-tailed weasel. It was literally bouncing all around the ditch, as if it was looking for something it couldn't find. Suddenly the light-bulb went off for us both as Evan and I looked at each other and said at the same time, "A nest!"

The weasel couldn't find what it was looking for, but it gave us a show in the meantime, jumping up and over the ditch, back and forth, even bounding off a nearby vertical wall with its nimble legs. After a few minutes, it loped off into the forest. The Junco then started alarming at us, as we went into the ditch and scanning the place with our eyes, eventually getting down on our knees and squinting into the deep grasses. Sure enough, tucked away in a little dirt and grass crevice, almost a cave, there was a little nest, with tiny little feather-balls shivering oh-so-slightly in the morning chill. We got out of there so the mom could calm down and instead put her energy into taking care of those babes.

If you love seeing wild animals and want to learn the secret of the "wild alarm system" then, my friends, you need to learn bird language.

How-To

Explain the Five Voices of Birds. Learn each of the five voices described below for yourself. The first four indicate normal non-life threatening situations, ranging from relaxed to stressed. The last voice marks a break into fear and panic. Jon Young's CDs titled *Learning the Language of Birds*, found in the *Seeing Through Native Eyes* series and *Advanced Bird Language: Reading the Concentric Rings of Nature*, offer story-filled explanations.

Then propose Bird Language Skits with gusto as "improvisational theatre." Ask for two or three volunteer actors or actresses for each Voice. Give them a little time to invent two skits: the first in Bird Language; the second in "Human Translation." Follow up each skit with a discussion of that voice.

The Five Voices of the Birds

1. Song. Who doesn't love bird song? Trills and warbles, the rising and falling of melodious voices. Have you ever noticed how on a cloudy day, a sudden sun break might release a renewed intensity of singing? Singing birds tell us they feel extremely comfortable, and males often advertise themselves to the females or stake out their territory.

Skit: Have two or three participants be birds to act out a scenario demonstrating singing in "Bird Language" by whistling or humming. Let the group guess the voice. Next act out the same scenario in human language: create a funny scenario that expresses the feeling and intent of bird-song. Humorous characters and funny situations really make the point. Imagine a boastful opera singer, singing loudly and grandly, with flourishes of the arm, "I am the most attractive man in the world. Ladies come and visit me!" Follow up with a discussion/explanation of this voice.

2. Companion Calling. A pair or group of feeding birds keep in contact with each other as they rummage around for tasty seeds and grubs. Since each bird, so intent on finding their food, calls to their vocal companion making sure no nasty surprises sneak up on either of them. Some birds even flash colors on their tail to tell mates and friends their whereabouts. Typically though, short chips and chirps in a regular, back-and-forth rhythm indicate everything is still okay. A bird struggling to eat a large worm might not be able to communicate to its neighbor on the other side of the bush. The neighbor starts chirping a bit more insistently, possibly even with a little panic, until the first bird responds again. Then the chirps become softer and again go back and forth, as if they're saying: "I'm here, over here, are you there?" "Yep, I'm here too, you still there?"

Skit: Have a few participants act out a pair of birds ground-feeding, finding big worms, chipping back-and-forth to each other without looking up, "Are you there," "Yep, I'm here," Have others guess what they're doing, and then go to "Human Translation." The actors might be a family at Disneyland, or maybe cars trying to caravan along a route, with passengers using cell phones. Or maybe a couple at a shopping mall, keeping track of each other. They have some amusing small talk back and forth until one friend gets hopelessly entangled in a rack of clothes. The other friend, unaware, keeps up the small talk. Since he can't see the entangled friend, he calls out earnestly for her, until he hears a reply back, "I'm fine, I'm fine, I just couldn't get out of that sweater." Follow up with discussion/explanation of this voice.

3. Juvenile Begging. Sometimes we call this begging, "Feed me! Feed me!" The babies and younger juveniles beg their parents for food. They get a large morsel shoved down their beaks, swallow, and then start loud begging behavior all over again. Whether in the nest or following Mom and Dad around, these young birds display incessant, agitated, and hungry begging.

Skit: Have two or three participants play baby birds in a nest, with one acting as a frenzied mother trying to feed screaming babies. The babies chirp loudly and insistently while the mother runs to and from the nest with food. Let them try and guess the voice. Then during the "English Translation," the nesters might become annoying kids shouting for every snack food under the sun, getting it, and then asking for more. Mom being stressed, and tired, feels about ready to pull her feathers out. Offer this highly amusing variation, when kids ask for non-food items: toys, video games, sports gear. Of course, it isn't only kids who beg and demand. Invite your participants to get creative. Follow up with discussion/explanation of this voice.

4. Male to Male aggression. Two males fighting over territory sound like rabble-rousing squawkers. They push and chase each other all over the place. By not actually fighting, they make sure no one really gets injured. The intensity and feeling in this voice could be confused with predator alarms—but if you hear other birds singing all around these two noisemakers, then there's really nothing going on to scare the other birds. It's just a lot of testosterone putting on a show.

Skit: Have two participants act out this scenario: birds chirping harshly at each other, standing each other off with nasty looks, and eventually butting chests and shoving with their bodies. You might have one eventual victor, while the other backs down or flies away in retreat. Have the audience guess the voice, and then do the skit in "Human Translation." Imagine two young men arguing over their "territory." "This is my side of the line, don't you even cross it or I'm gonna get real mad!" "Oh yeah, what do I care, I can do what I want, I'm my own boss!" Back and forth they go, being ridiculous with their insults and bumping chests. Nobody ever gets hurt and a couple other actors on the side just going about their daily life, get exasperated by their behavior, saying "If you just ignore them, they'll quiet down some time."

5. Alarm. This reaction perceives a threat. This particular squawk also alerts all the other birds and mammal species. Those who don't listen, usually end up being eaten by the owl, fox, coyote, or weasel. When you hear an alarm, watch what happens next. Sometimes everyone hides and goes silent. Perhaps one brave little bird will follow the predator, from a safe height of course, and keep pointing out with its beak and voice, "They're over here, look, look! Hungry wolf over here!"

Skit: Have a few participants act out a peaceful setting as feeding birds. Then one becomes a predator who enters the scene and provokes intense alarm calls as the birds flee for their lives. Diving predatory birds usually cause fleeing in silence. Hunting ground mammals may cause birds to fly higher, fly away, and alarm loudly. Have the others guess this voice, and then run the skit through the "Human Translation." The humans might be happily Companion Calling when suddenly they see a predator. Seeing actors dive for safety and cry out in panic can be highly amusing. The improvised skit might end up with a dramatic scene of victory for the predator, or an equally dramatic victory for those who hide, flee, and warn their friends. Follow up with discussion.

Inside the Mind of the Mentor

You may choose to act out these voices yourself with other instructors. This wonderful opportunity reveals your playfulness and role models fun improvisation and self-expression, without caring what others think.

During the discussions, people will often excitedly want to tell of when they've seen or heard this voice/behavior before. Let the stories flow and the whole group will internalize and learn so much more than you planned.

Once the skits have imprinted the idea of Bird Language, any activity, any game, any lesson, or any lunch, could be interrupted by sudden awareness of a change in bird behavior and intense curiosity about the cause. The whole energy of a group can change when someone suddenly sits up and points their ears, saying, "Did you just hear **that**?"

Unfortunately for your wildlife watching interest, most people will cause bird alarms when they excitedly run into the woods. If all of you want a chance to watch birds, and even mammals more closely, everyone will need to practice patience and slow movement. So when you make people aware of birds' Alarm Calls, you create the perfect hook to inspire practice of Fox-Walking and Sit Spot.

Watch out for a few hazards. First and foremost, please remember, we designed this activity to inspire empathy—the listening for the emotion behind a bird call. Many folks grow frustrated because they can't identify a particular bird's vocalizations. They want to identify the bird. We stress that you don't need to be able to identify every species by their calls in order to notice an alarm signal; however, the two studies blend and strengthen each other. Let any frustrated participants know that identification will come with time and study. Have them begin watching one extremely common bird, such as the American Robin until they can distinguish song from alarm. As they begin to understand the emotional nuances of companion calling, begging, and male aggression, rest assured that they have begun to internalize the auditory and visual cues of species identification as well.

Another hazard: interpreting the Five Voices of the Birds applies strictly to Passerine ground birds. Certainly all birds display some of these voices, but the passerines regularly pull off all five. Every bird in the Corvid family, which includes jays, crows, and ravens, act mischievous and sound vocally complex. They do not follow the rules presented here.

Alternatives and Extensions

Identification. Once you've presented the Five Voices skits, it can be fun to identify the particular voices of each of the common ground birds of your area. This practice will help participants draw their Maps with individual birds and their calls on it.

Make a Mix-Tape. To help with identification we recommend you find some bird vocalization recordings, which can be found at bookstores or online. Then make a "mix-tape": the authors of this book used to make them with actual tape cassettes, but nowadays the format would be CDs or digital playlists. Take the 5 most common ground-feeding birds in your area and put their recorded voices in a mix along with all your favorite songs. Then listen to the mix over and over, as you drive or do other work.

Fox-Walking and Sit Spot can be experienced with a focus on birds. How close can you sneak up on birds without causing the voice of alarm? What body language can you observe that shows nervousness before the actual vocal alarm call?

Thanksgiving: Circle of Thanks

CORE ROUTINES	**Core Routines:** Thanksgiving, Story of the Day, Mind's Eye Imagining, Expanding Our Senses
CHILD'S PASSIONS	Imagining, show-and-telling, telling secrets, keeping secrets, giving and receiving, seeking treasure, hugging, cuddling, holding hands
BOOK OF NATURE	The Whole Book, from the bottom up
NATURAL CYCLE	Northeast: Open and Listen, West: Gather and Share, Northwest: Reflect, North: Integrate
INDICATROS OF AWARENESS	Awe and Reverence, Caring and Tending, Quiet Mind

Story: *Community Thanks, by Daniel Evans*

One of the most wonderful programs I've been a part of is a nature-based alternative high-school. Their main classroom is a big hut with a dirt floor and a fire-pit in the middle. The program called "Community School" has been around Wilderness Awareness School about ten years now in one form or another. As the 'students' of this 'school' come and go, they are all different, all unique, and always amazing people to be with.

Some of these young people can track an animal until they touch it, others can tell when a bobcat is passing by what the birds are saying, and others can make a hand-drill fire in a matter of seconds. After a few months in the program, each one of them finds what it is that they most love to study, and then they focus almost entirely on that one subject.

Even though each person is so different, following so many different paths, one of the ways this group has found unity and togetherness is how they begin their day together. After getting a fire going (always using primitive methods such as bow-drill or hand-drill), each person takes some cedar they have gathered and says something they are thankful for. After they've spoken what they are thankful for on that particular day, they place the cedar frond in the fire. A magical hissing and popping happens as the oils of the cedar burn in the fire. As they go around the circle, everyone else carefully listens as each person speaks and then tosses the cedar in the fire. Also, no one has to speak. It's an option to not say anything out loud and instead be quietly thankful.

What I find remarkable about this simple and humble practice is that the these participants, no matter how tough their life is at that moment, always end up expressing gratitude for something.

How-To

Circle of Thanks. Simply gather in a circle and invite everyone to say aloud something they feel thankful for. You can do this to start the day and then again at the end of the day. You can do it going round the circle one by one, or "popcorn" style, allowing folks to speak when the spirit moves them. Changing the style, you can give thanks by saying just one word, or take a longer time to allow little stories to unfold. You can be grateful for elements of nature or for whatever happiness represents at the moment. Be serious or funny, reverent or light-hearted, all while steering participants to lift their hearts with a true sense of gratefulness. A circle of Thanks often results in a peaceful sense of community and connectedness.

Role-Model. Make sure to be a good role-model yourself. Be sincere in what and how you express gratitude and others will be inspired to follow.

Ceremony. The Circle of Thanks designs a way to enter your time together as a group and also bring your time to a close. By design, you leave the rest of your life at the gate and enter the intention of the gathering; then, at the end, a way of appreciating the time spent together, you release the group and go back to your individual life. As a routine, Circle of Thanks can become a gentle ceremony or rite of passage. If you practice a Circle of Thanks repeatedly over time, you may find it at first awkward, then comfortable and natural, and ultimately, it can become the most treasured and eagerly-anticipated part of the day.

Inside the Mind of the Mentor

Our friend Jake Swamp has published a book called *Giving Thanks*. You might get a copy of this beautifully illustrated children's book and perhaps read it with your audience as well. Jake Swamp based his book on the Mohawk tradition.

Jake tells us his Haudenosaunee People greet the day with Thanksgiving, begin each important gathering with Thanksgiving, and end every meeting the same way. Greeting your day with Thanksgiving upon waking makes a beautiful way to start every morning. Greeting your dreamtime with Thanksgiving forms a beautiful way to end every evening. Gathering family and friends in a Thanksgiving Circle creates a powerful way of uniting a group. A private Thanksgiving before important decision-making clears the way for maintaining balance and perspective. Giving thanks to the elements of the natural world roots our hearts to the land. Being aware of gratefulness develops another sensory antenna to add to seeing, hearing, smelling, tasting, and touching. Developed through practice, gratefulness becomes almost a sixth sense.

With any formal, ceremonious activity like this, you want to be especially careful about not stepping on anybody's toes regarding religious beliefs. Done appropriately, inviting people to be thankful should be so universal and simple and true that no one finds it objectionable.

Inviting expressions of gratefulness creates great opportunities to find out what motivates people, what rises in their awareness to be truly thankful for? Often, you can also get an early sense of who might be having a bad day by the way they handle a circle of thankfulness.

If people feel reluctant at first, try having your thanksgiving circle related to something specific, like water, or sun, or a favorite toy or beloved pet. Over time, expand to include other things of value. This works especially well with younger people. With consistency and time, their awareness will come around to true feelings of gratitude.

Alternatives and Extensions

It Doesn't have to be a Circle. Set participants in pairs or small groups to tell the Story of the Day in terms of people, emotions, or things they feel thankful for. You can also invite people to approach it on their own or at home by journaling, drawing, dancing, or freestyle rhyming. Many people write daily gratitude lists to keep their hearts feeling positive.

It Doesn't have to be Out Loud. A long pause—three minutes of silence, perhaps—while attending to what we feel grateful for can be an amazingly powerful, scary, awkward, and moving experience.

It Doesn't have to be Spoken. Thanksgiving lends itself wonderfully to singing, acting, and art. You can invent a rhythmic praise song with a simple refrain with improvised verses shouted or rapped out. You can gather natural objects you feel grateful for and just place them in the circle.

Enjoy the ascending model of the Thanksgiving Address (page 76). Invite your group to start with the ground and work their way all the way to the sky, naming things from the natural world they feel thankful for.

Setting Up The Learning Culture
ACTIVITIES

Activities that shape the culture of nature study,
set the tone, and create shared values
for your learning community

If you take part in a program using this Coyote Mentoring model, you will probably first encounter activities to create the Learning Culture. Why? Because these activities set the tone for all the learning that will follow. These activities excite, inspire and set parameters. They help create a landscape for everyone to travel through together. They set up the sign posts, the game rules, the agreements, and the basic *vocabulary* giving an inspirational taste of what they can hope to learn.

These activities "flip the switch," temporarily removing people from their day-to-day culture and rapidly relocating them. This different culture embraces nature studies, healthy serious fun, curiosity-based exploration, and personal-community respect. Setting up the Learning Culture activities will establish the culture of your learning community.

Nature Names

◎	CORE ROUTINES	Animal Forms, Exploring Field Guides, Mind's Eye Imagining
🏹	CHILD'S PASSIONS	Role-playing, Receiving Gifts
🌿	BOOK OF NATURE	Any and All species
↻	NATURAL CYCLE	Northeast: Open, East: Inspire, and South: Focus
🦌	INDICATROS OF AWARENESS	Inquisitive Focus, Awe and Reverence, and Caring and Tending

Primer

Some people think of animals and plants as each having a special "medicine." Their medicine represents a bundle of abilities and powers: cougar medicine means being silent, sneaky, independent, and strong; squirrel medicine includes climbing well or getting a lot of work done quickly, like gathering and burying pine-cones or acorns before winter sets in.

In ancient China, martial artists studied how animals move by sitting alone in the woods for hours until animals showed themselves. When martial artists needed to get fierce, they could "step into the mind" of Tiger, or if they needed to stalk silently through the dark, they could "become" the Crane standing in the water, and move so gracefully that they wouldn't make a sound or be noticed. The root of martial arts today comes from really, really, *really knowing* the wild animals themselves, until you can become them.

Today is a special day. We challenge you to "become" your own animal, and each one will be only for us. We're each going to pick a Nature Name out of a hat. You might pick a plant, bird, insect, or mammal, but remember, the name you pull out may have something to teach you, something very special, because it's only for you. Some people say we pick the name out of the hat; other people say the name picks *us*. Whatever name picks you, only you can figure out why.

How-To

Create a Master List. Start by using field guides to compile a master list of Nature Names you want to include. Make your list based on your bio-region and what may likely be encountered and learned about from direct experience in the field. You can choose all mammals, all birds, plants, or other species sets, or you can mix into one grand list.

Create Slips. Write them on paper, be as ornate as you wish, and cut them into bite-size bits of paper. Make sure you have enough for all participants and mentors. Yes, mentors need Nature Names too.

Pick Names. With your people in a circle, pass a hat or other receptacle around that holds all the Nature Names. As each person picks one, they announce their Nature Name to the rest of the group. This creates a naming ceremony, so you might want to add music and other elements to make the moment even more special: a drum beating in the background or a song softly sung by everyone as the hat goes around.

Reinforce. Some people will strongly associate with their name right away, and some may forget their Nature Name by the next time you meet. To establish the Nature Names firmly as part of your learning landscape, we suggest sharing them in circle at the beginning of each day or referring to them whenever it comes up. Some folks will even prefer to be called by their Nature Name all the time.

Inside the Mind of the Mentor

Having people receive Nature Names does a few beautiful things. First, animals and plants become teachers; in a short time, they are recognized for the gifts they offer us. Further, receiving a Nature Name provides the opportunity for a deeply meaningful, personal relationship with one particular species. Receiving the name of a creature prompts a natural curiosity and desire to learn about your namesake.

Often, learners will dive right into field guides to find out about their Nature Name; their face reflects their own personal understanding of the qualities of the animal and how they relate to themselves. "I really am Fox, because I *am* sneaky and very curious." This proud association can be built upon through research and experiences in the field, strengthening a human-creature relationship until it becomes truly magical.

Nature Names also creates peer-to-peer mentoring; people naturally learn from and share with each other about their names, thereby building collective knowledge of locally important species. Simply hearing a slew of local Nature Names every day provokes a lot of learning, but as individuals develop relationships with their namesake creatures, they often share new information, adding to group knowledge. Peers mentoring peers, yes!

Perhaps most important, care-taking attitudes toward Nature Names emerge through empathetic relationships, and empathy for wild creatures fosters a broader care-taking mind-set towards the whole natural world. The simple experience of having a Nature Name and combining it with field time, peer-to-peer sharing, and unified learning can change a life in a very personal and powerful way.

Alternatives and Extensions

Give Names with the Seasons. If you have a group during the school year, you might choose a new name each season/quarter from a different seasonally-focused species set. This gives a chance for everyone to learn about multiple species at the applicable and meaningful times. Examples: birds in spring, plants in summer, trees in winter.

Highlight Latin Names. Write only the Latin names on the slips of paper instead of common names, and challenge them to discover the identity of their Nature Name. Have a stack of field guides nearby, and watch as they dive in to discover their namesake, and learn to use an index along the way.

Nature Museum

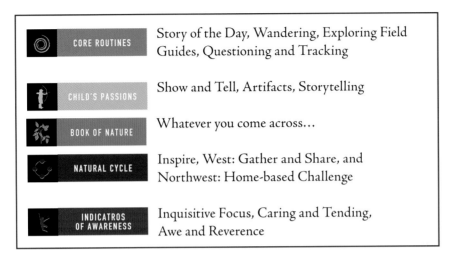

◎	**CORE ROUTINES**	Story of the Day, Wandering, Exploring Field Guides, Questioning and Tracking
🏹	**CHILD'S PASSIONS**	Show and Tell, Artifacts, Storytelling
🌿	**BOOK OF NATURE**	Whatever you come across...
	NATURAL CYCLE	Inspire, West: Gather and Share, and Northwest: Home-based Challenge
	INDICATROS OF AWARENESS	Inquisitive Focus, Caring and Tending, Awe and Reverence

Primer

We create a very special place that we will always want to keep beautiful: our Nature Museum. Our Nature Museum will be a collection of all the most memorable, favorite, or mysterious things we find in nature. What will make this museum really special comes back through the objects put there; you know each story—where it was found, who found it, and how it was found. So if you ever want to hear a story or remember a good time you had in nature, you only need to go to the Nature Museum.

How-To

Harvest Discoveries. This one is simple. Just encourage people to bring back the coolest things they find during their exploration into nature and create a beautiful space for them to be kept and displayed. You can create a space for the museum in whatever way you want; bookshelves or low tables often work well. Do make sure they harvest plants or other living things ethically and in the best interests of the landscape. Sometimes this means leaving some things that otherwise they would love to bring back for display.

Design a Museum. "Museum," a fancy word for any place to securely show and tell discoveries, can be inside or outside. With a little imagination, your Nature Museum could be a fully designed classroom layout of shelves, tables, wall boards, and computers, or "little altars everywhere," or even a little living zoo or herbarium. This place becomes a "museum" when your community gathers a collection that everyone treats with awe and respect. Nearby, you arrange a field guide library.

Role-Model. Be the role-model and keep a Nature Museum yourself. Bring back the enticing things you find and tell the Stories of the Days that go with them. Start a personal Nature Museum at your home. Your stories will imbue your objects with an aura of myth and magic. As members of your communities begin to do the same, the Nature Museum will become a very special place.

Inside the Mind of the Mentor

The Nature Museum is a marvelous addition in any gathering space, contributing much more to the learning landscape than can be put into words. Remember the two big things it can do: 1) Inspire curiosity and passion for exploring nature, and 2) hold stories of experiences in nature, always perpetuating the telling of Stories of the Day.

As your tables and shelves fill with an assortment of feathers, bones, colorful rocks, insect skeletons, hornet's nests, we highly recommend you place the Nature Museum somewhere in the flow of traffic and away from the rain, like right by the door so you see it as you walk in.

Essentially this "naturalist booby trap," triggers their curiosity and draws them straight into the wonders of nature. With the appropriate field guides nearby, participants will get drawn into what the Nature Museum holds, and they will be enticed to explore nature so they can add their own special object to the museum. The Nature Museum offers inspiration, naturally.

We use this activity like an extension of the Story of the Day. When folks come back with objects, you have the most golden opportunity to pepper them with questions about what they found, taking them deeper into their experience and knowledge. Where? How? What happened to it? Their displayed object physically represents their experience of that day and can be referred to through its story told again and again. The Nature Museum becomes a collection of "objects that teach on display"—just by having them around to look at, touch, smell, ask questions of, or hear stories about, the objects continually teach.

Alternatives and Extensions

Story the Landscape. You can also use stories to turn the entire landscape of nature you most often visit into a place full of objects on display that teach. Tell songline stories of experiences you had at this or that place, give places names according to such happenings. In this way, your living landscape will fill with story and myth that surrounds a person whenever they go out. The Nature Museum lives all round them; the local woods now hold that same magic. Of course this happens slowly as you and others develop relationships with your place.

Document the Collection. Have participants become curators of the museum, ask lots of questions, and use field guides to make information cards for each object. Even better: make info-cards with all the answers written on the back, and on the front have three or four really good questions about the object for any viewer to ask themselves before checking the answers.

Home Nature Museum. Inspire people to make nature museums at home and either bring objects to show or take pictures to share with you and others.

Animal Calls

CORE ROUTINES	Animal Forms, Listening to Bird Language
CHILD'S PASSIONS	Make Believe, Imitating, Being Loud, Codes and Secrets
BOOK OF NATURE	Any species, but especially Birds and Mammals
NATURAL CYCLE	East: Inspire and Southeast: Activate
INDICATROS OF AWARENESS	Aliveness and Agility, Awe and Reverence

Primer

Alright everyone, we get to develop our own set of secret codes. We need to pick sounds to communicate signals with each other so other groups won't know about our plans. Of course, if anyone else hears our sounds in the woods, they need to be hearing common nature sounds, like bird calls, cricket songs, or squirrel yelps. What do you think our call should be?

How-To

Choose a Sound and Synchronize. This activity is fairly straightforward. Work with your group to come up with nature sounds that have the specific purpose of helping to keep the group together. We use "sounds" in separate groups as the set-up suggests, but also in the big group. It's a great way to gather a disparate group together for an activity or announcement. Sometimes one mentor will just decide on a sound and get it going in the whole group.

Learning the Crow-Call. To show people how to do a decent crow-call, explain that there are two elements. Start with a plain "caw" sound. Have everyone try that. Then have everyone try the second element, a "coughing-up-hairball" sound. Then, just combine the two sounds together into one.

Create Sounds for Different Purposes. For instance, many times at Wilderness Awareness School the loud, "Kawww! Kawww! Kawww!" sound of a crow call can be heard to help gather everyone together. This works as well at adult programs as it does at children's programs.

Here's a list of some signals that you might want to develop:

- A "Gather everyone together" sound
- A "Let's all be quiet" sound
- A "Let's hide together" sound
- A "Let's all sneak away" sound
- A "Not everyone is paying attention" sound
- An "I think I hear something important" sound

Feel free to expand with your own concepts and ideas from this beginning list.

Role Model. For many people who lead this activity, they encounter a major stumbling block in their own reluctance to try to make animal sounds. Almost everyone can make this short list of sounds:

- Kaw! Kaw! – crow
- Chick-a-dee-dee-dee – chickadee
- Shneak! Shneak! Shneak! – sneak call of jays
- Ribbit, ribbit, ribbit – croaking of a frog
- Yip-yip-yip! – high-pitched yip of the coyote

Listening to electronic recording of birds and other animals can be a great source of inspiration for both you and the participants with this activity.

Inside the Mind of the Mentor

You should keep two key components to this activity in the back of your mind.

First, you want to get people to try making nature sounds as much as possible. This helps them imprint on a whole different set of stimuli from their personal normal like cell phone rings, car horns, TVs, and microwaves. By imprinting on the different nature sounds they will almost effortlessly start to pay more attention to their surroundings *especially noticing the nature sounds all around them*. Suddenly, the outdoor becomes a noisy place with information being communicated all the time.

Second, the participants literally create a unique language they just use with each other. This develops a group identity as well as cohesion and unity. The "secret codes" you start with may very well lead to people creating their own language.

Alternatives and Extensions

Sign-Language. In addition to audio signals, you can also create a group of hand signals or sign language unique to your group. People, and especially kids, enjoy using this silent mode of communicating for sneaking as a group or moving in "scout formation."

Sound Imitation. Play a sound-imitation game, where you go around the circle, with each person creating a sound of a different animal. Then everyone else has to imitate it then name the animal.

Follow the Animal Sound. In an open field or in a clear-floored classroom, have participants partner up and together choose an animal sound. Then blindfold one of the partners and take them, along with all other blindfolded partners to the center of the room or field. Then have the other partners create a perimeter encircling the blind-folded participants. Have them rotate around the room to hide their original position. Then when you say "start," the people on the outside begin calling their animal sound. Using ears only, the blindfolded partner needs to find the way to their partner.

Four-Directions

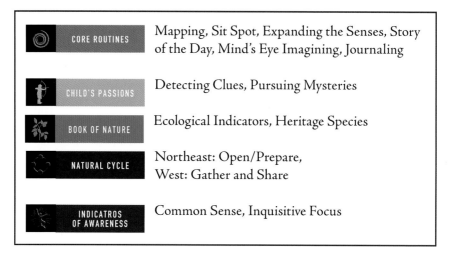

CORE ROUTINES	Mapping, Sit Spot, Expanding the Senses, Story of the Day, Mind's Eye Imagining, Journaling
CHILD'S PASSIONS	Detecting Clues, Pursuing Mysteries
BOOK OF NATURE	Ecological Indicators, Heritage Species
NATURAL CYCLE	Northeast: Open/Prepare, West: Gather and Share
INDICATROS OF AWARENESS	Common Sense, Inquisitive Focus

Primer

It was quite common in many places around the world for whole cities, towns, houses, and even rooms, to be laid out in the four cardinal directions of North, South, East and West. In many cultures today, the directions play a heavy role in ceremonies and stories to help people orient to the landscape around them. Besides increasing connection and awareness, this developing "sense of direction" establishes the most basic form of "lost-proofing."

How-To

Check In with the Directions. This activity offers a huge amount of room to play around with a basic concept. In the simplest form, you want to continually ask everyone "Where are we now?" Keep them aware and alert about the location of the Four Directions. The key is persistence. Just make it a core routine to continually check in, "Where did the sun rise today?" "Where's East?" "Where's Northwest?" Which direction is the wind coming from?"

Design the Meeting Place. This can be as literal as having a big E, S, W, and N taped onto classroom walls showing the directions. Or decorate the interior classroom with directional themes: focused materials, such as book-shelves might go in the South, and a focal point for sharing, like a blackboard, might sit in the West. On a fluid and dynamic long wander, deep into a natural area, ask participants to identify their location in space and time of day.

Follow Clues. This activity can be less explicit and obvious. Maybe set out symbolic item for each of the Four Directions at the place where you hold your program. These symbols could be exciting and fun nature objects that naturally draw people in. After folks feel familiar with the symbols, use questions so the participants will discover why we have four separate symbols and what their layout means.

Inside the Mind of the Mentor:

Where Are We Now? You are trying to create awareness of the Four Directions at all times. Make sure your learners understand their orientation at their starting point, help them keep that awareness as they move along. This can be done most simply by asking them what direction they are traveling in.

Start at the Edge. In the first place, not everyone knows one direction from the other. Start at that edge. Spend some time orienting East to where the sun rises, at mid-day the sun sits in the South location, and the sun sets in the West. The simple acronym, **E**at **S**limy **W**orms **N**ow helps some remember. Also, finding Polaris or the North Star is a great way to show people how to find North.

Alternatives and Extensions:

Eight Directions. Work on 8-directional awareness including the four ordinal directions of NE, SE, SW, and NW.

Compass Indicator. Combine this activity with both Mapping and Journaling to get a sense of the surrounding landscape. Get in the habit of beginning all maps and journal entries with a compass indicator.

The Natural Cycle. The story of The Natural Cycle adds depth and understanding to this learning journey. It can be laid out dramatically by gathering participants to form a circle with big rocks or logs placed at each of the four directions (help them find Middle, and adjust). Then walk round and round the circle tell the spiraling story of how the sun goes round the directions every day; and the seasons go round the directions every year; and the life of an alfalfa seed goes round the directions from sowing to harvest and beyond; and then get everyone engaged in seeing how the journey of a person's life goes round the same directions. These stories bring in a consciousness of the ancestral significances of the directions, which then brings metaphor and imagination into the times when they stop, look around, and ask "Where are we now?"

Home Practice. Have them take this home with them and practice finding East, South, West, and North at their house, at their Sit Spot, on the road.

Constellations. Combine this with a lesson on astronomy and the constellations. Which constellations lay in the South in summer? Which ones can be found in the Eastern night sky in winter? *The Stars*, a wonderful child-friendly book by H.L. Ray, the author of the *Curious George* books, will assist your efforts to turn folks onto the stars.

Eagle Eye

CORE ROUTINES	Sit Spot, Expanding the Senses, Animal Forms, Mind's Eye Imagination
CHILD'S PASSIONS	Scouting, Hiding, Sneaking, Challenges
BOOK OF NATURE	Hazards, Mammals, Plants, Trees, Birds
NATURAL CYCLE	East: Inspire, Southwest: Take a Break
INDICATROS OF AWARENESS	Aliveness and Agility, Awe and Reverence, Quiet Mind

Primer

Eagles have incredibly keen vision. From hundreds of yards above a field or sitting high in a nest overlooking a river, they can spot a small rodent or splashing fish. When they do, they lift and swoop right down to grab that little morsel of delicious food. Humans have good vision too, but we can learn a lot by watching eagles and hawks. Eagles and hawks don't even have

to move to spot something because they use their keen vision. If you practice using Owl Eyes—or Eagle Eyes—you'll be able to see more animals hiding from you. Do you think if we all went out and hid, you could stand still and spot us without moving or walking around?

How-To

Directions for the Eagle. This game is a sedentary variation on hide-and-seek. Play it in an area with some decent cover for hiding: bushes, ferns, tall grass. Be sure to check the area for hazards (like poison ivy) before playing there. One person will be chosen as the Eagle who must stand in his "Eagle Nest," about the range of his/her pivot-step. I usually start by having a mentor stay with the Eagle during the game as facilitator. The Eagle closes his/her eyes and counts to 60 while everyone else hides in a broad circle around the Eagle Nest (define the boundaries).

Directions for Hiders. All hiders or "voles/mice/rabbits" must hide themselves in such a way that **they can see the Eagle with at least one eye at all times.** This means no hiding completely behind trees, etc. They must also hide within the boundaries. The goal of this game moves the hider as close to the Eagle as possible and without being seen. This is the true test of invisibility.

Eyes Open. The Eagle opens her eyes, looks, and listens all around for everyone hiding, but she cannot leave the nest. When the Eagle sees something that might be a person hiding, he must describe the colors of the clothes or hair he sees and point to the exact location, it will be clear that the person has been seen. That person comes to the Eagle Nest and sits down, remaining silent not giving anyone else away. Again, the Eagle listens in the silence for any movements of other people hiding.

Sustain Pace. After a while, when the Eagle cannot see any more people, have her close her eyes and count to 30 while everyone quickly hides again, moving at least 5 steps closer to the Eagle this time. Keep playing like this until Eagle finds everyone or until one person remains. Ask the last person hiding to give a bird call so everyone may locate their number one hiding spot. In this way, the game stays interesting and fun for everyone involved, without lagging or becoming boring.

Inside the Mind of the Mentor

This is consistently one of the most popular games at our Youth Programs. We love it and often introduce it right off the bat because it inspires participants for a long time to come about 1) hiding, scouting, and invisibility; 2) using their eyes and ears in more focused ways; and 3) practicing patience in looking for animals in the woods.

We also really love this game and similar games because it gives energy-filled people, young and old, the experience of Sit Spot: sitting still outdoors. Hiding games "trick" people into breaking into new comfort zones where it is "okay" to be belly-to-the-dirt or in a thicket full of spider-webs and scratchy branches. They soon become at home in the natural world.

I can't tell you how many times hiders come back to the Eagle Nest after being seen not caring that they've been caught—instead they walk into the Nest talking excitedly of an orange and black caterpillar that crawled right by their face or the way the clouds moved so fast in the sky and made such cool shapes.

Left alone to sit quietly in nature, children discover Awe and Reverence, without any prompting. But since they likely won't sit alone in the forest without a good reason, hiding games such as Eagle Eye provide a space for this to happen. But of course from their perspective, they are just playing a game.

Also, this game gives an excuse to remind ourselves about Expanding our Senses—one of the most powerful Core Routines for a human to practice.

Alternatives and Extensions

Habitat Ecology. Learn about habitat ecology with Eagle Eye by playing this game in a range of environments, from tall grass fields to thick forests to rocky areas. You can turn this into a discussion about which animals it would be best to imitate and learn from when hiding in a certain area, and how different habitats compare, the pros and cons from the animal perspective.

Challenge Good Hiders. Have them wear brightly-colored bandanas on their heads when hiding, or stand on one leg, or hide in two's.

Challenge Mind's Eye Imagination. As they look for and describe colors they see, ask the Eagle which hider was wearing what color of clothes and the color hair for each hider. For really skilled Eagles, ask about the color of the hider's eyes.

Imprint Search Images. As you describe the boundary landmarks or ask the Eagle to describe to you where they see somebody hiding, ask them what kind of bush they are referring to: "You mean that sword fern or do you mean that bracken fern? What's the difference? The Bracken Fern stands taller and fluffier."

Firekeeper

CORE ROUTINES	Animal Forms, Expanding the Senses, Sit Spot
CHILD'S PASSIONS	Sneaking and Getting Caught, Challenges, Treasure-hunting
BOOK OF NATURE	Mammals, Ecological Indicators
NATURAL CYCLE	East: Inspire and Southwest: Take a Break
INDICATROS OF AWARENESS	Aliveness and Agility, Common Sense, Quiet Mind

Primer

There's a mythic story that has been passed down through the oral tradition of nature mentors in connection with this activity. It goes a little something like this ...

It is said that a long time ago, back when humans still talked to animals all the time, the humans on the earth would spend their winters shivering with cold. Why? Because they didn't have fire to warm their bodies and they didn't yet know how to make fire by rubbing sticks together. There was fire on the earth—one fire that always kept going, but the humans could never get near it because huge monsters called Gazoombutts guarded it. These monsters were enormous, very quick, and also greedy, wanting the fire all for themselves and never sharing the fire with anyone else, never letting anybody get near it.

However, the monsters had one weakness, they had no eyes. To compensate for their blindness, they could hear extraordinarily well, better even than deer or rabbits. They could hear a mouse's footsteps a hundred feet away. So all day and all night they used their hearing to guard the fire, catching any human who might try to sneak in and steal a bit of fire. Do you think you could sneak in and steal the fire from the Gazoombutts? Well, you're about to get your chance ...

How-To

Set up Playing Area. Have everyone stand in a large circle and use their shoes to mark the edge of the circle, or you can allow the circle to be an approximate size that everyone remembers. Depending on the terrain, you can invite everyone to take off their shoes and go barefoot so that they will be able to walk even more quietly.

The Goal. The goal of the game is for someone standing on the outside of the circle to stalk into the middle of the circle and steal the keys from under the nose of the Firekeeper without ever being heard and pointed at by the Firekeeper.

Select a Firekeeper. Ask one person to be the Firekeeper. The Firekeeper sits blindfolded on the ground in the middle of the circle.

Place the Fire. Find something to represent a good fire. Take your car-keys or something else noisy when handled, and place them about a foot out in front of the Firekeeper.

Catch Sneakers. If the Firekeeper hears someone sneaking in, he or she will point in the direction of the sound. If the point is accurate, you will announce it and ask the person to return to the edge of the circle. If their point was not accurate, tell them so. You will probably want to limit the number of "inaccurate" points to 6 or 7, so the Firekeeper will be forced to really listen and not just point everywhere. Also, ask the Firekeeper to make a clear point that goes out quick like an arrow, not waving in all directions. The Firekeeper can also "check the fire" every 30 seconds or so, by feeling to see if the keys still lie there.

Manage the Crowd. Each "sneaker" on the edge of the circle waits until you, as referee, point at them offering them a chance to sneak in. Allow only 2 or 3 sneakers at any time. This prevents the chaos of ten or twenty people sneaking in at the same time, a smaller number also makes the game challenging and exciting. People can hardly wait to have their chance to steal the fire!

Inside the Mind of the Mentor

This game will get participants Fox-Walking and sneaking. People seem to really "get" the importance of moving slowly and quietly. They realize how much noise they make when they move normally and they see how easy animals and other humans can hear their approach. They begin to understand they create disturbance and can choose to control and lessen that disturbance.

For these reasons, playing this game early on boosts the quality of all future sneaking. Their sense of balance comes alive, they become confident in their movement, and they feel inspired to sneak up on animals or humans. This game will cause participants, without being told, to make Fox-Walking a part of their everyday life.

This game emphasizes the power of listening, training the ears of the Firekeeper into finely-tuned instruments. As someone who has been a Firekeeper many times with the stealthiest of children sneaking toward me, I understand how this game stretches hearing as few exercises do. An intense need to hear subtle sounds expands our ability to hear.

This game also offers opportunity to take off shoes and expose bare feet to the earth. For many people in the modern world, this is a simple yet profound experience. Invite people to take their shoes and socks off for this game and introduce this primary connection to the earth in a safe and monitored environment.

Alternatives and Extensions

Vary the Surfaces. Play in as many different substrates to experiment how they each impact sound and hearing. Try wet and dry grass, sand, forest duff, concrete, even go inside and try carpet and hardwood floors. When people understand that different substrates react differently, they will start to recognize the diversity of ground-cover as they go through the woods with an eye towards a potential sneak. Their eyes and brains begin to see diversity in their landscapes, rather than one homogenous chunk of nature.

Play with Two Firekeepers. With especially sneaky people, raise the bar by putting two blindfolded fire-keepers in the middle, facing each other.

Sensory Awareness
ACTIVITIES

Activities that focus on expanding our senses,
through the use of blindfolds, hiding, sneaking,
and bird language

Sneaking through the forest, listening for bird alarms, looking for someone hidden, or being blind-folded—these activities greatly enhance peoples' connections to the world around them and actively involve several child passions. By exploring the activities in this section, the door to enhanced sensory awareness will begin to crack open and impressive results will follow.

In these activities, we really begin to Expand Our Senses, often in fun, mischievous ways that might include taking away our dominant sense: sight. Some mentors familiar with this curriculum even say that with the simple prop of a single blindfold, they can keep folks engaged, learning, and entertained for hours.

People really and truly love the games and activities that follow in this section. So beware ... you could easily over-do them. Use them regularly yet also sparingly, and always keep riding the edge.

Blindfold Drum Stalk

⊚	**CORE ROUTINES**	Expanding Our Senses, Animal Forms, Mind's Eye Imagining
⟐	**CHILD'S PASSIONS**	Taking Challenges, Stalking like Blindfolded Ninjas
⚘	**BOOK OF NATURE**	All
	NATURAL CYCLE	Northeast: Open and Listen, Northwest: Reflect, Southeast: Activate
	INDICATROS OF AWARENESS	Quiet Mind, Self-Sufficiency

Primer

Sandbar Sighting, by Evan McGown

A friend of mine drove out to the river for a quiet day of fishing. There's a great place with a sandbar island right on the edge of the river where we hold our Tracking Club. You can see all sorts of tracks and sign there, and if you're lucky, sometimes you'll even see the animal. Bear, cougar, hare, coyote, otter, eagle, salmon, deer, elk, and bobcat visit this place. On this particular day though, my friend reported a strange sight. Hunched over his tackle box, a slight and curious rustle in the nearby bushes caught his attention. Out stepped a blindfolded and barefoot young lady. She paid no attention to my friend and continued on down the trail, avoiding the blackberries and slipping through some more bushes to re-enter the forest.

Fortunately for my friend, he knew the young lady. Seeing her blindfolded was no surprise. In fact seeing her avoid thorny plants and walking down a trail with ease—while blindfolded—was no surprise either. This courageous girl had been practicing improving all her non-visual senses for years.

Try eating your dinner with your eyes closed. I guarantee it will taste better. A whole world opens up to us when we close our eyes. For opening up this other world, the next activity is one of the most powerful self-challenges we know of.

How-To

Set-up. Space your participants apart from one another and blindfold them. Explain this game as a solo experience that requires silence and listening. Put everyone at ease by ensuring them that you (and your team of mentors) will be watching to make sure everyone stays safe and doesn't fall off a cliff or into an underground cave full of starving Grizzly Bears. A good distance away from your group of participants, sit down with something loud and resonant to drum on.

Goal. Have the participants stand silently, "Until you hear the first drum beat." Then, they will navigate their way across the landscape towards the sound of the drum, until they touch the drummer. Remind the participants that this is not a race. If anyone wins, it will be the one who goes the slowest, because they will learn the most.

Drumming. The drummer beats infrequently, but often enough to inspire movement from the participants. Make a drumbeat every five or ten seconds. Be sure your spot will project the sound, such as from a high hill, or stand on a tree-stump.

When You Reach the Drum. Before beginning, instruct the participants after they touch the drummer, they will move silently away and sit and watch others arrive. Or, to avoid sniggering at the funny site of their peers struggling to walk blindfolded, ask them to sit and be quiet, keeping their blindfolds on until everyone finishes. Challenge the early-comers to sit so still and quiet a bird might come and land on their shoulder. With younger kids, another instructor may be needed to facilitate this.

Inside the Mind of the Mentor

Talking with folks after playing this game is always interesting. They will have many stories. Getting the opportunity to watch them move blindfolded lets you recall your story as well. I will usually have the opportunity to watch someone, in an amazing feat of blindfold sensitivity, walk over, around, or under an object without having ever touched it. The participants get excited when they hear these events; this is one of the goals, to get them excited about nature by stretching their other senses open. If one of your participants forgets about the drum because they're having an amazing time feeling grass seed heads or tree bark, consider the outing a wild success.

This activity can be a wonderful one to do at the beginning of a relationship with a learner, especially adults. It seems to wake people up to the moment, what is directly in front of them, and gets them out of their heads, which may be full of worry or thoughts about things they need to do at home. It shakes off the road-dust and brings them to the here-and-now. Also, unless someone has done this sort of thing before, this activity seems to humble us and press the "reset" button on what we thought we knew about awareness and nature. It "prepares the soil" and creates fertile ground for teaching lots of things: Fox-Walking, Expanding Our Senses, tree identification—what is that tree with the really smooth bark?—and more.

Conversely, this can also be a great activity, a wonderful "graduation test" to put peoples' awareness skills to the test. The great thing about this exercise, no matter how advanced you get; you will always learn something—about the natural world or about yourself.

During the debrief of this activity, I like to say, "It could be that the way you moved through this activity almost exactly reflects the manner you move through your life. Were you calm and patient? Did you rush forward and hit your face on branches? Is going the "fast" way and getting to the drum first really the point? Or did you move so slowly that you wish you had gone faster and kept up with others? What do you consider "success" in this activity? What do you consider "success" in life?"

Alternatives and Extensions

Level of Difficulty. Determine if your group's needs can be better served by setting up an easy course for touching the drummer as opposed to a difficult course where only a few will finish. Be aware, playing in a field or meadow can be quite difficult; it's actually harder to pinpoint where the sound is coming from. This game will teach you a lot about the way sound travels over land and around objects, or doesn't.

Challenge. To add challenge and up the ante, the drummer can move while drumming, the participants can go barefoot, or they can also carry a precious object like an egg or a cup of water. The intention is to go slow and simply experience every moment.

Wetness. With advanced and willing folks, you can push the edge by having them wear bathing suits. Then, make it so that the participants must travel through mud, pond sludge, shallow water, or other things that will get them squealing, "Ewww ... OH MY GOSH!" all the while laughing and giggling at their own foolishness. Upping the level of challenge over time can make this activity an evolving measure of people's self-confidence and ability to gracefully move through the forest.

Nutty Squirrels

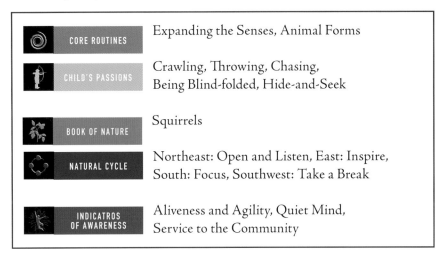

◎	CORE ROUTINES	Expanding the Senses, Animal Forms
⌁	CHILD'S PASSIONS	Crawling, Throwing, Chasing, Being Blind-folded, Hide-and-Seek
	BOOK OF NATURE	Squirrels
	NATURAL CYCLE	Northeast: Open and Listen, East: Inspire, South: Focus, Southwest: Take a Break
	INDICATROS OF AWARENESS	Aliveness and Agility, Quiet Mind, Service to the Community

Primer

(Note: This game was originally called "Tank," with tanks and tank-drivers, but we re-imagined it to send a natural-history-based message to young kids instead of a war-based metaphor. With older participants you may find it kosher to introduce it as "Tank" in order to simplify. However you do it, this is reliably a favorite activity, particularly for teens and adults.)

One of the hardest parts of being a young squirrel is leaving your mother to find your own territory. Your friends and neighbor squirrels will no longer be happy to see you, they will chase you away. Older and bigger squirrels also compete for new territory. Luckily physical fighting is rare; most squirrels argue with loud chattering and vigorous tail-waving. In this game, you be the Baby Squirrel whose Mother has decided to teach you early-on how to defend yourself when you look for territory. However, Baby Squirrels are born blind and don't develop the ability to see for a while. Your Mother thinks it would be funny if she taught you to throw nuts while you're still blind!

How-To

Pair up as Mother and Baby Squirrels. You'll need a minimum of three pairs to play, although larger groups work better. Ask for a volunteer Baby Squirrel, and blindfold the Baby.

Goal. Mother Squirrels guide their blind Babies with code-language to navigate the playing field, collect nuts, and fire them at other squirrels. Hit Squirrels go to the sidelines. The last squirrel left in the field, wins.

Set Up. Use markers to define your natural boundaries. Play this game barefoot by both partners, with their socks balled up, tossed into the middle of the playing field, to become Nuts. Remember to check the field for barefoot hazards before playing.

Set-up Signals. Before starting, partners agree on sound signals as their own secret code language with which the Mothers will guide the blindfolded Babies. Mothers very quietly stay close to their Babies at the beginning without touching them; Mothers don't want to draw other blind squirrels' attention to their Babies. Signals cannot be words; they need to be unique to each pair. Taps, squirrel-like chatters, and quick yelps work great.

Refereeing. To monitor larger games, you will need multiple instructors. When a sock-nut hits a Baby Squirrel, Baby and Mother must silently walk out of the playing circle and watch the remaining squirrels fight for their lives. If only the Mother gets hit, the Baby Squirrel stays in, now "on their lonesome" to do everything—with their blindfold still on. (Although best done with more mature participants, they absolutely LOVE this lonesome part). Watch the concentration of the last few blindfolded Babies as they listen for nearby footsteps and quietly Fox-Walk so they do not to betray their location. Watch for folks who demonstrate an uncanny ability to throw their nuts to hit the target, even before Mother Squirrel prompts them. Either their blindfold is loose or they're more than ready to become a fabulous birder-by-ear.

Last Squirrel Standing. The last squirrel standing wins the round. Have the squirrels on the sidelines—when they aren't rolling on the ground quietly laughing—remain quiet and throw miscast nuts back into the game-field.

Inside the Mind of the Mentor

People generally love the focus this game evokes. It requires a mix of silly mayhem and serious concentration. It's hard to believe that they can exist side by side, but the need to throw nuts accurately while blindfolded makes it so. Without this blend, the game will usually produce lackluster results.

Disclaimer/Warning. This game is best for older people (8 years old and up), and can simply end in disaster with younger kids. If your group has recently had aggressive streaks or lack of focus this game may exacerbate those situations.

Alternatives and Extensions

Advanced Play. Later rounds of Nutty Squirrels can have different twists to them. Try any of these: Mother Squirrel has had her voice taken away, now she only communicates directions through taps. For advanced players, if Mother Squirrel is sidelined by a hit, she can direct Baby Squirrel from the sidelines, using the non-verbal directions they've developed. The pairs might create clever signals to suggest directions like *turn right, turn left, duck,* or *throw.*

Real Squirrels. Of course, field observation of real squirrels lends itself nicely as a tie-in activity. Participants can research and observe mating, feeding, and aggressive behavior. Watching how squirrels and crows interact can be comedic as well.

The Wildlife is Watching

⊚	CORE ROUTINES	Sit Spot, Expanding Our Senses
🏹	CHILD'S PASSIONS	Hiding and Seeking, Getting Dirty
🌿	BOOK OF NATURE	Plants, Mammals, Birds
	NATURAL CYCLE	East: Inspire, Southwest: Take A Break, Northeast: Open and Listen
	INDICATROS OF AWARENESS	Quiet Mind, Awe and Reverence

Primer

How often have you sat and watched wildlife right in front of your very eyes? Never? A few times? If you asked the animals how often they've spied on you when you go walking out in nature, you'd be surprised at their answer. Many animals hide from humans by just being still and silent. Animals may be just five feet away, on the side of a trail, completely hidden by their natural camouflage. In this activity, you will do the same thing. You will learn about hiding, and also how to use your eyes and awareness to *really* see.

How-To

Create the Playing Field. Use a section of trail or path with very good hiding opportunities. Mark out a beginning and ending point along the trail. Between these two points, make sure your group has ample room to hide.

Create Roles. Divide your group into two. The hiders (the "wildlife") will have five or so minutes to camouflage and hide themselves within five (your choice) feet of the trail's edge. The seekers must remove themselves from the immediate area until the hiders feel completely hidden. You may use this time to review Fox Walk and Owl Eyes with them.

The Game. To begin, the seekers will Fox-Walk slowly down the trail, one at a time, a reasonable distance apart, and count *to themselves* how many of the hiders they've spotted. The seekers may stop in the middle of the trail at any time, *but they can only move forward*. Once they take a step, they can't go back. They may not touch the plants or point out any hiders they've spotted. When the seekers get to the predetermined end of the hiding zone, they can whisper into the ear of the awaiting instructor how many they spotted.

Once everyone has finished the walk, let those hiding show off their hiding places, their camouflage, or their strategy to stay hidden.

Switch up the roles of hiders and seekers and play again.

Inside the Mind of the Mentor

This game appeals to the universal desire to hide or seek. Like Eagle Eye it presents an opportunity to get familiar and comfortable with natural surroundings. While hidden deep in a thicket, people will see the intricate designs of the spider web right in front of them, or the myriad leaf shapes decomposing into the forest floor.

Draw out the time the "wildlife" stay hidden for as long as you think beneficial. Once you release the seekers, the hider's hearts will start to beat rapidly since they don't want to be seen. The more often they play, the more they will discover an alert but peaceful state of being. Undoubtedly, this will be useful when they begin to have real wildlife encounters.

Often younger kids will hide only if you put "camouflage" on them. I've seen many a child preoccupied with the avoidance of dirt suddenly embrace leaf mold and old fern fronds with passion when playing this game. As an amusing side-discovery, participants realize the difficult task of hiding in their typical street clothes. Over time, participants may trade out hot pink pants or white hats for earth tones. (You might suggest they start with these in gear lists for your shorter programs.) People who change their attire also demonstrate their desire to "fit in" with nature and may be ready for more focused explorations.

For the seekers in this game, this opportunity puts the Core Routines of Fox Walking and Owl Eyes to the test.

Alternatives and Extensions

Variety. Try shrinking or expanding the area to hide in and the time to hide.

Two Ways. Let the seekers move down the trail twice, the first time at their normal "city" walk and the second time using Owl Eyes and Fox Walk.

Camouflage. Precede or follow up with a lesson in camouflage and/or hiding techniques. Interests may be split between learning about other animals' techniques, and practicing camouflage themselves.

Head Honcho

CORE ROUTINES	Expanding the Senses, Listening for Bird Language
CHILD'S PASSIONS	Following the Leader, Imitating, Making Music, Whistling, Clapping, Stomping, Performing, Keeping Secrets, Helping Each Other
BOOK OF NATURE	All the rhythmic sounds in nature
NATURAL CYCLE	East: Inspire, Southwest: Take a Break, West: Gather and Share
INDICATROS OF AWARENESS	Common Sense, Aliveness and Agility, Service to the Community, Quiet Mind

Primer

You want a challenge? This game challenges *everybody* to use their Owl Eyes, the sharp wit and awareness of a tracker for the Head Honcho, and a poker-face and rhythmic abilities for the Tracker Detective. You can take the opportunity to review Owl Eyes with finger wiggles before starting.

How-To

Create the Circle. Everybody sits cross-legged knees just about touching, or stands at arm's length distance in a circle.

Choose Roles. First, ask a volunteer to be the Tracker Detective. Then ask this participant to leave the circle, go behind a tree, and cover their ears. They do this so that they won't know who the person is that you pick for the next role.

When you are sure the Tracker Detective can't hear the group silently picks a Head Honcho. His or her job starts a follow-the-leader rhythm circle using dance moves or bodily slaps, claps, snaps, any beat with a rhythm. The Head Honcho begins a simple movement, and then everyone else follows.

The Game. Invite the Tracker Detective back to stand in the middle of the circle. His or her challenge will be to identify the Head Honcho, using all of their senses to figure out who is leading the movement. Head Honcho changes the rhythm pattern about every 20 seconds. Everybody else copies the Head Honcho's movements, doing their best not to give him or her away (such as looking at the Head Honcho out of the corner of their Owl Eyes rather than directly staring).

The Tracker Detective in the middle has three guesses to figure out who changes the rhythm. Whether or not they get it, ask some questions to the Tracker Detectives to see what informed their choices. After each round, pick a new Tracker Detective and a new Head Honcho.

Inside the Mind of the Mentor

If participants sit in a circle to play, use this game for winding down the energy towards the end of the day, possibly leading into a Story of the Day Sharing Circle. Prepare to play it for a long time, because usually everyone wants a try at one or both positions. The constant rhythmic movement makes this a gentle, relaxing game, and seems to promote idyllic revelry on enjoyably warm days.

If they stand in a circle, you can use this game to break the ice in a group. What better way to create a community feeling than moving in synch all together and trying to keep a secret? Head Honcho practices leadership and receives personal affirmation as everyone enjoys the movements that originated from his or her creativity. Sometimes this turns into Physical Education when the Head Honcho does strenuous jumping jacks or toe touches ... whew!

Of course, the action puts Tracker Detective on the spot, so make sure you have a willing volunteer.

This game gives mentors a good opportunity to observe people in the circle as they follow the Head Honcho. Who seems to have a good grasp on Owl Eyes? Also, use questioning to find out what the Tracker Detective is paying attention to. Was he or she looking for movement ... locating the first change in sound ... reading facial expressions or body language ... or using intuition?

Alternatives and Extensions

Owl Eyes and Deer Ears. Use this game to expand on sensory awareness and to enable you to evaluate their continuing abilities in Expanding the Senses.

Jam Session. This game may evolve into forgetting the Tracker Detective part and simply enjoying the rhythmic synchrony. Consider the spontaneity to create a driftwood instrument rhythm jam spontaneously. A good time with such natural drums could go on and on for a long time.

Take the idea outside. Explore the sounds, rhythms, and reverberations of nature. Press your ear up against a tree with a woodpecker tapping on it. Listen to the different kinds of sound that come from rocks and minerals tapped together.

Bird Language Scenarios

⊚	CORE ROUTINES	Listening for Bird Language, Animal Forms, Expanding the Senses, Exploring Field Guides
	CHILD'S PASSIONS	Imitating Animals, Creating Stories, Acting Out Stories
	BOOK OF NATURE	Catchables, Hazards, Birds, Mammals
	NATURAL CYCLE	East: Inspire, Southeast: Activate, South: Focus
	INDICATROS OF AWARENESS	Aliveness and Agility, Service to the Community

Primer

Remember when we did the Bird Language Skits and had so much fun? Well, now we're going to take it to the next level.

How-To

Improv Set-Up. This activity extends and develops Bird Language skills learned from Bird Language Skits (refer to Core Routines—Bird Language). Simply put, give them a specific bird-life scenario to act out for each other. Using a common technique of improvisational theatre, give them a scenario and very little time to plan, and then enjoy watching them improvise. Don't help them. They need to apply their knowledge from the Bird Language skits. Small groups work best for this activity with six to eight participants per group.

Scenarios. These scenarios work well for this activity:

+ A mother bird tries to feed several baby birds, but she is keenly aware of a predator bird, like a Sharp-Shinned Hawk, nearby.

+ A pair of birds are feeding and companion calling when another couple of male birds fly into their territory. How does everyone respond?

+ A group of chickadees is feeding when a human enters their territory. As the human walks through, a weasel sneaks off through the bushes.

+ Several birds are singing their territorial songs when a jogger comes through. Then a few minutes later after the jogger passes, a person doing Fox-Walking and Owl Eyes walks through. How are the responses different?

These scenarios offer just a few basic ideas. Feel free to expand with your own scenarios or let the participants come up with their own.

Inside the Mind of the Mentor

This activity should be fun and actively engage the imagination. This is more important than whether or not they got the scenario "right" or "wrong." You can debrief the skits, asking participants what they saw or didn't see, what they might have done. Then, send them to Bird Language resources (referenced in Core Routines—Bird Language) to check on their accuracy.

Also, watch your participants to see which roles they choose for themselves. Who tries to be the "director?" Who wants to be the "star?" Who suddenly comes out of their shell when they get to be "on-stage?"

Alternatives and Extensions

Use it with Mammals. Take the basic premise of this activity but switch the subject matter: act out scenarios based on tracking mammals or how reptiles and amphibians respond to predators.

Use it with Sit Spot. Spend time at Sit Spots and then come back and act out individually the scenario of what happened.

Record. Have the participants illustrate, record, or film their scenarios, then enjoy reviewing them like you were a football team looking back on your plays.

Silent Stalker

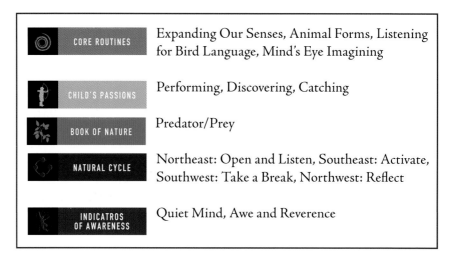

◎	**CORE ROUTINES**	Expanding Our Senses, Animal Forms, Listening for Bird Language, Mind's Eye Imagining
	CHILD'S PASSIONS	Performing, Discovering, Catching
	BOOK OF NATURE	Predator/Prey
	NATURAL CYCLE	Northeast: Open and Listen, Southeast: Activate, Southwest: Take a Break, Northwest: Reflect
	INDICATROS OF AWARENESS	Quiet Mind, Awe and Reverence

Primer

Watching the Stalker, by Evan McGown

Animals that hunt for a living must rely on their stealth. They need to sneak into a good hunting position and time their attack just right. Most of the predators are so much bigger, stronger, and faster than their prey, the food they eat. How come predators usually fail? Well I'm sure you know all about special adaptations, like the snowshoe hare's wide, large feet that allow it to weave and dance out of the grasp of the lynx.

But there's something else at play, a gift that all animals, including humans, have at their disposal. You can feel when someone is looking at you. For some people, they say the hair on the back of their neck stands up, for others they just have a sneaking suspicion so they turn to find someone staring back. Here's a true story from my life about this unexplained sense. It actually saved me.

After I graduated from high-school, I went on my first big road-trip. Everything was great, but near the end of the trip, I was in a large metropolitan city. Being in a big city with so many people packed together created new sensations for me. Well, I was hungry, and when I saw this line of people waiting for sub sandwiches being carried out huge and packed full of food, I knew where I was going for lunch. So I joined the line of people, which slowly moved towards the food counter. This place was packed.

Now, I had just started learning about Owl Eyes and Body Radar, but I was darn hungry and a little weary from weeks of traveling, so my awareness slipped a little. Luckily I noticed a sign on the wall of the restaurant. It said, "Beware of Pick-Pockets." Woah, I thought to myself. I had never had to watch out for pick-pockets before. I wondered how a Pick-Pocket might try to steal my wallet as I felt for my wallet in my back pocket to make sure it was still there … when suddenly I felt a strange sensation.

Without realizing why, I quickly turned my head around to see a man, who was standing against a far wall, *staring straight at me*. Looking at him, I thought he was out of a Mafia movie. He looked tough and mean … and he was staring at *me*. I looked away as if I hadn't really seen him and just played it cool. Suddenly, I felt the strange sensation again, but this time without realizing why, my head jerked to my right, to see another man, very similar in appearance, standing at the other wall, and again—*staring straight at me*. By now, I was a little freaked out. But I stayed in line, trying to keep calm, and staring straight ahead. Fortunately, I had something they didn't count on: my Owl Eyes.

So while staring straight ahead, I could see the guy to my right in my peripheral vision. But he didn't know I could still see him. He started making hand-signals in the direction of the other guy on the opposite wall. Then, pretending to cough, I turned my head backwards enough to see the other guy making gestures back. Okay, they were planning something. I couldn't just leave, although I badly wanted to get out of there; they stood right by the two exits. "What should I do?" I wondered. I just kept watching them in my Owl Eyes, and when I got to the counter to pay, I slipped my wallet into a different pocket. By then, I noticed the guy to the right was sitting at a table, and opposite to him there was an open table. Well, sometimes the safest place is in the eye of the storm itself. So I went straight to that table, and when the guy looked up from the newspaper he pretended to read—I stared right back at him, straight into his eyes, and said, "Hello." I saw his body language shift uncomfortably in reaction. Then he grunted and went back to his "reading."

As I ate, I pretended to read a bit of newspaper, but in reality I was constantly in Owl Eyes, watching them both for signals. I was ready to cry out for help at the slightest indication of some joint movement toward me. You never know what a Pick-Pocket might do if his trick is spoiled. I watched as the guy got up from the table, shot me one more look, and walked out of the place as if disgusted. I saw the other guy on the far wall also leave. They didn't seem happy. I guess they were worried I'd turn the cops onto them when I left.

Not only had my awareness skills kept me safe from their preying on me, but it also ruined their game for the afternoon. So I left, a bit shaken but still keenly aware that from now on, in this city or anywhere I went, I wouldn't let my awareness slip. I also left that little sub shop with a new appreciation and curiosity for the human powers of perception.

How-To

Set-up. All the players form a loose circle around a participant in the middle. The center participant picks a Prey animal to be, puts on a well-tied thick blindfold, and pretends to be hidden in a ring of trees. One participant in the circle must now be silently picked as the Predator, and everyone else becomes one of the Trees.

The Game. The Predator's job is to quietly raise hand and eyes, and using as much focus and hunger as he or she can internally muster, point to the Prey in the middle. The trees will just be peaceful, arms and eyes hanging down, watching the action with their Owl Eyes. The Prey in the middle gets to turn all around, staying in the middle of the circle, using Body-Radar to sense the area where the mean hungry Predator is poised and finally, point straight at them. The Prey person gets three guesses to "spot" the Predator by pointing back.

For multiple rounds, once your Prey is blindfolded in the middle, have the outer circle shuffle and find new spots before beginning again.

Inside the Mind of the Mentor

This game fascinates most anyone who plays. To children, as well as most adults, the possibility of a "Sixth Sense" seems irresistible. Even those who disbelieve in the concept of intuition can't resist playing. People with martial-arts training, hunters, bird-watchers, professional detectives, and most folks who have developed reverence for nature take to this game easily.

I watch for two things when this game is being played. First, everyone needs to be in their role. The acting required in this game is all internal. Exuberant Trees or meek Predators don't work.

Watching the Prey pointing is crucial. Think of ways to acknowledge success besides celebrating the occasional person who points straight at their predator: I encourage the Prey to slowly turn in the middle, to feel the whole circle before they point. I've seen two general patterns 1) in their turning, the Prey hesitates right in front of the Predator, or, 2) their first point lines up with the Predator, but to the opposite side of the circle. Is this a success? Possibly. You can tell the group what you noticed and ask them what they think. When someone feels disappointed because they didn't succeed after three tries, they usually feel thrilled to know they may have had success after all—even if they didn't realize it. But don't make up things about their body movements just to make them feel better. Call a spade a spade.

The point of this game is to get people experimenting with intuition for themselves, not to force people to "believe" something. This game seems to create a question for most people: Does a true intuitive ability exist in humans? Let each person decide for themselves. Some people decry this game and the premise it implies. Such tension drives people to question and search out answers for themselves. This also presents an opportunity to engage in open dialogue and critical thinking. If teens or adults become very curious about this phenomenon, we recommend a book for reading and discussion: *The Sense of Being Stared At*, by the English scientist Rupert Sheldrake.

Alternatives and Extensions

Hot/Cold. Being blindfolded is hard for some. Make this game easier by offering guidance to the Prey in the middle. Using terms like cold, warm, hot, or burning helps them out.

Discussion Starter. Because this game is such an experiential sensitivity enhancer, it creates a fabulous lead-in to exploring any topic involving birds and sensitivity.

Research. The relationships between all prey and predator species can be examined. Inspire research into the other sensory and physical adaptations that prey use to avoid predators or that predators use to catch prey.

Animal Form Games

ACTIVITIES

Activities built around playful imitation of animals for physical development, energy release, and empathy and imagination

Most of the activities in this section work great to begin the day, because they quickly engage people, release rambunctious energy, and set the tone of play and free self-expression. Energetic openers break down barriers between participants and through play, everyone gets to know each others' names and personalities.

Many of these activities carry the energy of the "Southeast"— that of a busy spring morning, excited bodily movement, and the joy of childhood. These can also be used to spill out an overabundance of raucous energy, or to bring about a celebratory feel of community at the end of the day.

Based on basic animal behaviors and predicaments, Animal Form Games invite participants to empathize with animals, to imitate their attitudes, and, to the best of their human-bodied ability in the throes of a game, practice animal ways of moving.

Otter Steals Fish

CORE ROUTINES	Animal Forms, Expanding the Senses	
CHILD'S PASSIONS	Tagging, Sneaking, Jumping, Lunging, Getting Away, Risk-Taking	
BOOK OF NATURE	Otter, Heron	
NATURAL CYCLE	East: Inspire, Southeast: Activate, Southwest: Take a Break	
INDICATROS OF AWARENESS	Aliveness and Agility	

Primer

Have you ever seen a Great Blue Heron catch a fish? Imagine this: Heron stalks into a river or lake quietly, picking up and putting down its skinny stilt-legs so slowly that it barely disturbs the water. It stands completely still for as long as it takes, maybe even an hour, until a fish swims right below it. Then "BAM!" Heron strikes like a bolt of lightning as its long, sharp beak spears the fish. Then it pulls the speared fish out of the water and in a quick acrobatic movement, throws the fish into the air, opens its beak wide, and swallows the fish whole. It's amazing to watch … I hope you get to see it someday.

As you can tell, Heron works long and hard to catch a fish, so you can bet it doesn't want anyone else to steal it. Sometimes, Heron or other fish-catching-animals will pull their catch to the shore and lay it down to eat it. This adds risk, because there are lots of things that might sneak up and try to steal that fish: Crow, Eagle, Fox, or the animal who loves fish as much as any other animal, and who is quick as a flash: Otter.

How-To

The Fish. You will need a small, soft article of cloth for this game that will become the fish: a bandana works best or a hat or glove also will work. One person starts out as Heron protecting its fish. Everyone else will be Otters waiting nearby and watching. Heron stands tall in the middle while the Otters circle him or her. The Heron holds the fish in hand and tells the Otters how many steps away they need to be in order to start the game (this gets important as the game re-starts a lot).

The Action. When the Heron feels ready, dropping the fish to the ground begins the game. Then it's simple: the Otters all swarm in and try to steal the fish from the Heron without getting tagged. If an Otter is tagged, he or she has to drop the fish and go back out to the edge of the circle and start again. The game becomes a frenzy of activity as Otters dive for the fish and the Heron frantically moves around, looking constantly in all directions and reaching to tag anyone close.

Successful Steal. To be successful in stealing the fish, the Otter must get the fish back to the original circle edge before getting tagged. Often this results in heroic full-body lunges. If someone succeeds in stealing the fish, they become the next Heron (unless they opt not to, as some participants will). If someone steals the fish but gets tagged on the way out, they give the fish back to Heron who gives new directions for how far away Otters must be.

Inside the Mind of the Mentor

This game is a flurry of fun, even if you just watch from the perimeter. It brings out the Awareness Indicator (from Chapter 11) of *Aliveness and Agility* as much as any activity we've encountered. It brings folks fully to the moment, gets their bodies moving in new ways, and teaches them to act quickly and decisively.

Playing this game yourself or watching people as they play it, the excited nervousness feels palpable as you ponder going in to try to steal the fish. The edge of risk, failure, apprehension, fear of being tagged all cause a state of fight or flight. But it is beautiful to witness as players summon the courage to push through small fear and crack into full-bodied exertion to take the risk, even if they don't steal the fish.

Therefore the quick-paced, moment-to-moment intensity in this game offers one of the best opportunities to gain insight into your players. Some will be very reserved and stay back, while others will go in without any thought or hesitation. You can tell which people have an easy time with adventures and adrenaline-pumping challenges, and who prefers more settled activities. You can see some who have natural athletic quickness and others grow quicker and more confident over time. You might notice some people depend on sheer quickness while others plot and plan very carefully, memorizing the patterns of the Heron's tagging strategies and finding the moments and places where the fish can easily be grabbed. Sometimes, participants will team up—without saying anything to each other—in order to create distractions so that others have a better chance to steal the fish.

Alternatives and Extensions

Otter and Heron Forms. Precede or follow-up this game by researching Heron and Otter. Look at their body forms, tracks, gaits, and typical postures, and then have everyone try to imitate these movements as they play the game.

Freeze Tag. Try this variation—if you get tagged, you don't go to the edge of the circle and start over, instead you freeze in place. After you play this awhile, you can try the more advanced version of this—if you lay frozen and accidentally get tagged again, you become unfrozen. Talk about confusion!

Tag and Out. To raise the stakes, alter the rules so that if you get tagged once, you are out for the whole round.

Run Rabbit Run!

⊚	CORE ROUTINES	Animal Forms, Mind's Eye Imagining
	CHILD'S PASSIONS	Running, Chasing, Being Chased, Playing Tag, Imitating Animals
	BOOK OF NATURE	Hazards, Catchables, Mammals
	NATURAL CYCLE	East: Inspire, Southeast: Activate, Southwest: Take a Break
	INDICATROS OF AWARENESS	Aliveness and Agility, Caring and Tending

Primer

If you are a Rabbit or a Hare, you have those big ears for a good reason. You must always listen for animals who want to eat you. Foxes, Coyotes, Bobcats, even Hawks and Owls eat Rabbits. Imagine you are a Rabbit, and you have a network of rabbit holes, and other little homes in thick brambles of blackberry or other plants. Of course you can't just stay in your safe little hole all day: you have to go out and find food, yummy dandelion greens and other fresh vegetables.

My friend Laura once watched a European Rabbit peacefully eating on dandelions in a meadow full of Rabbit holes. Suddenly a Mink appeared and leaped towards the Rabbit. The Rabbit was alert, however, with its ears constantly twitching to hear in all directions, and it heard and saw it coming in a flash and ran to the nearest hole like a burst of lighting. But just as Rabbit reached the entrance to the hole, the Mink was there to grab it and eat it down. Can you imagine if you lived in a world where this could happen at any given moment? What if you were a Rabbit who had to hop from hole to hole? Do you think you could survive and outsmart the Minks, Foxes, and Coyotes?

How-To

Create the Rabbit Holes. This very fun version of tag requires a bit of set-up that participants can help with: mark the outline of two or three circles on the ground using bandanas, coats, backpacks, whatever you've got. Make each circle about twelve feet wide, big enough for all participants to squeeze into while standing, but not too big. These circles are the "rabbit holes."

Set-up. Choose one person who will be the Fox (or other local predator of Rabbits). Have everyone else be Rabbits who stand inside one of the Rabbit holes. The goal of the game is for the Rabbits to continually run from hole to hole without getting eaten (tagged) by the Fox.

The Action. Rabbits run from hole to hole, trying not to get tagged. They strategize when to run, to which hole they go, etc. It's up to them to plot and choose and take risks. The Rabbits can leave a Rabbit hole at any time. If a Rabbit is tagged, it becomes a Fox, until only one Rabbit is left, who then has the choice to be the Fox in the next game.

Predators Must Always Circle the Edge. If all the Rabbits are safe in their holes, the Fox cannot just stand in between the holes, conveniently waiting for his prey. Instead, the Fox must circle around the outside of the Rabbit hole until a Rabbit pops out to run across the field to another hole. Ask the Foxes to really get into their character by panting, sniffing, baring their teeth, lightly growling, making a trotting motion with their hands as they circle the hole.

Inside the Mind of the Mentor

Animal Form tag-games such as this one strongly relay a bodily experience of what it feels like to be both the hunter and the hunted, predator and prey. Nothing compares to the feeling of being one of the only rabbits out of the hole, within grasp of a predator, with only your wits and your quickness to keep you out of their reach.

This creates an experience of empathy for the lives of wild animals that constantly live on the edge of life and death. For a brief period we step out of the box of the human way of life, and we taste, firsthand, what life is like for rabbits, foxes, mice, deer, coyotes … this game and others like it transform abstract notions of animals—from photos, stories, and zoo visits—into bodily empathy.

Alternatives and Extensions

Sitting Rabbits. A more challenging variation on the game has the rabbits sit down whenever they are inside a rabbit hole. It is much harder to make a running break from a sitting position, and it requires a different strategy and a different brand of patience.

Teach about Predators. The unfortunate slant people sometimes put on predators such as wolves portrays them to be mean, bloodthirsty, and evil killers. Games that feature predator and prey relationships provide the opportunity to teach about consequences in the life of predators: eating other animals is simply their way of surviving just as the rabbit's way of surviving is to run away and kill dandelions trying to grow. You can also mention that humans are predators, too, and our teeth structure is similar to that of foxes, coyotes, and other predators.

Population Dynamics. You can follow-up this game with a guided conversation, prompted by questions such as: "What happens to the foxes when only a few rabbits remain?" "What happens to the rabbits if no foxes or other predators were around?" Science has produced an abundance of evidence that predation on prey, such as rabbits and deer, actually benefits the prey species as a whole by 1) keeping populations at a sustainable level for the amount of vegetative food and other resources in an area, and 2) improving the gene pool over time by preying on the weakest, and therefore ensuring that the most fit and survival-strong genes get passed on. Predation makes both predator and prey species stronger.

Cougar Stalks Deer

CORE ROUTINES	Animal Forms, Expanding the Senses, Questioning and Tracking, Listening for Bird Language	
CHILD'S PASSIONS	Sneaking, Imitating Animals, Challenge	
BOOK OF NATURE	Mammals	
NATURAL CYCLE	Southeast: Activate, South: Focus, Northeast: Open and Listen	
INDICATROS OF AWARENESS	Aliveness and Agility, Quiet Mind, Common Sense	

Primer

Cougars hunt Deer by sneaking up from behind so stealthily that they remain unaware. A Cougar stalks slowly, moving low to the ground, making almost no noise as its hind foot lands exactly where its front foot had been. After a stalking Cougar gets close behind a Deer, they powerfully lunge onto the deer's back, biting into the neck. I bet you didn't know this: Cougars actually have nerve endings on the tips of their big canine teeth so that they can feel exactly where to put their teeth and bite, immediately severing the spine and killing the Deer quickly and painlessly.

The only protection a Deer has from a stalking Cougar is its sensory awareness. If it hears something and turns to see the Cougar moving, the Deer can bound off easily to safety and the hunt ends. However, deer have limited vision and can only clearly recognize moving animals. This means, you can stand completely still right in front of a Deer, and the Deer will not see you.! But don't get cocky—if the wind blows the right way, the Deer will smell you in a heartbeat! And if you make even the slightest noise, it'll be out of there in a flash.

So the trick for any Cougar sneaking up on a Deer in the open is the ability to stop moving and freeze in the same instant the Deer turns to look. Lions in Africa stalk low through the grass just like this, freezing whenever something looks their way, and then moving quietly closer when they look away again—until they get close enough to pounce and kill. Do you think you could do that?

How-To

This is a version of the classic game that many know as "Redlight-Greenlight."

Choose the Deer. One or two participants or instructors become Deer. Choose them and ask them to really get into the mind of grazing Deer. Have the Deer stand a little apart from everyone else. They will imitate the way Deer amble along, casually bending down to nibble on grass, occasionally springing their heads up and looking around when they hear a noise, always making sure they are safe. Except for when they raise their heads to look around, their backs are to everyone else, and they can slowly inch away from everyone else.

Create the Playing Field. The rest of the participants get to be Cougars. Have the Cougars form a starting line, at least fifteen yards from the feeding Deer.

The Action. Once you say start, the Cougars will silently and slowly stalk towards the feeding Deer, always watching the Deer so they can freeze in place as soon as the Deer turns its head to look around. The Deer can look back when they hear a noise, or every ten seconds or so. If a Deer turns while a Cougar is still in movement, that Cougar's hunt ends, and he or she begins again at the starting line. When a Cougar reaches Deer, it simply taps it on the shoulder this Cougar now becomes the Deer. The caught Deer obediently moves to the side, has a seat on the ground, and silently watches as the other Cougars continue the hunt.

Referee. You or another instructor will need to serve as referee to help the game run smoothly and fairly, i.e., to make a call on any arguments about people being seen or not seen moving, which of course will arise.

Inside the Mind of the Mentor

This game is awesome for learning stalking and body control because participants practice and test out their Cougar-Crawl or Fox-Walk. They will be challenged to always be physically centered, under control of their body, and able to freeze and hold a position, no matter what part of a step they are on. Along the way to gaining this self-control in movement, participants get frozen in many humorous awkward positions, as well as shaking legs and funny falls.

Also, this game emphasizes the use of the ears and eyes to catch movement, both on the part of the ever-watching Cougars ready to freeze and on the part of the Deer listening and looking for any movements. You can invite them to try Owl Eyes during this game.

Alternatives and Extensions

Change the Animals. If you don't have Cougars at all near where you live, or if you just want to change things, try changing this game into "Bobcat Stalks Rabbit," or "Housecat Stalks Robin."

The Smell Factor. Ask Cougars to arrange themselves so the Cougars always stalk from downwind. Guide them with questions to help them figure, in real time, the direction of the breeze, and where "downwind" would be. This awareness of their relationship to the wind gets participants tuning into their sense of touch regularly.

Make it Real. Challenge participants to touch an animal by using the stalking style of this game to sneak up on real animals whenever they have the chance: deer, robins feeding on the lawn, squirrel, even their own cat or dog.

Fire in the Forest

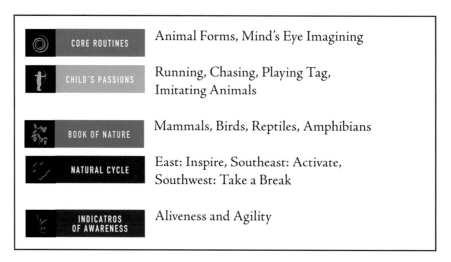

CORE ROUTINES	Animal Forms, Mind's Eye Imagining
CHILD'S PASSIONS	Running, Chasing, Playing Tag, Imitating Animals
BOOK OF NATURE	Mammals, Birds, Reptiles, Amphibians
NATURAL CYCLE	East: Inspire, Southeast: Activate, Southwest: Take a Break
INDICATROS OF AWARENESS	Aliveness and Agility

Primer

Do you hear that? It's the terrible sound of a crackling forest fire, coming straight towards us. There's a fire in the forest, and every animal is running away, trying to escape without being caught and burned by the fire.

There are all kinds of animals: mammals, like White-tailed Deer and Long-tailed Weasels and Deer Mice; birds, like Black-capped Chickadees, Pileated Woodpeckers, and Song Sparrows; reptiles, like Garter Snakes and Box-Turtles, and amphibians, like Bull-frogs and Rough-skinned Newts. But they all are running from the fire, trying not to get caught.

How-To

Create the Playing Field. For this game, you will need to mark a large rectangle or square as a playing field, using bandanas or backpacks to mark the corners and some of the sides. Make it at least twenty or thirty yards long, and as wide as you want: for this game, a wider field will make it easier to not get tagged, and a narrow field can make it very challenging. So choose somewhere in between based on your experience working with this group of participants.

Set-up. Have everyone stand on the line at one end of your rectangle, equivalent to the end zone on a football field. Tell them you need the names of three animals that live in those woods, and ask them to raise their hands if they want to be one of the animals. After three local animals have been chosen, explain the game. Everyone chooses to be one of those three animals during the game. They don't tell anyone else what animal they are; they just remember it in their mind. Choose one person to be "The Fire"; this person is "it" and stands out in the middle of the playing field.

The Action. The player who is Fire then starts the game by calling out one of the three animals. When you hear your animal name, you run through to the other end zone without getting tagged by the Fire. If you get tagged, you become a Tree on fire, and you are able to tag people running through—but, being a Tree, you cannot move from your roots; you can only pivot on one foot (you might need to demonstrate a pivot). If the Fire person calls out, "Fire in the Forest!" then all the animals have to run across to the other end zone without getting tagged by the Fire or any of the Trees. The game goes on like this, with animals running back and forth from end zone to end zone as they are called out. The game will eventually get quite challenging and extremely fun, as the Trees present an obstacle course reaching out to lick you with their flames.

The End is the Beginning. The last animal to be tagged gets offered the chance to be the Fire for the next game. Every time you start a new game, select three new animals who live in your area, letting the participants brainstorm and volunteer choices.

Inside the Mind of the Mentor

Besides the obvious fun of this tag-game, the magic is the way it slyly teaches about what animals live in your area. The process of choosing animals for the game often becomes a discussion through which participants learn what animals actually live in their area, what they look like, and how they move and act. Your people engage in the creation of a "Master List" of animals for this area without even realizing it.

"You mean we actually have fox in our area? I didn't know that?"

"Where do they live with all these houses around?"

"What's a vole? Oh … I think I might have seen one of those before."

"Isn't a garter snake poisonous … it's not? My mom told me they were."

During discussions that spontaneously emerge from choosing local animals, you will see players correct erroneous notions they had about animals living around them, while everyone comes to understand the animals that actually live in the places we explore. Most become naturally curious about what lives close to them, asking questions and eager to offer answers when they can. You can set parameters on the animals they choose by specifying Master Lists: "Choose three types of amphibians," for example, or mammals, or song-birds, or insects.

In this Master Listing process, you build a foundation of search images that can be drawn upon when you explore the natural areas around you. For instance, if you find a track, you can say, "What kind of animals live here that could have made this?" And you might just be amazed as they begin to rattle off information about the local species: "Well, we have mule deer, coyote, black bear … but black bear are too big to make this track." In this way, games and experiences in the woods build upon each other over time, gradually instilling a deep knowledge of place without the participants ever feeling their schooling.

Alternatives and Extensions

Play with the Names. It can be fun to make the names of animals very specific to your area. For instance, if someone volunteers "wren" as an animal, I might say "Okay, how about winter wren … that's the kind of wren that lives here." Another variation on this that can be fun for participants, if you make it wacky enough, introduces scientific, or Latin names. Have a field guide with you when you choose names and translate them into their Latin names. Be humorous in the pronunciation and get everyone to say out loud their animal's Latin name. This can be a fun way for them to learn "proper" names.

Practice Forms. Again, to the extent possible for humans trying to tag and avoid being tagged, you can get creative and imitate the actual movements and strategies of different animals. Infinite possibilities here for creative versions. Deer can bound, rabbits hop, raccoons amble, and ducks waddle. Birds could fly outside the boundaries. Could turtles burrow under mud? Could beaver be safe in their lodges? Research and find out.

Predator-Prey

◎	CORE ROUTINES	Animal Forms, Mind's Eye Imagining
↟	CHILD'S PASSIONS	Running, Jumping, Imitating Animals
❀	BOOK OF NATURE	Mammals, Birds
❖	NATURAL CYCLE	East: Inspire, Southeast: Activate, Southwest: Take a Break
✳	INDICATROS OF AWARENESS	Aliveness and Agility, Common Sense

Primer

Have you ever seen a Cat chase a Mouse? How about a Weasel or a Fox? What chance did the mouse have in those situations? Well, you are about to find out.

How-To

Set-up. This game turns into fun mayhem. Arrange your participants in a circle. Each person pretends to be Prey, and privately picks in their mind another person in the circle who they pretend is a Predator who wants to eat them. Next each participant privately picks another person who represents some protection, or a Protector. Once you shout "Go!" all the Prey must run to arrange themselves so they always keep their Protectors between them and the Predators.

Chaos is the Point. As invariably happens, the Protectors—who in their own mind are also Prey with their own Predators and Protectors—also run and try to hide behind their Protection, so the result is usually incessant running around in laughter-filled chaos. Play many rounds.

Inside the Mind of the Mentor

This game provides participants with the sense of never-ending change that abounds in nature, as well as empathy for prey animals. After a while, you just want it to stop. But for wild animals whose survival depends on eating while not being eaten, there is never a moment where full peace is guaranteed ... only occasional breaks, and even then you have to be alert and ready to move in a second.

Since the running can go on indefinitely, this game relieves excess energy in your group. It's interesting to observe that the running often settles down into an observable pattern (order from chaos), and energy conservation and survival strategy become more than a concept for participants.

Alternatives and Extensions

After a round or two, ask the participants to try to figure out if they can tell who thought they were a Predator, and who thought they were a Protector. This brings Owl Eyes into this very active game. Who says you can't be aware when you're running around like mad?

Conversations about hunting and defensive strategies within the realm of predator-prey relationships can be interesting and stimulate independent research and reading.

Deer-Bounding Challenge

CORE ROUTINES	Animal Forms, Mind's Eye Imagining
CHILD'S PASSIONS	Running, Jumping, Imitating Animals, Self-Challenge
BOOK OF NATURE	Mammals
NATURAL CYCLE	East: Inspire, Southeast: Activate, Southwest: Take a Break
INDICATROS OF AWARENESS	Aliveness and Agility

Primer

One time, walking to my backyard Sit Spot, I scared a deer who hid in the bushes. You know what it did? It was amazing. Suddenly it sprang straight into the air and jumped UP over the neighbor's fence, which was at least six feet tall. That's *this* high! It's like it was a four-legged turbo pogo stick: BOING! BOING! BOING! Deer have thin long legs just like pogo sticks, and with them they are able to jump into the air like *this* so that they can get away from predators. Forests often become thick with obstacles like fallen logs preventing straight-away running, so deer need to be able to bound high and come down delicately. And they sure can. Most gardeners know even their fence meant to keep deer from eating their vegetables, doesn't always do the trick. Some deer can simply bound right over a fence.

The foremost ungulate behaviorist, Fritz Walther, believed that bounding by deer and stotting by antelope had survival value because it helped the animals observe or detect predators. Instead of climbing trees or flying, deer can jump up and scan the ground around them.

So for humans who also want to be able to jump high, deer make the best teachers. Deer-Bounding will allow you to move through a log-filled forest just like deer, or it can make you soar like an NBA player on the basketball court. Want to play a fun game that will push you to bound higher and higher, just like a deer?

How-To

Create the Playing Field. Ask everyone to stand in a line. Then take a couple of your participants' backpacks (make sure its okay with them) and begin by stacking two of them on the ground about ten feet from the beginning of the participant-line. This stack of backpacks will be an ever-rising tower. The challenge is to Deer-Bound over the backpacks.

Teach the Deer-Bound. Before starting, teach the Deer-Bounding Form and demonstrate by bounding over the stack of backpacks. Give them a couple of minutes to bound around, practice getting as high off the ground as they can. Then have them return to a line.

Raise the Bar Incrementally. Start out easy, with just a couple of backpacks stacked. Give the signal for their turn to jump, after which they return to the back of the line to wait for their turn to come again. When it comes back around to starter, add to the stack of backpacks, making it a bit taller. Again, let each participant Deer-Bound over the bags one-at-a-time, and after that round make the stack even higher. Go on like this, going as high as participants can. When someone knocks the stack over, simply rebuild it. Throughout, continually encourage everyone to see whatever level they reach is a success.

Invoke the Mind's Eye Imagination. Before each turn, have them pause, close their eyes, and imagine a deer bounding high into the sky, over a fence. Ask them to feel the springy explosion of hooves leaving the ground. Have them become the deer in their mind and then open their eyes and go for it!

Inside the Mind of the Mentor

This activity usually carries an exuberant feeling of celebration and self-challenge, like the Olympics. With any healthy competition, put the emphasis on competing with yourself and challenging yourself, and encouraging and cheering for everyone else as they do the same.

This activity will improve physical fitness, and it will also light a fire in folks to interact physically with the natural world. Deer-Bounding can provide excitement around physical fitness and physical feats, prompting a new orientation to the world around them. After this or similar activities in which one animal form is emphasized, they often begin to interact physically by looking to animals as examples and teachers of different ways to move.

Alternatives and Extensions

Animal Forms Course. With or without the help of your participants, create a "course," a specific route through a section of your landscape. Let the route go through diverse terrain that will require different moves to traverse: a trail with logs that can be Deer-Bounded, turning into a thicket of bushes to be crawled through like a Raccoon, coming out into tall grass to be trotted through like a Coyote, and later stalked through as a Cougar low to the ground. You can show them animal forms ahead of time for each part, or you can walk through it with them, asking them, "What animal form would be best to use for this part?" and then allowing them to choose which animal forms to use.

Sleeping Fawn

◎	**CORE ROUTINES**	Sit Spot, Animal Forms
🏹	**CHILD'S PASSIONS**	Hiding, Laughing, Challenge
🌿	**BOOK OF NATURE**	Mammals
🔄	**NATURAL CYCLE**	Southwest: Take a Break
🦌	**INDICATROS OF AWARENESS**	Quiet Mind, Happiness

Primer

You may not believe it, but I was once half-scared to death by one of the smallest and cutest of animals. One day I was Fox-Walking out to my Sit Spot right as the sun was going down in the west. Because the light was fading, it was harder to see through the woods and I used my Owl Eyes to adjust to night vision and my Fox-Walk to keep from stepping on anything like a rusty nail in the dark (I was barefoot).

I walked along peacefully when suddenly—BANG! Something exploded from the spot of ground right in front of me, and my heart leapt out of my chest as I screamed—"Ahhh!" All in the same flash of a moment, this thing went springing into the air up to the level of my eyes and bolted away through the woods like a bullet. I had to laugh that a little baby fawn had scared me that much!

The spots on fawns, like Bambi, make the ultimate camouflage. Fawns, born with absolutely no scent until they grow older, combine this with their spotted camouflage and become almost invisible. They stay absolutely still, hiding from predators and even allowing them to come really close. I was only about two feet away from it when it bolted from me. I must have just gotten a little too close or smelled a little too bad.

How-To

Set-up. This game can be played in covered or open area, as long as each participant can find a place of his/her own big enough to lie very still on the ground with their faces visible. All of the participants are Fawns sleeping while their mother is away. The instructor is the Coyote or Wolf stalking around for prey.

The Action. This game is based on the fact that Deer Fawns will stay still and go unseen by predators that walk by, *unless* the Fawns move. The Fawns must remain completely still while the Coyote or Wolf wanders nearby sniffing around.

Funny-Face. You, as the Coyote, behave in true Coyote fashion, doing foolish, bothersome, and unexpected things, making faces, yelping, scratching, and fooling around in efforts to provoke movement or laughter, but may never touch the Fawn or use words. This can get really hilarious. When a Fawn is spotted moving, it must get up and go sit quietly in a designated area for Fawns that have been "caught" by the Coyote.

Story of the Day. Once all the participants have been captured, you can play again or also take the opportunity to chat about what it's like to be still and quiet for so long, or about having your own spot to sit still.

Inside the Mind of the Mentor

We've found no better way to connect folks to the earth than to have them lie flat on it and remain still. Although not the practice of Sit Spot in the sense of a place to be visited privately all the time, this game practices Sit Spot in the sense of lying silently for a long time and soaking up the landscape.

We want to prolong this Sit Spot time, so when you are the Coyote, walk away for ten minutes or longer before you even begin to prowl. For your players, this game develops the ability to be comfortable with stillness and quiet—another great primer for the full routine of Sit Spot.

It is important to note that this is a mellow game, one in which participants might possibly fall into a nap. This is a good thing. Try this one after lunch for an entertaining siesta or whenever there is a lull of energy that lends itself nicely to lying still. Observing the Natural Cycle of the day, this is a perfect Southwest game.

Also, your role-playing of Coyote gives you the chance to role model Coyote. Let loose, get silly, and have more fun than your participants by being fully alive with the happiness of a child.

Alternatives and Extensions

Sit Spot Lead-in. This can be a perfect activity to preface a more formal Sit Spot routine. You may wait to formally introduce Sit Spots to your participants: this game and similar ones may be something you repeat over a period of time to slow down your participants and build in them an aptitude for a conscious time of sitting alone.

Other Animals. Try mixing up the game by changing the predator to other ones in your area: wolf, cougar, or bears (yes, bears eat fawns).

Participant Comedians. Let the participants take turns as the predator when you trust that they won't abuse the role … you'll probably be surprised at the brilliance of humor that comes out.

Tracking Deer. This game may provide inspiration for tracking a deer to see if you can find and get close to one that might be hiding quietly (See 100 Tracks in a Row in Tracking Activities.) If you go into the woods right after this game, it can provide inspiration for Fox-Walking and Owl Eyes because you never know when there will be a deer just off the trail, frozen still until you walk by.

Tracking
ACTIVITIES

Activities that involve learning about animals, the six arts of tracking, questioning, and the following of mysteries.

Tracking ranks high among disciplines like music or chess—it is great for people to practice regularly because of the way it develops the brain's capacities for critical thinking. In tracking, you will never encounter the exact same situation twice. Every mystery to be solved is as fresh as every new day. Depending on the weather, when you see the tracks, your mood, and the mood of the animals, the tracking mystery varies endlessly.

The following activities have the potential to press the "on" button for the tracker inside, to unleash the curiosity-driven questioner who pushes learning as far as it can go and hunts down solutions to mysteries. These activities get the ball rolling (and potentially rolling very quickly) towards an insatiable appetite for learning the Art of Tracking.

Mudpuppy

Mudpuppies never lose their gills.
Mudpuppies also absorb oxygen through their skin.
They live in warm, muddy, or foul water.
Mudpuppies prefer shallow lakes and streams that
have slow moving water.
The mudpuppy's diet consists of crayfish, snails,
insect larvae, worms and small fish.
Mudpuppies can live to be more than twenty years.

Animal Cards

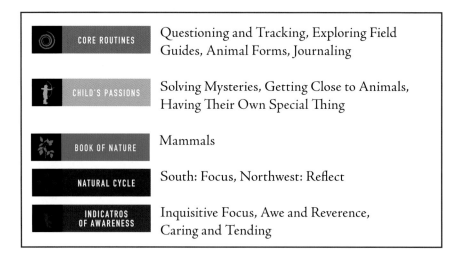

CORE ROUTINES	Questioning and Tracking, Exploring Field Guides, Animal Forms, Journaling
CHILD'S PASSIONS	Solving Mysteries, Getting Close to Animals, Having Their Own Special Thing
BOOK OF NATURE	Mammals
NATURAL CYCLE	South: Focus, Northwest: Reflect
INDICATROS OF AWARENESS	Inquisitive Focus, Awe and Reverence, Caring and Tending

Primer

To introduce this activity, check out the Nature Names in Setting Up the Learning Culture Activities.

How-To

Preparation. You will need to make up Animal Cards beforehand, each with one local animal's name in large type, as well as a physical description, what it eats, where it lives, its character traits/symbolism, and so forth. A picture of the animal—a photo, a sketch, a close up of its skeleton or other distinctive feature—will bring more life to the activity.

Getting Cards. Each person receives an Animal Card held firmly to their forehead or taped to their back so that everyone else can see their card. They will have to use their detective-minds to figure out the animal they represent.

Solving Mysteries. When each person has a Card, have them walk around and ask each other "yes/no" questions (and only "yes/no" questions) about their animal. Participants being asked questions can then read the information on the card if they don't already know an accurate answer. This game will be complete and successful when each person solves the mystery of their animal card.

Wrap-up. When they think they know their animal, have them come to an instructor and first tell them all the clues they gathered, and then tell what animal they have on their card. If they guess correctly, let them look at their card; if they haven't got it yet, encourage them and put them back on the trail of the mystery. After everyone has found their animal name, circle up and have a go-round where everyone talks about their animal a bit, proudly telling what they know about it.

Inside the Mind of the Mentor

This activity is wonderful for multiple reasons. First, it gets participants interested and connected with one specific animal. Secondly, and perhaps most poignantly, they learn to ask their own questions so they develop logical sequences of questioning by themselves. You can almost see their brains stretching as they search for questions to help them solve the mystery, and as they approach animals from many different angles, thinking of size, looks, habits, habitat, food, character, and track shape.

In this game, of course, each person will be exposed to the animals of all the participants and get more ideas for questions. In a half hour Animal Cards can provide a novice who knows only a few animals other than dogs and cats with a mental file-card bank of common wild animals of the area.

Alternatives and Extensions

Nature Names. This activity could be the way participants receive their Nature Names to last for the duration of the program.

Picking a Personal Mystery. You can set up a ceremonial way for them to pick their Cards, rather than just handing them out. You could set the cards face-down in a circle on the ground and ask participants to walk one-at-a-time around the circle until their Body Radar attracts them to one card that will become their personal animal mystery.

Animal Medicine. You may choose to write a few words on the card about the symbolism or legendary character traits commonly linked with that animal. People are often charmed by the idea of animals as guides or teachers, who bring to mind special "medicine" or ways of handling life.

Insight into People. The animal that each person gets, as well as their reaction to it (i.e., disappointment vs. pride), can give you memorable insight into those you mentor. Once the trickster child who liked to push the edge of boundaries drew the Fox card; I laughed at how perfect it was for him. Another time, a quiet and reserved girl picked Spider, and the symbolism written on the card confirmed for her the validity of her quiet, complex, and wise ways.

Doorway to Field Guides. Animal Cards can be easily expanded into Exploring Field Guides to find more information. If you dwell on one animal you can search through multiple Field Guides for different approaches to information about it—some have photographs, some have sketches, some show tracks, some show its ecological niche and habitat companions.

Doorway to Animal Forms. Similarly, encourage people to identify and practice imitating their animal's typical movements, postures, sensory abilities, and survival strategies.

Stick-Drag Game

◎	**CORE ROUTINES**	Questioning and Tracking, Expanding the Senses, Listening for Bird Language, Mapping
🏹	**CHILD'S PASSIONS**	Chasing, Following Mysteries, Playing Detective, Role-Playing
🌿	**BOOK OF NATURE**	Mammals and Birds
	NATURAL CYCLE	East: Inspire and South: Focus
	INDICATROS OF AWARENESS	Agility and Aliveness, Inquisitive Focus, Common Sense

Primer

Human hunters long-ago used a special type of hunting, called Persistence Hunting. Scientists say this represents one of the oldest forms of hunting, but it's also one of the riskiest. If someone has not trained well enough, they could die. Basically, on a very hot day, you chase after an animal for hours until it overheats and collapses. I once saw a video of an African San Bushman tracker and hunter do this. He waited for a very hot day—over 110 degrees Fahrenheit—and then went out tracking in the sandy lands. He picked up the very fresh trail of one of the biggest animals they hunt—a kudu. He jogged after the tracks until finally he saw the herd of these huge beasts. Then the chase was on.

He started jogging after them. Soon it became apparent which one was the weakest and most vulnerable and he followed that one. The sun got hotter and as he chased this animal, barefoot, across the hot sand, hour after hour passed. Often the Kudu would get so far ahead he would have to track as he ran along. For five hours he ran and ran, never stopping for a break. Then the tracks began to show that the animal was getting tired and soon enough the sweating hunter stood eye-to-eye with this handsome animal who cannot sweat like us humans, but whose hairy body keeps all the heat locked up inside, until they overheat. After more than six hours, the hunter had done it. He then used his spear to kill it and took its meat back to his people. When he returned, there was singing and feasting.

Some biologists say this form of hunting helped humans evolve. Today humans have such hairless bodies—and the capacity to sweat—as well as the mode of walking on two feet, rather than four like nearly all the other mammals on earth. Four-legged animals move much faster than two-leggeds over short distances—like the sprinting cheetah, or the deer that bounds away into the forest after you spook it. However, at lower speeds two legs work much better for long-distance running, stamina running. Humans have even been known to hunt cheetahs in this same manner and beat horses in 100-mile races—out-running them over a long distance. Scientists from different specialized areas, including genetics, archaeology, and biology theorize that Persistence Hunting helped determine the biology of all humans, having originated in similar savannas of Africa. Some people also say that our ability to read—to see a shape or symbol and instantly match it up with complex ideas and images—came from thousands and thousands of years studying tracks and hunting animals on these African savannas. Interesting to think about, huh?

Now, put all those same human abilities of tracking, running, and sweating to the test. I will be the 800 pound Kudu, and you will be the persistence trackers. Do you think you can track me down?

How-To

Set-up. Lead into this game using the story above or with a similar scenario/ story, and then explain that you will only have a two-minute head start; while they close their eyes and ears, you take off running.

Dragging a Trail. As you run, you will drag a stick behind you on the ground, making sure to leave a noticeable trail in the ground. This game plays most easily in a sandy location, but it can also be played in forests or fields: just make sure you have a sharp-point on your stick and apply enough pressure to leave a trail. Also, make sure the stick is sturdy or else it might snap on you. You might want a partner to help out. Stick-dragging leaves me hunch-backed and cramping as I run along, not the most comfortable way to run.

Tactical Evasion. Give a crow call to let participants know it's time to start chasing. Continue running, even after they begin tracking you, and go on as long as you desire or until you feel truly exhausted, as in the scenario. As you drag the stick, occasionally make trailing challenging: go over some rocks or hard-packed dirt for a bit before returning to soft, easy-to-track soil. You can make this really fun for your participants by looping around behind them, crossing back over your trail, or going in a circle and hiding so that they walk right by you as they follow your trail, eventually hiding and surprising them with a shock. Or, if you want to build up their confidence—and you just can't take anymore running—sit tight until they track themselves straight to where you "collapsed."

Inside the Mind of the Mentor

This activity can get people really excited about tracking. Something magical and exhilarating happens when you follow a set of tracks to the very animal that made them, even if it's group leader. Also, the heavy stick-drag provides easy success and confidence with tracking. For beginners and novices alike, this can open up the world of tracking to them, making it real, meaningful, and accessible.

This activity also provides a genuine simulation of the adrenaline-pumping hunt, allowing people to connect with this ancient part of our humanness. The thrill of this game sometimes stays with people for a long time to come. This game also fosters empathy for animals, both those that hunt for their food and those that are constantly threatened by being hunted.

Trailing someone for a long time across a landscape gets people noticing and thinking about the lay of the land in ways that they haven't before. When I have done this exercise as a tracker, my mind automatically starts to imagine a bird's eye view of a map of the land as I try to anticipate where the stick-dragger might have gone. You can also emphasize the involvement of bird-language, so they track you not just the dragging stick track, and notice the bird disturbance you create in each moment.

Alternatives and Extensions

Repetition. You can play this game repeatedly over the course of months or years, gradually making the stick drag more and more subtle as people learn to see better and follow tracks better.

Role Reversal. You can let participants be the Kudu, which provides a completely different yet incredibly vivid experience.

The Real Thing. If large mammals in your area are seasonally hunted, pretend to be a common prey species—elk, bear, wild pig, or deer.

All Six Arts. This game is an excellent lead-in to the study of animal trailing, and the complementary studies of track identification, gait and behavior

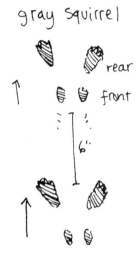

gray squirrel

rear

front

6"

raccoon

front

rear

interpretation, track aging, and ecological tracking, and empathy. Encourage people to "get inside" the mind of the animal and ask "if I were this animal, where would I go? What would I be eating? Where would I sleep?"

Tracking while Being Tracked. For adults, you can also pump up the dramatics of the scenario. Pretend it's a "Fugitive Chase," some kind of criminal man hunt adds the element of forcing the trackers to think of themselves not just as predators, but prey as well, and to look at not just the tracks but to broaden their awareness and keep all their senses alive so the fugitive cannot take them by surprise. Bring props if you want to make it realistic, such as water-guns (then, if you want, you can double-back and hide out in the grassy knoll, waiting to squirt them).

Search and Rescue. Conversely, stir the protective instinct in everyone, adult or child. The scenario could be all about catching up with a lost child or person before they get hypothermic or freeze to death. Maybe you need to reach them to give them vital medicine they need to stay alive. In another rescue scenario, you can sit in your grassy knoll dripping with ketchup and turn this into a wilderness first aid lesson.

Tracking Expedition

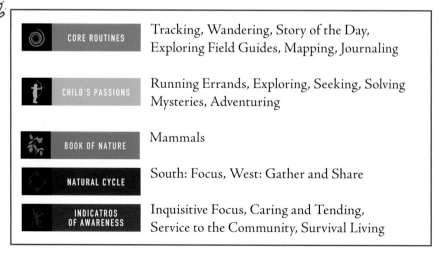

CORE ROUTINES	Tracking, Wandering, Story of the Day, Exploring Field Guides, Mapping, Journaling
CHILD'S PASSIONS	Running Errands, Exploring, Seeking, Solving Mysteries, Adventuring
BOOK OF NATURE	Mammals
NATURAL CYCLE	South: Focus, West: Gather and Share
INDICATROS OF AWARENESS	Inquisitive Focus, Caring and Tending, Service to the Community, Survival Living

Primer

I'm really glad we've all been starting to learn how to read and identify the tracks of wild animals, because today, we've got a real job to do. It's time to put our skills and knowledge to use. The Department of Fish and Wildlife has asked us to go to this area and take note of all the animal sign we can find, especially those of any endangered species. Some people want to clear cut this forest and the Department of Fish and Wildlife needs to know its value to local animals.

We'll keep a special eye out for tracks and signs of a few special species on their list; you never know—maybe even live sightings. But we will also challenge ourselves to find the tracks, signs, or live sightings of as many different animals as possible. We'll split up into groups and cover different areas, and at the end of the day come back and share with everyone else what we find.

We'll take lunch and water with us, and spend the whole day outside … just tracking! Ready? Well, grab your gear and let's go.

How-To

Leader Prep. You will want to figure out ahead of time these things—*what species* you will focus on and *why*. Create a *need* for people to go out and track. This could be accomplished by telling inspiring tracking stories, but it will be more potent if you find a true need or service for their tracking efforts.

Many schools across the country do this by contacting local government biologists. In our experience they have been glad to give us places to track that might help their efforts. Besides the above example, it could be something more local, such as "The neighbor's chickens are being killed by something and she wants us to figure out who is doing it, what trails they're using, and how they're getting into the wire cages." You can generate questions to fulfill needs for the school principal, some other authoritative figure, or your personal curiosities. You can hook up with Nature Mapping (see resources and programs list in back of book) or other non-profit organizations that could provide you with professionals who will lead your group, and require specific recording techniques. This is the "errand" phenomenon in action.

Pre-trip. Develop a list of focus questions about the place you will be exploring: things you want to figure out about that place and its wild animals. Using field guides and journaling, have every person research questions of interest to them, as well as the local hazards. If you focus on one or two species, you may want to journal the track and sign so as to develop a "search image" in everyone's brain.

On Location. Divide up into tracking teams based on any criteria you choose (age, skill, personal energy, subject focus). Teams fan out into the landscape, either wandering, following a route, or a little of both. Their goal is to capture as much information about their target species or area as they can.

Wrap-up. Come back early enough so that each team can present a story of the highlights of their day: amusing moments, discoveries, species seen, and signs seen. Create maps that include where tracks and signs were found. Then you can begin to draw out connections to these stories happening within the overall landscape. Piece together the findings of all the several groups into a unified picture of what's happening in that place, at that time.

Inside the Mind of the Mentor

As Tom Brown, Jr. accurately says, "The greater the need, the greater the result." If you want people to be excited and persistent in learning tracking, find a true need for them to track. Talk to local scientists, park managers, and land-owners to see what kind of tracking projects you can form. It's not hard. Most people are happy to further the education of others, and some will even come along to help out and learn themselves. And of course, they will be thankful for your services.

Every game or Core Routine in this book can be done while on Tracking Expedition. Indeed, during the time between finding and following tracks, these activities serve to hone awareness, interest, and curiosity. I usually plan out a few games or activities to serve the higher purpose of creating better observations and excitement for my tracking team.

For most people, especially younger ones, their favorite way to convey this experience afterwards to others downplays the expedition and claims they walked around a lot and played some games. However little they tell to their parents, you and I know a lot of primary education happens on expeditions: balancing on logs, looking under leaves for beetles, following bobcat tracks, sitting peacefully by a river eating lunch, envying the person who found the skull, telling jokes to their friends, and watching in silent wonder as a red-tailed hawk screamed and soared in the sky above them.

With most groups, especially those with younger kids, things will go more smoothly if everyone has a "role" or "job" to do on the expedition. This also reinforces the ideas of community niches and complementary talents. Some examples: someone to keep a Master List of mammal tracks and sign, a map navigator, a Story of the Day "teller," someone keeping their eyes out for hazards, a first aid person, field guide carrier. Look and you will find roles.

Another way to generate a need to learn tracking is by returning it to its original use: to hunt for food. Many people are now offering programs that conduct hunts in a sustainable and sacred manner, offering it as a basis for learning life skills, developing emotional relatedness to the world and transitioning into adulthood. Tracking Expeditions in this setting are group-learning experiences focused around this sobering task of learning about an animal in order to take its life.

Alternatives and Extensions

Flip the Script. Don't create focus questions or look at field guides before you go. Let their curiosity lead on an all-day, wandering version of Tracking Expedition. Just tell a good tracking story and then follow their lead. Their observations throughout the day can then be approached later with applied questions and field guides.

Empower Leadership. With teens and adults, and more advanced younger kids, turn the leadership of expeditions over to them once they get the hang of it. Let them decide what the focus questions or species should be, let them pore over maps and decide where different groups should go, let them facilitate the end-of-day debrief and pull out all the hidden connections and stories that the collective tracking of the group indicates.

What you track will only be limited by your imagination and interest. Focus expeditions on ecology, geology, birds, edible plants, amphibians, rare species, or all of these. See Wildlife Survey activity in the Ecology and Community activities section.

100 Tracks in a Row

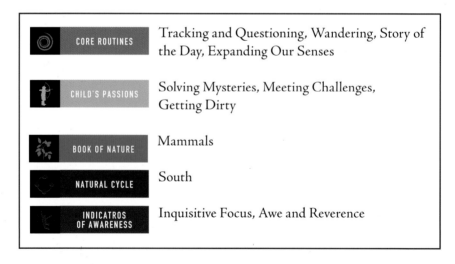

CORE ROUTINES	Tracking and Questioning, Wandering, Story of the Day, Expanding Our Senses
CHILD'S PASSIONS	Solving Mysteries, Meeting Challenges, Getting Dirty
BOOK OF NATURE	Mammals
NATURAL CYCLE	South
INDICATROS OF AWARENESS	Inquisitive Focus, Awe and Reverence

Primer

Blood-Tracking, by Daniel Evans

Once I accepted a challenge to find 100 animal tracks in a row in an hour. "That's easy," I thought. I was on a river sandbar. "Everyone knows how easy it is to find tracks on sand."

I partnered up with two other friends, and we walked along until we found a set of fresh deer tracks. They headed away from the water and toward the forest. Off we went. At first the counting came really easy. Within the first minute, we got 25 crisp, beautiful "heart-shaped" tracks right in the moist sand. But the deer's tracks headed off towards the larger cottonwood forest, maybe moving from a feeding area towards a more hidden place so it could lie down for a while.

The ground was now scattered here and there with the old, decomposing leaves of the cottonwood trees. Every time the deer stepped onto a leaf, it cracked a heart-shaped depression into the leaves. I thought that was really cool to track an animal by following its prints on leaves. We counted 50 tracks so far, and had only searched for five minutes.

As we got closer to the forest, the leaves became thick and abundant, and the ground became firmer. Most of the leaves weren't cracking anymore. I thought, "Uh-oh, maybe this is harder than I thought." But after a few minutes of trying to measure how far each step of the deer took, and so predict where the next track would be, my friend used his eyes, and solved the problem: the deer still had sand stuck to the bottom of the hooves. Near where we predicted the next step to be, we saw small dustings of sand, about the same size as a heart-shaped track. We found 25 more tracks this way, but it took us almost 15 minutes and lots of detailed looking and measuring.

Only 25 more to go! By now we stood underneath the big cottonwoods, their thick buds were almost ready to open up for spring. The sand on the deer's hooves had worn off and the ground was firm. The challenge seemed impossible. Our heads were on the ground, looking for a grain of sand, a slightly depressed leaf, or a crushed grass blade. That's how we discovered the blood on the ground. Looking ahead we found another drop. "Hey, our deer must have gotten scratched back there pretty deep by a blackberry." We followed our blood drops until we saw … a few feet away from our heading, a nice patch of sand with, guess what—our deer's track in it! We scratched our heads; our blood drop trail was 10' away. What was going on?

We went back to where we had first spotted the blood, now we walked instead of crawling on our bellies like snakes, we saw red drops everywhere. When we smelled the red drops, it actually smelled like a sweet spice. It wasn't blood—it was Cottonwood sap, dripping out of the spring buds of the trees above us. We laughed and got back on our bellies and found the last 15 tracks with just a minute left. It was tough … but we did it!

How-To

Challenge your participants to find 100 tracks in a row.
Start with Success. Usually, people find deer tracks easy to follow and give quick success, so start there. Initial success inspires further learning and builds self-confidence. However, this depends on your local fauna as well as the local tracking conditions. Maybe you'll follow 100 frog tracks on the river-bank. Whatever provides both success and challenge along one trail—go for it.

Set-up and Props. Groups of no more than three can work together nicely for team versions and provide big lessons about the value of different perspectives and ways of seeing. This activity can also be done solo. Decide if you will have a time limit to increase the excitement; it may also distract from detailed looking. Teams should mark behind each track with a small twig, toothpick, or Popsicle stick. Bring tape measures or "tracking sticks": braches carved or marked with pen/paint to indicate the average length of step of the animal you're following. Simply hold the stick alongside each new track to approximate the whereabouts of the next one.

On the Trail. Once a team finds the animal's beginning track, they move either forward or backward along its trail. All team members need to agree on the existence of each track before marking it and moving onto the next one. Walk around, observing and only jump in to encourage or help when someone or some group gets utterly frustrated.

Debrief. Talk out the experience afterwards. Who learned what? How were challenges overcome? Celebrate everyone's efforts, no matter how far they got. Honor and acknowledge not a number of tracks, but rather the quality of observation, perseverance, or teamwork you observed.

Inside the Mind of the Mentor

This activity inspires people to get down on their bellies and really study beyond their surface judgments. They begin to recognize the meaning that rests in the small and subtle markings, and begin to look at everything with a closer, more thoughtful gaze.

Morning is an excellent time for this activity, when everyone can find fresh, crisp tracks. If you haven't gone over tracking protocol before do this first (emphasize the importance of *not* stepping on tracks). Nobody likes to have their tracking trail be mistakenly wiped out by a series of misplaced steps.

Questions from the Six Arts of Tracking can break a locked intellectual focus and return sensory awareness: "Who is it?" "Where do you think it is going?" "Why do you think it is going this way?" and "Could it be watching us right now?"

Alternatives and Extensions

Fewer Tracks. Start with finding fewer tracks and eventually move up to more.

Target Species. Choose specific species of your area; research where you'll find them.

Map Drawing. Draw a map of your tracking area, and mark each animal's trail on it.

Math Lesson. Use the gait measurements as a doorway into a gambit of possible math challenges.

Track Journaling

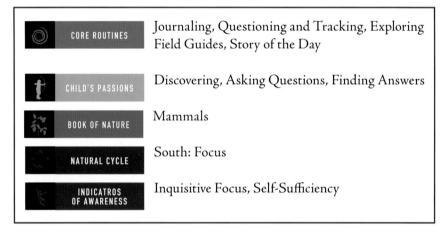

CORE ROUTINES	Journaling, Questioning and Tracking, Exploring Field Guides, Story of the Day
CHILD'S PASSIONS	Discovering, Asking Questions, Finding Answers
BOOK OF NATURE	Mammals
NATURAL CYCLE	South: Focus
INDICATROS OF AWARENESS	Inquisitive Focus, Self-Sufficiency

Primer

Finally, Finally, by Evan McGown

After you spend some time tracking and probably do a few of the other activities in this section first, people need to record their observation and explore natural mysteries they have found.

One of the best ways to become a great tracker is to draw the tracks you find—especially the ones you don't know. One of my good friends once found some tracks on the edge of a pond that flipped him out—they looked like a set of deer hooves in a regular walking pattern, except each one was only the size of a large jelly bean! What on earth was this, he wondered. He thought, "It's either some sort of miniature deer that a mad scientist shrunk down or a tiny Chihuahua dog with little deer hoof-shoes strapped on to its feet!" He couldn't figure it out.

So he took out the pocket notebook he always carries and spent at least a half-hour drawing the tracks in as much detail as he could. He also sketched quick pictures and maps of the trees, bushes, and water all around where he found the tracks.

My friend spent the next eight YEARS carrying that notebook everywhere with him, always asking any tracker he could find if they knew what had made those tracks. No one did. He showed his drawings to a few of the top trackers in the world, and even they didn't know. He researched in libraries, searched on the internet, and finally found what the only possible explanation could be: a Duiker, which is a very tiny antelope that lives in Africa. How could it have gotten inside the U.S.? Maybe someone had one as a pet and it escaped—you never know—stranger things have happened.

One day, eight years after he found those tracks, I was walking with my friend out in the field with a bunch of kids. The kids began looking at something on the ground, and I walked over to see. It was pretty cool to me, and I stood there watching with the kids for a while. Then my friend finally walked over, and stared at the ground. He seemed frozen for a minute of intense concentration, and then he began yelling. "OH MY GOSH!" he screamed, pulling his hair out, his eyes popping out of his head. "OH MY GOSH! I CAN'T BELIEVE IT! EVAN ... YOU JUST DON'T KNOW ... I MEAN ... OH MY GOSH!" I looked at him, sort of worried. "What's wrong?" When he finally calmed down enough he told me and the kids the story: after all those years of searching, he had finally figured out what had made those tiny deer tracks! In fact, he had now even seen them being made. That's how he knew for sure. If you watch an animal make tracks, then you can be absolutely certain about that track.

What was the track? I could tell you, but I'll have to ask my friend first. Here's a hint: they were in a drying puddle of water. He had worked really hard for those eight years, always holding the question to figure out those tracks, so solving the mystery was one of the most exhilarating experiences of his life.

Instead of me telling you the end of his story, why don't we let you experience this sense of adventure and mystery yourself. Would you believe that all around are tracks, some no one else has ever seen before? Now it's your turn. Ready?

Alright, trackers (or nature detectives), we'll go out in the field and hunt for cool tracks and mysteries. We'll draw in our journals whatever mysteries we find, and then we'll come back to our field station to see if we can crack the code and solve the mystery. Everybody will get to dive into our magical field guides, compare sketches, and maybe make some new ones. By the end of the day, you just might solve the mystery! Or ... it might take you eight years. Regardless, it will be fun, and we'll all get to share and hear each other's stories.

How-To

Get in the Field. With this activity, you take the natural excited energy of those people you mentor (East) and now get them focused (South) outside. Find some track or sign in the field, even if you don't know what animal made it: then, either have everyone sketch it, or find a bunch of tracks in a large area and let each person sketch one. A community will learn more together if they each research a different type.

Journal for Detail. Use the "Six Arts of Tracking" (found in Introducing Core Routines activities) to guide your note taking, include the answers in your journal. Use questioning to cause yourself and others to really see the tracks, in their fine details. Notice every detail: which toes are the largest, which nails are the sharpest, is it a right foot or left? Draw the pattern or gait of the tracks. Are the front and rear tracks the same in size and shape? Shade in the deeper parts of the tracks, get on your belly and lay your head on the ground so you can see if parts of the ground are actually raised up as a result of the track. Wild dogs like coyotes, foxes and wolves will actually pull soil into a high peak in-between their four toes. You can draw a cross-section of the track to show this.

Observe the Big Picture. After zoning in on the micro-elements of the track, look at the bigger context of ecology for that track. Draw a quick bird's eye view map of the surrounding ten or twenty feet, including plants, trees, different soils, rocks, other animal tracks, everything there. And always, when you draw a map like this, find and mark North on your drawing. Based on that, note which direction the animal was moving.

Research. Ideally, you have a set of tracking field guides that everyone can share, or each person has their own. Have people flip through them until they find pictures of tracks similar to theirs. It's best for this to be a quiet activity with each person conducting their own research in the field guides and then quietly sketching and writing down information. Challenge them to research and journal everything they learn about their animal. Create a need by reminding them that each person will present what he and she found at the end.

Create a Post-Field Journal. Based on the tracks they find, when they've looked through field guides and tracking books enough that they have at least an idea of what made the track, ask everyone to do a final drawing. The actual journaling process here doesn't have to be complicated or sophisticated. Here are some ideas of what people can include in their journals:

+ Sketch and describe the animal tracks found in the book. Then compare side-to-side with their field drawing.
+ Name of their best guess of who made the tracks.
+ Alternative choices and why rejected.
+ Sketch and describe the animal itself.
+ Sketch and describe the animal's scat.
+ Description of surrounding habitat.
+ Significant behaviors of the animal: nocturnal/diurnal, carnivore/herbivore/omnivore, food-gathering strategy, sleeping habits, times for mating, ask people to expand their list of questions.

This list only begins the possible research. Ask people to add more information than this list. Encourage them to use multiple sources.

Group Sharing Time. To wrap up this activity, each person presents information to the others using the journal as a visual model. Post the journal pages on a board near your Nature Museum for more leisurely study. This showcases the diversity of people' styles of journals and allows everyone to learn about each other's discoveries.

Inside the Mind of the Mentor

While some people will jump right into Track Journaling, others will drag their feet. It might seem too much like homework. Two excellent strategies help get participants get around these blocks.

One is role-modeling. If you pull out your journal in the field and do everything (and more) that you ask everyone else to do, they will notice. They will also notice if you don't. When you all return, jump into the research right along with everyone else. If you have your nose in a field guide while you quietly sketch and write down information, then everyone else is a lot more likely to do so as well. Then role-model presenting your information to the group. In addition, you get a great excuse to further your own tracking and learning while also mentoring others.

The second strategy for inspiring Track Journaling: wander around, offer support, and ask participants probing questions to facilitate their process. "What animal do you think it might be?" "Which field guide do you think will be most helpful?" "How many toes did you observe for this animal?" Use these few questions and you will think of many more.

Another thing to keep in mind is some of the people may be artistically gifted and others very self-conscious about their ability to draw or sketch. Remember, the key, people who journal about tracking will find out more about what they discovered; therefore, some may end up being very heavy in sketching/drawing and others may be very heavy in text. However, make sure each journal has at least some sketching and some text. And let them get creative to make it their own.

Finally, this activity works best with older kids, teens, and adults. However, it is entirely possible to do this with young kids as well. For younger kids, have them try to find pictures that match what they found. Then they can make drawings (perhaps with crayons or paints) of the animal or the tracks from a picture in a book.

Alternatives and Extensions

Other Species. Try this same activity, but journal tracks of birds, reptiles, or amphibians.

Digitize. Turn this into a multi-media research project. Use the web and have people design computer-based journals.

Mind's Eye Sketching. Make this into an activity that develops the Mind's Eye by having people close their eyes after looking at tracks in the field, or in the field guides, before writing or sketching in their journals. This way they are not simply copying information out of books. They are stretching their imagination and forcing themselves to imprint search images accurately from the actual tracks they find.

Report. Turn the journal into a long report involving several days of research. Final reports could be several pages with pictures, text, and diagrams.

Camera Stalk

◎	**CORE ROUTINES**	Expanding Our Senses, Questioning and Tracking, Sit Spot, Wandering
🏹	**CHILD'S PASSIONS**	Hunting Elusive Animals, Self-Challenge
🌿	**BOOK OF NATURE**	Mammals
	NATURAL CYCLE	Southeast: Activate, South: Focus, Northeast: Open and Listen
	INDICATROS OF AWARENESS	Inquisitive Focus, Common Sense, Self-Sufficiency, Quiet Mind

Primer

Hunting with a Camera, by Evan McGown

Jim Corbett was a hero. He grew up in the jungles of India, learning to track and hunt from his older neighbors. He became so artful in tracking that he could look at a Tiger track in the mud and tell you whether it was male or female, about how old it was, and whether it was hurt. He could identify individual tigers by their tracks just as you can recognize your friends when you see their faces.

Corbett became famous and revered throughout India for hunting tigers that killed and ate humans from villages near jungles. Corbett was the only man who could consistently show up, track the tiger, identify such nuances from its tracks such as a wounding in the leg (wounding often seemed to be the reason the tigers sought out easy human prey), and then shoot the animal dead. He wrote books telling of his many adventures hunting man-eating tigers. The books give fabulous insights into tracking, and are thrilling to read.

As years passed, Corbett realized these creatures, which he had come to love and revere as one of the most beautiful and graceful creatures on earth, were declining in population due to destruction of their native forests. He didn't want to hunt them anymore, but the thrill of the hunt couldn't keep him away. So he continued to hunt, except he no longer used guns—he used a camera instead. He would use all the same tactics he used to hunt the man-eaters: tracking them for days and studying their patterns, listening to the bird language of the forest for signals and secrets, and very patiently sitting still in a tree for long-periods of time—until finally he'd get a beautiful shot of his beloved orange-and-black-striped fellow-creatures. He went on to use these photographs and the stories of his experiences to convince others of the need to preserve forests so these animals could have their homes protected, and he succeeded. The very first preserved jungles in India are named in his honor, where his beloved tigers still roam today.

The thing I forgot to tell you about his camera, though, it had NO ZOOM-LENS. He lived in the early 1900's, when cameras were a lot less advanced than cameras today. No zoom meant that he had to get REALLY close to the animals in order to get a good photo.

Do you think you could take an old camera, with no zoom-lens and get a full-frame photo of some wild animal? It could be a bird, it could be mammal, it could be anything you want. Are you up to the challenge?

How-To

Set the Bait. Tell a story or simply set this up as an enticing challenge too good to refuse.

Buy Cameras. Buy some cheap, no-zoom disposable cameras, the "old" kind that use real film and only have so many pictures. If you're working with adults, you may have them buy their own. If it's youth, you may want to provide each with a camera.

Happy Hunting. Set the ground-rules for the challenge: it has to be a wild-animal that is not caught, it has to be a full-frame shot so they need to be close, and they have as many chances as they have exposures on the camera. This activity need not be completed in a single day, although there's always the chance that someone could. Assign this activity to be completed almost entirely in non-program personal time; it may take months for them to finish off the entire roll of film. Keep the fire of inspiration stoked by periodically asking about their Camera Mission.

Research. If they are struggling, entice them with some field-guide research that helps them get to know the habits and habitat of the animal(s) they are tracking. Even if they aren't struggling, take the opportunity to engage them in learning about the tracks and sign that animals leave, or about the bird language clues that will tell them about approaching animals.

Celebrate Success. When they finally get that full-frame shot, acknowledge it and celebrate their efforts. Let them tell the story to a big group of peers or elders, the full story of their trials and errors, and ultimately their success. Frame the photo for them and give it as a gift, or somehow make this success special. This is not an easy thing to do, and if someone has persevered to succeed, that's something to really give them credit for. The rest of the community will be inspired by this person's role-modeling.

Inside the Mind of the Mentor

This activity, one of Jon Young's favorite missions to give to people (particularly adults), creates a fun and real need for people to learn and experience many things: long, timeless wanders through nature, the birth of millions of questions about animals' lifestyles, the study of tracks, bird-nest locations, habitat, bird language, and natural camouflage and scent-covering, and of course our favorite practice— sitting still in nature for long periods of time.

Camera Stalk sends people on an errand through which they will learn many lessons in a completely self-sufficient manner. They will learn how to Fox-Walk properly; the value of sitting still and being accepted by the birds and squirrels; what bird calls really mean; what times of day certain animals are active—they will learn all this and much more, 100% by *their own experience*. This activity works as a major Southeast motivating power tool, because it activates people into direct experiential learning that otherwise might not seem desirable.

Even if this activity does not reach youth with the intense level of study and experience that it might for an adult, what could be better than engaging kids in looking at the world through the eyes of a photographer, where everything is potentially beautiful? Of course, they'll also be running around everywhere looking for critters: you can bet they'll quickly learn that salamanders live under logs or rocks, or how to stay still enough for a butterfly to land on them.

Alternatives and Extensions

Camera Game. Joseph Cornell has a great game that he calls "Camera." It's of a similar spirit, but with a different emphasis. It's simple: have people partner up. One person is the "camera" while the other is the photographer. The camera closes their eyes and is led to a nice photo by the photographer. With eyes still closed on the camera, the photographer arranges them to get the proper picture, perhaps giving an expansive view of the land or getting them on their knees and craning their neck to get a close-up of a bright-colored mushroom. When the camera is in the right position, tap the ear or the back of the camera's head. This button opens the "shutter"—the camera person's eyes. The photographer decides how long the shutter will remain open, and then taps them again to close their eyes again, and then takes them to the next photograph. After a dozen or so photos, switch roles and go again.

Preparing for the Real Hunt. If you have an older youth or adult who passionately wants to hunt and kill a wild animal, this activity is a great way to train them. If they want to hunt a deer, give them the challenge to first get a full-frame photo of a deer with a no-zoom camera. Such an exercise will not only humble them in their outlook on hunting, it will also train them in everything they need to know to do a real hunt: disguising their scent, moving downwind, camouflaging, patience to sit still, how to move when the wind moves. Whatever the gaps in a person's awareness, this little mission will fill them in like spackle, preparing them physically and mentally for what will perhaps be one of the most powerful experiences of their life.

Plants And Wandering
ACTIVITIES

Activities for learning plants in a meaningful manner, as well as skills of wandering, aidless navigation, and lost-proofing

We often group the study of plants along with the skills of wandering and navigation, because the two go hand-in-hand. If one becomes equipped with knowledge of edible plants and skills of wandering without getting lost, one can roam the wilderness with practically nothing—in the warmer seasons—for months. Plants live practically everywhere. So wherever you wander, a meaningful relationship with plants will make them your constant friends and allies.

Although we encourage the use of both maps and compasses on a daily basis, the wandering and lost-proofing exercises presented here emphasize *aidless* navigation. Offer yourself and others this goal: to be able to move across the land in the old way, using no more than the sun, natural landmarks, and your wits to orient and find your way. The natural world will become an open book that you can enjoy and explore with confidence and familiarity.

Plant Concentration

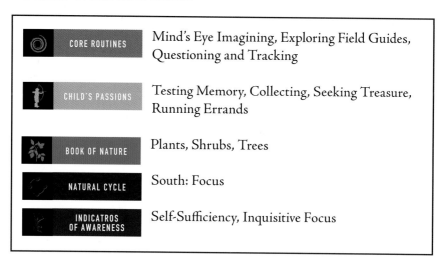

CORE ROUTINES	Mind's Eye Imagining, Exploring Field Guides, Questioning and Tracking	
CHILD'S PASSIONS	Testing Memory, Collecting, Seeking Treasure, Running Errands	
BOOK OF NATURE	Plants, Shrubs, Trees	
NATURAL CYCLE	South: Focus	
INDICATROS OF AWARENESS	Self-Sufficiency, Inquisitive Focus	

Primer

Spying Skills, by Evan McGown

The first medicines of humans came from the plants they collected. Peppermint was discovered to settle an upset belly and bad gas. Plantain was found useful for soothing insect bites. Today, researchers hunt all over the world for new medicinal plants. It is told that one explorer who was sent into the jungles of South America used a twelve year old native girl as his plant guide. She could identify a hundred and fifty different species of plants from just the smallest torn leaf. Can you imagine that: a hundred and fifty different plants, just from *a piece* of a leaf. She could tell you when to harvest it, what part to use, and what its medicinal value was—whether it made good medicine for eye infections, stomach aches, a bad cold, or to stop bleeding and treat a wound. She gained all this knowledge by the time she reached twelve years old.

Right here where you live there are dozens, maybe hundreds of plants that you can either eat or make into medicine. But you've got to really know plants, as this girl did, so you don't poison anyone with the wrong plant! We're going to play a game to help you know plants.

The FBI, the CIA, and other agencies use this game to train spies. Why? Well, just like a good herbalist or survivalist or tracker or scout, spies have to be able to see something once and remember exactly what it looked like. That way they can report every little detail. And they never can be sure what will be important to remember, so they remember everything. I remember watching a movie called *Bourne Identity*. It's about a guy who was trained as the highest level of spy, but then he hit his head and couldn't remember how he had come to have such amazing recall. There's one scene where he is sitting in a restaurant, trying to get the person with him to understand his dilemma. He says something like, "Look, right now, without looking around, I can tell you what the people in the booth behind us are wearing, how old they are, and what they ordered for lunch. I can tell you the license plate number of every car that was in the parking lot when we walked in, and I can tell exactly where every single exit is in this building and which way I would leave in an emergency. In a flash I know all of this stuff ... but *I don't know how I know it all*! It's like my brain has been trained to notice all this whether I want to or not."

Well, the game we're about to play will lead you down his path. I love this game so much because it teaches us how to identify edible and medicinal plants, AND it also trains and sharpens our awareness to the highest degree possible—equal to the world's greatest spies, trackers, and scouts. Ready to play?

How-To

Harvest Plant Parts. Secretly collect five to twelve plant leaves or fragments, seeds, fruits, bark chunks, berries, or sticks, but keep them hidden in a bandana or in your pocket. Pick a smaller number of plant-parts (about five) for younger kids, and a larger number (up to a dozen or so) for older kids and adults. Remember to collect only plants that have already littered their parts onto the ground, or are in such quantity that a missing leaf is not detrimental.

Create the Playing Field. Asking everyone to turn their backs so that you can set up the game without them seeing, place the plant parts on the ground, preferably on a bandana. Arrange them in some meaningful pattern, the Four Directions for example. Spread the items over only as much space as can be covered by your bandana.

Cover and Explain. Next, cover the items with a second bandana so they remain hidden. Then invite everyone to gather around and explain the game. Tell them, "Underneath the bandana I gathered an assortment of parts from plants from this place. I will lift the bandana off the items, but only for thirty seconds. Memorize everything you see under the bandana and where it is. Take a "mental photograph" of the items underneath, not only noticing individual details, but also the arrangement of the parts as they have been laid out."

Replicate. After the thirty seconds is up, cover the items back up. Then everyone (great to do this in pairs or groups) has four or five minutes, you decide: they need to gather the same plant parts and arrange them exactly as they were under the bandana. After time is up, ask them if they want one more chance to see the items and add or change their own replication. Most will say, "Yes!" Even as their witness, notice how fascinated you feel watching how sharply they observe the second time. You have turned something "on" inside their brain. All the gaps in their brains soak up the information they missed before, like liquid spackle that fills all the holes. Now they go off again, with lots of side glances at other group's piles, and comparisons of similar findings within their group, and make their final arrangements.

Review Results. Choose any way you like to review results. It can be cooperative or competitive, but the aim is to encourage and enjoy the development of spy-like instant-accurate memory.

Inside the Mind of the Mentor

Even a quick ten-second peek usually "burns" the image of most of your plants into the minds of people. This game, and variations on it, makes people happy and excited to practice Mind's Eye Imagination to imprint search images. It gives new meaning to the phrase "learning by heart."

Plant Concentration has powerful ecological linking advantages as well. People will become familiar with plant associations, discovering that certain plants always grow near each other, or for another example, grow only in shade. I like to throw in a few tricks. Plants gathered in a different ecological zone that can't be found right here create an "aha" moment for players when they eventually do see them again.

Also, I like to use this game with adults as a demonstration of how we learn and pattern our brains. After the first assemblage of a replication, I like to ask them what they each feel unsure about, what things they would look for if they could have another glimpse. We discuss these, as people share what their burning questions are: "I vaguely remember that plant, but I have no recall of what shape its leaves were or how they grew off the stem!" Then, when everyone gets to see the items a second time, it's obvious what happens: people's questions drive what they notice, learn, and remember. This is the clearest example I've found of directly observing how our brains pattern, and how important and fundamental our questions and curiosity feed the process of learning.

Also, a trick for this game you can offer after one or two tries: when revealed, count the total number of items. This provides a check-list to reference when trying to remember everything you saw.

Alternatives and Extensions

Haggle. I create a really strong need for the participants to succeed in this game, by haggling with them over how much time they're allowed to peek under the bandana. Just as I'm about to pull it up, I begin haggling again to their exasperated groans. When I finally lift it, they really want it!

Play Anywhere. Of course, you can play this game with any items, wherever you are. Spy trainers probably do this. In a restaurant, use a napkin to cover up such items as forks, toothpicks, or things from your wallet. Suddenly anywhere becomes a potential training ground, and a dull moment waiting for food can become a potent moment for "brain food."

Group by Theme. Create "themes" under your bandana. Only fern fragments, leaves from edible, medicinal, or poisonous plants, plants currently decaying, just sticks, or just seeds.

Arrangements. For additional challenge, the participants have to arrange their plants in the same pattern that you've laid them out—a few lines, grouped by type, or maybe in a circle associating each item with a parallel quality of the Natural Cycle.

Follow-up. After playing, pick one of the plants and get to know it better. Journal it; discover its strategy for survival.

Eating Wild Edibles

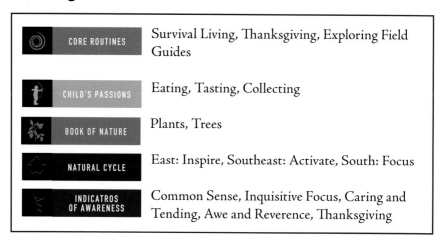

CORE ROUTINES	Survival Living, Thanksgiving, Exploring Field Guides
CHILD'S PASSIONS	Eating, Tasting, Collecting
BOOK OF NATURE	Plants, Trees
NATURAL CYCLE	East: Inspire, Southeast: Activate, South: Focus
INDICATROS OF AWARENESS	Common Sense, Inquisitive Focus, Caring and Tending, Awe and Reverence, Thanksgiving

Primer

Surviving on Greens, by Evan McGown

I remember the first time I went out by myself on a survival trip. I only wore shorts. I went out into the sizeable forest that a friend of mine owns, and I started wandering around. Soon I got hungry. That's when I started to notice the few edible plants I knew. I didn't know very many. But I knew Dandelion and I found it growing in one sunny spot where a road used to be. I also found some Plantain there, so I threw a few of its leaves into my pocket in case I got stung by fire-ants or a yellow-jacket. I even found a patch of my favorite—chickweed. The leaves look like little mouse-ears and they are delicious.

Farther on, I saw a tree I had just learned, a persimmon tree. They produce these delicious little orange fruits. I gathered a couple of them, and then I saw another tree, although it wasn't a wild one: an old apple tree. But I made sure it wasn't a poisonous look-alike. Luckily, just the week before my friend taught me how to identify apple trees by the little spurs on their branches.

As the night went on, it got pretty cold. I shivered in my shorts as I tried to make a bow-drill fire. But I had waited too long. It got too dark, and I had to sit without a fire that night. When I tried to sleep, well, that's another story. Let's just say I learned a lot about being comfortable in uncomfortable situations. But, despite a sleepless night, I had plenty to eat. As I ate all my wild greens and fruits, my body seemed to warm up from the calories. I was so appreciative that someone had taught me how to go into a wild place and find food. My life really has never been the same since!

Have any of you ever eaten wild plants? What about a wild-greens salad? Any berry-pickers out there? Maybe we could put together a whole meal of wild plants, just like I did that night. That's right, we could leave our lunches in their bags and boxes today, and just go out and harvest everything we eat from nature: a wild feast. The whole plant world is our grocery store and everything's free. Well, almost. The only price is intimate knowledge of the plants. Would you like to learn some plants so that you find food wherever you go? Let's go for it, but let's be sure we don't collect any non-edible plants or poisonous ones by mistake.

How-To

Do Your Homework. Eating Wild Edibles with the people you mentor depends on how familiar you, the instructor, have become with wild edibles. See the Resources under Plants in the Book of Nature chapter for field guides that can help you know your plants—poisonous, edible, and medicinal plants in your area.

Gather and Eat a Wild Edible Salad. You can gather casually as you wander through your day. Or set aside a specific time where everyone focuses on foraging and meets back to put all the wild edibles in a big bowl. Toss with a little oil, serve in special bowls, and chew in silence and gratitude.

Cook up a Wild Feast. If you have a program that includes camping overnight, make a Feast. Gather enough for a wild salad or another dish you might prepare by the evening fire. This can be like Story of the Day except with food. Get creative and diverse: make yummy pine-needle tea, stir-fry dandelion roots, mash up berries into a delicious jam, roast cat-tail rhizomes over the fire, make salad out of edible flowers with wild greens, or grind acorns into flour. When done safely, working with wild edibles can be extremely fun, satisfying, and provide learning and exciting projects for a long time.

Dandelion. If you don't know anything about plants, there is an easy place to start—the delicious Dandelion. Often called a "weed" by the uninitiated, this introductory edible is found in almost every yard in North America. As an old organic farmer once told me, a weed is a name for any plant that you don't want to be where it is. After experiencing Dandelion's gifts, you'll likely be happy with it in most places.

Plant ID with a Real Plant. Eating Wild Edibles provides a fertile opportunity for us to learn about plants and develop new relationships with creatures that live even under our feet and noses. It gives participants a meaningful reason and a need to learn plant identification. Bring the people you work with to a plant that you know to be edible. Explore the plant with them, telling them you think this might be an edible one but you want to make sure. Ask them and yourself—using your own genuine beginner's mind curiosity—some of the following rudimentary botanical questions as you determine its true identity.

+ Are the leaves opposite, alternate, or basal?

+ Are the leaves compound, simple, or palmate?

+ Are the edges of the leaves serrated (toothed) or smooth?

+ Is the plant flowering?

+ What color is the flower?

+ Is it symmetrical?

+ How many petals does it have?

You can explore field guides with your participants to match your answers up with a plant. Not every field guide covers the edibles, so demonstrate how to go deeper, into another book if necessary. When you feel certain, take a nibble. How does it taste? How would you describe the taste?

Gratitude for Plants. While eating from a plant, role model both a genuine thankfulness for this food plant and also a Caring and Tending ethic. You could ask: what would happen if we ate all the leaves or berries from this plant? Do any other animals depend on this plant for food? How few or how many of the neighboring plants match this one? How many leaves or berries do you think we should take from this plant so it will continue to live and other animals can share it, too? What do you appreciate most about this plant? Can you imagine a world without this plant or other edible plants in it?

Asking Permission. If you work with kids, we strongly recommend laying a ground rule regarding edible plants: a young learner **never eats anything unless they've asked permission** of an instructor or parent who knows the plants. They need to first show what they plan to eat to make sure it is edible.

Of course, this might not apply to some of the common berries after you've been eating the very same ones for weeks, but for everything else, make it mandatory to ask.

Inside the Mind of the Mentor

The inspirational power of being able to eat wild foods, which people harvest themselves, opens the doorway to learning about and appreciating all types of plants. The joy of snacking on a dandelion can provide a meaningful opportunity to learn about photosynthesis, root structures, vitamin content, comparative nutrition, and other aspects of a plant's life. This appreciation can then transfer to all nearby plant-life

Alternatives and Extensions

Journaling. You can ask participants to sketch the plant before eating so that they can remember it really well.

Learning Wild Edibles can sink in with great power when coupled with learning about similar-looking plants that can kill you. The potential of their own death catches peoples' attentions very quickly. See the next exercise, Meeting Poisonous Plants.

Meeting Poisonous Plants

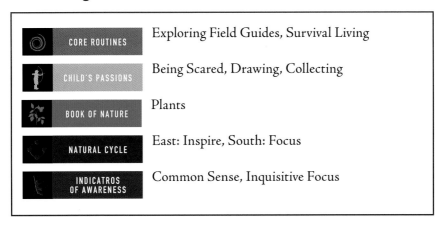

CORE ROUTINES	Exploring Field Guides, Survival Living	
CHILD'S PASSIONS	Being Scared, Drawing, Collecting	
BOOK OF NATURE	Plants	
NATURAL CYCLE	East: Inspire, South: Focus	
INDICATROS OF AWARENESS	Common Sense, Inquisitive Focus	

Primer

Wild Iris, by Evan McGown

Edible plants can look a lot like poisonous ones, and some plants contain such deadly poison that just putting them to your lips could cause you to go to the hospital or even die.

One time, my friends and I spent an entire afternoon gathering edible plants. That night we were going to cook them all up in a wild edible feast. I was psyched. My job was to harvest greens for a salad. I harvested Dandelion, chickweed, sheep sorrel, yarrow, plantain, salmonberry flowers, violet flowers, and lots of other delicious things. While I did this, another of my friends dug up some roots to cook for a stir-fry. And another of my friends had the fun job: he went into a nearby swamp in a canoe and harvested the edible young shoots of cattail plants. These were also going to go into the stir-fry. Yummm, yummm ... I could already taste the delicious foods that we gathered with our own hands.

We all met back at my friend's house to cook. As we were washing everything off, my friend who harvested the cattails pulled out a shoot, and said, "Look at how beautiful this shoot is! And I bet it's yummy, too!" Then he took a bite of it, because we all read that you can do this with cattail. Then another friend took a bite. Just as they were handing it to me to taste, the first friend suddenly grabbed his throat. "Oh my gosh ... something's happening to my throat! It's burning like a bunch of hot needles." Then the second friend started to feel the same thing. "What's going on? This is cattail, right? Could you have harvested the wrong thing?" We rushed to our field guides and looked for any look-a likes that might be poisonous. Sure enough, there it was, a picture of a plant almost identical to cattail, and right next to its picture, a skull-and-crossbones sign. My friends had not eaten cattail—they had eaten the poisonous Wild Iris. "Oh my gosh, are we going to die?" they asked. I read the details about the poisoning, and it said that the result is usually just illness, and death only when consumed in large quantities. Needless to say, my friends still freaked out. They washed their mouths out, and hours later, the tingling and burning in their throats started to fade. They ended up fine, but things could have been a lot worse!

After that, we all looked really, really hard at any plant we wanted to eat. We studied and made drawings and researched field guides of all the poisonous plants in the area. Whenever we saw one, we pointed it out to others. The good news is that you'll find relatively few poisonous plants compared to all the edible or medicinal ones, but you better know those few.

Before we make a wild plant salad, we need to learn all the poisonous plants. We definitely want a Wild Feast, so let's go out and get to know some of the poisonous plants around here. That way you'll keep yourself and everyone else safe and happy. No tingling or burning throats for us.

How-To

Side-by-side. Understand that botanical comparisons use advanced levels of knowledge (see below, Inside the Mind of the Mentor). Using a plant press, side by side in-the-field observations, and field guides, introduce poisonous plants and their look-a-likes. Give ample time to draw, research, or do leaf rubbings of these plants in individual journals. This continually on-going activity tests knowledge and awareness of poisonous plants as we introduce new edibles to our learners.

Comparative Plant Press. Harvest two plants that look the same, but one is poisonous, one edible. Then press them, mount and label them, and put them on display. Make an easy plant press with two heavy duty cardboard sheets, paper towels, and some strong rubber bands. A sample of leaf, flower, or shoot gets sandwiched between two paper towel sheets on one of the pieces of cardboard. Additional samples can be added, layers easily separate by paper towels. Cover the plant samples with the remaining cardboard and fasten tight with the rubber bands. The plant will soon dry out, flatten, and be preserved. Moderately heavy books on top of these lightweight presses can speed the process.

Inside the Mind of the Mentor

Although always wanting to waken others to the culinary delights of wild plants, I've seen enthusiasm tempered drastically by the dawning awareness that poisonous plants exist. Poisonous plants present an incredible opportunity to introduce botanical knowledge to those you mentor. Making distinctions between edible and poisonous look-alikes often settles into primary knowledge when learners see the differences in flower parts or leaf structures. Once people have that knowledge and awareness it acts like a scaffold to hold more information, more plants, for the next level of knowledge and awareness.

For beginning and intermediate participants, I start by going over the most toxic of the local plants. But I also make a point to balance this hazard-based approach by simultaneously introducing the friendliest edibles. If there are edibles that have poisonous look-alikes, I won't tell someone about those (and therefore open the possibility to harmful confusion) until the other person has very high skill in plant identification and differentiation.

Note: Many organizations and communities across the country advocate that people learn poisonous plants first before learning wild edibles. There is merit in this position, but we feel it is also vital that people do not learn to fear plants. Use your best judgment to find a balance between the two.

Alternatives and Extensions

Meeting Poisonous Plants is best interwoven throughout the Eating Wild Edibles activity.

Songline

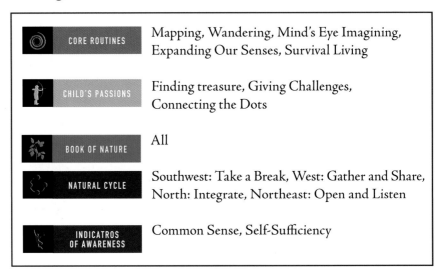

⊚	CORE ROUTINES	Mapping, Wandering, Mind's Eye Imagining, Expanding Our Senses, Survival Living
	CHILD'S PASSIONS	Finding treasure, Giving Challenges, Connecting the Dots
	BOOK OF NATURE	All
	NATURAL CYCLE	Southwest: Take a Break, West: Gather and Share, North: Integrate, Northeast: Open and Listen
	INDICATROS OF AWARENESS	Common Sense, Self-Sufficiency

Primer

Songline in Fast Forward, by Ellen Haas

Gary Snyder, an adventurous writer and poet, tells a story about a visit he took to the Australian Outback. He went as the guest of aboriginal people whose ancestors had lived there for thousands of years. Only very recently these people began to include in their cultural ways modern things like pickup trucks.

He took a ride in the back of a pickup truck with one of the elders and as they bounced along dusty clay and sand roads going through the great desert toward the elder's home, they passed rock outcroppings, gnarly trees, and distant evidence of water holes. Gary tells of being at first surprised, then bewildered because his host bumping along with him suddenly changed into a storytelling dynamo, pointing at these landmarks as they whizzed by, and keeping up a non-stop, fast, detailed, stream of legends and stories about how they had been created, what their many names were, who had had fights and love affairs—everything, but so fast that it seemed crazy.

After a while, Gary realized why. In the elder's culture, it was a deep-set custom to walk on foot through the landscape and as the people came to a significant landmark, they told and sang its story. In their leisure time, these stories would then get made into beautiful art whose symbols would hold the story. The children learned their history, and found their way because these stories contained all those clues about landmarks. Everything in the landscape had a story, and all the stories connected to each other. Anthropologists call this wonderful cultural tradition "Songlining."

Gary Snyder realized that he was following the route of a traditional Songline and his host felt compelled to honor everything they passed with its story. Because they rode in that pickup truck instead of walking the Songline route, the story about each place came out of his mouth like a tape running at Fast Forward speed!

Let's us try to create a kind of Songline as we go along today. Let's go on a treasure hunt using a Songline map to find our way.

How-To

Set-up. Divide people into two groups and include an instructor in each group. Each group will be given a "treasure" to hold onto (your choice). Then, they hide that treasure somewhere for the other group to find. How will they find it? The group will also create a written Songline for them, filled only with clues that reveal landmarks and directions in the landscape. As you go to bury your treasure, follow a route, and create a series of clues that lead from one cool place to the next, until you find a good place to bury your treasure, camouflaging any signs of disturbance. Both groups will then meet back at the beginning, swap Songlines, and try to find the other group's hidden treasure.

Making the Songline Map. The clues in the Songline will be imaginative names, or descriptions of places in the landscape. Have the group begin by looking around from their starting point. Look for obvious to not-so-obvious landmarks or unique places that stand out. The map is not a drawn map but a written one containing a set of directions to landmarks. One might say, "First head towards the Standing Tower Rock, turn away from the sun

and walk twenty five steps. Next, look for the Tree Ring Circus. Walk into the middle and look between Grandma Cedar and her grandbaby. Head for Uncle Joe the mossy stump and look under his hat." This is what we call a Songline. If your group just can't seem to find the hidden treasure, the other group might need to re-translate for you, from where you got stuck. The above example would translate to "First head towards the tall, thin rock standing on end, turn away from the sun and walk twenty five steps. Next, look for the circle of trees. Walk into the middle and look between the biggest and the smallest cedar trees. Head towards the mossy stump that looks like it has a face and find the treasure under the huckleberry growing out of the top of the stump." If you want to, you can turn it into a Dr. Seuss-like rhyme that will undoubtedly tickle and delight kids of all ages.

Inside the Mind of the Mentor

Games like this, especially started when children are young, create an exceptional awareness of their surroundings. As they get older and they wander farther and farther, they begin to see each section of the landscape as unique and of distinct character. It's harder for them to get lost because they notice and connect to specific places they have walked through previously.

Not only this, but the landscape also becomes alive as living, imaginative beings who speak to our imaginations and our image-based and story-based way of thinking. Some psychologists refer to this as *participation mystique* with one's landscape, noting that such a relationship is common in nature-based cultures. As we re-story the landscape, we allow it speak to more than just our rational minds.

A note for working with kids: when it is Songline-making time, some kids may want to set up impossibly obtuse challenges for the other team. Use this opportunity to help them learn to see and speak with subtlety. If they want to refer to a part of the forest as a "black hole" for no reason other than no one will figure it out, help them make it tricky but translatable.

Alternatives and Extensions

Songlines Every Day. Create Songlines as often as you can when you go outdoors with people. Set this up as a technique they can use any time they're walking alone and don't want to get lost. Instead of chatting as you walk along a trail, make it a game to create a Songline. This will keep your attention on nature and your imagination fired up. The group forms their story and line of travel together, has lunch or snack, and then you test your memory by simply playing the Songline backwards! Do this everywhere, all the time. Over time, people will become lost-proof.

Mildy Toxic Hairy Cat's Ear

Common Edible Dandelion

Get Lost

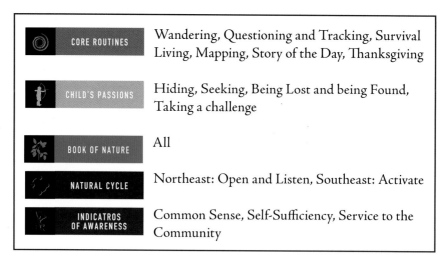

◎	**CORE ROUTINES**	Wandering, Questioning and Tracking, Survival Living, Mapping, Story of the Day, Thanksgiving
	CHILD'S PASSIONS	Hiding, Seeking, Being Lost and being Found, Taking a challenge
	BOOK OF NATURE	All
	NATURAL CYCLE	Northeast: Open and Listen, Southeast: Activate
	INDICATROS OF AWARENESS	Common Sense, Self-Sufficiency, Service to the Community

Primer

The primer for this activity simply works through the surprise element: do not let participants know your intention. You need to distract them from thinking about orientation at all. Do this by going out for a Wandering filled with engaging fun until, suddenly, you find that you are lost! Your distractions worked if they experience disorientation.

How-To

Wander. Wander with your group until you've gone into territory new and unknown to them. Wander a bit off trail until you think your wander-mates have become distracted from paying attention to where they've been going. For kids, this might not require going very far. With adults, it might mean a sizeable hike. But wherever you go, make sure you know the area well enough to navigate out regardless of whether anyone else has paid attention.

Put Forth the Challenge. Then, announce to everyone that you abdicate leadership; you will pretend you have no idea how to get back. As a group, they need to find the way back home. If they don't, well ... we'll just be lost!

Prompt Dialogue. Get the group talking about how to get home. What will their strategy be? Do they have a leader? Help facilitate conversation over remembered landmarks. Help everyone express their voice. Choose when to step in and "save the day" if necessary.

Inside the Mind of the Mentor

In this activity, you want to generate a need for people to be aware of their surroundings at all times. During wanders, if you occasionally spring on them that you all are "lost" and they need to find the way back themselves, they will begin to pay attention to bearings, directions, and landmarks, especially when you lead the group.

As a consequence of this sudden challenge, group dynamics really gel or get pushed to break down. Your presence is crucial to keeping it a positive learning experience. I find that non-cohesive groups just need reminding that they do have skills for working things out together. I might have different participants take turns being the route finder while the others act as council that advises. Once they start to find familiar turf, their excitement will build up, and you might find yourself running after them. Be prepared to explain yourself to family members who ask, "Why is my child so excited about getting lost today?"

Alternatives and Extensions

Survival Priorities. The Survival Priorities activity can be played during this game, as well as going over protocol for what happens when you really are lost.

Body Radar. Encourage Body Radar and Expanding Our Senses as you go.

Songline and Map. If you feel you generated a greater need for awareness of surroundings, follow up with the Songline activity on another day. Upon safe return home, use Story of the Day time for participants to draw a Map of their route.

Just Kidding ... You can really take this activity to another level by NOT letting them know you're *pretending* to be lost yourself. This will definitely push some edges. When you tell them at the end that you really did know where you were, will they believe you? Will they ever trust you again? Be sensitive to the possible implication of doing this.

The Lost Test

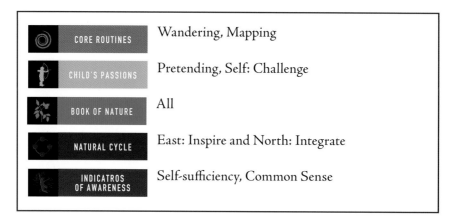

CORE ROUTINES	Wandering, Mapping
CHILD'S PASSIONS	Pretending, Self: Challenge
BOOK OF NATURE	All
NATURAL CYCLE	East: Inspire and North: Integrate
INDICATROS OF AWARENESS	Self-sufficiency, Common Sense

Primer

Pretending to be Lost, by Daniel Evans

I used to practice getting lost as a kid. As I wandered the canyons and mesas where I grew up, I pretended search parties looked frantically for me. In my imagination, just as everyone gave up, I would walk out of the bushes and say, "See, I wasn't lost, I just went on a long walk." Even when my parents took me to the mountains or the desert, I would take any opportunity I could to walk by myself, to pretend I was lost, of course.

I never really experienced the excitement of being scared or the happy relief of rescue because I actually memorized as many details as I could along my walk. I watched the sun's angle, all the interesting rock formations I passed, and I saw each group of trees as unique. I think I felt too afraid of getting lost, so I paid attention really well.

For those of you who have never had the chance to go walking alone in the woods or try your hand at getting lost, now is the time to test your skills in the Lost Test.

How-To

Find and Create the Playing Field. Set up the Lost Test playing field—before the participants show up. You need to find a place with a few important characteristics. 1) It needs relatively dense vegetative cover and a trail for everyone to string themselves out on. 2) It has to be okay for your participants to bushwhack off-trail. Bring your participants to a starting point, a well-worn trail or logging road perhaps. The participants will each pick a spot on this trail, a good distance apart from each other and make a marker on the trail at their starting point. First they walk into the vegetation alone a predetermined number of paces (dependent on age, skill, thickness of cover, or presence of hazards). When they cannot see where they started from, they will turn around, and find their way back as close to their marker as they can get. Instruct people not to "trail-blaze" or mark their path in any way, such as with broken branches. Give them an appropriate time limit and monitor their return.

Story of the Day. When they have all returned, gather around to hear their Story of the Day. This may seem simple, yet it's amazing how fear enters and confuses, how landmarks that made sense going one way become completely strange coming back the other way, how detours around impassable spots can disorient people, how what seems "straight" really isn't—all kinds of observations can be expected.

You will require support. Consider it necessary to have extra help for this adventure. Have your helpers spread out into the playing field at a distance farther than the players plan to walk. You need this insurance in case someone really does get lost. Set a time limit, and send your best tracker hunting when participants don't return. Equip folks with emergency whistles, walkie-talkies or functioning cell phones. Do whatever you need to do to be absolutely sure you don't really lose anyone.

Inside the Mind of the Mentor

Again, with this activity as with the last, we create a need for people to pay attention to their surroundings by consciously practicing wandering and lost-proofing techniques. The Lost Test helps by safely shocking kids and adults alike into cultivating awareness of their place in the world. If anyone comes out onto the starting trail in a completely different place than they left, help them discover where their awareness lapsed. Did they ever notice the sun, can they distinguish between plant species (or is it just a sea of overwhelming green?) Was there panic involved? Depending on what you find out, you've just set up some future individualized lesson plans.

For those already quite comfortable and reliable in the woods, this activity can serve as a testing, to make sure they feel ready for the responsibility of leadership, and of spending more time in the woods alone.

Alternatives and Extensions

Raising the Bar. The more participants try this, the further they can go. Set them up in a place where they need to circle around impassable spots and find a new way back. To vary a familiar setting a bit, have them go in and then return blindfolded, or vice versa.

Buddies. Younger children can pick an older child as a buddy for the first time trying this, if needed to reassure you and them about their safety.

Aidless Navigation. All of the mapping and wandering activities serve to reinforce a person's awareness of their place on this earth. Regardless, go over what to do anytime you plan to go somewhere where someone might get lost. This is of utmost importance. Definitely also role-model and inspire everyone to learn the basics of using a compass and a contour map. Also get familiar with other Aidless Navigation techniques through the great stories Jon Young tells in Part 3 of the "Seeing Through Native Eyes" tape series, under the topic of Wandering and Aidless Navigation. The other Six Arts he reviews, in addition to Songlining, are:

1. **Sight lining.** Line up three objects in a straight line. Look at them. Sight down them, and see that this Doug fir tree, that mossy rock, and in the distance, that dead snag, line up to make the perfect straight line. Now, walk to the mossy rock, and look back to the Doug fir tree, and say, "I'm still in a straight line. Now I'll walk from the mossy rock to the dead snag, and I'll make sure that I can still see everything in a line." Then pick a new object in the line for the next steps, and so on.

2. **Backtracking.** "I'll find my way back. I'll just backtrack." Simple, right? No. Tracking is difficult. If you can already back-track yourself out of any landscape, you don't need to be studying these skills to start with.

3. **Trailblazing.** Break branches in the direction in which you travel … drag a stick … pile rocks … hang surveyor's ribbon, etc.

4. **Bird's Eye View Mapping.** Internalize the mental map. The very first thing I did when I moved to my new home in Washington was to get a county map. I found where I lived and marked it with a pen, and I stared at it and stared at it. And I said, "Which way is this river? Which way is that river? Where are the mountains from here? And if I wandered this way off my property, where would I end up? What road

would I cross? Would I even encounter a road?" I do this in every new place I enter, whether for a trip or as a new home. I buy maps, draw maps, and ask a million questions until I start to feel like I have a map living inside my head.

5. **Celestial Navigation and Landmarks.** Use sun and stars to orient, as well as larger landmarks in the landscape such as distant mountains or the ocean coast.

6. **Intuition.** Something learned over years by practicing the above techniques over and over and over.

Combinations. You can combine this activity with Mapping, Songlining, Body Radar, Wild Edibles, and Story of the Day.

Plants and Wandering Activities | 451

Trees And Survival Skills
ACTIVITIES

Activities for learning trees in a meaningful manner,
as well as the skills, abilities, and ingenuity of
primitive wilderness survival

If you want to know how to survive in the wilderness, you'll end up getting to know trees *really* well. Whether we need to make shelter, fire, tools, or crafts—we turn to trees. Conversely, if you want to get to know trees really well, nothing else matches learning to use and appreciate their individual qualities through the ancient skills of primitive survival.

These activities are not meant to and do not thoroughly transmit any of these skills, such as fire-by-friction, survival shelters, or water purification. Many wonderful resources in the Suggested Reading already do this well. Instead, these activities provide a starting place, an inspirational doorway into the never-ending journey of learning.

Survival teaches us about trees, while it also teaches about ourselves and how to develop many virtues: common sense, ingenuity, self-confidence, perseverance, mindfulness, and a fresh, grateful perspective on the conveniences of the modern world.

Survival Priorities

◎	**CORE ROUTINES**	Survival Living, Questioning and Tracking, Mind's Eye Imagining, Thanksgiving
	CHILD'S PASSIONS	Imagining, Taking Challenges, Creating Stories
	BOOK OF NATURE	Trees, Plants
	NATURAL CYCLE	East: Inspire, and North; Integrate
	INDICATROS OF AWARENESS	Self-Sufficiency, Caring and Tending, Common Sense, and Awe and Reverence

Primer

Once with a group of friends, we spent a weekend testing our skills in the wilderness. We went out into the rain of early Spring with nothing but knives, the clothes on our backs, and one blanket each. We wanted to make fire, build shelters, purify water, and feel good about how much we ate. Since we went as a large group, we divided into teams for making a primitive fire and building shelters. It was so helpful to have a village of people who had been studying survival skills, because doing any of these things by yourself when it's raining can be really hard work.

By the end of the first day, our hard work had paid-off: we drank our purified water and planned a meal of wild berries, nettles, cattail, and bird eggs for the next day. We sat around the fire that night, proudly congratulating ourselves, and looked forward to our first night out sleeping in the shelters we had built with our own hands.

By the next morning, however, my group realized we still needed some learning. We needed a roof that didn't soak us with rain.

How-To

This Survival Priorities activity works well as a follow-up to the Survival Scenario activity from the Introducing the Core Routines section. This can also be done as a stand-alone. We want people to figure out what they need and in what order of importance.

Question and Prioritize. While you make plans for a survival trip, actively question participants about what they would do in a survival situation. Brainstorm a list. Then try to find out how they would prioritize what they need to survive. Do the participants worry about food before fire or water? If it is raining or snowing outside, will locating shelter for everyone or building a fire be more important?

Rule of 3s. Keep these guidelines in mind. We call this commonly-shared tool the "Rule of 3's":

- **3 minutes**—On average we can survive **without air** for only 3 minutes.

- **3 hours**—We can only survive 3 hours **without adequate warmth**. Hypothermia can set in and cause death.

- **3 days**—We can survive up to 3 days **without water**, but many people are relatively incapacitated after 1 day. This rule becomes very bio-regionally specific. In a desert environment on a hot day, the air dehydrates your body, and few people can truly make it 24 hours without water.

- **3 weeks**—Believe it or not, the average person can go up to 3 weeks **without food** and still survive.

Based on this new information, what would your survival priorities be? Through questions, drills, and presenting different scenarios, use the Rule of 3's to get this important information across to people.

Inside the Mind of the Mentor

The name of this game will be creating a space for dialogue. You want to get people to seriously imagine themselves in a tough situation and start working out what they would really need to do.

With a little opportunity and coaching, you will begin to see people's ingenuity arise. Ask them questions about the immediate area? How would you build a shelter and where? What would you use to gather water? With true need and your questioning, you help people develop their improvisational intelligence, their MacGyver "working with what you got" mentality. It's fun to watch what creative ideas the folks come up with.

Watch for those who want to pick food over everything else. Play their scenario out to its grim finish for them. Depending on your environment, shelter or fire followed immediately by water will probably be the wisest order of priority. If necessary, humans can go without food for weeks.

An important note: your priorities depend on the environment—the time of year, weather, temperature, distance to water, and likelihood of rescue. For instance, in a tropical environment, a warm shelter might be less important than protection from snakes or biting insects. Likewise, in some very hot places, water might trump everything. When would shelter from wind be important? When would it be wisest to simply stay awake and keep moving?

Alternatives and Extensions

Use What You've Got. Bring out 3 objects, say a carving knife, a bandana, and a shoe-string. First, have people list out as many possible survival uses for each one, and then have them choose which one they would most want to have in a survival situation. Walk in to your meeting place with a broken TV under your arm. How could this be made useful?

Learn Some Skills. Any activity that involves learning and applying survival skills works as an obvious extension of this activity (shelter, fire-making, water boiling, edible plant identification, aidless navigation, or plant-aids that repel insects).

Meet-A-Tree

◎	CORE ROUTINES	Sit Spot, Wandering, Expanding the Senses, Questioning and Tracking, Mind's Eye Imagining
	CHILD'S PASSIONS	Being blindfolded, Tricking, Solving mysteries
	BOOK OF NATURE	Trees
	NATURAL CYCLE	Northeast: Open and Listen, East: Inspire
	INDICATROS OF AWARENESS	Care-taking, Awe and Reverence

Primer

For many cultures, there comes a time when teenage boys and girls antici-pate going through special experiences which cause them to grow up into responsible men and women. These experiences often involve a high degree of challenge, putting their skills and character through intense testing.

We have been told of one such challenge put to young people as part of their coming-of-age rite of passage. Each young person gets blindfolded and led out of their village, miles into the wilderness, into regions where they never spent time before. When they arrive, they were taken to a tree and asked to sit with that tree and get to know it very well. So each youth would sit at their own tree blindfolded, day and night, for three or four days. Then they were led back to the village, blindfolded the whole way.

Once they returned, they could remove their blindfold. Then they receive their challenge: walk out into the hundreds of square miles of wilderness surrounding their village, and from the hundreds of thousands of trees, walk to their specific tree. Remarkably, year after year young people could do this. But to them, it probably wasn't remarkable; it was required. When a young person succeeded, the elders and the mentors knew they were ready to be a mature member of the people.

How-To

Partner-up. People team up with partners, and decide who will be blind-folded first.

Guide. Then guide the blindfolded person by hand or body-direction in a confusing or circuitous pattern to a tree in the area. Even though you want to disorient them, still be a compassionate and gentle leader: consider what it will be like when your turn comes. The tree becomes "their tree."

Get to Know Your Tree The blindfolded person then gets to know the tree as well as they can using all of their senses—other than their eyes. They get as much time as they want. Remind the person when they are first led to their tree, to circle the tree, hug it low and high, rub their skin against its textures, and smell it. Invite them to listen for Bird Language that might mean some-thing, territorial aggression that might indicate a nest, or a woodpecker find-ing bugs that might indicate its age or height. Encourage them to be creative in the use of their senses to get to know the tree. When finished lead them back to the starting point, again in a confusing or circuitous pattern. Then take off their blindfold and put the challenge before them: find your tree.

Switch It Up. After the first person successfully finds their tree, switch part-ners and let them have a go.

Story of the Day. Follow-up with a group Sharing Circle, and seize the opportunity to work the Art of Questioning.

Inside the Mind of the Mentor

This game activates the sense of touch beautifully. This can be such a peace-ful activity for some. I've seen young folks and adults alike just linger on their tree for minutes, exploring all the details of the branching, bark, root, and moss growth. It really does feel great to spend some time alone with trees … and the blindfold gives them permission to touch and smell in a way that might normally seem foolish.

People who weren't able to find their tree often want to start over and go again, and may need some active involvement on your part for them to find success. Most often, they didn't become familiar enough or aware of all the nuances that a tree's base can contain. On their second try, have them feel longer and describe out loud all the sensations they encounter. Guide them with sensory questions of all sorts. Help them remember the terrain on the way there and back. Or show them three trees, one of which is theirs.

Alternatives and Extensions

Tree Introductions. Follow up by taking the whole group around to meet all the trees. Participants can introduce their trees as new friends and tell something special about them. The introductory part builds good etiquette training, and opens an opportunity for Thanksgiving.

Multiple Trees. For advanced learners have the partners lead them on a Meet-A-Tree course where they have to meet multiple trees and find them in the order that they visited them.

Do It On Your Own. For participants who seemed especially touched by this activity, providing additional opportunities for them to be truly alone with trees can be an amazing way to develop their sensitivity. Perfect time for Sit Spot.

Tree Tag

CORE ROUTINES	Expanding Our Senses, Exploring Field Guides, Journaling, Mind's Eye Imagining
CHILD'S PASSIONS	Playing Tag, Solving Mysteries with Clues
BOOK OF NATURE	Trees and Shrubs, and everything else
NATURAL CYCLE	Southeast: Activate
INDICATROS OF AWARENESS	Aliveness and Agility, Inquisitive Focus

Primer

Who would like to play a game of tag? Alright, are you sure? Okay … I'm warning you, for this game you better know a little bit about the trees around here. But don't worry … if you don't, you'll learn quickly. Ready?

How-To

Set-up the Playing Field. You'll need a place with open running room and a nice variety of shrubs and trees on the border or spaced throughout like an orchard, open forest, or meadow with trees and shrubs growing at the edge. Set up some outside boundaries.

Call Out Tree Descriptions. Gather up and choose a volunteer to be the starting Chaser. The Caller (you) begins the game by shouting, "You're safe if you're touching a (insert tree name or identification clue … such as "an evergreen tree" or "an oak-tree" or "a tree that makes fruit you can eat"). These tree types become the "base" where people must touch to be safe. Once a runner finds the right tree, and tags it, they can't leave it until the next round begins. If a runner has tagged the wrong tree, they're fair game for the Chaser. The Caller can give out additional clues during the round if needed.

Play On. Anyone who gets tagged becomes a Chaser for the next round. Chasers must re-form near the center of the playing field after each round. For each new round, call out a new "base," a different type of tree. The game ends when everyone has been caught and turned into a Chaser.

Inside the Mind of the Mentor

This activity is a nice way to work previous botany lessons into an active game. Depending on the age or knowledge of the participants, one might use tree names, descriptions of plant parts, medicinal or edible clues. Add a complication: mention certain lichen, moss, mammal, or bird species currently hanging out in one of the trees.

This game can help people get familiar with using field guides. Knowing that you will play this game, pull out field guides beforehand. Help a participant state a question or observation and then empower them to research for the answer. The time before the game starts, when everyone gathers around books and trees is priceless. The mentor's next job helps everyone construct mental images that they can quickly recall once the running action begins.

Alternatives and Extensions

Field Guides. In its full version, this game relies on good local field guides. Depending on a learner's level, every variety of learning becomes possible, from learning plant families to leaf structures to botanical terms. Have each learner pick out a tree that interests them for further research. Or, have a pile of tree field guides handy, and after you call out a tough clue, give them a minute or two of "safety" to look through the field guides for help.

Circling the Edge. If your people seem inexperienced with field guides, change directions and play this game using clues easily found in books, and currently on or just beyond the edge of their knowledge. This sets up a motivating desire to use the field guides later when you introduce a research time-out in the middle of game time.

Beyond Trees. Why limit yourself to just trees and shrubs? This can be the ultimate awareness tag game as well. Give the participants a few moments to study the landscape and then fire away with any sort of question or detail you can think of: Running water. Unnatural litter. A plant whose Latin name is "Plantago major." A cumulous cloud. A Snag. Quartz. Something with a square stem. Challenge their ecological knowledge: Food for a robin. Moss on a tree. A spot of sun. A dry place. A look-alike dandelion. Something that can heal nettle stings. A mouse tunnel in the grass. Stretch your own imagination.

Shelter Building

⊚	**CORE ROUTINES**	Survival Living, Sit Spot, Thanksgiving
⚒	**CHILD'S PASSIONS**	Building, getting dirty
🌿	**BOOK OF NATURE**	Trees
⟳	**NATURAL CYCLE**	South: Focus, West: Gather and Share, North: Integrate
✺	**INDICATROS OF AWARENESS**	Self-Sufficiency, Service to the Community, Awe and Reverence

Primer

The Village Scene, by Daniel Evans
Once, with an active group of six and seven year olds, a shelter-building

experience turned into the greatest game of "primitive" house. Since it was summer, these kids needed nothing more than a simple lattice house of branches and logs erected among the cedars. They built that quick as a wink. So, they soon took their magnificent power of Make-Believe and turned the whole area into their village.

They directed themselves in a series of tasks needed to keep the village happy. They were builders, hunters, and rope makers, and still had lots of time for just relaxing and having good conversation and games. I don't think those children even needed me there. They were home already!

How-To

Use What You've Got. If your group has researched shelter building styles already, and has a specific plan, then find an area that satisfies your material needs. Otherwise, you should be fine with downed branches, logs, and plenty of leaf mulch.

Site Location: Pick a spot where the shelter remains unseen from trails, like you're in the middle of the wilderness. Depending on the season or length of time you'll use the shelter, you may want to consider needs like good drainage, sunlight, wind protection, and safety from hazard trees. This activity assumes you have permission from the landowner.

Build. To build, basically let the fort-building instincts of the participants take over. However, you can offer some suggestions on building and insulation. Look to our primitive skills resources for more detailed information on great shelter-building, but here's a basic idea:

First—find or make a backbone
Second—put ribs on the backbone
Third—create lattice-work over ribs that can hold debris
Fourth—pile leaves and other debris on, as much as possible

Sleep in it! If you work with folks who can spend the night, decide to build a shelter they will sleep in. This creates an extra motivator and really gives them a need to do their best, and their experience of sleeping in a primitive shelter will not be soon forgotten. For kids and adult beginners, this can be a goal they work towards over a period of time.

UnBuild. On public land, if left standing to slowly decompose through the year, your shelter will be considered by most other people a public liability and an eyesore. If you work with kids in a daylight program, after you finish with your shelter, celebrate and give thanks to the trees, then turn it into an animal home. Remove the supports and let it collapse. If you build your shelter in a public space, removal might be done at the end of the day or week.

Inside the Mind of the Mentor

This is such an organic and naturally primitive process, about the only thing needed by the mentor, once you accomplish the initial set-up, will be helping people build something that fits the scope of their energy and focus. Building shelters can be a carefree magical experience, where learners grow in awe of their group handiwork. It can also be an experience in which the mentor needs to dig down below the surface and help individuals, or the group, find out and express what needs aren't being met.

Taking breaks to look and survey your progress is good. I provide alternate, non-distracting activities for those who truly aren't interested.

For older groups who build shelters to sleep in, limiting the amount of time to complete will really inspire a focused bundle of energy and teamwork.

If you have the opportunity to sleep in, or at least spend a long day enjoying your finished shelter, this activity has hit a home-run. When people feel "at home" in nature, they form new pathways for expressing appreciation and thanksgiving.

Alternatives and Extensions

Pressurized Scenario. If you want a quick shelter lesson that really emphasizes survival, create a dramatic scenario such as "Oh my gosh a huge storm is rolling in; we only have 20 minutes to build a shelter so all of us can fit inside … or else we'll be left out in the midst of a giant thunderstorm! Quick, let's get going!" This creates an amazing intensity. Everything is suddenly heightened: learning that occurs, team-communication successes and break-downs, leadership skills, and physical activity. People usually feel astonished at what they can do. Such an intense need will allow them to do things they never thought possible. This very important and vivid lesson works magically for kids of all ages—this includes adults too.

Fairy Shelters. For limited time lines or with fairy lovers, try building miniature shelters. I like to have kids build one over a rubber chicken. We then pour water over it to see if the chicken stayed dry during the night.

Crafts. Some additional crafts that lend themselves to shelters are learning knots and making cordage from fiber plants.

Shelter Hazards. There are many lessons that trees can teach. Journaling and learning the trees of your area that are susceptible to root or trunk rot and falling branches becomes a necessity for the serious shelter builder. Tell them to go out for a whole day and follow the woodpeckers.

Five-Minute Fire

◎	CORE ROUTINES	Survival Relationship, Questioning and Tracking, Mind's Eye Imagining, Story of the Day
	CHILD'S PASSIONS	Self-Challenge, Collecting Wood, Burning Things, Playing out Scenarios
	BOOK OF NATURE	Trees
	NATURAL CYCLE	Southeast: Activate, North: Integrate
	INDICATROS OF AWARENESS	Self-Sufficiency, Awe and Reverence

Primer

Imagine this: all of us go out in the woods for a walk on a fine crisp fall day. Our outing was fun, the picnic food tasted great, but the weather turned cold and rainy, so we start heading back home. Unfortunately, at the river crossing, your beloved mentor or parent or spouse slipped off the log bridge and fell into the icy river. They managed to swim to shore, but now they're in very real danger of freezing to death. You all realize the heaters in the cars are too far away so you better start a fire here. But alas, all of the matches got wet except for three.

You have five minutes to gather everything you need to start a small sustaining fire. Go!

How-To

Getting Started. This activity assumes you have permission to make fires, an appropriate space, and trust in the people you are working with. As soon as you can set this scenario, divide a large group into small groups, and everyone understands the boundaries of their "fire area." Ten per group works, but if you have extra help, fewer works better. The participants will run off and get busy collecting, debating, and arranging wood. Shout out the minutes remaining as the clock ticks.

Lighting. At the end of the five minutes, they must try lighting their fires. Hand out three matches to each group. With younger people, you will strike the match, but ask first, where the group wants you to place the match. Have them reveal their fire starting strategy to you. Shortly, the participants will discover if their materials and arrangement worked.

Changing Plans. Back in the scenario for a moment, you suddenly might "discover" just 3 more matches for each group, and give them another 5 minutes to learn from their mistakes and the collective wisdom of the group.

Burning Out. Take everyone on a tour of each group's fire area to discover what did and didn't work. Burn up the remaining gathered wood if you can, or disperse it. Make sure each fire feels cold and wet before you move along. Teach etiquette for putting out fires.

Inside the Mind of the Mentor

Welcome to what is often the "two-hour" fire activity. Any mentor has their hands full with this one, for it strikes a primal chord with pretty much everyone. Fire! People will often want multiple chances, or lessons on all the fine arts of fire making: such as tinder and kindling arrangement, or why grass doesn't burn, or the difference between wet wood and dry wood. Most groups usually need help with momentary organizational dysfunction, such as arguing over who lights the match; and ethical challenges like trampling plants in their blind determination to save the fictional victim. I've gotten in trouble with parents of younger children who weren't able to make the distinction between imagination and reality, meaning the story I used to set up this activity was too strong and too scary.

Asking the right questions after their success or failure is the key component to translating their enthusiasm with fire into a skill. Small groups afford you the opportunity to observe the particular dynamics that need tweaking, and thus the questions you can be asking.

If you are fortunate, this activity's closure will coincide with a meal time, and everyone can gather around one fire (add a coal from the others) for good cheer and story-sharing.

Alternatives and Extensions

Fire Lessons. Many valuable lessons can be taught around fire making, such as ethical harvesting techniques, which trees have dry twigs in downpours, where to find pitch, how and when or whether to ring a fire, how to use matches and lighters effectively and safely, how to tend fires by arranging kindling, tinder, and logs, and how to be sure fires are out.

Finding the Appropriate Edge. For advanced learners, do this activity in the rain, or use only materials they've never tried before. Allow only one match or create a competitive race with the instructors.

For intermediate learners, group them with beginners so they can pass on good techniques and astute observations, or challenge them to use wood only from plants they can name.

For beginners, give them longer than five minutes, or be prepared to offer fire-making instructions between attempts.

Journals and Field Guides. This 5-Minute Fire Activity lends itself nicely to many field or classroom based lessons. Make a collection of fire twigs that people can use to find and match up with the proper tree. To raise their awareness of this renewable resource providing our warmth, ask them to guess the age of the parent tree that provided the kindling. Also, bring back leaf and twig samples for sketching and field guide research.

Community And Ecology
ACTIVITIES

Activities that inspire team-building and appreciation of human ecological connections with the rest of nature

Can we stretch our imaginations and visualize animals gathered together in ancient councils discussing the attitudes and behaviors of human beings? Many legends from around the world recount versions of this story. Can we humans learn anything about how to treat each other from observing the relationships of the plants and animals around us? Does the key to restoring ecological balance lie in how we appreciate our kinship with the rest of the natural world?

The activities in this section may not answer these questions, but at least they do ask them. By trying out team-building, taking on different roles, and exploring local ecology, people will develop appreciation of how everything connects to everything else. This section takes a deep look at our roles and relationship with each other and our local bio-region.

Blindfold Caterpillar

CORE ROUTINES	Expanding the Senses, Mind's Eye Imagining, Animal Forms
CHILD'S PASSIONS	Helping each other, Pretending, Taking Challenges
BOOK OF NATURE	Things to Catch and Tend; Caterpillars, Centipedes, and Millipedes
NATURAL CYCLE	East: Inspire, Northeast: Open and Listen, West: Gather and Share
INDICATROS OF AWARENESS	Common Sense, Service to the Community, Quiet Mind

Primer

Have you ever watched a caterpillar move along or looked closely at a centipede's legs? First the head wiggles forward and then each section follows the leader part by part. It's like watching a slow ripple. Do you think that as a group you could move together like a caterpillar?

Let's see how your parts can work together as a group. Are you ready for a challenge? How about a blindfold challenge?

How-To

Blindfold Caterpillar works as a simple Animal Form activity to begin to shape a group of individuals into a single coordinated community. It gives everyone, including you, an insight into some of the stresses and strains of acting together as one body with a group mind.

Being a Caterpillar. Divide people up into teams of at least three, eight at the most. Each team will become a Caterpillar and each will have a sighted mentor or group leader at the lead. Give everyone a blindfold and a small paper cup filled to the brim with water. Get them lined up, each with one hand on the shoulder of the teammate in front, and the other hand trying not to spill the water in the cup.

Walking with Grace. Now the whole blindfolded team will walk as one body, following your leader's voice as you guide them around an area. Take them through some obstacles. Urge them to find a way to move along gracefully. How do they do it? How much water remains in everyone's cups? Perhaps, if you repeat the activity, they will spill less.

Change the Leader. Every few minutes, switch the head of the line by sending the leader, blindfolded again, to the back and moving the next person up to lead. Ideally, everyone should get to be at the head of the caterpillar.

Debrief. At the end, take off the blindfolds and talk about how many parts make up a whole. Where does "leadership" actually come from? How do mental logic and physical instinct work together? What does blindness activate? Why do people feel different in their comfort with such close touch? Who enjoyed it? Who felt frustrated? Why?

Inside the Mind of the Mentor

I admit it is serious fun to walk quietly alongside the Caterpillars and observe how they navigate the uneven terrain with their many feet—and each other's personalities. Blindfold Caterpillar is designed to reveal group dynamics. You're likely to notice a few human types, such as:

+ Those who can't resist being in charge, even from the back of the line

+ Those who freeze when put in the leadership position

+ Those with natural grace and rhythm

+ Those with a natural tendency to stumble all over

+ Those great at encouraging others

+ Those who are forgetful or neglectful of the ones ahead and behind them

+ Those who want to "do it right"

+ Those who "go with the flow"

+ Those uncomfortable with the touching required to stay together

+ Those who enjoy the closeness involved

Take mental notes as you watch your group evolve itself into a moving body. These will give you foresight when it comes time for meaningful group unity.

Alternatives and Extensions

Variations. This is a simple activity, an ice breaker, and it can be used with any number of variations like:

+ Let the group decide when to change the head and who to put up front.
+ Let them see but not talk.
+ Take away the water cup. What use do people make of a free hand?
+ On long courses, offer your Caterpillar mini-challenges and reward them with water refills.

Other Teamwork Challenges. People often encounter similar group challenges in their lives, so while they're at camp, in scouts, doing ropes courses, and even at some schools, these personal challenges can be safely recognized.

Study Social Groups in the Animal World. Tell some stories, watch some films, check out books, or experientially look into social animal groups such as bees and colonizing ants. Learn together how to tend a beehive, or an ant colony and study them over time. What can they teach about community?

Group Secret Spot

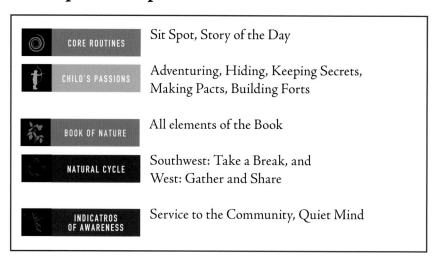

CORE ROUTINES	Sit Spot, Story of the Day
CHILD'S PASSIONS	Adventuring, Hiding, Keeping Secrets, Making Pacts, Building Forts
BOOK OF NATURE	All elements of the Book
NATURAL CYCLE	Southwest: Take a Break, and West: Gather and Share
INDICATROS OF AWARENESS	Service to the Community, Quiet Mind

Primer

Have any of you ever had a secret base? How about a tree house or tree fort? Our job will be to go out and find one for our group. It will be a special place for all of us to go and spend time. We can keep it secret from other groups, and we can even come up with a secret code name for our base. Let's go find one far away from everybody else.

How-To

Find a Group Secret Spot. This activity is very straightforward and self explanatory. It works with participants of all ages, especially if you have sub-groups of a larger group, which will require separate meeting places for each. Put simply, you need to find a place that your entire group of participants likes and considers their secret group Sit Spot. Throughout the program, this will be a special place for just your group. Having a regular place far out in the natural world where your group goes for a break will work wonders for building unity and connection to place.

Criteria. Pick a place off the beaten path. This minimizes human distur-bance and also creates a sense of secrecy, which lends a sense of group bond-ing, just as with tree houses or "clubhouses." Old tree stumps work great, as do rock formations or overhangs. It's really important to find a safe place with no hazards such as yellow jackets, venomous snakes, or large mammals already using your Group Secret Spot.

Come to Consensus. The act of finding a place that everybody can agree on can be quite daunting. If the Spot really will be the group's base for a long program, then it will matter to everyone that they pick a good place. This provides an excellent opportunity for your group to work on consensus, dis-cussion, and democracy. Consensus means that your group makes no deci-sion until everyone agrees; a simple democratic majority isn't enough. What happens if five participants really like one place but four really don't? Do you find a new place or can you find a way to compromise?

Name the Landscape. Add a further element of imagination and fun by having the group come to consensus on the name for their new place. Of course, you won't call it "Group Secret Spot." "Secret Base," "Fort," "Hiding Spot," or perhaps "Secret Huckleberry Swamp Fort" would all work as better names. Encourage creativity, silliness, and imagination and realize this consensus requires imagination and identity. Who takes this seriously and who allows others to guide them? Again, watch the group dynamic. The hidden goal in this activity: people realize that the process of coming to agreement is as important as deciding on a name.

Inside the Mind of the Mentor

While searching for a base, keep a keen eye on everyone. Who is really into the activity? Who feels bored, just going along? Does anybody think to watch out for dangers when finding a spot?

Coming to unanimous agreement about what makes a perfect Secret Spot or name will press the group to form a group identity. With use, this Secret Spot has the potential to bond the group as they develop it into a comfortable, safe, private home with its own special language.

Alternatives and Extensions

Extensions for this activity seem almost endless. We give you just a few:

- Map your Group Secret Spot.
- Build a group fire circle and group shelter at your Spot; create a "survival village" where natural tools and primitive crafts are abundant in various stages of completion.
- Have everyone find their own Sit Spots near the Group Spot.
- Do a Wildlife Survey of the area around your spot.
- Play Meet-a-Tree, Tree Tag, Eagle Eye, or other games at your Spot.

The list goes wherever you take it ...

Wildlife Survey

◎	**CORE ROUTINES**	Questioning and Tracking, Wandering, Mapping, Exploring Field Guides, Listening for Bird Language, Story of the Day
	CHILD'S PASSIONS	Seeing Animals, Discovering, Running Errands, Exploring
	BOOK OF NATURE	Ecological Indicators and everything else
	NATURAL CYCLE	South: Focus, West: Gather and Share
	INDICATROS OF AWARENESS	Inquisitive Focus, Service to the Community, Caring and Tending, Awe and Reverence

Primer

All right everyone, we've been given a mission. We have a new job to survey this park (lake, forest, mountain, desert, wetland, or whatever you've got) top to bottom and find out what lives here. We need to find as many different kinds of wildlife, plants, and trees as we can. All of them need to be positively identified by track, sign, or sighting and listed with their common and Latin names. We have exactly X number of hours so grab whatever you think we'll need and let's go.

How-To

Survey Team. Doing a bio-blitz style Wildlife Survey can do wonders for bringing groups together and for tying together all the different pieces of Coyote's Guide. One of the best ways to do a Wildlife Survey of your area is by running a big competition or race between two or more small groups. Depending on your people and place, you can make up a scenario for who gave you this "mission," but for the competition, see which group can positively identify and make a Master List of the greatest number of species in your place in the same amount of time. Motivation becomes one of the keys to making this activity a success. Competition in a time limit creates one form of motivation, but since everyone wins from playing along, some people prefer win-win scenarios—perhaps everyone gets ice cream, no matter what their survey results.

Compose Groups. Our species list from The Book of Nature offers eight divisions of species. Assign individuals within a group, or groups, to find examples of all of them.

For example, one participant will look for Hazards, one will look for Catchable amphibians and reptiles. Mammals, Edible and Medicinal Plants, Trees, Birds, Heritage Species, and Ecological Indicators will each have one person assigned. This way each team has a complete group of wildlife surveyors and each participant has their own task. Of course, depending on your numbers, you can also have multiple searchers for one species, or you can drop a few of the species.

Supply Field Guides. Acquire enough field guides so everyone surveying has good access to them. Make sure participants get their noses into field guides—this essential part makes this activity a success.

Go Find. Send at least two groups out to find as many examples of all the species as they can in a time limit. They should actually observe the species, find their tracks and sign or hear their calls or song. They can feel positive about their identifications, and double check them in field guides. When they have confirmed their finds, have each group get together and make a Master List of all the species they have discovered.

Report and Count. After the allotted time, the groups present their Master Lists to each other, sort of a variation of the Story of the Day, and see who found the greatest number. At the end, reflect with the participants on the sheer number of animals, plants and trees they discovered. Pause here, give thanks for all the many life forms that share this place with them.

Inside the Mind of the Mentor

This is quite similar to the Tracking Expedition activity (in the Tracking Activities section), but with a different focus. The focus this time develops community and interrelationships. This version also creates a broad, overall awareness of a place rather than a careful, focused, species-specific search. Although very similar, we present them both here to emphasize that you can undertake similar activities with very different underlying intentions.

Nearly every activity in this book could be shaded to emphasize any one of the eight approaches to nature education laid out in the Book of Nature. It's up to you and your intentions for what energy or results an activity will yield. Once you have a strong "vocabulary" of all the activities, you can improvise, and shade the same games with very different feelings and moods.

During the course of Wildlife Survey, people will be awed by how many different species live in the area. They will develop a much deeper knowledge of their environment. Inevitably, many questions will arise about the relationships between this great multitude of plants and creatures, all living in the same place.

Encourage this questioning and pull out relationships in a manner that gets the different groups intermingling and talking, asking questions about what others found, creating strong, new interrelationships in the group. "You mean the deer ate all of the foliage on the plants, so you couldn't see any leaves? Gosh, I wonder if we missed a lot of that plant we were looking for just because we couldn't see the leaves?" Or, "That's where you found the most earthworms? Funny, that's where we also found all those Robin tracks and scat-piles."

Be prepared for some people to feel frustrated or bored and lose focus during part of the time you do this activity. That might be a time to change roles in your group so the participant who looked for mammal tracks now looks for trees. Or, take a break and play a game. Of course, towards the end of the game, you might just remind them that the other groups probably stopped to play a game of Eagle Eye or Firekeeper and they all need your group to do their job.

Alternative and Extensions

This activity goes really well with the next activity: Exploration Team. Combining the two can give you days of activity for your groups or teams.

Instead of looking for many different species all at once, change the focus and instead just look for as many mammals as you can find, or as many edible plants, or as many birds. This can be done with any of the Book of Nature groups.

Combine this activity with Mapping and have the participants place where they found each species on a group map of the area.

In the classroom, have participants do a survey like this using field guide resources for a different bio-region than their own. Then compare and contrast with local species.

For information about the Bio-Blitz concept—mustering lots of people to do a cross-species ecological count in a short time—and for support in running a Bio-Blitz in your area, contact Karen Dvornich with the University of Washington NatureMapping Program at http://depts.washington.edu/natmap/

Exploration Team

CORE ROUTINES	Mapping, Wandering, Questioning and Tracking, Listening for Bird Language, Story of the Day, Journaling
CHILD'S PASSIONS	Adventuring, Discovering, Exploring, Telling Stories
BOOK OF NATURE	Ecological Indicators, and everything else
NATURAL CYCLE	Southwest Wander, West: Gather and Share
INDICATROS OF AWARENESS	Inquisitive Focus, Service to the Community, and Caring and Tending

Primer

All right everyone, we've been given another mission. We're going to form an Exploration Team to thoroughly explore and map this area. Specifically, we need you to create a good map for those who assigned us this mission. At the end of the day, we have to share what we found with the other groups, with our invited guests, and Elders.

In order for this to work out, each person in our group will have a job so that we make a good exploration team. Raise your hand for a job that captures your interest.

How-To

Exploring. This activity, like the previous one, has the potential for an all-day or even multi-day event. The above primer is a customizable scenario. Inspire

your Exploration Team to simply wander and explore an area for an extended period of time. Choose a focus that fits your land, your people, and your situation. It could be checking for dangers and hazards to young children or Elders, finding food resources, locating campsites or good hiding places, mapping out and creating new trail systems, or envisioning sites for a retreat center. You might even pretend you have landed on a new planet. The emphasis, however, fits wandering as a team with a fun sense of wonder and connection rather than specifically finding different species. Instead of motivating with competition, try to build up excitement for adventure and discovery.

Working as a Team. Each team member will volunteer to play a role on the Exploration Team, so emphasize the different roles they need to fill before you can begin. You might base roles on historical expeditions, such as Lewis and Clark or the settlers who came to your valley. It's up to you to define roles best suited to your own situation. Also consider roles corresponding with qualities of the Natural Cycle:

- East: Someone looks out for Hazards.
- East: Someone makes sure the group remains in constant communication even when dispersed.
- Southeast: Someone makes sure the group is Fox-Walking.
- South: Someone records the assigned findings.
- South: Someone draws the Map.
- Southwest: Someone makes sure that everyone drinks water and takes care of themselves.
- Southwest: Someone navigates with map and compass, making sure the group doesn't get lost.
- West: Someone prepares to speak for the group at the end Story of the Day.
- West: Someone keeps an eye on whether everyone engages as a community.
- Northwest: Someone makes sure the group develops a Songline of its travels.
- North: Someone makes sure the group stays on task and gathers nuggets of wisdom as assigned.

- Northeast: Someone makes sure the group pays attention to Bird Language and creates a ceremonial beginning and end to the day.

Most of these examples come from our mentoring approach. Roles can be assigned by using the Natural Cycle, or the Book of Nature, or anything that you like. Create a team where everyone is vigilantly conscious of their contributions to the welfare of the group as a whole.

Story of the Day. After you have completed the exploration phase of the activity, come together for a celebration, to which invited guests and community Elders have been invited. Welcome your returning scout groups, and give them time to shows their findings, their maps, and to report their Story of the Day.

Inside the Mind of the Mentor

This will really be a great activity for you to push the edges of the people you mentor. Rather than letting them choose roles for themselves, you can assign roles. This gives you an opportunity to test each person's ability to adapt to and stretch an area of personal discomfort. Perhaps the group's noisy person will be in charge of making sure your group moves quietly. Or, maybe you put someone who is reluctant to serve in a leadership role in charge of making sure everyone remembers their role. However, be careful of pushing participants' edges too far. Pick and choose appropriately.

This activity also tests everyone's focus. How focused can your group stay? How often do you have to remind them of their roles? What motivators can you think of to keep them in their roles? Thinking of these questions ahead of time can help keep the experience valuable for everyone.

Finally, this experience actually peaks with the "performance" at the end. Let each team present their Story of the Day in front of invited guests and Elders. Feel free to help facilitate this process, but let the participants put their story together in their own way. If they struggle and don't put on much of a performance, it can be a powerful learning experience.

Alternatives and Extensions

Turn this activity into a Scout Mission where your Exploration Team shouldn't be seen or heard by other groups, but must really scope out a place and gather as much info as possible.

Plan on meeting up with other exploration teams out on the trails during the day and swap stories.

Make this an overnight expedition with Exploration Teams going out multiple times.

Capture the Flag

◎	**CORE ROUTINES**	Animal Forms, Expanding Our Senses
	CHILD'S PASSIONS	Playing Games, Running, Jumping, and Chasing
	BOOK OF NATURE	NA
	NATURAL CYCLE	East: Inspire, Southwest: Take a Break, and West: Gather and Share
	INDICATROS OF AWARENESS	Service to the Community, Aliveness and Agility, Quiet Mind

Primer

Let's Play Capture the Flag! (Usually all that's needed...)

How-To

Capture the Flag, in one form or another, has grown to be a familiar and famous game loved worldwide by children of all ages. We have added twists to incorporate some of the Core Routines, build teamwork, and still let everyone have tons of fun.

Create the Playing Field. In the basic version, divide a large group into two teams. Each team has one side of a playing field for their territory. A neutral line divides the middle of the field, and if crossed, puts you in your opponent's territory. Each team also has a flag either hidden or visible (you choose) at the far edge of their territory.

The Game. When in your own team's territory, you are safe. If you get tagged on your opponent's territory, you must go to Jail at the back of your opponent's territory. The goal is to get into the opponents' territory and move their flag back to your side. If you accomplish this and don't get tagged, your team wins.

Jail: If you get captured and put in jail, you can be freed if a member of your own team makes it all the way to the opponents' jail and tags you. Then the two of you have "free walk-backs" to your own territory.

Inside the Mind of the Mentor

Keep it simple and make sure the participants have fun. This is an active game that can be great for the participants, particularly if they are in a high energy state. We use it often when instructors feel burned out or overwhelmed by a group. Be sure and watch for participants who try to get out of playing or who fake injuries. Work the game out so that everybody participates.

Alternatives and Extensions

Variations: Capture the Flag emphasizes speed and teamwork. Since some participants can feel a little left out if they are not good runners we've added a few twists to make this more of a Nature and Awareness game.

Play the game in a forested area. Players consider themselves automatically captured at the moment they get spotted on their opponents' side. This encourages silence, sneaking, and strategy.

Have the players use Animal Forms. Instead of just plain running—this adds a bit of Simon Says to the play and requires a Referee. Examples include: Stalking on all Fours like a Cougar, Running like a Coyote, or Bounding like a Deer. To really keep them on their toes, switch the Animal Forms several times in the middle of the game.

A version especially for groups of kids. Have the participants play as normal, but with lots of kids against fewer teachers or a group of parents. See if they can use superior numbers to make up for the speed and intelligence of the smaller number of adults. This really builds unity. And if they win—which they just might (darn those rascals are quick)—they will never forget the time they used teamwork to beat their teachers.

Have people pair-up and tie their wrists together with bandanas. Then blindfold one of the pair. Now, everyone has to work with their partner to play the game.

Multi-Day Adventure. We have seen yearlong programs culminate in a multi-day version of this that pushes all naturalist and stealth skills to the max (See Primer Story: *Scout Camp Blows My Mind*, under *Introducing Core Routines Activity: Mapping*). Find a large piece of land you can have all to yourself, create multiple teams, a common safe-base for all teams to come and eat or fulfill other needs. Use this as a task you build towards all year with skills of camping, survival, awareness, camouflage, mapping, etc. The larger adventure proves to be especially good for older teens and adults.

Ideal Ecological Vision

◎	CORE ROUTINES	Mind's Eye Imagining
🏹	CHILD'S PASSIONS	Imagining and Pretending
🌿	BOOK OF NATURE	Heritage Species, Ecological Indicators
〰	NATURAL CYCLE	Northwest: Reflect, North: Integrate
⚘	INDICATROS OF AWARENESS	Caring and Tending, Service to the Community, Awe and Reverence, Quiet Mind

Primer

Have you ever wondered what this area looked like completely covered with old-growth trees? How many salmon (or catfish or bass) really used to swim in these rivers? What was it like when whole herds of bison roamed the prairies? How bright were the stars before electricity lit up the night? How silent was the day before cars and airplanes?

If we could travel through time and see this place as it was a long time ago, what would it be like? How many years back do you want to go? 100? 1000?

Let's go for a walk and see …

How-To

Many of the activities in the Activity Guide section of this book are straightforward and can be done with a minimal amount of preparation. This is not one of those activities. It requires time, effort, and can be tricky to pull off. However, it can be extremely rewarding for the whole group, including the mentors.

Preparation: The first part of this activity consists of preparation and the preparation consists of research. You need to look into your bio-region's history and find out what it was like in pre-modern times. How plentiful were the game herds? What did people use for food and medicine? Exactly how big around were the old growth trees back then? What were the forests, rivers, deserts, and mountains really like in pre-modern times?

You can find the answers to these questions or you can engage your participants to find the answers by creating a whole unit on Indigenous Cultures and Native American History.

Here are some facts to inspire your research:

+ In old times, legend reports salmon runs with salmon so thick you could walk across streams and rivers on their backs.

+ The specific chemistry of nitrogen in salmon found its way from carcass to scavenger and finally into the trees of the forests for miles around the rivers.

+ Acorns from oak trees fell in such profusion in many areas of the country that acorn mush was the staple food for the fall and winter and enough acorns for winter sustenance could be gathered in a matter of days.

+ The term "two birds with one stone" comes from Native American descriptions of bird migrations, especially waterfowl and passenger pigeons. It was said, the numbers of birds flying over were so great you could throw a stone and kill one bird as the stone flew up and kill another as the stone fell down.

+ Anthropological studies reveal in some of the harshest climates most hunter-gatherer people spent only 15 to 20 hours a week gathering food and taking care of their survival needs. They used the rest of their time developing complex cultural and artistic achievements.

By researching your area, you should be able to find similar facts or stories about natives who resided in your bio-region. Once you and your participants have discovered these, take your new information out to the field.

Into the Field. When your group has researched enough, prepare them for the field component of this activity by letting them know your group will now explore their local area as if it were in pre-modern times. This requires a little bit of a serious tone, a quiet mind-set, and some serious imagination.

As you begin your walk, encourage the participants to really try to see with their Mind's Eye Imagination what the land around them looked like. Feel free to have them share with each other if they have an insight or discovery.

Here are some scenarios:

+ Find the biggest tree around (or an old-growth stump) and have the participants all explore it with their sense of touch. Then have them imagine a whole forest around them.

+ Ask participants to check out a local body of water or some moving water. Let them imagine what the aquatic wildlife was before. Also, have them imagine what it would be like to drink from any stream or river they came across without having to boil the water first.

+ Let everyone imagine that there are no stores at all to go and buy food, medicine, or clothes. They can only use what grows on the land around them. Then show them some local edible or medicinal plants and trees. Have them imagine being able to take care of all their needs in pre-modern times just from their local bio-region.

Make sure that the participants have fun with this activity by engaging their imaginations. Be open to what everyone has to say and realize they may already hold a variety of points of view on this subject.

Story of the Day. At the end of your time in the field or when you have returned home or to the classroom, have people share their reflections. You might have them draw what they imagined. Also, have them think about specific things they can do to help with restoration of their local bio-region. This could lead into an excellent next lesson on native plant restoration or reintroduction of endangered species or salmon ecology.

Inside the Mind of the Mentor

This activity gets participants feeling and understanding the impact humans have had on the landscape, especially in modern times. We don't want them to come away overly disheartened, complaining, and blaming others over the way modern humans treat the world around them. Instead, we want to create hope and motivation to actively protect and restore the bio-region where they live. We want them to become active members in their community to create the change they want to see. It can help to have everyone make lists of ways they can help with on-going ecological restoration or preservation in their area, or contribute to education that help shift peoples' awareness and perspectives on nature.

Alternatives and Extensions

Combine this activity with a lesson on the Indigenous People of the area in which you live. Better yet, if the native people still inhabit the area, invite in a willing wisdom-holder to share about their culture and the ancestral connection to the land.

Make this a world safari activity and have different people give reports on the "ecological ideal" of places around the world. Have participants emphasize places where the "ecological ideal" still exists.

Lead people on a "Storyteller's Mind" journey of what the land might look like in 10, 20, 50, or 100 years into the future. Emphasize the positive impacts that could happen if more humans discover a personal connection with nature and move toward living sustainably and taking positive political and environmental action.

Coyote in Context

EPILOGUE *Written by Jon Young*

Weaving The Web

Has someone said this to you lately?

"How do I thank you enough for saving my life?"

Or ... "How do I thank you for saving my child's life?"

Over the past twenty-five years, I have heard this a lot—so have many of my friends who are skilled Coyote Mentors. Before undertaking this journey, take to heart the secret they all know—since the dawn of human existence, Coyote Mentoring has always danced to the music emanating from a vibrant village culture.

In 1983, I began to work with Coyote Mentoring in an intentional way. Since then, I have had the opportunity to work with children in many settings. I was a park naturalist bringing nature into classrooms, and bringing classes into nature. I was able to work with live animals in the classroom, to explore artifacts from the old native cultures in the lands where I worked, to bring young people out on canoeing adventures in beautiful settings, and to lead exploratory journeys into the landscape.

COYOTE MENTOR
A person practicing the art and science of Coyote Mentoring.

COYOTE MENTORING
Conscious facilitation of the expansion of people's awareness through all major and minor senses into deeper relationships with the world around and within them for all aspects of their environment—this includes family, community, and nature. Like coyote, the process of Coyote Mentoring works from the edge and beyond the edge of perception.

CULTURAL MENTORING
This refers to the effects on people's learning by cultural elements. Whereas mentoring can be a conscious choice by an individual facilitating another's learning journey, Cultural Mentoring often facilitates learning as a side effect or unintended consequence of experiences gained while exposed to the surface area of a cultural element. Cultural Mentoring is also referred to as "the invisible school."

This was not always a setting suitable or respectful of Coyote Mentoring—though I always tried, the settings were not always suitable for Coyote Mentoring. Having been mentored my entire life on the coyote path; conventional educational situations did not work well for me. My instincts as a Coyote Mentor are like artifacts, tracks left on my soul from my experience in a series of traditional cultures that supported my journey of nature connection. Over the years, I have come to see that nature connection is always strongest where the culture supports Coyote Mentoring consciously or, more often, unconsciously.

Soon after founding my first Coyote Mentoring experiment with young people, I was joined by an amazing elder named Ingwe, who had grown up among the Akamba tribe of East Africa. As a child, he was immersed in an authentic experience with two key elements working in powerful balance: Coyote Mentoring and the regenerative mentoring culture of the native tradition. Ingwe quickly wove strands of his culture around my little network of sprouting nature kids. He began to call them his grandchildren and identified himself as the Grandfather. He called me their older brother; parents who spent time with us, he called their aunts and uncles. He wove in the magic of the storyteller. He crafted an initiation journey, rites of passage, and important moments of honoring and village celebration. All of this was done in the context of a modern, suburban setting. Our backdrop was homes, back yards, fire circles on farm lands, and parks for wandering and camping.

Something remarkable began to emerge that I had not noticed before. As the effect of nature connection, Coyote Mentoring, and the seeds of a healthier culture formed, children and adults both began to thrive in this new environment. They developed inner quietness, a calm presence, a lust for adventure, deep curiosity and that twinkle in the eye that says so much. There was much laughter, there was hope, there were tears of joy and sorrow—and all these feelings were freely expressed. There was health, humor, vitality and love. There were stories of adventures, of addictions dropped, of unhealthy habits willingly left behind, of courage to overcome obstacles, restored hope, joy and love—and in so many, many stories the expressed conviction of lives, marriages, and families saved.

It then became clear to me: without the cultural pieces that Ingwe invisibly wove together, the power of Coyote Mentoring diminished. Outside the context of the woven culture, I often felt I was walking through mud. Here I saw many sad faces, many gray and sullen complexions. They looked tired and worn. I would bring out a wild corn snake, and see repulsion in their eyes, and only a few faces showing mild interest. I couldn't engage them, and I wondered if I was even speaking their language. Gradually it became clear to me that although Coyote Mentoring holds great power, culture deeply impacts any learning journey.

Culture is inevitable. It happens, one way or another. It is continuously woven around our hearts and minds, culture is like a vast invisible web that shapes our dreams, our ambitions, and ultimately our lives. It is the vessel in which our thoughts, perceptions, and emotions are formed through the subtle, recurrent influences of our everyday experience.

Cultures grow out of our relationship with the land and all its beings, including humans. It is how we grow our food and build our houses. It is our corporate slogans. It is the stories we tell about our personal journeys through the landscape of our lives. Because each one of us decides how to nurture those relationships, and how we wish to conduct our journey, we are all participating in the daily creation of culture—together we weave through each other's lives and shape the world in which we live.

At some point in history, western culture's journey radically altered man's relationship to nature and to himself. With time, nature became the resource on which mighty nations were built through the invention of corporations, the development of science and the application of increasingly powerful technologies. After centuries of warfare, our nation states eventually found ways to further their mutual interests through global treaties and organizations. The unique culture that has emerged out of this historical period is the culture in which children around the world are now coming of age, a

WHY REGENERATIVE?
We use the word "regenerative" frequently in our work as Cultural Mentors. It is a core mission for the positive aspects of our work to be regenerative—which means to be 'marked by regeneration' or 'tending to regenerate.' In turn, regenerating is, according to definition 'to give fresh life or vigor to.' Regeneration is most definitely a core aspect of our vision, mission, values, and goals as Coyote Mentors.

Culture consciously or unconsciously informs education, shapes learning experience, brain patterning, and therefore beliefs, values, and behaviors. Many aspects of culture are 'regenerative' for the positive—or, for the negative. People tend to subconsciously model many aspects of their culture. Violence, for instance, can beget violence in the next generation unless the cycle is facilitated in a new direction.

Fundamentally, culture influences the level to which people connect to nature. Nature connection is the core experience that result in restoring or renewing, thus regenerating one's natural living instincts. Regenerative culture is a culture that regenerates itself.

REGENERATIVE LIVING, PERMACULTURE DESIGN & COYOTE MENTORING

As a Coyote Mentor, it is important to anticipate shifts in people's values. When people experience a concentrated amount of Coyote Mentoring, they will reach a point of nature connection where their awareness grows to include the impact of their personal lives on all others. A values-shift occurs, and people with fresh, new awareness begin to seek strategies of living that match their ethics. One such match is that of Permaculture design where "The only ethical decision is to take responsibility for our own existence and that of our children" (Mollison, 1990). Working with a core set of design principles, individuals can design environments that reduce negative impact or even enhance ecosystems. Regenerative living means to work integrally with the natural world, thus improving the ability for the land, the water, the air, the wildlife, the food systems, the economy, and the culture to support life in a positive way.

world described as "the global village."

Richard Louv points out in his introduction to *Coyote's Guide* that many children today are truly suffering from nature separation. Many species supporting this global village are suffering too, as are the environments that support them. There is a growing body of evidence that suggests the culture we are all creating day by day is increasingly incapable of satisfying the spiritual needs and desires of our children; the environment we shape is increasingly unable to tend to their physical and emotional needs. We can see it in their faces. We can see it in the way they carry themselves. We notice it in the health of their bodies. We may hear it when we listen to their concerns and fears.

As a Coyote Mentor you now have the power to help our children heal by guiding them to healthier, lasting relationships with their natural surroundings. Through this deepening connection to place, in time, a child will develop a profound sense of empathy for all the beings in the neighborhood. If guided in the right way, a strong desire will eventually arise in the child to tend to the needs of nature. As the child's relationship to the land changes, this becomes the seed of a new culture beginning to form.

Coyote Mentoring is to the child what water is to the seed. To thrive, the young sprout also requires the support of a nurturing environment, good soil, the right combination of elements. This is culture. Just as we have a choice to take the dried, cracked earth and treat it with mulch, water, fertilization and time, we can chose to take the dried, cracked elements of our culture and influence them with what we call cultural mentoring.

If you use coyote mentoring tools in the absence of a healthy culture, it is the equivalent of watering a seed and dropping the sprout on pavement. You might get lucky. The sprout might blow on a breeze onto a soil capable of sustaining it a while. But ask any farmer, and they'll tell you it's better to prepare the soil, and anticipate the needs of the growing seedling as it matures to a productive part of the ecosystem.

Cultural Mentoring does just that. A circle of mentors

forms a cultural basket to hold all the necessary elements to nurture the village. Together they engender healthy children through Coyote Mentoring, and they create a healthy, vibrant culture that repeats for generations, gaining power over time, revitalizing both humans and their ecosystems. This is a Regenerative Mentoring Village.

In this regenerative village, a team of diverse mentors analyze the equally diverse needs of those they're mentoring. They understand that a child will have one set of needs, whereas the parents have another. And they take into account the many elements that make up a regenerative mentoring village. Every village contains dynamic variables, including economics, ethnicity, environment, history, geography, and more. This process of intentionally creating an evolving and earth-based culture is called Regenerative Community Design.

We encourage all of you who undertake the Coyote Mentoring journey to deepen your understanding of the culture that surrounds you and your children. We encourage you to consider how you might shape that culture, so you cultivate not only the hearts and minds of our children, but the very soil in which they grow. Only through this comprehensive undertaking, can we bring our children into their own full power.

When we apply the cultural mentoring tools with all eight aspects of this Coyote's Guide, then we have what I call: "Eight Shields Dancing"—a role for all ages, all skills, all people.

The stories from our own communities speak for themselves. After a recent winter storm passed one of these communities, I received a story from Alan, a mentor-in-training enrolled in one of our holistic cultural and Coyote Mentoring programs. His story illustrates what I'm getting at, and with his permission I share it here:

The barn was crammed with people who had come from all around the coastal hills of California. There were people of all ages, from all walks of life. I saw entire families, groups of friends, people arriving alone or in the company of newcomers. They had come from all directions to gather here—from isolated homes in the surrounding grasslands, from the diversity of San Francisco, from the expanding core of Silicon Valley, and from wild streets of Santa Cruz.

REGENERATIVE COMMUNITY DESIGN
An important partner of Coyote Mentoring, the process of Regenerative Community Design recognizes the impact of both Coyote and Cultural Mentoring and intentionally designs community interaction and cultural elements to provide surface area in a patterned and predictable way. This results in the creation of a Regenerative Mentoring Village. The Eight Shields Cultural Mentoring system provides the engineering blueprint for this process.

REGENERATIVE MENTORING VILLAGE
This is a designed and facilitated context for Coyote Mentoring to occur. Like a village, there are needs, set roles, processes, commitments, spaces, and social calendars. Not needing a specific locus or centralized property, a Regenerative Mentoring Village is spread out over a region and its scope and overall size is usually determined by relatively easy access due to local transportation influences.

Eight Shields Dancing

A community development goal
for the organic evolution of a
Regenerative Mentoring Village
based on the Eight Shields
Cultural Mentoring blue-print—a
checklist and inventory for things
to be considered in developing a
supportive community around
Coyote and Cultural Mentoring.
Eight Shields Dancing can also
be a short-to-mid-range program
goal where all systems within
Coyote's Guide—for all ages
and experience or interest—may
run at roughly the same time, in
roughly the same place.

**Eight Shields
Cultural Mentoring**

A set of cultural facilitation
principles and concepts
arranged in a pattern based on
eight categories or "shields."
Coyote's Guide takes these eight
shields into consideration in
the design of the book and its
Coyote Mentoring elements.
This blueprint is a checklist
and inventory for things to
be considered in developing a
supportive community around
Coyote and Cultural Mentoring.

News of this month's community dance had spread through emails and list servers and from there through word of mouth that moved like a mist through the rolling prairies, through the fir woodlands, along cool creek beds lined with redwood forests and on to the dusty streets of the big cities. People hadn't come this far to be chilled by the damp air wafting through the floorboards. They didn't come to admire the rows of corn decorating the rafters. And if they just wanted a good night out, they could have chosen from a dozen other places that weren't located right on the coast highway, with the erratic roar of traffic rattling through the barn walls.

Yet these people keep coming back to this place every month. Where else can I walk into a room where everyone is smiling so much their faces hurt. Every set of eyes you make contact with are welcoming and bright. There are children running around everywhere. Kids are playing tag in a free-range subculture. The parents don't care where their children are, because they know they are safe, even in such close proximity to the highway. People are in their power here. They move with confidence and certainty. Their bodies are happy. An energy is moving, looking for release. The musicians over on the west side of the barn are churning out classic American fiddle tunes. Adults with flushed faces thread through the raised arms of the smallest of the children. The music is barely audible through the pounding of hundreds of feet stomping across the barn floor, the caller laughs with the sound system inadequate to its task.

Earlier that afternoon, I had been out tracking deer with a group of people from my learning group. Our task was to draw the stories of the deer from the land in any way we could, and to remember pictures and feelings, images, tracks and sign and smells that would touch the oldest part of our brains. We had all wandered off in different directions. Some trotted along the road, some grazed next to the marsh, and others relaxed in a deer bed for a nap in the sun. I was a doe gently moving along the meandering deer run, eyes softly focused, relaxed and alert. I sensed the breeze, the scent of parched grass and a need to find comfort in the shade of the willow thicket.

A couple of hours later the twelve of us all met in a meadow, forming a circle in this sheltered bowl, laying in the grass and reliving our day. We had all sensed that the robins had been singing when the deer had come through, leaving fresh tracks throughout the area. There had been not a hint of predator on the wind, no humans around to disturb them. Life had been good for the deer on the day they made their trails. This was our artistic impression of the day, revealed to us through consensus, a certainty that we all knew to be true through experience, using our body as our sensors. There was no logic to our impressions, and we took comfort in the full acceptance of what was.

At some point a light went off in my head. Jon had told us he would draw the story of the day out of us in a way we hadn't experienced before. He now struck a chord on his guitar and we all raised our hand when the chord matched our feeling. We whistled. We laughed and joked. We hummed little phrases of music and gradually they melded into a dance tune.

Back in the barn, the musicians from the meadow had been training the rest of the barn dance band, like messengers bringing the story of the day to the fire and dancing to honor the deer and their gift to the people. The song hit the groove running. We knew in our body that we were playing it right. The dancers were swept up. The caller fell into a trance of sorts and forgot to end the dance. He turned to us and asked, "How would you feel about playing this a little longer?" We nodded eagerly. The caller jumped out on the dance floor and led the dancers into a stomping line dance out of the barn into the glow of the full moon. We danced out the back and returned through the side, everyone's faces were glowing. We ended the dance tightly forty-five minutes after the first note, with four stopping strokes of the fiddle bow. All of us cheered. We knew that the deer nation had been honored as powerfully as we could have hoped for.

Driving home late at night, we barely missed a deer that leapt in front of our car. The driver of another car said that they kept having a powerful feeling he would see a deer on the way home. We all had a feeling something was going on with the deer, as if these animals were called to our presence by our song. In the morning the local farmer sent word he had a deer that needed to be taken. Everyone was amazed at the synchronicities. We all knew what needed to be done.

It took six of us all day working with stone knives to transform that deer into a hide ready to tan, into sinew ready for bowstring and

When a community gathers to celebrate a sacred passage from childhood to adulthood, that young adult's focus changes to accept and explore maturity. Only a clean separation with childhood will cause a young woman or man to fully embrace their adulthood. As a society, we have fallen short of our developmental potential. Before the paradigm will shift, young people standing on the edge of adulthood must be given the opportunity to reach for the promise of their genetic heritage. That promise is unlocked with the Rites of Passage ceremony where parents release their child and the community welcomes a new member into adulthood.

Gail Burkett, "An Imperative"
Author of *Gifts From the Elders: Girl's Path to Womanhood*

Throughout history, a young man also learns at a deep emotional level his inseparable relationship with nature as well as his responsibility to fiercely protect it. This is precisely what hunting does for young men. If the future of hunting is in doubt, so is the future of the earth and its creatures, which is why we must recover hunting as a universal rite of passage.

Randall L. Eaton,
From Boys to Men of Heart

cordage, into meat for the freezer and a rack of smoking jerky. It took us three days to brain-tan the skin into velvety nap smelling of smoke and earth. Several months later, we received a message that some Apache women down in Texas needed naturally tanned hides for a coming of age ceremony for a young Apache woman there. Might we donate our hide?

It didn't take much for us to say yes. It was a natural opportunity for reciprocity. The lineage of tracking and awareness skills we had been learning for the last year had been passed to us from Jon Young, passed to Jon from Tom Brown, Jr., and passed to Tom by Grandfather, an Apache scout. Something had come full circle and the gift was received with gratitude for the richness of the story that it held."

My friend Alan shared this story of a few encounters in his journey through a Coyote Mentoring program for adults. He may not have realized the extent to which the collaborators of our coastal hillside region had gone to weave a cultural basket that stirred everyone's heart in a dance that went far beyond the barn, deep into the land. This is how it feels to be a part of a thriving village environment where everybody is a Coyote Mentor, and where there is a cultural fabric in place. This is the invisible school, hidden in plain view. This school is an intentional culture that can be facilitated by cultural mentors. In the past decades, we have wrapped a bundle containing many of the maps and the tools used by indigenous people to generate a healthy culture that is ideally suited for Coyote Mentoring and healthy, happy children.

We do this because we believe in the urgent necessity of embracing everything we've learned up to this moment. Together we can form a vision of a diverse, abundant, and lasting web of cultures where many generations can thrive and grow to their greatest potential. Here coyote can again work the edges of the fields and meadows of our awareness. And the soil, once hard-pan and cracked, will become a soft, rich loam so coyote can leave a trail where our children may freely follow.

Your journey as a mentor to
facilitate nature connection in
children and adults alike is just
beginning. As your powers grow,
you will begin to discover a need
to foster a village culture that
holds, protects, and integrates
the accumulated understanding
of what it means to be a human in
deep connection with nature.

Cultural mentoring forms a bridge
so we can live fully in the modern
experience while dancing to the
land's ancient heart beat that lies
within each of us. The work of
the cultural mentor in creating
Regenerative Mentoring Villages
is the subject of our next book.
You can follow progress on that
work, and other developments
in cultural mentoring, at http://
www.8shields.org.

SUGGESTED READING

Guides to Nature Education

Acorn Naturalist Resources for the Trail and Classroom. Tustin, CA: Acorn Naturalists. (www.acornnaturalists.com)

Berry, Thomas. The Dream of the Earth. San Francisco, CA: Sierra Club Books, 1988.

Boal, Augusto. Games for Actors and Non-Actors. London, England: Routledge, 1992.

Bringing the World Alive: A Bibliography of Nature Stories for Children. Great Barrington, MA: The Orion Society.

Burkett, Gail. Gifts from the Elders, Girls' Path to Womanhood. NY: Universe, Inc. 2004.

Caduto, Michael J. and Joseph Bruchac. Keepers of the Animals: Native American Stories and Environmental Activities for Children. Golden, CO: Fulcrum Publishing, 1991; Keepers of the Night, Native American Stories and Nocturnal Activities for Children, 1994.

Cohen, M. J. Reconnecting with Nature: Finding wellness through restoring your bond with the Earth. Lakeville, MN: 2007; Connecting with Nature: Creating Moments That Let Earth Teach, A Field Guide. Eugene, OR: World Peace University, 1989. (www.ecopsych.com)

Cornell, Joseph Bharat. Sharing Nature with Children, 20th Anniversary Edition; Sharing Nature with Children, Volume 2. Nevada City, CA: Dawn Publications. (www.sharingnature.com)

Gallagher, John. Wildcraft! An Herbal Adventure Game. Board Game. Carnation, WA: www.LearningHerbs.com, 2006. (www.LearningHerbs.com)

Gardner, Howard. Intelligence Reframed: Multiple Intelligences for the 21st Century. New York, NY: Basic Books, 1999.

Kohl, Judith and Herbert. Illustrated by Roger Bayless. The View from the Oak. The Private Worlds of Other Creatures. San Francisco, CA: Sierra Club Books, 1977.

Lachecki, Marina, Joseph F. Passineau, Ann Linnea, and Paul Treuer. Teaching Kids to Love the Earth. Minneapolis, MN: University of Minnesota Press, 1991.

Liu, Eric. Guiding Lights – How to Mentor and Find Life's Purpose. New York, NY: Ballantine Books, 2006.

Louv, Richard, Last Child in the Woods: Saving Our Children from Nature-Deficit Disorder. Boston, MA: Houghton Mifflin, 1990. Also see Childhood's Future, and Web of Life, Weaving the Values that Sustain Us. (www.cnaturenet.org)

Moore, Robin C., and Herb H. Wong. Natural Learning, Creating Environments for Rediscovering Nature's Way of Teaching. Berkeley, CA: MIG Communications, 1997.

Nabham, Gary Paul, and Stephen Trimble. The Geography of Childhood, Why Children Need Wild Places. Boston, MA: Beacon Press, 1994.

Orion Society's publications. An environmental education organization working for a profound change in our ways of living in the natural world. Their publications expand our understanding of our relationship with nature. Nature Literacy Series includes, Stories in the Land: A Place-Based Environmental Education Anthology with an introduction by John Elder; Into the Field: A Guide to Locally Focused Teaching by Clare Walker Leslie, John Tallmadge, & Tom Wessels, with an introduction by Ann Zwinger; Place-Based Education: Connecting Classrooms & Communities, 2nd Edition with Index, by David Sobel. (www.orionsociety.org)

Orr, David W. Earth in Mind, On Education, Environment, and the Human Prospect. Washington DC: Island Press, 1994.

Project Wild: K-12 Curriculum and Activity Guide, A Wildlife-Focused Conservation Education Program for K-12 Educators and Their Students. A Program of the Council for Environmental Education. Outstanding classroom activities, available through training workshops. (www.ProjectWild.org)

Project Wet: Water Education for Teachers. (www.ProjectWet.org)

Repoley, Robert and Barbara English. Kamana for Kids, The Young Naturalist, Book One: Hazards, Book Two: Awareness. (www.WildernessAwareness.org)

Runyon, Linda. Shiloh, NJ: WildFoods, 1997. Wild Cards: Wild Food Identification Card Game. Educational Cards.

Sobel, David. Beyond Ecophobia: Reclaiming the Heart in Nature Education. Great Barrington, MA: The Orion Society, Nature Literacy Series, 1996. Also see Place-based Education: Connecting Classrooms & Communities, and Children's Special Places: Exploring the Role of Forts, Dens, and Bushhouses in Middle Childhood.

Spolin, Viola. Improvisation for the Theater. Evanston, Ill., Northwestern University Press, 1963.

Van Matre, Steve. Earth Education – A New Beginning. Greenville, WV: The Institute for Earth Education, 1990.

Walker Leslie, Clare and Charles E. Roth. Keeping a Nature Journal. North Adams, MA: Storey Publishing, 2000.

Young, Jon. Kamana Naturalist Training Program, Kamana One: Exploring Natural Mystery; Kamana Two: Path of the Naturalist; Kamana Three; Kamana Four. Shelton, WA: OWLink Media, 1996. (www.WildernessAwareness.org)

Field Guides

We encourage you to explore your own regional resources.

Bodie, Edmund D. Venomous Animals (Golden Guide). NY: Golden Press, 1991.

Brockman, Frank and Rebecca Merrilees. Trees of North America, a Golden Guide. NY: Golden Press, 2001.

Burroughs, William J., Crowder, Bob, Robertson, Ted, Vallier-Talbot, Ealeanor, Whitaker, Richard. The Nature Company Guides–Weather. Sydney, Australia: Weldon Own Pty Limited, 1996.

Ehrlich, Paul R., David Dobkin, and Darryl Wheye. The Birder's Handbook: A Field Guide to the Natural History of North American Birds: Including All Species That Regularly Breed North of Mexico. New York, NY: Simon & Schuster, 1988.

Elbroch, Mark. Animal Skulls: A Guide to North American Species. Mechanicsburg, PA: Stackpole Books, 2006; Bird Tracks and Sign: A Guide to North American Species, with Elanor Marks, 2001; Mammal Tracks and Sign: A Guide to North American Species, 2003.

Elias, Thomas and Peter Dykeman. Edible Wild Plants: A North American Field Guide. NY: Sterling Pub. Co., 1990.

Elpel, Thomas J. Botany in a Day: Herbal Field Guide to Plant Families. Pony, MT: HOPS Press, 2000.

Fichter, George S. Golden Guide to Fresh and Salt-Water Fishing. NY: Golden Press, 1987.

Forrest, Louise Richardson. Field Guide to Tracking Animals in Snow. Mechanicsburg, PA: Stackpole Books, 1988.

Foster, Steven and James A. Duke. A Field Guide to Medicinal Plants and Herbs (Peterson Guide). Boston, MA: Houghton Mifflin, 1999.

Foster, Steven, and Roger Caras. A Field Guide to Venomous Animals & Poisonous Plants, North America, North of Mexico (Peterson Guide). Boston: Houghton Mifflin, 1994.

Harrison, Hal and Roger Tory Peterson. Peterson Field Guide to Birds' Nests (Eastern and Western). Boston, MA: Houghton Mifflin, 1988.

Kays, Roland W. and Don E. Wilson. Mammals of North America. Princeton, NJ: Princeton University Press, 2002.

Kircher, John C., Roger Tory Peterson and Gordon Morrison. Peterson Field Guide to Eastern Forest. Boston, MA: Houghton Mifflin, 1988 and Peterson Filed Guide to the Ecology of Western Forest, 1993.

Lehr, Paul, et al. Golden Guide to Weather: Air Masses, Clouds, Rainfall, Storms, Weather Maps, Climate. NY: Golden Press, 1987.

Levi, Herbert and Lorna. Golden Guide to Spiders and Their Kin. NY: Golden Press, 1981.

Meuninck, Jim. Basic Essentials: Edible Wild Plants & Useful Herbs. Old Saybrook, CN: Globe Pequot Press, 1999.

Murie,Olaus J. and Mark Elbroch. A Field Guide to Animal Tracks. Boston, MA: Houghton Mifflin, 2005.

Newcomb, Lawrence. Newcomb's Wildflower Guide. Boston, MA: Little, Brown, 1977.

Peterson, Lee Allen and Roger Tory Peterson. A Field Guide to Edible Wild Plants of Eastern and Central North America. Boston, MA: Houghton Mifflin, 1978 and A Field Guide to Edible Wild Plants, 1977.

Petrides, George and Olivia. Peterson Field Guide to Western Trees. Boston, MA: Houghton Mifflin,1998.

Pojar, Jim and Andy MacKinnon. Plants of the Pacific Northwest Coast: Washington, Oregon, British Columbia & Alaska. Edmonton, AB, Canada: Lone Pine Pub., 2004.

Pyle, Robert Michael. National Audubon Society Field Guide to North American Butterflies. NY: Knopf, Distributed by Random House, 1995. The Thunder Tree. CO: Houghton Mifflin, 1993.

Reid, Fiona A. A Field Guide to Mammals of North America, North of Mexico. Boston, MA: Houghton Mifflin, 2006.

Reid, George K. and Herbert S. Zim. Golden Guide to Pond Life. NY: Golden Press, 1987.

Ridpath, Ian and Tirion, Will. The Monthly Sky Guide. Cambridge, England: University of Cambridge, 1996.

Sibley, David. Field Guide to the Bird of Eastern North America and Field Guide to the Bird of Western North America. London, U.K.: Christopher Helm, 2003; Sibley's Birding Basics. New York, NY: Alfred A Knpof, 2002.

Thayer, Samuel. The Forager's Harvest: A Guide to Identifying, Harvesting, and Preparing Edible Wild Plants. Ogema, WI: Forager's Harvest, 2006.

Tilford, Gregory. Edible and Medicinal Plants of the West. Missoula, MT, Mountain Press Publishing Co., 1997. From Earth to Herbalist: An Earth Conscious Guide to Medicinal Plants. Missoula, MT: Mountain Press Publishing Company, 1998.

Zim, Howard and Hobart Smith. Golden Guide to Reptiles and Amphibians. NY: Golden Press, 2001.

Zim, Howard and Lester Ingle. Golden Guide to Seashores. NY: Golden Press, 1991.

Zim, Howard and Robert Baker. Golden Guide to Stars. NY: Golden Press, 2001.

Guide Books

Anderson, M. Kat. Tending the Wild: Native American Knowledge and the Management of California's Natural Resources. Berkeley, CA: University of California Press, 2005.

Beard, Daniel Carter. The American Boy's Handy Book: What to Do and How to Do It. Mineola, N.Y.: Dover Publications, 2003; The Field and Forest Handy Book: New Ideas for Out of Doors. Boston, MA: D.R. Godine, 2000.

Beard, Linda and Beard, Adelia, B. The American Girl's Handy Book: Making the Most of Outdoor Fun. Lanham, MD: Derrydale Press, 2002.

Belitz, Charlene and Lundstrom, Meg. The Power of Flow: Practical ways to transform your life with meaningful coincidence. New York, NY: Three Rivers Press, 1998.

Brill, Steve. Identifying and Harvesting Edible and Medicinal Plants in Wild (and Not So Wild) Places. NY: HarperCollins, 1994.

Brown, Tom, Jr., with Judy Brown. Tom Brown's Field Guide to Nature and Survival for Children. Illus Heather Bolyn and Trip Becker. NY: Berkley Books, 1989. Also see Tom Brown's Field Guides to Wilderness Survival, Nature Observation and Tracking, City and Suburban Survival, Living with the Earth, Wild and Edible and Medicinal Plants, The Forgotten Wilderness.

Couplan Ph.D., Francois and James Duke. The Encyclopedia of Edible Plants of North America. New Canaan, CT: Keats Publishers, 1998.

Elbroch, Mark and Mike Pewtherer. Wilderness Survival. Camden, ME: Ragged Mountain Press/McGraw-Hill, 2006.

Elpel, Thomas J. Participating in Nature: Thomas Elpel's Field Guide to Primitive Living Skills. Pony, MT: HOPS Press, 2002.

Gatty, Harold. Finding Your Way without Map or Compass. Mineola, NY: Dover Publications, 1999.

Halfpenny, James. Field Guide to Mammal Tracking in North America. Boulder, CO: Johnson Books, 1986; Winter: An Ecological Handbook. Boulder, CO: Johnson Books, 1989.

Hamm, Jim. Bowyer's Bible. New York, NY: Lyons and Burford, 1993.

Heath, Robin. Sun, Moon, Earth.. Wales, Wooden Books, 1999.

Hemenway, Toby. Gaia's Garden: A Guide to Home-scale Permaculture. Los Alomos, NM: Chelsea Green, 2001.

Herrero, Stephen. Bear Attacks: Their Causes and Avoidance. New York, NY: Nick Lyons Books, 1985.

Hickman, Mae, Maxine Guy and Stephen Levine. Care of the Wild Feathered and Furred: Treating and Feeding Injured Birds and Animals. Santa Cruz, CA: Unity Press, 1978.

Hughes, K. Wind and Wolf, Linda Daughters of the Moon, Sisters of the Sun–Young Women &Mentors on the Transition to Womanhood. Gabriola Island, BC, New Society Publishers, 1997.

Jacke, Dave and Eric Toensmeier. Edible Forest Gardens. White River Junction, VT: Chelsea Green, 2005.

Kroodsma, Donald. The Singing Life of Birds: The Art and Science of Listening to Bird Song. Boston, MA: Houghton Mifflin, 2007.

Klein, Hilary Dole and Adrian M. Wenner. Tiny Game Hunting: Environmentally Healthy Ways to Trap and Kill the Pests in Your House and Garden. NY: Bantam Books, 1991.

Law, Ben. The Woodland Way: A Permaculture Approach to Sustainable Woodlot Management. Hampshire, U.K.: Hyden House, 2001.

Liebenberg, Louis. The Art of Tracking: The Origin of Science. Claremont, South Africa: David Phillip Publishers, 1990.

Martin, Alfred G. Hand Taming Wild Birds at the Feeder. Chambersburg, PA: Alan C. Hood & Company, 1991.

Mollison, Bill and Reny Mia Sley. Permaculture: A Designer's Manual. Tasmania, Australia: Tagari Publications, 1997.

Moore, Robert L. and Max J. Havlick Jr. The Archetype of Initiation. Philadelphia, PA: Xlibris Corporation, 2001.

Plotkin, Bill. Nature and the Human Soul, Cultivating Wholeness and Community in a Fragmented World. Novato, CA: New World Library, 2008.

Ray, Paul H., Ph.D., Anderson, Sherry R., Ph.D., The Cultural Creatives: How 50 Million People Are Changing the World, NY: Harmony Books, October, 2000.

Rezendes, Paul. Tracking & the Art of Seeing: How to Read Animal Tracks and Sign. New York, NY: Harper Collins, 1999.

Ridpath, Ian. Star Tales. New York, NY: Universe Books, 1988.

Schacter-Shalomi, Zalman and Miller, Ronald. From Aging to Saging: A Profound New Vision for Growing Older, New York, NY: Warner Books, Inc, 1995

Smith, C. Lavett. Fish Watching: An Outdoor Guide to Freshwater Fishes. Ithaca, NY: Comstock, 1994.

Stokes, Donald and Lillian. Stokes Field Guide to Animal Tracking and Behavior. USA: Little, Brown and Company, 1987. Stokes Guide to Observing Insect Guides. USA: Little, Brown and Company, 1984. Stokes Guide to Bird Behavior Volume 1. USA: Little, Brown and Company, 1983.

Tilton, Buck. Backcountry First Aid and Extended Care. Guilford, CT: Globe Pequot Press, 2007.

Wescott, Dave. Primitive Technology: A Book of Earth Skills—From the Society of Primitive Technology. Salt Lake City, UT: Gibbs Smith Publisher, 1999.

Wiggington, Elliott. The Foxfire Books: Hog Dressing; Log Cabin Building; Mountain Crafts and Foods; Planting by the Signs; Snake Lore, Hunting Tales, Faith Healing; Moonshining; and Other Affairs of Plain Living. Garden City, NY: Doubleday, 1972.

Young, Jon and Tiffany Morgan. Animal Tracking Basics. Mechanicsburg, PA: Stackpole Books, 2007.

Natural History and Science

Abram, David. The Spell of the Sensuous: Preception and Language in a More-than Human World. New York, NY: Pantheon Books, Random House, Inc., 1996.

Asimov, Isaac. Beginnings: The Story of Origins—of Mankind, Life, the Earth, the Universe. NY: Walker and Company, 1987.

Balick, Micheal and Paul Alan Cox. Plants, People and Culture: the Science of Ethnobotany. NY: Scientific American Library, 1996.

Benyus, Janine M. Illustrated by Juan Carlos Barberis. The Secret Language and Remarkable Behavior of Animals. New York, NY: Black Dog and Leventhal Publishers, Inc., 1998.

Carson, Rachel. Silent Spring. New York, NY: A Crest Book with Houghton Mifflin Company, 1962. Also see The Sense of Wonder.

Chesanow, Jeanne R. Honeysuckle Sipping: The Plant Lore of Childhood. Camden, ME : Down East Books, 1987.

Corbettt, Jim. Jungle Lore. New York, NY: Oxford University Press, 1953.

Cronon, William. Changes in the Land: Indians, Colonists and the Ecology of New England. New York, NY: Hill & Wang, 1983.

Day, Gordon M. In Search of New England's Native Past: Selected Essays. Amherst, MA: University of Massachusetts Press, 1998.

Deitrich, William. Natural Grace, the Charm, Wonder, & Lessons of Pacific Northwest Animals and Plants. Seattle, WA: University of Washington Press.

Deur, Douglas and Nancy J. Turner. Keeping it Living: Traditions of Plant Use and Cultivation on the Northwest Coast of North America. Seattle, WA: University of Washington Press, 2006.

Duensing, Edward. Talking to Fireflies, Shrinking the Moon: Nature Activities for All Ages. New York, NY: Plume, 1990.

Etling, Kathy. Cougar attacks: Encounters of the Worst Kind. Guilford, CT: The Lyons Press, 2004.

Gallagher, Winnifred. The Power of Place: How our surroundings shape our thoughts, emotions and actions. New York, NY: Harper-Collins, 1993.

Goodall, Jane. My Life with the Chimpanzees. New York, NY: Pocket Books, 1996.

Gore, Al. Earth in the Balance: Ecology and the Human Spirit. New York, NY: Rodale, 2006; An Inconvenient Truth: The Crisis of Global Warming. NY: Viking, 2007.

Gibbons, Euell. Stalking the Good Life, My Love Affair with Nature. NY: David McKay Company, Inc. 1971.

Giller, Paul S., and Bjorn Malmqvist. The Biology of Streams and Rivers. New York, NY: Oxford University Press, 1998.

Goodenough, Ursula. The Sacred Depths of Nature. New York, NY: Oxford: Oxford University Press, 1998.

Gould, Stephen Jay. Dinosaur in a Haystack: Reflections on Natural History. New York, NY: Harmony Books, 1995; The Panda's Thumb: More Reflections on Natural History. New York, NY: Norton, 1980.

Heinrich, Bernd. Bumblebee Economics. Cambridge, MA: Harvard University Press, 1979; Mind of the Raven: Investigations and Adventures with Wolf-Birds. New York, NY: Cliff Street Books, 1999; The Trees in My Forest. New York, NY: Cliff Street Books, 1997; Winter World: The Ingenuity of Animal Survival. New York, NY: Ecco, 2003.

Jensen, Derrick. A Language Older Than Words. New York, NY: Context Books, 2000. Kruckeberg, Arthur R. The Natural History of Puget Sound Country. Seattle, WA: University of Washington Press, 1991.

Kyselka, Will. An Ocean in Mind, Honolulu, HI: University of Hawaii Press, 1987.

Lieber, Arnold L., M.D.. How the Moon Affects You. Mamaroneck, NY: Hastings House, 1996.

Logan, William Bryand. Dirt: The Ecstatic Skin of the Earth. NY: Riverhead Books, 1995.

Luoma, Jon R. The Hidden Forest: The Biography of an Ecosystem. New York, NY: Henry Holt, 1999.

Margolin, Malcom. The Ohlone Way: Indian Life in the San Francisco – Monterey Bay Area. Berkely, CA: Heyday Books, 1981.

Marchand, Peter J. Autumn: A Season of Change and Life in the Cold: An Introduction to Winter Ecology. Hanover, NH: University Press of New England, 1996.

Martin, Alexander C., Herbert S. Zim and Arnold L. Nelson. American Wildlife & Plants: A Guide to Wildlife Food Habits. NY: Dover, 1951.

Matthiessen, Peter. Wildlife in America. NY: Vicking, 1959.

McLuhan, Touch the Earth, A Self-Portrait of Indian Existence. New York, NY: Simon and Shuster, a Touchstone Book, 1971.

McGarr, Paul and Stephen Rose, eds. The Richness of Life: The Essential Stephen Jay Gould. New York, NY: 2007.

McPhee, John. Basin and Range. New York, NY: The Noonday Press, Farrar, Straus and Giroux, 1980. Also see The Control of Nature, Coming into the Country, The Pine Barrens, and A Sense of Where You Are.

Minnis, Paul and Wayne Elisens. Biodiversity and Native America. University of Oklahoma, 2000.

Moore, Robert, L., and Max J. Havlick. The Archetype of Initiation: Sacred Space, Ritual Process, and Personal Transformation. Philadelphia, PA: Xlibris Corporation 2001.

Nabham, Gary Paul. Cultures of Habitat: on nature, culture, and story. Washington, DC: Counterpoint, 1997.

Nash, Roderick Frazier. The Rights of Nature, A History of Environmental Ethics. Madison, WI: The University of Wisconsin Press, 1989.

Peattie, Donald Culross. A Natural History of North American Trees. Boston, MA: Houghton Mifflin, 2007.

Perlin, Joh. A Forest Journey: The Role of Wood in the Development of Civilization. Boston, MA: Harvard University Press. 1991.

Pollan, Michael. The Omnivore's Dilemma. New York, NY: Penguin Books, 2006. Also see The Botany of Desire.

Ponting, Clive. A Green History of the World: The Environment and the Collapse of Great Civilizations. New York, NY: St. Martin's Press, 1992.

Pyle, Robert Michael. Wintergreen: listening to the Land's Heart. Boston, MA: Houghton Mifflin, 1996.

Rue III, Leonard Lee. Way of the Whitetail. Stillwater, MN: Voyageur Press, 2005. Also see The World of the White-tailed Deer. Philadelphia, PA: Lippincott, 1962. Sacred Tree, Reflections on Native American Spirituality. Produced collaboratively by Judie Bopp, Michael

Bopp, Lee Brown, and Phil Lane. Illustrated by Patricia Lucas. Lethbridge, Alberta, Canada: Four Worlds Development Press, 1984.

Seton, Earnest Thompson. Animal Tracks and Hunter Signs. Also see Wild Animals I Have Known. Cutchogue, NY: Buccaneer Books, 1926.

Shipman, Wanda and Marna Grove. Animal Architects: How Animals Weave, Tunnel and Build Their Remarkable Homes. Mechanicsburg, PA: Stackpole, 1994.

Standage, Tom. A History of the World in 6 Glasses. NY: Walker & Company, 2005.

Thomas, Lewis. Lives of a Cell: Notes of a Biology Watcher. New York, NY: Viking Press, 1974. Also see The Lives of a Cell and The Medusa and the Snail: More Notes of a Biology Watcher.

Tudge, Colin. The Tree: A Natural History of What Trees Are, How They Live, and Why They Matter. NY: Crown Publishers, 2006.

Turner, Nancy J. Keeping it Living: Traditions of Plant Use and Cultivation of the Northwest Coast of North America. Seattle, WA: University of Washington Press, 2005.

Walters, Mark Jerome. Courtship in the Animal Kingdom. NY: Anchor, 1989.

Watts, May Theilgaard. Reading the Landscape of America. Rochester, NY: Nature Study Guild, 1999.

Wessels, Tom. Reading the Forested Landscape: A Natural History of New England. Woodstock, VT: Countryman Press, 1999.

Williams, Hill. The Restless Northwest, a Geological Story. Pullman, WA: Washington State University Press, 2002.

Wilson, E.O. ed. and Frances M. Peter, assoc. ed. Biophilia. Boston, MA: Harvard, 1984. Naturalist. Washington, DC: Island Press, 2006.

Young, Karen Romano. Small Worlds, Maps and Mapmaking. New York, NY: Scholastic Nonfiction, 2002.

Nature Writing – Literary Stories, for kids of all ages.

Abbey, Edward. Desert Solitaire. Tucson, AZ: University of Arizona Press, 1988. (The Southwestern desert, with an attitude!)

Barrett, Andrea. The Voyage of the Narwhal. New York, NY: W. H. Norton & Company, 1998. (Early navigation in the arctic ice.)

Baylor, Byrd. The Other Way to Listen. New York, NY: Scribner, 1978; Your Own Best Secret Place. New York, NY: Scribner, 1979; Coyote Cry. New York, NY: Lothrop, Lee, and Shepard, 1972. (Wonderful illustrated books for children.)

Berry, Wendell, edited by Norman Wirzba. The Art of the Commonplace: Agrarian Essays of Wendell Berry. Washington, DC: Counterpoint, 2002; Meeting the Expectations of the Land: Essays in Sustainable Agriculture and Stewardship. San Francisco, CA: Northpoint Press, 1984; The Unsettling of America: Culture & Agriculture. San Francisco, CA: Sierra Club Books, 1996. (A wise, quietly spiritual proponent of connection to place and sustainable living.)

Bonello, Kurt L. When Pappy Goes Hunting. Bonello Studios, 1995. (A sensitive portrayal of deer hunting for children's understanding.)

Brown Jr., Tom. The Tracker: The True Story of Tom Brown Jr. as told to William Jon Watkins. Englewood Cliffs, NJ: Prentice Hall, 1978. Also see The Search, The Vision, The Quest, The Journey, and Grandfather, New York, NY: Berkley Books. (Seminal books by Jon Young's mentor.)

Carter, Forrest. The Education of Little Tree. Albuquerque, NM: University of New Mexico Press, 1976. (Youth. A wonderful picture of growing up in the hills of Kentucky.)

Dillard, Annie. Pilgrim at Tinker Creek. New York, NY: Harper & Rowe, 1974. (Dense and quirky observations from Virginia. Also see An American Childhood.)

Duncan, David Jame. The River Why. Toronto, NY: Bantam Books, 1984. Also see River Teeth, God Laughs and Plays. (Hilarious story of fishing and vision quest.)

Egan, Timothy. Good Rain: Across Time and Terrain in the Pacific Northwest. New York, NY: Vintage, 1991. (Compelling narrative natural history of the Pacific Northwest.)

Ehrlich, Gretel. The Solace of Open Spaces. New York, NY: Penguin Books, 1985. (Personal observations in the American West.)

Eiseley, Loren. The Immense Journey. New York, NY: Vintage Books, 1946. Also see The Unexpected Universe. (An imaginative naturalist explores evolutionary history.)

Emerson, Ralph Waldo. Nature. Boston, MA: James Monroe and Co, 1936. (American transcendentalist who found God in nature. Henry David Thoreau's mentor. See his essays in collected works.)

Fuller, Alexandra. Don't Let's Go to the Dogs Tonight, An African Childhood. New York, NY: Random House Trade paperbacks, 2001. (Chaotic childhood midst the heat and smells of Southern Africa.)

George, Jean Craighead. Julie of the Wolves. Boston, MA: G. K. Hall, 1973; My Side of the Mountain. New York, NY: Puffin Books, 1998. (For youth, strong stories of wilderness survival.)

Gilbert, Elizabeth, The Last American Man. NY: Viking, 2002. (The story of Eustace Conway who lives and teaches off the land in Appalachia.)

Gould, Stephen Jay, Oliver Stacks and Stephen Rose. The Richness of Life: The Essential Stephen Jay Gould. NY: Vintage, 2007.

Hardy, Thomas. The Return of the Native. New York, NY: New American Library, 1959. (A classic story of the power of nature, set in the desolate heath of England.)

Hunter, Paul. Breaking Ground. Eugene, OR: Silverfish Review Press, 2004. (Muscular poetry about farming life in Ohio.)

Kingsolver, Barbara. Prodigal Summer. NY: Harper Collins Publishers, 2000. (Also nature-based works: Poisonwood Bible; Homeland and Other Stories; Small Wonder; Essays; Animal, Vegetable; Miracle: a Year of Food Life.)

Kipling, Rudyard. The Jungle Books. New York, NY: Barnes and Noble Classics, 1894. (A magnificent read for all ages. Beyond Disney's Mowgli. Richly charactered storytelling set in Africa and India.)

Krutch, Joseph Wood. The Desert Years. Tucson, AZ: The University of Arizona Press, 1951. (Stories from the Arizona desert. Also see The Voice of the Desert and Grand Canyon: Today and all its Yesterdays.)

Le Guin, Ursula. Buffalo Gals and other Animal Presences. Santa Barbara, CA: Capra Press, 1987. (Brilliant animal fiction and fantasy, centered on Coyote.)

Leopold, Aldo. A Sand County Almanac. NY: Oxford University Press, 1949. Also see his many essays. (A compelling declaration of "the conservation ethic.")

London, Jack. The Call of the Wild and Other Stories. New York, NY: Oxford University Press, 1990. (Great tales of the Yukon, one from the point of view of the dog. For youth and adults.)

Lopez, Barry. Arctic Dreams: Imagination and Desire in a Northern Landscape. NY: Bantam Books, 1989. Crow and Weasel, illustrated by Tom Pohrt, San Francisco, CA: North Point Press, 1990. Patriotism and the American Land. Great Barrington, MA: The Orion Society, 2002. Also see Giving Birth to Thunder; Sleeping with His Daughter; Coyote Builds North America; Of Wolves and Men; Winter Count; Desert Notes; River Notes; and Home Ground. (Myth, politics, and landscape from the Arctic southward.)

Lueders, Edward. Writing Natural History, Dialogues with Authors. Salt Lake City, UT: University of Utah Press, 1989. (Makes a strong argument for writing about nature. Includes a terrific essay by E. O. Wilson.)

Lynch, Jim. The Highest Tide, a novel. New York, NY: Bloomsbury Publishing, 2005. (For youth and adults. An endearing coming of age story about a boy who pays attention to tidal life.)

Maxwell, Gavin. Ring of Bright Water. New York, NY: Penguin Books, 1987. (Youth and Adults. Otters and country life in Scotland.)

Momaday, N. Scott. House Made of Dawn. New York, NY: Harper and Row, 1968; The Way to Rainy Mountain. NY: Harper & Row, 1968. (Evocative writing, Kiowa heritage.)

Mowat, Farley. Never Cry Wolf. Boston, MA: Black Bay Books, 2001. (Youth and Adult, funny, wise stories of living among wolves.)

Muir, John. Essential Muir: A Selection of John Muir's Best Writings. Berkeley, CA: Heyday Books, 2006. Also see Travels in Alaska, My First Summer in the Sierra, The Yosemite, The Wilderness World of John Muir. (Pioneering adventures in the West.)

Murie, Margaret E. Two in the Far North. Seattle, WA: Alaska Northwest Books, 1997. (Growing up in untamed Alaska, accompanying Olaus Murrie's discoveries.)

Norton Book of Nature Writing, The. Edited by Robert Fince and John Elder. New York, NY: W. W. Norton & Company, 1990. (An outstanding chronological collection of prose essays that define the nature writing genre–full of scientific observation, personal narrative, awe and reverence, and literary value.)

Nelson, Richard K. The Island Within. New York, NY: Vintage Books, 1989. Also see Heat and Blood: living with Deer in America; Make Prayers to the Raven: a Koyukon View of the Northern Forest; Shadow of the Hunter: Stories of Eskimo Life. (Anthropology among the Northern Koyukon.)

Oliver, Mary. New and Selected Poems. Boston, MA: Beacon Press, 1992. (Nature poetry, full of stunning imagery and personal response.)

Olson, Sigurd. Open Horizons. NY: Alfred A. Knopf, 1956 & 1969. Also see The Singing Wilderness; Runes of the North; Wilderness Days; Reflections from the North Country; Of Time and Place. (Beautiful story of growing into love and conservation of the Boundary Waters Wilderness.)

Powell, John Wesley. The Diary of John Wesley Powell: Conquering the Grand Canyon. (Amazing journaling while discovering the Grand Canyon, 1834-1902.)

Powell, M. Norman. Echoes of Kenya & Other Short Poems. Shelton, WA: OWLink Media, 2002; Ingwe. Shelton, WA: OWLink Media, 2001. (Stories from our Grandfather, Ingwe.)

Pyle, Robert Michael. Wintergreen, Rambles in a Ravaged Land. Seattle, WA: Sasquatch Books, 2001; The Thunder Tree: Lessons from an Urban Wildland. Boston, MA: Houghton Mifflin, 1992; Chasing Monarchs: A Migration with the Butterflies of Passage. (Delightful writing on butterflies & boyhood, Colorado and Washington.)

Raymo, Chet. Natural Prayers. Saint Paul, MN: Hungry Mind Press, 1999. (Majestic personal musings on astronomy.)

Sachs, Maryam. The Moon. New York, NY: Abbeville Press, 1998. (Covers all aspects of the moon, from the mythical and magical to the scientific.)

Schachter-Shalomi, Zalman and Ronald S. Miller, From Aging to Saging: A Profound New Vision for Growing Older, New York, NY: Warner Books, Inc, 1995. (Creating a world-wide network of "Spiritual Eldering.")

Silko, Leslie Marmon. Ceremony. New York, NY: Penguin Books, 1986. (Pueblo landscape and myth, New Mexico.)

Standing Bear, Luther. My Indian Boyhood. Lincoln, NE: University of Nebraska Press, 1988; Land of the Spotted Eagle, 2006. (Stories from his Sioux heritage.)

Stegner, Wallace. Angle of Repose. Garden City, NY: Doubleday, 1971. (One of many richly developed novels of life in the American West.)

Stokes, John, ed. Thanksgiving Address: Greetings to the Natural World. Onchiota, NY: Six Nations Indian Museum, 1993. (A little book containing the powerful Mohawk Thanksgiving Address.)

Swamp, Jake. Giving Thanks: A Native American Good Morning Message. New York, NY: Lee & Low Books, 1995. (An illustrated children's version of the Thanksgiving Address.)

Steinbeck, John. The Log from the Sea of Cortez. New York, NY: Penguin Books, 1995. (The Great American novelist writes with a profound sense of place. Also see The Grapes of Wrath, East of Eden.)

Thoreau, Henry David. Walden; or, Life in the Woods. NY: Dover Publications, 1995. (A classic, full of keen awareness and "adolescent bravado.")

Tolle, Eckhart. A New Earth: Awakening to Your Life's Purpose. NY: Penguin, 2005.(A strong message for building a better world.)

Van der Post, Laurens, The Lost World of the Kalahari. New York, NY: Morrow, 1988; Testament to the Bushmen. 1984. (An artistic and political voice for the soul and culture of the Kalahari Bushmen.)

Wallace, David Rains. The Klamath Knot. San Francisco, CA: Sierra Club Books, 1983. (Brilliant, captivating writing evolution's story in Klamath, Oregon.)

Williams, Terry Tempest. Refuge: An Unnatural History of Family and Place. New York, NY: Pantheon/Random House, 1991. (A naturalist and activist's touching account of the effects of the flooding Great Salt Lake.)

Words from the Land, Encounters with Natural History Writing. Trimble, Stephen (Ed.). Salt lake City, UT: Peregrine Smith Books, 1989. (Selected writing with biographical introductions.)

Zwinger, Ann. The Nearsignted Naturalist. Tucson, AZ: University of Arizona Press, 1998. (A tour of ordinary and astonishing natural places.)

Zwinger, Susan. The Last Wild Edge: One Woman's Journey from the Arctic Circle to the Olympic Rain Forest. Boulder, CO: Johnson Books, 1999.

Multimedia Resources

Advanced Bird Language: Reading the Concentric Rings of Nature. Audio CD Series. Jon Young. Shelton, WA: OWLink Media, 2005. (www.WildernessAwareness.org)

Art of Mentoring and Coyote Teaching, The. Audio CD. Jon Young with Ellen Haas. Shelton, WA: OWLink Media, 1995. (www.WildernessAwareness.org)

Bay Area Mycological Society's Webpage of Mushroom Poisoning Stories. www.bayareamushrooms.org/poisonings/index.html

Birding by Ear: Eastern and Central Region. Audio CD Series. Richard K. Walton, Robert W. Walton and John Sill. Boston, MA: Houghton Mifflin, 2002.

Birds, Birds, Birds! An Indoor Bird watching Field Trip. DVD Bird and Bird Song Guide. John Feith. Madison, WI: Calculo, 2005.

Branches of Mentoring. Audio CD. Michael Meade.

Connecting with Nature by Michael J. Cohen. Charley Scutt, 2007. DVD. Project Nature Connect. (www.ecopsych.com)

Cornell Lab of Ornithology, Macaulay Library (Free Bird Sounds Archive) (www.animalbehaviorarchive.org)

David Fischer's Webpage on America's Poisonous Mushrooms. (americanmushrooms.com/toxicms.htm)

Folklore and Legends of the Akamba. Audio CD. M. Norman Powell. Shelton, WA: OWLink Media, 2003. (www.WildernessAwareness.org)

Into the Forest, Nature's Food Chain Game. Card Game. Oakland, CA: Ampersand Press.

John Gallagher's herbalist training website: http://www.herbmentor.com

Learning the Language of Birds. Audio Cassette. Jon Young. (www.owlinkmedia.com)

Life of Birds. DVD. David Attenborough. London, UK: BBC Warner, 2002.

Life of Mammals. DVD. Dir. David Attenborough. London, UK: BBC Warner, 2003.

More Birding by Ear: Eastern and Central Region. Audio CD Series. Richard K. Walton and Robert W. Walton. Boston, MA: Houghton Mifflin, 2002.

North American Mycological Society's Mushroom Poisoning Case Registry and Volunteer Emergency Mushroom ID: www.sph.umich.edu/~kwcee/mpcr/

Planet Earth: The Complete BBC Series. DVD. David Attenborough. London, UK: BBC, 2006.

Poison Control Centers: www.1-800-222-1222.info/poisonhelp.asp or call 1-800-222-1222

Primitive Skills and Wilderness Survival. DVD Series. Tom Elpel. (www.Hollowtop.com)

Reclaiming Our Natural Connection. Audio. Jon Young. Owlink Media, 2008. (8shields.org/products)

Sharing the Joy of Nature. Video. Joseph Cornell. Nevada City, CA: Sharing Nature Foundation (www.sharingnature.com/BooksandResources.html)

Seeing Through Native Eyes: Understanding the Language of Nature. CD Series. Jon Young. Shelton, WA: OWLink Media, 2005. (www.WildernessAwareness.org)

Seeing Through the Eyes of the Ancestors. Audio. Jon Young. (8shields.org/products)

Seeing Through the Eyes of the Children. Audio. Jon Young . (8shields.org/products)

The Great Dance. DVD or VHS. (www.sense-africa.com)

The Moon in the Well. Book and Audio CD. Erica Helm Meade.

The Spirit of the Leopard. Audio CD. M. Norman Powell. Red Bank, NJ: Redhawk Productions,1995. (www.WildernessAwareness.org)

Thayer Birding Software (by Region). (www.thayerbirding.com)

Tracking: Mastering the Basics. DVD. James Halfpenny. Gardiner, MT: www.TrackNature.com, 2004.

Tracking Pack One. Audio CD. Jon Young. Shelton, WA: OWLink Media 1998. (www.WildernessAwareness.org)

Western Birding by Ear. Audio. Richard K. Walton, Robert W. Walton and Roger Tory Peterson. Boston, MA: Houghton Mifflin, 1990.

"Wilderness First Responder (WFR)" course from one of the following:

Solo - www.soloschools.com/index.html

Wilderness Medical Associates - www.wildmed.com/

Wilderness Medical Institute - www.nols.edu/wmi/

INDEX

(Page numbers in *italics* indicate front matter. Page numbers in **bold** indicate a sidebar or illustration.)

8 Shields Institute

www.8shields.org

The 8 Shields Institute is an organization led by Jon Young.
Since founding Wilderness Awareness School in 1983, Jon
Young has inspired many programs and individuals to utilize
the skills of Coyote Mentoring around the globe.

The 8 Shields Institute works with a collaborative network of affiliates and partners to
gather and disseminate skills of Coyote
Mentoring and provide best practices in all of
their trainings and programs.

The 8 Shields Institute trains groups and
individuals around the world to utilize Coyote's
Guide to create communities based on deep
nature connection.

Please contact us if you would like to become
an affiliate of Coyote Mentoring or find an

photo: Andreas Ochsmann

affiliate in your region or are seeking personal mentoring in nature connection.

OWLink Media

www.owlinkmedia.com

OWLink Media offers products that support positive
connections with nature, community, and self, including
original books and audio from Jon Young.

OWLink Media

For those inspired by *Coyote's Guide* who are looking
for more resources to support the nature connection
journey, we have a number of great products,
including Kamana, our naturalist training program,
and the many audio products that feature Jon
Young's captivating storytelling.

Order online at www.owlinkmedia.com.

photo: Andreas Ochsmann

WILDERNESS AWARENESS SCHOOL

Since 1983, Wilderness Awareness School has offered year-round Coyote Mentoring programs that empower youth and adults to become naturalists, stewards, and mentors.

"I highly recommend Wilderness Awareness School to everyone who cares about children and the Earth and wants to join an amazing community..." -Stephanie Etley

COYOTE MENTORING TRAINING PROGRAMS

Learn to connect kids and adults with nature! Practice Coyote Mentoring with our experienced staff on our 40 acres in the foothills of Washington's Cascade Mountains.

Coyote Mentoring
Gain first-hand experience with the basic principles of Coyote Mentoring in this fun-filled weekend workshop.

Art of Mentoring
Delve deeply into the principles during the week-long programs that immerses you in a vibrant mentoring culture.

Anake Outdoor School
A nine-month immersion program where you live within our mentoring culture and explore all aspects of our curriculum as part of a supportive community of fellow learners.

Our online store offers a full selection of unique and exciting products—great gifts for the naturalist in your life, and field-tested tools for your learning journey.

The Kamana Naturalist Training Program is a home study course that gives you the outdoor skills and knowledge of place essential to be a strong, confident naturalist and outdoor leader.

www.wildernessawareness.org